What Oth

MUSINGS II is an answer to the prayer of all those who want to know God better and who have a deep desire to serve Him.

Through these powerful insights, God uses Pastor Brian to hold high His mirror. As we look into it, we find ourselves plunged headfirst into the depth of God's word. We're challenged to see the scriptures in a different light, which in turn creates in us a deeper hunger to know God more personally. Through these THOUGHTS OF THE DAY, we gain a better understanding of how we can respond to His expectations, each one wrapped in His love for us.

All my colleagues with whom I shared *Musings* have always testified that it is spiritually simple and yet remarkably profound. My prayer is that your eyes would be open wide as you read these new insights found in *MUSINGS II*.

Pastor Carlo Thomas
President, New World Missions

Musings II

A Daily Devotional

Brian R. Weeks

Musings II

A Daily Devotional

Published by Spring Mill Publishing, LLC

Sharpsburg, MD

ISBN 9781711836683

Acknowledgments

A book is never written by one person.

In fact, the more I write, the more I realize that what I type is not really me but the Holy Spirit wanting to express principles and concepts on His heart. Therefore, Holy Spirit, thank you for allowing me that privilege.

Once again, I am overwhelmed at the hours and hours of time Anne Kaminski has put into editing this book as well as my previous three books. Her work takes more into account than sentence structure, spelling, and punctuation but considers the whole context. This means that certain concepts and comments are tagged for clarification or further development, or just plain sense-making. This can take hours and hours. I've said this before, and it's true, without Anne this book and others would never have been published. Thank you, Anne...

Thank you to my wife Donna, who never complains about how much time I spend at my computer but who does urge me to go to bed earlier.

I'm thankful for the opportunity to share the thoughts that fill my mind, and I hope that something people read may be a blessing to their lives.

Day 1

THOUGHT OF THE DAY: New Year's Prayer

This is a new year! Will it be different from last year? Will we continue to live in our ruts and routines? Could this be our Year of Jubilee? Could this be the year that each of us will determine to pursue a place of greater intimacy with our God, Father, Son, and Holy Ghost? Will this be the year when people see us and say that we have "been with Jesus"? Will this be the year that as Jesus said, "If you have seen me you've seen the Father"?

May this be the year that we all realize who we are and what we carry. Yes, we carry the presence of God wherever we go. We don't need to pray for the anointing to come because it's already a reality.

May the goodness of God overshadow and overwhelm you this year! May you live beyond the ordinary and live in the extraordinary!

Day 2

THOUGHT OF THE DAY: I don't know what to do

I can't begin to tell you how many times I've been at a place where I just don't know what to do.

Haven't we all been there? To be honest, it's not one of my favorite places, because it usually means I'm in the middle of a storm or trial. When I come to this place I can get overwhelmed emotionally, and it can cause me to withdraw and procrastinate or avoid altogether what I'm facing. Being overwhelmed can then create anxiety where I feel compelled to do something, even while I know that crisis decisions are most always bad ones.

So when we don't know what to do, we need to follow Jehoshaphat's example in 2 Chronicles chapter 20. He found himself surrounded by his enemies and severely outnumbered; it says he was surrounded by "a great multitude." His initial response was fear.

What is our response when we face situations so big and so complex that unless God intervenes a huge mess will ensue? What did Jehoshaphat do? He got everyone together to pray. We don't want just any answer; we need an answer from heaven. So in his prayer he says in verse 12, "We don't know what to do, but our eyes are upon You."

Once we pray, we need to wait for an answer. That's often the most difficult thing to do. It's better to do nothing than to do something without the heart and mind of God. Saul made the mistake of not waiting for Samuel. When asked why he didn't wait, he said, "I felt compelled."

Father, hear our heart's cry – "We don't know what to do, but our eyes are upon you."

1

Day 3

THOUGHT OF THE DAY: There's a wedding

Hey! There's this wedding, and it's like no wedding you've ever seen. Not only have I been invited, but I've been told to invite you!

We've all seen elaborate weddings on television and in magazines: weddings of the rich and famous, weddings of royalty. Aren't they spectacular? But they don't even begin to compare to the wedding to which we've been invited.

In fact, we've all been instructed to simply go out and invite other people to this wedding. It's not our role to persuade people to come; we're simply supposed to invite them. Even Jesus said, "Come and see." All the time we invite people – those we know and those we don't - to all kinds of events. Why not this one?

Here's how Matthew puts it in 22:9: "Therefore go into the highways, and as many as you find, invite to the wedding." One translation says, "Invite the guests of honor to come."

He tells them to just go, and as many people as they encounter along the way, to invite to the wedding. We find their response in verse 10, "So those servants went out into the highways and gathered together all whom they found, both bad and good." Notice the word servants and that these servants end up inviting "both the good and the bad." I think we need to expand our idea of the people to whom we're willing to reach out.

The rest of the verse says, "And the wedding hall was filled with guests."

Can we even begin to comprehend the vastness and splendor of this wedding? I love how Luke expresses it in 14:20, "Go out into the highways and hedges, and compel them to come in, that my house may be filled." Luke heard Jesus say, "You have to compel them to come."

We're supposed to be excited and passionate about inviting people. If we're blasé about it, the results will never fill the "house," but if we're excited and fully convinced it's an opportunity of a lifetime – people will come.

Go ahead; invite people with love and passion... Tell them they just have to come!

Day 4

THOUGHT OF THE DAY: Are you an encourager or a discourager?

Let's be honest; when we see certain people coming towards us, there's a smile on our faces and joy in our hearts! On the other hand, when others approach us, we have a very different attitude.

Are you ever somewhere and when you spot someone and see that they haven't noticed you, you avoid them?! Yup, it's true. Would Jesus do the same? Would he avoid them?

And yet maybe the person we avoid is in need of encouragement. Our problem here is obvious. We're self-focused. We're too busy meeting our own needs, and it doesn't even cross our mind that just maybe the person we seek to avoid needs to touch the Jesus in us. Maybe they're desperate for a simple word of encouragement.

Perhaps we're missing opportunities to genuinely be the voice of encouragement to those who are in a place where they really need it. Have you ever had a day when you could've used a word of encouragement?

Maybe the person we're avoiding is the person to whom the Holy Spirit is sending us.

In the verse below insert your name in place of Timothy's.

• 1 Thessalonians 3:2: "We sent Timothy (your name), our brother and minister of God, and our fellow laborer in the gospel of Christ, to establish you and encourage you concerning your faith."

Prophetic people (those who breathe the breath of life on others) need to be encouragers.

• Judas and Silas, who themselves were prophets, were used by God to encourage and strengthen the believers in Antioch. (Acts 15:32)

Yes, we all have "bad days," but we aren't called to "build our house" or set up camp there.

Barnabas' name means "son of encouragement." The church is in desperate need of encouragers. All of us are called to be Barnabas.

Perhaps today you'll see someone who needs a simple word of encouragement. Go change the world.

Day 5

THOUGHT OF THE DAY: If we all did a little...

Have you ever met someone whose entire life is lived by faith and who's not concerned about their own needs but is instead compelled to do everything possible to expand God's kingdom?

Many of you have. In fact, many of you know him – he's Pastor Carlo from Haiti. After he arrived on Saturday night and as we were driving, I asked him to tell me his needs. His famous first word is often "Well..."

This time his reply to me was, "I have so many needs, I must prioritize them." I asked him a second time, because I know that he would never speak of his needs without being asked.

His first need was for $175 a month. This would pay for the propane gas to cook five days' worth of food for 185 children. The children who attend his schools are seldom fed at home and so will take food home to share with their families. It was easy to say that we would meet this need for cooking fuel. Indeed, how could we say otherwise?

Last night I asked him, "What is your next greatest need?" His reply came with a voice I have never heard before. He said, "that Jericho Bible College wouldn't die."

Jericho Bible College is a two-year program to teach, train, and mentor men and women who in turn, train, teach, and mentor others. Every two years he moves it to another area in Haiti to offer that same training to people in a different part of the country.

Hearing this about the school, my heart sank and tears filled my eyes, and "wouldn't die" rung in my ears. When I asked what specific amount would allow Jericho to survive, he told me that for the entire year $450 would be sufficient.

He said that he had thought of asking us for help, believing that once people here in the United States heard of the need, we would certainly respond.

We admire people like Pastor Carlo, so can we demonstrate this by helping just a little? If you wish to, drop me a line. I can let you know the options available to send funds.

Thanks so much for being the great people you are!

Day 6

THOUGHT OF THE DAY: I have heard the cry once again

Twenty-three years ago, I heard a cry, a deep groan coming from the people of the city of Fall River.

The cry was coming from God's children who were in bondage, those who didn't know God. Many weren't even looking for Him and couldn't care less whether or not He was real. What they did know was that what they were living wasn't life.

I could see thousands of people who had once been in church and yet were now part of those rejected by the church -- misunderstood, not fitting the "mold." They needed an arm around them, not a list of do's and don'ts.

Then I saw thousands of people hurting, broken, and wearing old tattered clothes. They lived from soup kitchen to soup kitchen, former veterans who were never able to put their lives back together, street people who through circumstances we would have a hard time comprehending, left churches because they didn't fit in or they never felt accepted. These were people the church hoped wouldn't attend their religious, family churches.

Twenty-three years ago, I heard their cry. I started a new church in Fall River but grew weary because I needed help. I ended up disobeying God, who had given me a three-year plan. After only one year I gave the church away to another pastor. Happily, that church is still reaching the broken today.

Once again, I heard the cry in 2009, and this time God has sent others who have heard the same cry. Have you heard this cry?

Perhaps you are being led to be a part of this rekindled vision: an answer to the cry of thousands of people who want to be loved, honored, assigned value, and given purpose. There are those who are groping in the dark looking for the God who loves them.

Have you heard this cry? Is something in your heart crying out to love the hurting and broken?

Exodus 2:23–25: "Now after a long time, the king of Egypt died. The people of Israel were sad in their spirit because of being slaves. They cried for help. And because of their hard work, their cry went up to God. God heard their crying and remembered His agreement with Abraham, Isaac and Jacob. God saw the people of Israel and He cared about them." (NKJV)

• People were in bondage and their lives were broken.
• They cried out. They are still crying out.
• God heard.
• He remembered.
• He responded because He CARED ABOUT THEM. He cares about you...

Matthew 11:27-27 from the Message Bible says it well: "Are you tired? Worn out? Burned out on religion? Come to me. Get away with me and you'll recover your life. I'll show you how to take a real rest. Walk with me and work with me—watch how I do it. Learn the unforced rhythms of grace. I won't lay anything heavy or ill-fitting on you. Keep company with me and you'll learn to live freely and lightly."

Luke 10:2: "The harvest truly is great, but the laborers are few; therefore, pray to the Lord of the harvest to send out laborers into His harvest."

Perhaps God is calling you to be a person He can count on to labor in His kingdom?

Yes, I can go to various places all over the world, but can I go into my own backyard? You're needed wherever your backyard is...

I heard the cry once again. Have you heard this cry?

Day 7

THOUGHT OF THE DAY: Are we ready to hear new things?

We are creatures of habit; many of us don't like change. We cling to stability, but sometimes it's a subtle way of staying in control. Others of us like change (we kind of pride ourselves in our willingness to change, in fact), which can also create problems. Micah 6:9: "The Lord's voice cries to the city."

Can you hear His voice? It's time to truly follow the Holy Spirit like we've never done before.

I can hear people say, "I'm in."

What if the Lord tells us what He told the rich young ruler?

- Luke 18:20-23: " 'You know the commandments: Do not commit adultery, Do not murder, Do not steal, Do not bear false witness, Honor your father and your mother.' And he said, 'All these things I have kept from my youth.' "

- The rich young ruler responded by saying he'd done everything God had asked him to do. So when Jesus heard his response, he said to him, "You still lack one thing. Sell all that you have and distribute to the poor, and you will have treasure in heaven; and come, follow Me."

- Yet he was lacking something he couldn't see. That causes me to ask what we're lacking? It's interesting that Jesus says, "to sell everything and DISTRIBUTE IT TO THE POOR."

- Would I/we have the capacity to hear what Jesus said to the rich young ruler? Is there something we're holding onto which is stopping us from living a totally abandoned life?

- Are we ready to hear new things? In Isaiah 48 God tells Israel that one of their problems was their stubbornness. (A few translations use the word rebellion.)

- What is God after in each of us? He may be after our excuses.

Isaiah 48:6-8 tells us to get ready to hear new things.

- "You have heard; see it all. And will you not declare it? I announce new things to you from this time and hidden things that you have not

6

known. Now they are created, and not from of old, and before today, and you have not heard them so that you could not say, 'Look! I knew them.' Neither have you heard, nor have you known, nor from of old has your ear been opened." (the Lexham English Bible)

Father, grant us the willingness to surrender even when in our natural mind it doesn't make sense. In Jeremiah 38:17 Jeremiah said to Zedekiah, "Thus says Yahweh, the God of hosts, the God of Israel, 'If only you will go surrender to the officials of the king of Babylon, then you will live, and this city will not be burned with fire, and you will live, you and your house.' "

What would He want us to surrender?

For some it's their ministry, because it's become their own and not His. It's caused them to have a false identity. Some have been told to move on (let the ministry go), and they haven't. Some have been told to give financially, and they haven't.

Can you hear these excuses in your head?

We all know something new is coming. Will we be able to respond? Are we ready to hear new things?

Day 8

THOUGHT OF THE DAY: Mixed emotions

Like most of you, for the past two days I've been asking the Lord what He wants to say to me about this new year.

I didn't write yesterday, because I was having all kinds of mixed emotions. I've been feeling a sense of anger, grief, and sadness coupled with a deep burden to see people restored. I'm pleading with God that He'll help people focus on who they are, not who they're not.

The account that keeps coming to mind is the story of the man in the synagogue with the withered hand. In this verse we see Jesus say to him, "Step forward." I know the Holy Spirit is saying the same thing, that regardless of people's opinions and who's standing around watching, that this is the year to step forward.

If you recall, the man with the withered hand was being observed by the Pharisees who were watching to see if Jesus was going to heal on the Sabbath. Clearly there's an urging in my spirit that we must "step forward" into the things of God and not be hindered by people like the Pharisees. Our focus needs to be on the needs of people and having a deep sense of compassion for the hurting and broken. We're not just to pray but to care for them as we're led and are able.

Go ahead, "STEP FORWARD."

While this was on my heart, I also felt grief, anger, and sadness. This morning I was led to read the story of the man with the withered hand in the books of Matthew, Mark, and Luke.

Each of them saw the man being healed, but Mark captures exactly how I'm feeling. Mark 3:3-5: "Jesus asked the man to come and stand in front of the congregation. Then turning to his enemies, he asked, 'Is it all right to do kind deeds on Sabbath days? Or is this a day for doing harm? Is it a day to save lives or to destroy them?' But they wouldn't answer him. Looking around at them angrily, for he was deeply disturbed by their indifference to human need, he said to the man, 'Reach out your hand.' He did, and instantly his hand was healed!" (TLB) The New King James Version says, "And when He had looked around at them with anger, being grieved by the hardness of their hearts, He said to the man, 'Stretch out your hand.' And he stretched it out, and his hand was restored as whole as the other."

Clarke's Commentary interprets hardness of heart (TLB says, "indifference") to mean "callousness, deadness; blindness" and Gill's Commentary says that Jesus was "troubled in his human soul." The statement in verse five really grips me: "For he was deeply disturbed by their indifference to human need."

Oh Lord, seize us with the compassion that ran through your heart that we might not just see people in need, but actually be "doers" of good.

We can't allow our mixed emotions to paralyze us into doing nothing! James 1:22 says, "But be doers of the message and not hearers only." (LEB)

It's time to do.

Day 9

THOUGHT OF THE DAY: "He saw the city and wept over it." (Luke 19:41)

What breaks your heart?

Can I ask the question again: WHAT BREAKS YOUR HEART? Have we become indifferent? Have we become Pharisees and Sadducees? What do I mean by that question? They were those who attended church, knew the scriptures, had their strong convictions, but lacked compassion. Have we lost our compassion?

What breaks your heart? Perhaps it's time to ask for a heart transplant.

"He saw the city and wept over it."

Day 10

THOUGHT OF THE DAY: When our lives are upside down

There are times/seasons of our lives when everything is a mess. Everything around us is in chaos. No matter where we turn, everything looks bleak. Yet in spite of our circumstances, we have hope.

The prophet Habakkuk, who seeing the state of Israel and the coming destruction brought on by the Babylonians, writes the following:

• Habakkuk 3:17-19 from the Amplified Bible: "Though the fig tree does not blossom and there is no fruit on the vines, [though] the product of the olive fails and the fields yield no food, though the flock is cut off from the fold and there are no cattle in the stalls, Yet I will rejoice in the Lord; I will exult in the [victorious] God of my salvation! The Lord God is my Strength, my personal bravery, and my invincible army; He makes my feet like hinds' feet and will make me to walk [not to stand still in terror, but to walk] and make [spiritual] progress upon my high places [of trouble, suffering, or responsibility]!"

These verses are taken from the end of what is commonly known as the "Prayer of Habakkuk." Habakkuk's name in Hebrew means to "embrace." His name defines how he lived his life, EMBRACING GOD… He embraced His love, His mercy, and God's faithfulness to His people.

Habakkuk sees the pathetic state of Israel, understands the situation and what more would take place, and writes this as a song: "Yet I will rejoice in the Lord; I will exult in the [victorious] God of my salvation! The Lord God is my Strength."

Yes, in the middle of chaos, when everything is a mess, when our lives are upside down – we need to sing. From the Message Bible – "I'm singing joyful praise to God. I'm turning cartwheels of joy to my Savior God. Counting on God's Rule to prevail, I take heart and gain strength."

Day 11

THOUGHT OF THE DAY: Learning to be content

I know that so many of us are facing strenuous times, yet too often we allow circumstances/situations to steal our contentment. To be content is to be satisfied; to be at peace.

Paul in writing to the Philippians says: "For I have learned to be content, whatever the circumstances may be. I know now how to live when things are difficult and I know how to live when things are prosperous. In general and in particular I have learned the secret of facing either poverty or plenty. I am ready for anything through the strength of the one who lives within me." (4: 11-13, Phillips)

It's important that we see that learning to be content is a process. Whether things are going well or not, we can live lives where we're at peace. Jesus tells us that worrying/fretting doesn't change our circumstances. The Word says "to rejoice in the Lord always!" (Phil. 4:4) We're learning to do that...

People (our children, family, friends, coworkers, etcetera) are watching us. They're looking for a faith that is real in all circumstances. Too often when things are not going well, we act, or at least look like, the Grouch from the Muppets.

Peter writes:

- 1 Peter 4:12-13: "And now dear friends of mine. I beg you not to be unduly alarmed at the fiery ordeals which come to test your faith, as though this were some abnormal experience. You should be glad, because it means that you are called to share Christ's sufferings." (Phillips Translation)

How do we learn to be content? The last verse in Philippians four above tells us: "I am ready for anything through the strength of the one who lives within me."

Day 12

THOUGHT OF THE DAY: Surprised answer

Yesterday I suggested that "perhaps it's time to ask for a heart transplant." So I said to the Lord, "Well, if I need a heart transplant, then give me one." It was one of those halfhearted prayers, because I really felt that I was in a good place. I should've recognized that this was a sure indication that I was trouble.

So I got up this morning and sat pondering what the THOUGHT OF THE DAY might be and had the "bright idea" to pray. What happened next surprised me. Tears filled my eyes, and my heart began to swell with grief and sadness, which is still there. I heard, "Well, you asked for a transplant." Oh Lord, I'm so sorry that I didn't see my true condition.

It wasn't but a few moments later that He reminded me of the Church of Laodicea, the church that no one wants to be identified with because they're "neither hot or cold." Surely that's not me! So I clicked on my bible program and began to read. I came to Revelation 3:18, and this is what I read as I looked it up in the Living Bible; "My advice... to get medicine from me to heal your eyes and give you back your sight." The phrase "give you back your sight" really resonated with me.

Now what? Off I go to get some eye salve.

I keep on saying, "I'm so sorry." As I close my eyes, I see a pharmacist standing behind a counter. He has a warm and loving smile, and he's holding a white bag in his hand. He whispers to me that the order was called in some time ago and has been here waiting for me to pick up. Then he says with tears running down His face and His voice quivering and broken, "I'm so glad you've come!"

Day 13

THOUGHT OF THE DAY: It's time to be healed

Every morning when I awake, I'm aware that there are so many of us who are in need of healing. In Psalm 147:3 it says, "He heals those who have a broken heart. He heals their sorrows." (NLV)

It's time we seize and apply this scripture. Honestly, there are parts of all of our hearts that need healing. There are deep sorrows in all of us that directly affect the way we live. They affect our relationships, how we view life, how we do life, our commitment to the Kingdom of God, to the church, to one another, even how we make excuses.

The brokenness and sorrow in many of us is so deep that it's like having a deep pain whose source the doctors can't discover. It's like waking up in the morning knowing something is wrong but not knowing quite what. What we do know is the impact on our lives. Yet if we really want to be honest, our broken hearts and sorrows (at least for many), have come from our being part of the "church." We read in Zechariah 13:6: "And if anyone asks them, 'What are these wounds on your chest?' the answer will be 'The wounds I received in the house of my friends.' " (NRSV) Yes, I was wounded by the church.

Many wonderful brothers and sisters have lost their way because they were wounded in the church. Many love God but want no part of the church. Others go to church because they know they should but have no desire to be hurt again. There are even those who are serving and sacrificing, but it's from a place of obedience, and all the while they're hurting, broken, and full of sorrows.

It's time to be healed! How can healing come? Jesus said because the Spirit of the Lord was upon Him (us) that "He has sent Me to heal the brokenhearted, to proclaim liberty to the captives, and the opening of the prison to those who are bound; to comfort all who mourn, to console those who mourn in Zion, to give them beauty for ashes, the oil of joy for mourning, the garment of praise for the spirit of heaviness." (Isaiah 61) The only way to healing is the anointing!

It's time to be healed! Perhaps churches could put a Sunday aside, or perhaps a home group. Perhaps you could open your home and invite people in for an evening of healing. It just has to happen!

11

No matter where we've been broken and no matter where sorrow has entered our lives – It's time to be healed!

Day 14

THOUGHT OF THE DAY: Why am I here?

How often are we in places and in circumstances where we don't want to be? More often than not we spend too much time, energy, and emotion grumbling, complaining, and pouting when we're in circumstances we don't like.

We often blame others for where we are, and it might be that we didn't do anything wrong but still ended up in a horrible place. What did Joseph do to be thrown into a pit, sold as a slave, and then end up in prison? What did Daniel do wrong to end up in Babylon and later in the lion's den? What did Peter and John do wrong to end up in prison? What did Paul do wrong to spend 5.5 – 6 years there? What did Jesus do to be beaten and crucified? Then there's Jonah. What did he do to end up in the belly of a whale? What about Samson?

Perhaps the question we should be asking the Lord is why we're there. What divine plan and purpose does God have in mind for us? What is He working in or working out of us? What are we to learn/glean from where we are?

Paul wrote Colossians, Philemon, Ephesians, and Philippians from prison. Joseph ended up in prison so he could be in position to become Pharaoh's right-hand man. The same is true about Daniel. Paul from prison writes, "But I want you to know, brethren, that the things which happened to me have actually turned out for the furtherance of the gospel." (Philippians 1:12) Then we read in Roman's 8:28: "And we know that all things work together for good to those who love God, to those who are the called according to His purpose."

Can we say ALL THINGS? Can we say that the things which have happened to us have actually turned out to further the gospel? Yes, even Jonah and Sampson in their disobedience ended up fulfilling God's purposes.

Jesus says to Peter in John 21:18: "Most assuredly, I say to you, when you were younger, you girded yourself and walked where you wished; but when you are old, you will stretch out your hands, and another will gird you and carry you where you do not wish." In other words, Jesus said that he would bring us to places that on our own we wouldn't otherwise choose.

When I end up in circumstances and places I don't like, I am learning (notice I use the word learning) to try and ask the Lord a four-word question - Why am I here? Also: What divine purpose have You intended?

Instead of looking for a way of escape, I'm learning to follow the road before me. Hebrew 12:2 says, "keeping our eyes fixed on Jesus, the pioneer and perfecter of our faith." (NET)

Why am I here?

Day 15

THOUGHT OF THE DAY: Welcome to Peniel

Hasn't there been a deep cry in your heart for months? Hasn't there been a deep groaning where you've been trying to understand where you are?

Haven't we all been trying to find the right words to express how we're feeling?

I think what Paul writes in Philippians 3:10 captures our heart. He says, "that I may know Him and the power of His resurrection." Lord, we want to KNOW YOU AND THE POWER OF YOUR RESURRECTION... Earlier in this chapter Paul writes in verse eight: "Nothing is as wonderful as knowing Christ Jesus my Lord. I have given up everything else and count it all as garbage. All I want is Christ."

Did we see that Paul said, "I have given up everything and count it all as garbage."? Lord, nothing matters but knowing you.

So in His love for us He brings us to the place called Peniel. It's a place where we're alone and no one is there, and it's our time to wrestle with God. Genesis 32:24 says, "Then Jacob was left alone; and a Man wrestled with him until the breaking of day." Jacob did not just wrestle for a few hours; he wrestled until daybreak. Isn't that where we are?

The key for us is what Jacob said in verse 26: "I will not let You go unless You bless me!" I WILL NOT QUIT. I will continue to press in until I am changed.

Peniel is not only where Jacob saw God face-to-face; it's where God changed his name from Jacob to Israel. This is our place of change!

Welcome to Peniel!

Day 16

THOUGHT OF THE DAY: It's time to truly honor

What does it mean to honor? In Philippians 2:3 Paul tells us that to honor is to esteem others more than ourselves. When we're with people we're meant to assign them great value.

What if today we all started honoring everyone we met? The New Living Testament says it this way: "Be humble, thinking of others as better than yourself." The ICB says, "Be humble and give more honor to others than to yourselves." In the JFB commentary it says, "esteeming each other superior to yourselves." Instead of fixing your eyes on the areas in which you excel, fix them on those in which your neighbor "excels" you - this is true "humility."

Over the past number of months we've had the opportunity to serve the people in our community. I've struggled with the terminology that we typically use to describe the homeless. Sometimes we say the broken, the displaced, street people, the less fortunate, etcetera. While each of these words might describe their condition, it doesn't describe them. These are wonderful people who need to be loved, honored, and valued. I had been asking the Lord to give me a word or a phrase that I could use when speaking about them.

Then I remembered Brennan Manning's book called Ragamuffin Gospel where he writes about the paralytic in Matthew chapter nine. After Jesus heals him, the Pharisees begin their critique.

Why did they do this? They were honoring themselves and their own opinions and also devaluing those who weren't like them. In verse one of Matthew nine Jesus says, "For I did not come to call the righteous but sinners to repentance." Manning says the Greek word "kalein" has the meaning/sense of inviting an honored guest to dinner." (Page 26)

I'm overwhelmed. Now when I see people, I can view them as the guests of honor that Jesus has invited for dinner. Now I can esteem them BETTER than myself.

It's time to honor!

Day 17

THOUGHT OF THE DAY: Kingdom thinking

Luke 6:29 says, "To him who strikes you on the one cheek, offer the other also."

Did Jesus really mean to let them hit us again? Sadly, I thought so. When my son was in second grade, I taught him this principle in a literal way, which set him up to be picked on for a few years. Then...one day his anger and resentment took over. Several years passed before the Lord resolved my error.

So what was Jesus saying? Let me offer you a couple of thoughts:

1. Was Jesus saying that we must be willing to maintain our relationships even if it means getting hurt again? If we severed every relationship in which we got hurt, we wouldn't have any relationships.

Luke's account differs from Matthew's. The big difference is that Luke says to "offer the other cheek." I see this as our responsibility in order to initiate the rebuilding/preserving of the relationship. Luke says, "offer the other also." Often when we're hurt, we pull away or put the responsibility on the one who hurt us to take the steps to restore the relationship. With kingdom-thinking we are to initiate the process of restoration. KINGDOM THINKING – UGH!

2. Was Jesus saying that we need to confront the person who hurt us? Rather than being passive, we need to address what happened. All too often when we get hurt, the issue is never addressed or only partially addressed. Therefore, when we don't confront people, we enable them to continue to hurt others.

So not only do we have to get healed, we need to speak up and ensure that others seek healing for their own wounds. KINGDOM THINKING – UGH!

Day 18

THOUGHT OF THE DAY: "Simon, I have something to say to you." (Luke 7:40)

My heart is pounding. I can hear this whisper – "Brian" (put your name here), I have something to say to you." There is such anticipation! I'm praying that I have the capacity to hear what He wants to say and to also respond.

I can hear the Lord say, "There is so much I want to say to my sons and daughters." He's saying, "We need to be able to hear differently." He wants us to be able to hear Him speak "new" things. In Exodus 34:24 it says, "Enlarge your borders." We're still trying to mingle new wine with old wine. We're still trying to sow a new cloth with an old cloth.

I can see 1 Samuel 3:10: "Now the Lord came and stood and called as at other times, 'Samuel! Samuel!' And Samuel answered, 'Speak, for Your servant hears.' " Literally, I can see the Lord standing beside you! He comes to some just after you get in bed. I see even as you read this, Him standing beside you. He's calling you by name. His voice is full of such deep affection. He's saying, "I have so much to say to you. Please listen; your life will never be the same." It's like Song of Solomon 2:10: "My beloved spoke, and said to me: 'Rise up, my love, my fair one, and come away.' "

These are new days. We, the church - as individuals and corporately - are all in a place of transition. This has been and is a difficult time because we are trying to know and understand "new" while still trying to fit it into the old. What used to work is not working. Old habits and behavior patterns die hard. We're afraid. We don't want to make a mistake. We feel awkward. We're unsure.

What a great place to be!

Have a piece of paper nearby and have the courage to write down the things you hear. Often hearing God is like a puzzle: we get one piece at a time. Have the patience to wait for all the pieces before you draw a conclusion. Take every thought (piece) and "muse with it." Too often we hear and either do nothing or fail to take time to get the clarity we need. These are great days!!!

Can you hear Jesus say, "I have something to say to you?"

Day 19

THOUGHT OF THE DAY: "You did not choose Me, but I chose you and appointed you that you should go." (John 15:16)

Think for a moment: of all the millions of people on the earth, God chose you! It says that WE DID NOT CHOOSE HIM! Please don't read on yet, but close your eyes and think about that. It screams that you are special.

In Ephesians 1:4 the Amplified Bible says, "Even as [in His love] He chose us [actually picked us out for Himself as His own] in Christ before the foundation of the world, that we should be holy (consecrated and set apart for Him) and blameless in His sight, even above reproach, before Him in love."

God chose us because He loved (and still) loves us; He picked us out. I often get a picture in my mind of an orphanage, and there we are. After the Father looks around at all the children, He turns and with tears streaming down His face, looks at us and asks, "Would you come home with me and be my son/daughter? I've been looking for you since the foundation of this world."

Paul goes on to say in Ephesians 1:5: "For He foreordained us (destined us, planned in love for us) to be adopted (revealed) as His own children through Jesus Christ, in accordance with the purpose of His will (because it pleased Him and was His kind intent)." (AMP)

In His love He adopted us to be His "kids." Our being chosen was NOT an accident!

John 15 says that not only did He choose you, but He personally appointed you. Appointed you to do what? Appointed (some translations say ordained) "TO GO." Go do what? Go and be a reflection of our Father. That we would love the world (people) as He did and does. That as Jesus said, "He who has seen Me has seen the Father." (John 14:9) We are appointed to go and be a reflection of our Father in everything we do, don't do, and everything we say and don't say, such that people would see Abba.

What a privilege and honor to be chosen, appointed, and sent…"You did not choose Me, but I chose you and appointed you that you should go."

Day 20

THOUGHT OF THE DAY: Our capacity to believe is linked to our capacity to dream

"So Jesus stood still and called them, and said, 'What do you want Me to do for you?' " (Matthew 20:32)

The scripture is taken from the story of Jesus leaving Jericho where two blind men are calling out to him. I can see that in our blindness we do the same thing.

It says, "Jesus stood still"… If we could only envision that when we call His name, He stands stills – we have captured His attention. Next, He calls them as He's calling all of us. The question Jesus poses after this is staggering: "What do you want Me to do for you?" Imagine that you're with the Lord and he asks you, "What do you want Me to do for you?" How would we answer this question?

The need of the two blind men was obvious – they needed to see. Our need? To see! We are blind to the dreams that have been written and kept stored in heaven for each of us. I can see bank vaults, and inside them are shelves full of scrolls. These scrolls were written before we were born, and each contains a dream/vision that was written specifically for us.

How do we know what to believe for, however, when we've limited our capacity to dream?

Perhaps our inability to dream is because our focus has been on what we could do and not what God can and will do. It's been based on our ability and not the Lord's. We see ourselves as limited, while God sees us as unlimited. We see ourselves by what others have said about us, not what God says about us.

We've all made the mistake of taking the dreams we've received and trying to fulfill them. Notice I said that we've tried to fulfill them. When the dream or dreams didn't come to pass, we stopped dreaming. The dream wasn't the issue! We were the issue.

It's time to dream again. Time to rekindle the dreams you have had. This time allow God to expand your dream. You see, our dreams were incomplete before - incomplete because so many of them were based on us and were therefore restricted. Can you hear Jesus say, "What do you want Me to do for you?"

Our capacity to believe is linked to our capacity to dream.

Day 21

THOUGHT OF THE DAY: "Not so, Lord! For I have never eaten anything common or unclean." (Acts 10:14)

Many chronological bibles date the action of Acts 10 at approximately A.D. 40. Using the same bible version, Jesus died in A.D. 29. Peter has been ministering to his Jewish brothers for approximately 14 years. While he was very happy in "his ministry," here in Joppa in A.D. 40, his life and ministry are turned upside down.

Can anyone raise their hand? Peter's transition was dramatic and supernatural!

Peter could have missed the shift/transition if it wasn't for the Holy Spirit's persistence. It says in verses 9–13: "The next day, as they went on their journey and drew near the city, Peter went up on the housetop to pray, about the sixth hour. Then he became very hungry and wanted to eat; but while they made ready, he fell into a trance and saw heaven opened and an object like a great sheet bound at the four corners, descending to him and let down to the earth. In it were all kinds of four-footed animals of the earth, wild beasts, creeping things, and birds of the air. And a voice came to him, 'Rise, Peter; kill and eat.' "

We find Peter's response in verse 14: "Not so, Lord! For I have never eaten anything common or unclean." Peter could have missed God's divine transition because of his inability to hear something new. Imagine that: 14 years of ministry and God has something new for Peter. Peter could have missed God's divine transition because he was used to the old way of doing things, which is something which can happen to us. Peter wouldn't have budged except for what we see in verses 15 -16, "And a voice spoke to him again the second time, 'What God has cleansed you must not call common.' This was done three times."

I believe we'd all agree that God is up to something new. Do we have the capacity to be able to hear something so outside of our "box" that our whole world and the way we've done ministry can be dramatically and supernaturally changed? Notice I didn't say altered, but CHANGED.

Such is awkward, frightening, bewildering, and exciting all at the same time. We are now entering the land of total dependency. All our old methods and old patterns don't work here, nor can they. We're entering the place we have desired, which is to be truly led by the Holy Spirit and not by our own thoughts or ideas. This is the place of the supernatural.

This is the place where we see the Holy Spirit working. This is where WE stop working. Haven't we all desired to come here?

The Holy Spirit will be persistent! Will we be willing to hear? Will we be willing to be dramatically transitioned? Will we let go of the old? Will we let go of the familiar and comfortable in exchange for the new and uncomfortable?

I am confident we will say – "Here I am Lord, send me." (Isaiah 6:8)

Day 22

THOUGHT OF THE DAY: "Follow me." (Luke 9:59)

As I awoke this morning, I asked the Lord what He wanted to say. After a few moments I could picture Jesus standing in front of each of us and saying simply, "Follow me." It sounds like a very simple request. Can you see him standing beside you saying that?

It really is a simple request, isn't it? Yet in both Matthew eight and Luke nine we find Jesus asking two people to follow Him. They both respond by saying yes, "BUT." Verse 59 says, "But he said, 'Lord, let me first go and bury my father.' " It is believed that the father was not actually dying, so what the disciple was saying was that he would follow later. Verse 61: "And another also said, 'Lord, I will follow You, but let me first go and bid them farewell who are at my house.' " Jesus, I will follow you, BUT I have to go see my family.

Now is Jesus against families? Not by any stretch! So what's the problem? The answer is that they were making excuses. We'll follow when it's convenient. We'll follow when it fits into our plans. I'm busy right now. It's not a good time. How often has the Lord said to come and follow him, and we have said YES...BUT...!

The days we've all entered are unprecedented. We've been asked to be a part of history. Our problem? Making excuses. Waiting for a time when it fits our schedule or when we feel like it. What if we all responded? I know we would experience the presence and power of God like never before. We would be filled with amazing joy.

What do we have to lose, I might ask? When He calls "COME, FOLLOW ME," let's simply say, "You lead, and I will follow" ...

Day 23

THOUGHT OF THE DAY: Another look at receiving

I am just beginning to realize that not receiving is a subtle form of rejecting.

I'm just beginning to realize that the enemy has used rejection in our lives to keep us from receiving all that God has for us. I believe all of us have difficulty receiving in one way or another. Our problem is not in giving, it's in receiving.

We find it easier to love others than to receive their love. When God loves us unconditionally, we feel like we have to earn it. Because we have a performance mindset, we're unable to simply receive, not only His love, but everything that He has for us. Think about it: isn't our inability to receive a form of rejecting?

Our incapacity in this area hinders us from RECEIVING more. We've all been frustrated when we pray, often thinking that we don't get the results we're believing for. Well, there's a second part to believing! It's receiving. Mark 11:24: "So listen to what I'm saying: Whatever you pray for or ask from God, believe that you'll receive it and you will." (VOICE)

Jesus is clearly saying that real believing is having the confidence that you will indeed receive. Lately I've seen that so much of our praying is not believing, but instead hoping. Something has shifted... It's nothing that I've done or could do, because like you, I've tried. The Holy Spirit has birthed and is birthing something that we've never had before - the ability to really believe because we now have the capacity to receive.

The Holy Spirit is moving... He's doing in us what we've been unable to do. If this is the beginning, can we imagine what it will be like as we mature in this?!

"So listen to what I'm saying: Whatever you pray for or ask from God, believe that you'll receive it and you will."

Day 24

THOUGHT OF THE DAY: "But you shall receive power" (Acts 1:8)

Do we really believe that we've received power? I'll ask it again - do we really believe we HAVE RECEIVED POWER?

This is not just any kind of power, but the same power that raised Jesus. Ephesians 1:20 says it plainly: "This is the same mighty power that raised Christ from the dead."

Jesus, in speaking with the Sadducees, said something we need to consider - Matthew 22: 29: "You are mistaken, not knowing the Scriptures nor the power of God." I want to encourage all of us to spend time mediating/musing over the scriptures that refer to the power of God. We're familiar with the power of God in our academic minds but don't really know it in our spiritual minds. Sadly, we spend too much time living in our natural mind rather than in our spiritual one.

BUT THINGS ARE CHANGING!

Paul's prayer in Ephesians 1:19 is my prayer for all of us - "I also pray that you will understand the incredible greatness of God's power for us who believe him." The NIRV says in verses 19-20: "And you will know his great power. It can't be compared with anything else. It is at work for us who believe. It is like the mighty strength God showed when he raised Christ from the dead."

I love the phrase, "And you will know his great power" – This is a power you've ALREADY RECEIVED!

Day 25

THOUGHT OF THE DAY: Don't let go of your dream

Run. Go get your watering can and pour water on your dream. This water will refresh your dream. It will revive it. This water will cause your dream to grow.

So many of us haven't watered/nurtured our dream. We all know if the same were true of our plants, that they'd eventually die. The water that's available to us can also bring dead plants back to life, just like dead dreams.

Go get the watering can, because God has come to revive your dreams. I can actually feel wind blowing on my face and neck. Go get your watering can, because God is about to rekindle, refresh, and revive your dreams.

There was an old song by Sam and Dave called "Hold On, I'm Coming." The key lyrics in the song are "Just hold on, I'm comin', Hold on, I'm comin'." The question concerns what we're doing while we're holding on. Perhaps our answer is in Galatians 6:9: "And let us not get tired of doing what is right, for after a while we will reap a harvest of blessing if we don't get discouraged and give up." (TLB) There are two key words here: tired and discouraged. When these set in we let our guard down and can become lethargic. Soon our dream is swallowed up by the concerns of life.

So go get the watering can, because God is about to pour out in such a way that we won't be able to contain everything He's determined to do. Zechariah 8:15: "So again in these days I am determined to do good to Jerusalem and to the house of Judah. Do not fear."

GOD IS DETERMINED! DO NOT WHAT? Yes, FEAR.

Go get the watering can! Isaiah 44:3: "For I will pour water on him who is thirsty, And floods on the dry ground."

Day 26

THOUGHT OF THE DAY: The place of surrender

In each of us there's a place of surrender. In fact, we'll visit this same place a number of times during our walk.

21

This is the place where we totally and unconditionally surrender everything to the Lord. It's where we give ourselves without reservation no matter the consequences. Jesus did this in the Garden of Gethsemane - Matthew 26:39 "He went a little farther and fell on His face, and prayed, saying, 'O My Father, if it is possible, let this cup pass from Me; nevertheless, not as I will, but as You will.' " We'll never know the cross (another place of surrender) until we go to the garden.

Earlier Jesus declares that He's had to come not to do His will, but His Father's. As we all know, there's a significant difference between saying you're willing to do God's will and actually doing it. The place of surrender is where we live out Matthew 22:37: "Jesus replied, 'You must love the Lord your God with all your heart, all your soul, and all your mind.' " (NLT)

The verse says you MUST!

In 1972 when Donna was 20 years old and I was 24, we had been married 11 months. It was Christmas Eve, and Donna told me that her water had broken. We were so excited but had no idea what the next 40 hours would hold. We jumped in the car and drove to a home in Middletown, Rhode Island. That's right, we drove to a home in order to have home birth. We called the sixty-something year old midwife before we left and she eventually met us on Maple Street.

Donna's labor started out like any other but lasted 36 hours. For eight hours Donna pushed. She was so tired she fell asleep between contractions, and I would wake her just before the next one. Our son would crown and then retrieve back into Donna's cervix. This went on for eight hours. Something was wrong. By this time Donna was bleeding, and the look on the midwife's face said it all – we were in trouble. She left the room, and I decided to go to the bathroom and pray. On the way there I heard the midwife say to the couple who owned the home, "I think the baby is dead." I knelt down and wrapped my arms around the old sweaty toilet and prayed. "Lord, if my son dies it won't change a thing. I will love and serve you all my life. If Donna dies, it doesn't change a thing. I will love and serve you forever. If they both die, I will love and serve you forever."

I left the bathroom and within two minutes Josh came out far enough to remove the birth cord from his neck and then retracted back into Donna's cervix. With the next push, the cord was removed from his neck again, and back into the cervix he went. The third time when the cord was removed from his throat, he came out. He was a bit blue and wasn't breathing. Then after what seemed to be minutes, he cried, and then peed.

This was the first, but there have been many times since, when Donna and I have together surrendered.

God is looking for a people who are willing to go to the place of surrender, because He knows that you "Love the Lord your God with all your heart, all your soul, and all your mind."

It is in the place of surrender where we put the Lord above all things. I know many of you are at this place again, but where else would you really want to be? As with Jesus in the Garden of Gethsemane, God will strengthen you. "Then an angel appeared to Him from heaven, strengthening Him." (Luke 22:43)

Remember, you are not alone in the place of surrender!!

Day 27

THOUGHT OF THE DAY: Where is the move of God?

Where is revival? Where are the signs and wonders? Where are the miracles?

The answer is quite simple and profound – the move of God is in you!

A number of months ago I was asking God these same questions and was speaking with Him about how I couldn't wait for revival. He said, "Stop waiting." Then He said, "You (meaning all of us) carry revival." We keep waiting for someone else to spark revival when each of us carries that anointing within us.

It was then that I could see that no matter where I went, I carried revival. I began realizing that we are the temple of the God, so we don't have to go to a meeting, because we ARE the meeting. I began to realize that as the ark of God carried the presence of God, we too are the ark of God.

I am in no way suggesting I have all of this figured out and that I fully comprehend it all, but I've begun. You're welcome to join me. You don't need a certificate of ordination hanging on your wall, because you've already been ordained, not by human hands, but by heavenly ones.

On a daily basis wherever we go, in fact, we're literally carrying the presence of God, His move, His revival. Awareness of this has helped me to develop a God-consciousness which causes me, before I go into a store, for example, to turn to the empty seat in my car and say, "We're going in now. Help me to see what you might be doing there."

We need to stop looking for the move of God and realize that we're carriers of it!

Remember how when Jesus shows up, those who were demonized began manifesting? He didn't say a word. See Mark five and Luke 4:31-

34: "Then He went down to Capernaum, a city of Galilee, and was teaching them on the Sabbaths. And they were astonished at His teaching, for His word was with authority. Now in the synagogue there was a man who had a spirit of an unclean demon. And he cried out with a loud voice, saying, 'Let us alone! What have we to do with You, Jesus of Nazareth? Did You come to destroy us? I know who You are—the Holy One of God!' "

We need to know who we are!

Listen, we've all been waiting for who we're going to be instead of realizing who we are NOW. Sure, the anointing increases, but here's a key: "Use what you have." The more we exercise our faith, the more it increases.

God is looking for people He can work through. Ezekiel 22:30 says, "So I sought for a man among them who would make a wall, and stand in the gap." He is still looking. Second Chronicles 16:9 says, "For the eyes of the Lord run to and fro throughout the whole earth, to show Himself strong on behalf of those whose heart is loyal to Him." Isaiah 6:8-9: "I heard the voice of the Lord, saying: 'Whom shall I send, And who will go for Us?' The answer: then I said, 'Here am I! Send me.' " For what reason? "And He said, 'Go, and tell this people' "

God wants to and IS moving! He's moving through ordinary people who He's already anointed. You want a move of God, then be one. You want revival, be it.

Where is the move of God? It's in YOU!

Day 28

THOUGHT OF THE DAY: Revival before judgment

I am often asked where I believe we are in relationship to the coming judgment of God.

I am convinced that God is holding back His judgment. Why? Because He delights in mercy. I know that when judgment comes many people will turn to the Lord, but I'm convinced that God will, and in fact has begun to pour out His Spirit as He promised in Joel. I do believe He's trying to awaken the church. Joel 3:9 says, "Wake up the mighty men and bring them down to the Valley of decision" – Joel 3:2: "Bring them down to the Valley of Jehoshaphat." Verse 14: "Multitudes, multitudes in the valley of decision!"

Can't we hear God saying – "Realize who you are," realize that you've been empowered, realize you are the church. As I have sent others, I'm now sending you. It's not about your ability. It's about my ability in you.

In Jeremiah 31 it says that God will gather His people and that they'll come streaming to the goodness of the Lord (verse 12). Romans 2:4 says that it's the "goodness of God which leads you to repentance."

I believe that God is and will send new wine. He's trying to show us that the old isn't working. After this next move of God worldwide, then judgment will come.

All of us hold the key to revival because we all carry it. So the question is, what are we going to do? Will we continue as we are, or will we become who we were created to be?

Day 29

THOUGHT OF THE DAY: Are we safe yet?

I've begun to look once again at the message and ministry of Jesus. It can be summarized very simply in three words: Kingdom of God.

In Luke four Jesus gets up early to pray, and when his disciples find him, they bring him back to pray for all the people who've come to be healed. If you remember, Jesus refuses and says to them in Luke 4:43: "I must preach the kingdom of God to the other cities also, because for this purpose I have been sent."

Now if the purpose of Jesus being sent here was to preach the Kingdom of God, two things come to my mind. One is, what was the message of the Kingdom of God, and two, are we preaching it? As I once again look at this, I realize that most of our churches haven't understood nor have they lived out this message of the kingdom. In the four gospels, the Kingdom of God and the Kingdom of Heaven are mentioned 86 times.

When we look at Jesus' ministry, we quickly conclude that it was radical. When I reflect on the years I've been a believer, I ask myself if the ministry I've done looks like Jesus' ministry?

I've come to realize that one of the primary missions of the church is to equip, train, and send people into the Father's vineyard. I think we've instead built cocoons where we teach people about Jesus and every once in a while, leave our "safe harbor" to do a community event or offer a mission trip. Our children's programs and our schools seem to have one primary goal – keeping our children safe. I wonder what kind of church Jesus would have built?

Jesus spent the majority of his time with people we avoid or people we only visit occasionally. Jesus really didn't have a ministry; he had his life. Perhaps we could spend some time in the gospels to really look at what Jesus said and did.

Look, I'm not throwing rocks at the church. I'm just trying to become the church that Jesus died for. I'm not saying everything we've done has been a failure or for nothing. I'm just saying that I want people to look at us (his Church) and say that its people remind them of Jesus.

We are entering uncharted waters. I certainly don't have all the answers, but I know this – IT'S TIME FOR RADICAL CHANGE...

Are we safe yet?

Day 30

THOUGHT OF THE DAY: Walking past the wounded

Each day we journey down roads similar to the road from Jerusalem to Jericho. More often than not we run across someone who's been stripped and is wounded and half dead. This is the parable of Luke 10.

How often do we meet people robbed of their dignity and stripped emotionally and mentally by the world? These are people who live each day wounded and hurting. They're people just like you and me. They've been beaten and wounded. Ever been so stripped and wounded that it's taken the very life out of you? We just want someone to care.

In Luke 10 the priest and the Levite saw the wounded man. I'll say that again, they saw the wounded man, and they avoided him. It says in verses 31 & 32 that they "passed by on the other side." Too busy? Didn't care? I have enough of my own problems? Full of religion but absent of true religion? Fill in the blank.

Thank God for the Samaritans, who are often the most unlikely people! Verse 33 says, "But a certain Samaritan, as he journeyed, came where he was. And when he saw him, he had compassion." The difference between the priest, the Levite, and the Samaritan was compassion. Twelve times in scripture we see that Jesus was motivated by compassion. First Peter 3:8-9: "Finally, all of you be of one mind, having compassion for one another; love as brothers, be tenderhearted, be courteous; not returning evil for evil or reviling for reviling, but on the contrary blessing, knowing that you were called to this, that you may inherit a blessing." We were called to be a blessing and to love and have compassion.

Back to Luke 10 and verses 34-35: "So he went to him and bandaged his wounds, pouring on oil and wine; and he set him on his own animal, brought him to an inn, and took care of him. On the next day, when he departed, he took out two denarii, gave them to the innkeeper, and said to him, 'Take care of him.' " Lessons – he bandaged wounds and sacrificed time and comfort (walking while the wounded man rode). He made sure he was cared for, and yes, he spent his own money.

Over the past two years I've been in stores, restaurants, churches, on the street, in homes, and even conducting prophetic meetings, and see hurting and wounded people, and the Holy Spirit will tell me to go and pay for their groceries, pay for their meal, or just give them money. I was in a meeting some time ago when God told me to give a particular person a large sum of money. I told God I couldn't afford it, and He said, "You can't afford not to do it." Listen, we can have compassion and care for people without money, but we need to be willing to give money when prompted.

Matthew 25:44-45: "Lord, when did we see You hungry or thirsty or a stranger or naked or sick or in prison, and did not minister to You? Then He will answer them, saying, 'Assuredly, I say to you, inasmuch as you did not do it to one of the least of these, you did not do it to Me.' "

Today is a new day. Let's not pass by the wounded.

Day 31

THOUGHT OF THE DAY: Our God is able

This morning I keep hearing over and over again Luke 1:37: "For with God nothing will be impossible." The NCV says, "God can do anything!" Go ahead and say it, NOTHING IS IMPOSSIBLE; say it again, NOTHING IS IMPOSSIBLE. Our biggest challenges are staying out of God's way, being willing to wait and do nothing but trust, and doing what He tells us to do and nothing more. OUR GOD IS ABLE...

In 1 Samuel 13:5 it says, "Then the Philistines gathered together to fight with Israel, thirty thousand chariots and six thousand horsemen, and people as the sand which is on the seashore in multitude." How did Israel react? Verses 6-7: "When the men of Israel saw that they were in danger (for the people were distressed), then the people hid in caves, in thickets, in rocks, in holes, and in pits. And some of the Hebrews crossed over the Jordan to the land of Gad and Gilead."

Come on now. What would we do? This isn't like hearing some strange noise outside our home. This isn't like being behind in our rent or mortgage. Verses 7-9: "As for Saul, he was still in Gilgal, and all the people followed him trembling. Then he waited seven days, according to the time set by Samuel. But Samuel did not come to Gilgal; and the people were scattered from him. So Saul said, 'Bring a burnt offering and peace offerings here to me.' And he offered the burnt offering."

That the people were afraid is an understatement! Saul was given instructions by Samuel to WAIT. He was told to wait seven days, and when Samuel doesn't read his clock correctly, Saul takes it upon himself to DO SOMETHING. We know the feeling – I HAVE to do something. Now this is what follows in verse 10: "Now it happened, as soon as he had finished presenting the burnt offering, that Samuel came." Samuel asks the big question in verse 11: "What have you done?"

How many times do we regret not waiting just a little while longer? Here is Saul's EXCUSE. He said, "When I saw that the people were scattered from me, and that you did not come within the days appointed, and that the Philistines gathered together at Michmash, then I said, 'The Philistines will now come down on me at Gilgal, and I have not made supplication to the Lord.' Therefore I felt compelled, and offered a burnt offering."

He felt compelled. Samuel responds in verse 13: "And Samuel said to Saul, 'You have done foolishly. You have not kept the commandment of the Lord your God, which He commanded you.' " The consequences were awful: "But now your kingdom shall not continue. The Lord has sought for Himself a man after His own heart." (verse 14)

God takes away the kingdom from Saul. Now this wasn't Saul's first sin. His repeated behavior eventually cost him his kingdom. What was God really after - a man with the right heart.

If he'd only waited a little while longer. The problem wasn't that Samuel came late (someone else's fault). The problem was that he didn't have the right heart to know that OUR GOD IS ABLE. THAT NOTHING IS IMPOSSIBLE.

Today and in the days ahead, please remember that it's not what WE can do! It's our GOD who IS ABLE!

Day 32

THOUGHT OF THE DAY: Has your God been able to deliver you?

This was the question Nebuchadnezzar asked Daniel as he ran. It says, "very early in the morning." (Daniel 6:19)

From inside the cave Daniel yells, "My God sent His angel and shut the lions' mouths, so that they have not hurt me, because I was found innocent before Him; and also, O king, I have done no wrong before you." (Daniel 6:22)

There is a confidence we can have when we're walking in obedience. The enemy is always looking for ways to accuse us. Daniel 6:4 says, "So the governors and satraps sought to find some charge against Daniel concerning the kingdom; but they could find no charge or fault, because he was faithful; nor was there any error or fault found in him." Our God is full of mercy, but when we walk through life as Daniel did, there is a greater confidence we can have. In John 14:30 Jesus says, "I will no longer talk much with you, for the ruler of this world is coming, and he has nothing in Me."

I am not able to say that YET... but oh, how I'm asking the Holy Spirit to direct my thoughts and decisions. Let's strip Satan of every legal right he has to accuse us!

Yes, God is able to deliver us, but if He chooses not to, I want the heart of Daniel's three companions. In Daniel 3:17-18 they tell Nebuchadnezzar after refusing to worship his image - "If that is the case, our God whom we serve is able to deliver us from the burning fiery furnace, and He will deliver us from your hand, O king. But if not, let it be known to you, O king, that we do not serve your gods, nor will we worship the gold image which you have set up."

Whether God chooses to deliver us or not, we must purpose in our hearts that we will not compromise. Remember that Joseph did it right and still ended up in prison because it was vital to God's plan and Joseph's growth. I'm not contradicting myself; I'm being honest with the scriptures.

Has your God been able to deliver you? Undoubtedly we can all say, "Yes, over and over again." Lord you have been so faithful – we have to say THANK YOU...

Day 33

THOUGHT OF THE DAY: I don't know what to say

How often have we been in situations among friends, coworkers, strangers, bosses, or people who have prestige or authority, and we've found it difficult to express our faith or conviction regarding the topic at hand?

There have been times we know that we should say something, but we just can't "find" the words or think that they'll come out wrong or that we'll look foolish. Well, we've all been there, but there's a solution that Jesus shares with us in Luke 11.

First, I think we all can agree that there are various reasons we react this way.

- We're still in the process of understanding our identity.
- We're still understanding that we carry the power and presence of God.
- We're still understanding that we've been sent to represent the Kingdom of God as ambassadors.
- We're still relying on our own strength and ability.
- We're still understanding that all the resources of heaven on earth are available to EACH of us.
- We're relying on OURSELVES...

The bottom line is that we're all growing and learning and that our Father is meanwhile so in love with each of us. Our inabilities don't cause Him to love us any less. He's ever trying to encourage us to become who He created us to be and presents us with opportunities so we can be challenged, so we can grow.

Now here is Jesus' instruction to us with regard to overcoming our inabilities in these areas. Luke 12:11-12: "Now when they bring you to the synagogues and magistrates and authorities, do not worry about how or what you should answer, or what you should say. For the Holy Spirit will teach you in that very hour what you ought to say."

It seems simple! Don't worry and the Holy Spirit "WILL TEACH YOU IN THAT VERY HOUR WHAT YOU OUGHT TO SAY." It's interesting that it doesn't say to speak what we think we should say.

Therefore the seventh item on the list should read, "We have preconceived thoughts/ideas what we think we should say." The effect is to limit the work of the Holy Spirit, because we're unable to see what really needs to be accomplished.

It's true that in any given moment I may not know what to say, but... the Holy Spirit DOES!

Day 34

THOUGHT OF THE DAY: It's time for TOTAL ABANDONMENT!

We've all been and are being stirred and provoked. There is a "holy dissatisfaction," a yearning, a discontentment, a desire for more. More of the Holy Spirit, more revelation, more power, more zeal, more love, more compassion, more of everything that God has for us. This is the answer to your prayer. God is doing something in us that we could not do.

The only thing that stands in the way is our old man. By holding onto our own lives we're in fact losing our true lives. Luke 17:33 says, "If you grasp and cling to life on your terms, you'll lose it, but if you let that life go, you'll get life on God's terms." (MSG) Isn't that the case - that we've been doing a lot of our lives on our own terms?

In Matthew four we see Peter, Andrew, James, and John being called by Jesus. I know you're hearing the same call! It says in Verse 20, "They immediately left their nets and followed Him." Then verse 22: "and immediately they left the boat and their father, and followed Him."

What's holding us back from abandoning everything and simply following what the Holy Spirit is showing us to do? I'm not saying leave your jobs, etcetera, but make the bold move into an abandoned life style.

This isn't a life of knowing where you're going or what's going to happen. That doesn't take faith. Hebrews 11:8 tells us that "By faith

Abraham obeyed when he was called to go out to the place which he would receive as an inheritance. And he went out, not knowing where he was going." Did you notice that he was called out to the place where he'd receive "an inheritance?"

Yes, you're receiving the same call as Abraham. You're being asked.to leave where you are, and when you do, you'll receive an inheritance. This isn't the full inheritance, but things you've been promised and things that have been reserved for you. You've known God had more for you, the problem was that in the place you were, you couldn't receive it.

I can sense your excitement.

Aren't we all tired of being stirred and not responding? What do we have to lose? The answer is "lots." Sure, we'll be saved, but we'll miss what we've been created for. Just say, "Yes, Lord. Do what I can't." Then take a single step.

It's time for TOTAL ABANDONMENT!

Day 35

THOUGHT OF THE DAY: Today we HONOR

When I awoke this morning I heard, "Everyone you meet today, everyone you see today, you must honor."

Everyone was created by our Father, each one created for a purpose, each having the potential of being our brother or sister in Christ. As I write this, though, I can see my judgmental spirit. I can see how I so easily judge people by what I see: I don't like the way they look. I don't like their body language. I don't like their tone of voice. With these prejudices in my heart, how can I truly love and honor them?

How often is it that when we cross paths with someone, our first interaction isn't positive? And under those conditions what we probably do is to develop a negative attitude toward them. Of course, we never actually greet them with a "lousy" attitude. Of course, we're always gracious, loving, and warm. We never have a bad day. We're always carrying the love of Christ. We're always loving people the way Jesus did and the way He would.

Oh, am I ever carnal! James talks about a fountain of water and how it can't be both sweet and bitter. And yet, how often is ours?

All that changes today! Today we begin living out Philippians 2:3, which says, "Let each esteem others better than himself." This means we place greater value on someone else than we put on ourselves. Honor is loving and assigning value. The (ERV) says, "In whatever you do, don't let selfishness or pride be your guide. Be humble, and honor others more than yourselves."

When Paul wrote the church of Corinth, he said that he "determined not to know people after the flesh." (2 Corinthians 2:2). If we allow ourselves the liberty of looking at people in our flesh, we'll never truly love or honor them.

Today AND tomorrow we determine to HONOR.

Day 36

THOUGHT OF THE DAY: The cry of God's heart – if you only knew!

For years we've known theologically that God loves us. This was particularly true when we first accepted Christ. We were in awe that He would so freely give His life in such a brutal fashion to forgive us and accept us as His son or daughter.

As years have gone by, however, we somehow began trying to EARN His approval. Much like the Church of Ephesus, we lost our first love. We have been lied to by the evil one, and even our own minds have deceived us. We started out rejoicing that we were forgiven and that there was a PLAN for each of our lives. It was so simple, and we were overwhelmed. Today as I awoke, I kept on hearing, "If you only knew."

The Song of Solomon is a book we rarely even flip through, but so critical to knowing this reality. Song of Solomon 7:11-13 says,

Come, my beloved, let us go out into the fields and stay in the villages. Let us get up early and go out to the vineyards and see whether the vines have budded, whether the blossoms have opened, and whether the pomegranates are in flower. And there I will give you my love. There the mandrakes give forth their fragrance, and the rarest fruits are at our doors, the new as well as old, for I have stored them up for my beloved. (TLB)

If we would take the time and rise up early before the clutter of the day and walk with him through His kingdom, we would see the "flowers in bloom." Here we could learn to receive His love. Oh, if we only knew!

A number of years ago I was walking down the stairs at our home on the most magnificent spring day. There was a warm gentle breeze caressing my face, the flowers had just started to break through the ground, and an incredible fragrance filled the air. I said, "Lord what a beautiful spring day," and He answered back by saying, "You have missed a lot of springs." If we only knew!

That day on my front steps the Holy Spirit put in my heart not to miss another day of "walking with Him." He put a determination in me to enjoy and cherish each day. I have not done this perfectly, but in this journey, I've come to understand that when I was born again, I entered the Kingdom of God. In John 3:5 we see, "Jesus answered, 'Most assuredly, I say to you, unless one is born of water and the Spirit, he cannot enter the kingdom of God.'"

Though many of us are waiting to die (in our natural bodies) to enter His kingdom, this clearly implies that it's at the point of being born again that we have that privilege. We HAVE in fact, ALREADY died – the old man is dead; crucified with Christ. Not only have we entered the kingdom, but we can see it. John 3:3: "Jesus answered and said to him, 'Most assuredly, I say to you, unless one is born again, he cannot see the kingdom of God.'"

WE CAN SEE THE KINGDOM. It's here, and we can see spring. Oh, if we only knew!

Back to Song of Solomon. Did we notice verse 13 – "There the mandrakes give forth their fragrance, and the rarest fruits are at our doors, the new as well as old, for I have stored them up for my beloved." God has stored away for us. It's even at our door. Fruits of love, mercy, grace, affection, power, gifts, His presence, and so much more. We can all sit before Him and allow Him to show us the things He's stored away for each of us. First Peter 1:4 tells us we have "inheritance incorruptible and undefiled and that does not fade away, reserved in heaven for you."

Sadly, though, we've all been waiting to receive our inheritance instead of enjoying it now. If we only knew!

If we only knew HOW MUCH HE LOVES US!

Day 37

THOUGHT OF THE DAY: Don't sweat

How much time have we all spent in striving? How much time have we all spent fretting and being anxious about things over which we have no control? How many hours, days, and even weeks have we spent worrying? Even when it comes to ministry, we've spent too much time striving and worrying! In Ezekiel 44 the sons of Zadok were given the following instructions. Ezekiel 44:16-16:

They shall (priests) enter My sanctuary, and they shall come near My table to minister to Me, and they shall keep My charge. And it shall be, whenever they enter the gates of the inner court, that they shall put on linen garments; no wool shall come upon them while they minister within the gates of the inner court or within the house. They shall have linen turbans on their heads and linen trousers on their bodies; they shall not clothe themselves with anything that causes sweat.

We're not supposed to sweat. We aren't to lose our peace when pressure comes. When we determine that we won't allow situations or circumstances to steal our peace and joy, we'll discover we're no longer sweating.

Take off the wool and stop sweating.

Day 38

THOUGHT OF THE DAY: "They will take you where you do not want to go."

This quote is taken from John 21:18: "I tell you the truth. When you were young, you put on your own belt. You went where you wanted to go. But when you are old, you will put out your hands. Others will put your belt on for you. They will take you where you do not want to go." (WE)

Haven't we all discovered that as we've gotten older the Holy Spirit has allowed us to go places we wouldn't have chosen? Why? This isn't easily answered, but in summary, it's been for our equipping, our training. It's put things in us and taken things out of us. It's so we could have empathy, compassion, understanding, insight, and so on, not only for ourselves, but more importantly for others. In Hebrews 2:18 we read "Since he himself has gone through suffering and testing, He is able to help us when we are being tested." (NLT) Yes, He's also allowed or has even led us into situations so we could help others.

Haven't we all asked or at least thought, "How come I go through these things and others don't?" In John 21 when Jesus is talking to Peter about how he'll be taken places he wouldn't have chosen, Jesus says very simply that he is to "follow him." In verse 19 when Peter is looking at John laying on his breast, he responds, "But Lord, what about this man?"

We're not to compare ourselves with others, but simply follow. We need to embrace the heart of Peter and John after they were arrested and beaten. Acts 5:41: "So they departed from the presence of the council, rejoicing that they were counted worthy to suffer shame for His name."

Lord, we praise you for having taken us to places where we didn't want to go and will praise you when you do it again!

<u>Day 39</u>

THOUGHT OF THE DAY: "What shall I give you?"

In 1 Kings 3:5 it says, "At Gibeon the Lord appeared to Solomon in a dream by night; and God said, 'Ask! What shall I give you?' " Imagine for a moment that God appears to you asking the same question.

Our answer would reveal a lot about what's really in our heart. So what would our answer be? Would we ask for ourselves? Would we ask for something temporal or something eternal?

You see, in reality we're being asked that question each time we pray. Just considering this idea makes me pause. Even in these few moments I can see that many of the things I ask for are short-sighted. Many things I ask for are about making things better for myself so that my life will be more comfortable. I give God His assignment and am very "reverent" as I give Him my to-do list, which, not incidently, often includes who God needs to fix!

I remember when I was first married, I had a huge closet where I'd pray. Almost daily I'd pray for my wife and ask the Lord to touch her so she would be used for His kingdom's sake. One day the Lord said to me, "You keep on praying that you want me to touch your wife for my kingdom's sake, yet what you're really asking is that I would change her for your sake. You want her conformed into the image of what you want her to be. You want me to change her so your life will be better."

Now I don't want you to get the wrong idea. Donna was a marvelous wife; I just wanted a few adjustments. And yes, it's true; they were for my sake and not really for the kingdom.

So here's the question. "What shall I give you?"

Often our prayer is like a "honey-do list." You know, honey do this and honey, do that. As I'm writing this I'm asking what I should ask for. I'm getting a very small glimpse of the immense magnitude of the responsibility we've all been given. Here in 1 Kings 3:12 it says, "Behold, I have done according to your words," and in Daniel 10:12 God says, "Then he said to me, 'Do not fear, Daniel, for from the first day that you set your heart to understand, and to humble yourself before your God, your words were heard; and I have come because of your words.' " Back in 1 Kings when Solomon answered God, this is what he asked for: "Therefore give to Your servant an understanding heart to judge Your people, that I may discern between good and evil." (verse 8) In both cases they pray not for themselves, but for understanding to know what they should do for the good of others – in other words, to have God's heart.

God's response to Solomon is in verses 10-13:

The speech pleased the Lord, that Solomon had asked this thing. Then God said to him: "Because you have asked this thing, and have not asked long life for yourself; nor have asked riches for yourself, nor have asked the life of your enemies, but have asked for yourself understanding to discern justice, behold, I have done according to your words; see, I have given you a wise and understanding heart, so that there has not been anyone like you before you, nor shall any like you arise after you. And I have also given you what you have not asked: both riches and honor, so that there shall not be anyone like you among the kings all your days."

I love the two statements "I have done according to your words" and "I have come because of your words." Our words can reach God and He will respond. In Jeremiah 29:12 he writes, "Then you will call upon Me and go and pray to Me, and I will listen to you." Psalm 91:15: "He shall call upon Me, and I will answer him."

Jesus said to pray, "Your kingdom come, your will be done," and only after to ask about our daily needs. Paul writes to the Ephesians that they should understand to whom they're praying: "...Him who is able to do exceedingly abundantly above all that we ask or think." (3:20) It's important we pray with that same understanding and mindset.

I can hear these words ringing in my head - "What shall I give you?" Oh Lord, show us how to pray. Help us understand the rest of Ephesians 3:20: "according to the power that works in us." Yes, we have this power in us that when we pray – and because of it, supernatural things will happen.

"What shall I give you?"

Day 40

THOUGHT OF THE DAY: Depressed: discouraged: in debt

In 2 Kings 4 Elisha runs into a widow whose husband has died. He was a prophet and had faithfully served God. She sees Elisha and cries out, telling him that not only is her husband dead but to make things worse, though they had been serving God, they were in debt. Many of us have all been there and are even there now.

She cries out to Elisha for help, and Elisha says to her, "What shall I do for you?" Tell me, what do you have in the house?" Listen to her response: "Your maidservant has nothing in the house but a jar of oil." (2 Kings 4:2) When we are depressed, discouraged, and in debt, our situation steals our ability to see by faith. It creates within us a negative and pessimistic attitude, and wherever we go that attitude follows.

When asked by Elisha she said, "I have nothing." We get so discouraged we forget what we do have and who it is who's asking us – "What shall I do for you?" Often when we get depressed, we lose all motivation. We have a pajama-mentality, so overwhelmed we do nothing. Elisha's solution was "Go, borrow vessels from everywhere, from all your neighbors." The solution is to go – to take action.

Don't let discouragement, depression, and debt steal from you what you do have. Who is it that says to us, "What shall I do for you?"

Day 41

THOUGHT OF THE DAY: Being double-minded
I'm awake but extremely exhausted. Last night I dreamed, and in my dream, I couldn't make up my mind. It was like being on a ship in a storm tossed to and fro.

James 1:8 speaks of the "double-minded man, unstable in all his ways." The amplified says, "(for being as he is) a man of two minds (hesitating, dubious, irresolute), [he is] unstable and unreliable and uncertain about everything (he thinks, feels, decides)." It speaks of how very exhausting this condition is.

When I dream like that, there's a reason. The Lord is prompting me to do some "poking around" in my life. Clearly, He sees that I'm walking in the amplified version of James 1:8 and yet am not really aware of it. I can hear the Lord say "Make a decision," in fact, not only one decision, but more than one.

I'm writing this because I can see a sea of faces. We're all walking around slamming into each other like bumper cars because we're double minded.

So, my dear friends, perhaps God is speaking this to you as well?

Day 42

THOUGHT OF THE DAY: Most of our dreams are too small
Why is this? We don't comprehend:

- How much we're loved
- That we're joint heirs
- That we're forgiven
- That we're complete
- That He really is FOR us
- His power that's available to us
- It's not who we're GOING to be, but who we are NOW
- HOW PROUD HE IS OF US

Day 43

THOUGHT OF THE DAY: We can walk with God

We read in Genesis 3:8: "And they (Adam and Eve) heard the sound of the Lord God walking in the garden in the cool of the day, and Adam and his wife hid themselves from the presence of the Lord God among the trees of the garden."

This verse implies that they were familiar with God walking in the garden, and it doesn't take much to assume that they had walked with Him. Sadly, as is often the case when we sin, we run FROM God and His presence instead of running TO Him.

We've often thought that because of Adam's sin, the privilege of walking with God was lost until Jesus restored it with his death. We read in Genesis 5:22, however, that "Enoch walked with God three hundred years" and in Genesis 6:9 that "Noah walked with God." Then there's this promise in Exodus 33:14: "And He said, 'My Presence will go with you, and I will give you rest.' " Then there's Jesus in John 8:16: "For I am not alone, but I am with the Father who sent Me."

Yesterday morning when I sat to spend time with God, I heard, "I have been waiting for you to realize that I love walking with you. Each morning when you awake, I am there – I have been watching over you all night just as you would watch over your own children, and I couldn't wait for you to wake so we could enjoy each other's company."

Enjoy your walk!

Day 44

THOUGHT OF THE DAY: "Behold, I will do a new thing." (Isaiah 43:19)

I remember when the Holy Spirit spoke this to me a few years ago. I had no idea how life-changing this and the verse previous to it would be to my life, for all intents and purposes turning it upside down. "Do not remember the former things, nor consider the things of old." (Isaiah 43:18)

I've had to be willing to let go of the past, the old way of doing life, doing church. Just when I think I'm doing reasonably well – a dangerous place - the Holy Spirit comes and says, "Well, that was a good start."

Perhaps you'd allow me to share this one thing with you. For over 40 years I've had such a passion for the Kingdom of God that in my zeal I didn't see a very important part of His kingdom. My desire to build His kingdom was so strong, that I often acted at the expense of my family. Don't misunderstand; there are lots of time that your family will need to sacrifice, BUT... In my zeal I perhaps rarely, if ever, asked the Holy Spirit if

I should choose my family or choose serving someone else, the church, etcetera.

We've all preached God, family, ministry. Sadly, though, there's preaching it and then LIVING it. Part of me is afraid to even write this because there are people who will misunderstand what I'm saying. How will they misunderstand? They'll continue to use their family as an excuse not to be committed to the purposes of the Kingdom of God. So please hear me; ask the Holy Spirit how this THOUGHT OF THE DAY applies to you.

I'm writing this from Great Neck, New York. Our daughter asked us to come and celebrate Christmas with her and her fiancé's family. We really do not know them, so this is a wonderful opportunity. Sounds like an easy choice. Actually, it wasn't. I've been away for two weeks and haven't ministered in my home church in three, and was away a lot even before that. Not easy when there's a very important Christmas women's meeting that my wife agonized over not being at. But we knew that the Holy Spirit was saying to go. Yet we wouldn't have done this in the past. Yes – "Behold I do a new thing."

I'm sitting here needing to ask those whom I have pastored to forgive me for perhaps making you feel guilty that you chose family or that you neglected family because you felt that's what I wanted you to do. As much as I thought I had given liberty; perhaps I didn't.

Yes, God is doing a new thing. Please find the balance by asking the Holy Spirit what he thinks.

Father, help us to be willing to forget the way we've done things and be willing to live a new way. We pray that Your kingdom come!

Day 45

THOUGHT OF THE DAY: Do we have the capacity to be able to hear something different/something new?

It's good to have yourself grounded. It's good to hold onto the truths that are absolutes. It's good to be fully persuaded. However, is there room for the Holy Spirit to show you something beyond your boundaries?

We're creatures of habit and routine, and yes, we're at times stubborn. We like what we believe. We like our "little world" and find it unfortunate that people don't think the same as us. It's truly hard to teach us "old dogs new tricks!"

The question remains, however... is the Holy Spirit trying to lead us in a different direction? Is He trying to expand our insight/revelation? I didn't say we're to abandon our convictions. What I'm asking is, are we willing to change? Are we willing to be challenged? Are we willing to allow the Holy Spirit to expand our thinking/insight/revelation?

Peter had this dilemma in Acts 9:9-15. I'm thankful God is persistent:

The next day, as they went on their journey and drew near the city, Peter went up on the housetop to pray, about the sixth hour. Then he became very hungry and wanted to eat; but while they made ready, he fell into a trance and saw heaven opened and an object like a great sheet bound at the four corners, descending to him and let down to the earth. In it were all kinds of four-footed animals of the earth, wild beasts, creeping things, and birds of the air. And a voice came to him, "Rise, Peter; kill and eat." But Peter said, "Not so, Lord! For I have never eaten anything common or unclean." And a voice spoke to him again the second time, "What God has cleansed you must not call common." This was done three times.

I just love Peter's brief conversation with the Lord. We often have the same problem. The Holy Spirit is speaking in prophetic language, yet it's our natural minds which are trying to comprehend what the Holy Spirit is saying.

Two things: It might be good to go back and review the prophetic words we've all been given. Secondly, we need to be willing to hear things outside of our normal/habitual way of thinking/hearing.

This word to Peter changed the entire world. Such a simple word, but look at the results. The gospel was given to the Gentiles, and the Holy Spirit was poured out. A revival started that's still occurring today.

Imagine. You might be given a word to change one life, ten lives, a hundred lives, or perhaps thousands.

Do we have the capacity to be able to hear something different/something new?

Day 46

THOUGHT OF THE DAY: "Those who refuse to help the poor will not receive help when they need it themselves." (Proverbs 21:13 – ERV)

Loving, honoring, and helping those in need is not just a concept for Thanksgiving and Christmas. Last night we were warm and had food to eat, even while there were people in each of our communities who slept in boxes or were in some sort of indescribable living conditions. They may have even gone to sleep not having eaten. Today they awoke with one thing on their mind: trying to survive another day.

Most of us will run around during the next week or so buying one more present. And yet perhaps you'd consider a different kind of gift? Find an organization or agency that is daily doing all they can to personally love, honor, and help those in need. If you don't know of any, we'll be glad to get you in touch with some of these unseen, yet heroic organizations, agencies, and shelters.

"Those who refuse to help the poor will not receive help when they need it themselves."

Day 47

THOUGHT OF THE DAY: The orphanage

Several years ago a number of us went to the Ukraine on a missions trip. We had a young woman who was part of our church community in Massachusetts doing full-time mission work there. To this day, the impact of that trip has changed my life forever.

You might ask what it was that changed my life. The answer is: visiting the orphanages. The images of what I saw are so deeply etched in my mind. There are many days when I close my eyes and am transported back to those precious moments.

When we first arrived, it was a hot and humid day, and I was dressed as a clown. I can remember that when they opened the doors, dozens of children came streaming outside. They were probably 5 to 9 years old and were wearing underpants and hats on their heads – that was it. They followed me with great interest. The rest of the team was swarmed by these little people, many of them calling "Mommy" and "Daddy" to our team members. Several had dirty faces and scraggily hair. They literally clung to our team and followed us no matter where we went. As we left these little ones we headed for another orphanage.

My heart was forever broken.

This morning I'm back there remembering the faces of these children. Faces say so much. They ask, "Will you love me?" "Would you care for me forever?" "Will you take me home?" "Can I be your child?"

Our closest friends were so impacted by this trip they ended up adopting two precious girls who now years later are 15 and 16 and have grown into amazing young women. I can't imagine my life without them. Each time I see them I remember walking around the orphanages wishing I could adopt all the children and take them home.

There are so many days, and today is one of them, where I see myself lost and confused and wanting to be adopted, and praising God that I was. Yes, although I had parents, I was lost and confused in my soul. I was spiritually lost and living with no hope. I was in a spiritual orphanage. If you could've seen me, I was the little boy who was so dirty (having lived in this world), and the dirt was all of my sin. I was an angry little boy who would have been passed by in an orphanage, so much was I dirty and angry and full of problems.

Yet our heavenly Father walked through the orphanage of this world and saw me and saw you and with the biggest smile and tears running down His face, pointed at me/us and said, "I want that little boy/girl!" Though Satan tried to convince Him not to adopt us, He insisted all the more. We read in Galatians four, "You can tell for sure that you are now fully adopted as his own children because God sent the Spirit of his Son into our lives crying out, 'Papa! Father!' " (Message Bible)

I love the phrase "fully adopted." Ephesians 1:4-6: "just as He chose us in Him before the foundation of the world, that we should be holy and without blame before Him in love, having predestined us to adoption as sons by Jesus Christ to Himself, according to the good pleasure of His will, to the praise of the glory of His grace, by which He made us accepted in the Beloved." (NKJV)

That's right, God saw us before the world was created and decided to adopt us that we would "be holy and without blame," and it was His joy to make us "accepted in the Beloved."

This little boy was adopted in 1970.

Day 48

THOUGHT OF THE DAY: He's calling you

Shh/ssh/hush/shush – please be quiet, because I can hear Jesus calling to each of us. I can sense that he just wants to be with us. He has something to say –

I'm being serious. HE'S CALLING YOU!

We have some amazing examples in scripture of how God calls to us when things in our lives are upside down.

· John 20:1: "Now on the first day of the week Mary Magdalene went to the tomb early, while it was still dark" – Jesus had died

I love the phrase "while it was still dark." How often in our lives when things are the darkest, does he call to us by our name? "Jesus said to her, "Mary!" Can you hear Him? "He is calling you." (verse 16)

He calls to us when we cannot see.

· Mark 10:49: "Then they called the blind man, saying to him, 'Be of good cheer. Rise, He is calling you.' "

"Be of good cheer." Now, this is important: "Rise;" don't stay immobilized – don't stay stuck. Why? Because "He is calling you." What would have happened if the blind man had stayed seated?

Can you hear Him? "He is calling you."

He calls to us when we're grieving and don't understand. We're questioning why He's delayed coming; why He didn't answer our prayer the way we wanted or expected.

· John 11:28: "The Teacher has come and is calling for you." At the tomb of Lazarus, He called. Can you hear Him? "He is calling you."

He calls to us when we're depressed and disappointed, and when He does, the key is what Elijah had to learn on the mountain - listening for the still small voice. Too often we look for God or can't hear Him because it's too noisy.

· 1 Kings 9:12 -13: "a still small voice. So it was, when Elijah heard it, that he wrapped his face in his mantle and went out and stood in the entrance of the cave. Suddenly a voice came to him."

Can you hear Him? "He's calling you."

Day 49

THOUGHT OF THE DAY: I am honored

When I awoke this morning, I was overcome with a sense of honor. Can we grasp the honor we have in knowing the Lord?

In my silly mind I could see the angels clearing their throats getting ready to sing. My daughter sang for years, and I've been around enough worship teams warming up their vocal cords to recognize the very unusual sounds coming from them as they prepare. I could see the scripture in Luke 2:13-14: "And suddenly there was with the angel a multitude of the heavenly host praising God and saying: 'Glory to God in the highest, And on earth peace, goodwill toward men!' "

As I write this I can't help but sit here and praise, and the more I praise, the more tears fill my eyes and run down my cheeks. There's no need to continue because I've been enveloped with the joy of His presence. Perhaps you too can join with the angels and right now at this moment clear your voice and worship Him.

Revelation 19:4: "And the twenty-four elders and the four living creatures fell down and worshiped God who sat on the throne, saying, 'Amen! Alleluia!' "

I'm honored that I might fall down and sing.

Day 50

THOUGHT OF THE DAY: What did Joseph and Mary have in common?

They were people who "pondered" (thought and considered) what was happening in their lives and how they should respond.

Luke 2:18-19: "And all those who heard it marveled at those things which were told them by the shepherds. But Mary kept all these things and pondered them in her heart." Roberson Word Pictures (RWP), says "Pondering (sunballousa). An old Greek word. Placing together for comparison. Mary would go over each detail of the words of Gabriel and of the shepherds and compare the sayings with the facts so far developed and brood over all of it with a mother's high hopes and joy."

Matthew 1:19-21:

But Joseph, her husband, being [a] righteous [man], and unwilling to expose her publicly, purposed to have put her away secretly; but while he pondered on these things, behold, an angel of [the] Lord appeared to him in a dream, saying, "Joseph, son of David, fear not to take to [thee] Mary, thy wife, for that which is begotten in her is of [the] Holy Spirit. And she shall bring forth a son, and thou shalt call his name Jesus, for he shall save his people from their sins." (Darby)

Perhaps today or as soon as we can, we should take some time to ponder where we are. What is the Holy Spirit saying to us? What do the circumstances in our lives have to do with the purposes of God? Joseph could've followed the law and divorced Mary but by "pondering" it, gave the Holy Spirit an opportunity to show him what he should do. There is what may appear right to us, and then there is God's heart and mind on the matter.

Let's learn from Hebrews 4:1-3: "Therefore, since a promise remains of entering His rest, let us fear lest any of you seem to have come short of it. For indeed the gospel was preached to us as well as to them; but the word which they heard did not profit them, not being mixed with faith in those who heard it."

Day 51

THOUGHT OF THE DAY: Where are your accusers?

Time to get your dancing shoes on – because the moment we sin, the provision for forgiveness is available. YES, THE VERY MOMENT OF SIN IS THE SAME MOMENT OF FORGIVENESS!

I love the story of the woman who was caught in adultery. (In our current culture it is no big deal, but in that culture, it warranted death. And yes, in God's kingdom-culture, this sin and all others are worthy of death when we do not repent.) Here is John 8:9-11 as they bring the woman to Jesus:

They said this to test him, so that they might have some good grounds for an accusation. But Jesus stooped down and began to write with his finger in the dust on the ground. But as they persisted in their questioning, he straightened himself up and said to them, "Let the one among you who has never sinned throw the first stone at her." Then he stooped down again and continued writing with his finger on the ground. And when they heard what he said, they were convicted by their own consciences and went out, one by one, beginning with the eldest until they had all gone. Jesus was left alone, with the woman still standing where they had put her. So he stood up and said to her, "Where are they all—did no one condemn you?" And she said, "No one, sir." "Neither do I condemn you," said Jesus to her. "Go home and do not sin again." (J.B. Phillips New Testament)

Did you see the statement, "they persisted in their questioning?" That is how Satan works; he's persistent in accusing us. But praise God, the Holy Spirit is also persistent: always reaching out, always calling. I can hear the words of Jesus saying, "Come to me."

In this story Jesus asks, "Where are your accusers?" We don't have to live a life listening to accusations. We don't have to live a life hounded by Satan who is the "accuser of the brethren." (Revelation 12:10) Jesus said to the woman and He says to us "Neither do I condemn you." Yes, he said, "Go and sin no more," but if we sin, there's immediate provision.

As I'm asking myself why I'm writing this, I just keep on hearing that there are many who need to hear this today, and others will need to have this placed in their hearts for another time.

Finally, Hebrews 9:14: "How much more will the blood of Christ, who through the eternal Spirit offered himself without blemish to God, purify our conscience from dead works to worship the living God!" (NRSVA)

Where are your accusers?

Day 52

THOUGHT OF THE DAY: Where did you sleep last night?

It was 10:45 p.m. and I was getting out of my car in downtown Fall River near the two overnight shelters. A young woman in her early twenties approached me for a cigarette. I said, "I'm sorry I don't smoke." She replied that there was nothing to be sorry for. She had on a wind breaker. I reached in my pocket and handed her five dollars.

With tears in her eyes she thanked me and asked what was I doing out so late. I told her that I was the night supervisor at the shelter inside the Baptist Church. She asked if she could come in for the night. I apologized but told her that she needed to apply at the other shelter on North Main Street. With that she put her head down and walked off into the frigid night air.

Where did you sleep last night?

I met Pastor Tom, and we went inside the church to supervise the shelter from 11:00 p.m. to 7:00 the next morning. When we got inside, we were greeted by three people from our church who had been there since 7:00 p.m. when the shelter opened.

You want to talk about feeling proud of people! Our small church community has taken on the responsibility of caring for the people in the shelter every Tuesday for the next two months. Couple that with our monthly food pantry! I am one proud pastor for the people God has sent to love those in need.

Once inside we found that the lights had just been turned off for the night. There were men in one room and women in the other whose whole lives fit inside one bag. The rooms were dry and a little chilly but provided a place to sleep. From the time we arrived, one person was snoring so loudly (perhaps the loudest I've ever heard) that a number of the men couldn't sleep. They got up, visited the bathroom, and returned to bed. This was a pattern until after 2:30 a.m. when finally, someone woke the person. Imagine walking the streets all day? How tired would we be?

Where did you sleep last night?

In the kitchen were day-old donuts and a couple sheet cakes sitting on the counter. This was the evening snack, and yes, their breakfast. We had to wake everyone up at 6:00 a.m. They'd run out of coffee so went without until someone came at 6:15 to bring the night to a conclusion. They had cereal and donuts for breakfast, then folded their rollaway beds and brought them to where they're stored for the day. They swept, cleaned, and made sure that everything was picked up. My eyes filled with tears seeing their sincere care for the place that had been provided for them. By 7:00 a.m. they were all gone, having picked up their bag of belongings to carry with them throughout the day.

Where did you sleep last night?

For as many who were in the shelters last night there were many more huddled somewhere trying to make it through the night.

Where did you sleep last night?

As I got in my car and drove away last night, I was filled with such gratitude that I was driving back to a home and a bed. I was filled with gratitude for having the privilege of being able to care for people right here in the city God has planted me in.

Where did you sleep last night?

Day 53

THOUGHT OF THE DAY: Can you hear the whisper?

There's a whisper coming from God's throne: "Come over here to Macedonia and help us." (Acts 16:9) Let's rephrase this: "Come over here to NAME YOUR COMMUNITY and help us."

Perhaps you've been hearing this for a while. Matthew 9:37: "Then he said to his disciples, 'The size of the harvest is bigger than you can imagine, but there are few workers.' " (CEB) What a great translation: "The size of the harvest is bigger than you can imagine." Can you hear the whisper, "Come over here and help us."

This section of scripture written in Acts 16:6 is where Paul was being frustrated by the Holy Spirit to preach the word in Asia. It says "They were forbidden by the Holy Spirit to preach the word in Asia."

Are you being frustrated by the Holy Spirit? Are doors or opportunities not opening for you? Perhaps you want to go in one direction, and God wants you to go in another. Some people have been frustrated so long they've given up doing anything. Others have just copped an attitude. Can you hear the whisper, "Come over here and help us"?

When Jesus first met His disciples, he said simply, "Come follow Me." Jesus is asking us again to follow Him. It's time to resubmit our visions and dreams to him. It's time to return and do the simple things. You are needed! In Ephesians 4:16 it says that, "Every joint supplies, according to the effective working by which every part does its share." Can you hear the whisper, "Just do what I'm calling you to do."

Never have I seen so many needs in and out of the church. If it is truly a place where God has called you to rest, then rest. You're not to get burned out, but there is this whisper: "Can you come over here and help us? The size of the harvest is bigger than you can imagine."

Day 54

THOUGHT OF THE DAY: Convenience or Commitment?

We're all hearing the Holy Spirit say that He's looking for a people through whom He can work. Sadly, so many of the Father's children get burned out, discouraged, and hurt, and the fire and passion so many had at one time needs to be rekindled. Many have stopped going to church; others have settled for a gospel of convenience. They go to church having no expectation of a divine encounter.

In Joel three the prophet says, "Wake up the mighty men," and then they were to go down to the Valley of Decision. That's what's happening: the Holy Spirit has been poking and prodding, saying, "YOU CAN MAKE A DIFFERENCE!" We have heard, and now we must do.

In 2 Chronicles chapter 34, while repairing the temple, the law which had been lost was found. Here they find the book of the law, and Josiah is so moved by what he reads that he makes a DEEPER COMMITMENT. In verse 31 and 32 it says, "Then the king stood in his place and made a covenant before the LORD, to follow the LORD, and to keep His commandments and His testimonies and His statutes with all his heart and all his soul, to perform the words of the covenant that were written in this book. Once he made the commitment, He asked the people to make the same commitment And he made all who were present in Jerusalem and Benjamin take a stand."

Look up. We can't ask others to do what we're not doing. I love that the king asked God's kids to TAKE A STAND.

Convenience or commitment? "YOU WILL MAKE A DIFFERENCE!"

Day 55

THOUGHT OF THE DAY: "I will cry out to God Most High, To God who performs all things for me. He shall send from heaven and save me." (Psalm 57:2-3)

I've clung to this verse so many times in my life, and it's truly been my life line. There have been so many times that I've tried this and tried that. I've prayed and fasted, but it didn't work. Just when I'd almost lost all hope, God showed up and does what only He can do.

Yes, Job was right when he said, "For He performs what is appointed for me, and many such things are with Him." (23:14)

Day 56

THOUGHT OF THE DAY: I continue to be amazed

This past Saturday I was blessed to be in Cambridge, New York at St Luke's Episcopal Church where Father Jim and his lovely wife hosted a prophetic day. There was a diverse crowd there: people from many different churches. We all saw God move in incredible ways. We experienced very intimate worship, prophetic words, and the power of God move on people as even couples who were prayed for together were touched at the same time. People who had never been touched by the Spirit were touched for the first time.

While this was so wonderful to be a part of, God went beyond what we were expecting.

The Holy Spirit had me give a brief teaching on unity and being in one accord. We saw several scriptural examples of what happens when there's unity, and the room was filled with such a presence! The two visiting pastors as well as Pastor Jim and all the people there repented of the disunity that has existed between them and other churches. They gathered in groups and prayed, repented, and spoke of a new beginning. The session ended, and we had lunch.

Upon our returning for the last session, there were a few prophetic words, but it was clear that it was time to lay hands on people. The anointing was so strong I could barely stand (seriously). Everyone present could see and feel that God was doing something very special.

Just a short time ago, I spoke with Father Jim who yesterday (Sunday), had his annual meeting. As he spoke he told me that something had genuinely happened to people's hearts. They were all talking about the need for unity. The people who didn't attend Saturday's meeting were being exhorted by those who did that THEY HAD TO HAVE UNITY - not only unity in their church, but unity with the other churches in Cambridge.

If you could have heard the joy in Father Jim's voice. He has been sharing on unity for a long time. He said, "THEY GET IT!"

What a joy for me to be there and to hear what God continues to do! I continue to be amazed!

Day 57

THOUGHT OF THE DAY: Learning to refocus

Here's a verse we all love: "Many are the afflictions of the righteous, But the Lord delivers him out of them all." (Psalm 34:19) The problem is not the verse but our focus on the first part of it: MANY ARE THE AFFLICTIONS OF THE RIGHTEOUS...

The reality is that everyone goes through trials. Scripture says it "rains on the just and the unjust." Sadly, however, our focus is on the first part of the verse and not the second, which continues, "But the Lord delivers him out of them all."

How many times have we been in situations that seemed impossible, overwhelming, and yes, have lasted for years. Then... there is that word... BUT... "But the Lord delivers him out of them all." Yes, I know all too well that the how and when of the methods God implements to deliver us are often not what we expected or the way we would've done it, but how often do they work out better than what we'd desired?

And perhaps the greatest value of the trial is the internal changes in US. We are changed, molded!

We also need to allow verses 15-18 to be sown deeply into our hearts. "The eyes of the Lord are on the righteous, and His ears are open to their cry." The righteous cry out, and the Lord hears and delivers them out of all their troubles. The Lord is near to those who have a broken heart and saves such as have a contrite spirit."
- God's eyes are ON US
- God's ears are open to OUR CRY
- He hears & delivers

• He is NEAR when our heart is broken and saves us when we have contrite spirits

I know many of us are going through some very difficult times! I want to encourage us to refocus – "THE LORD WILL DELIVER US OUT OF ALL OUR TROUBLES!"

Day 58

THOUGHT OF THE DAY: Are we following Jesus?

Jesus said, "Follow me, I will make you fishers of men" (Matthew 4:19) Was this word for 12 men or was this a word to all of us who follow Jesus? If the latter, how is this being accomplished?

Jesus said FOLLOW ME... I WILL... MAKE YOU... FISHERS OF MEN!

Are we following Jesus?

Day 59

THOUGHT OF THE DAY: Pharisee or disciple?

In Matthew 5:20, Jesus' first sermon known as the Sermon on the Mount, he said, "For I say to you, that unless your righteousness exceeds the righteousness of the scribes and Pharisees, you will by no means enter the kingdom of heaven."

The Pharisees were external worshippers who weren't concerned with the heart; Jesus was.

A few verses later Jesus gives an example of what he meant. "Therefore if you bring your gift to the altar, and there remember that your brother has something against you, leave your gift there before the altar, and go your way. First be reconciled to your brother, and then come and offer your gift." (Matthew 5: 23-24)

It's Sunday morning; I'm bringing my tithe, and then...I remember. Not a convenient time. Let's look at what Jesus said again – "and there remember that your brother has something against you." It says we remember that we have a brother who's been offended or thinks he's been offended or hurt by us – we must go to him.

Here is where we come up with excuses. Jesus says we must go and before we offer our gift, we need to attempt to reconcile. Be aware that while we can go, the person has to be willing to be reconciled. Proverbs 18:19 says, "A brother who has been insulted [offended] is harder to win back than a walled city." (EXB)

If they don't desire reconciliation, then we're released of our accountability. Jesus didn't say it would be easy. He simply said, "Go."

When we remember... are we a Pharisee or a disciple?

Day 60

THOUGHT OF THE DAY: There is no one like you!

When I awoke this morning, I was so overwhelmed with His presence. I knew He was with me, and I knew He was with you too. Can we begin to comprehend? We're on the cusp of seeing God move like we've only dreamed of. Oh Lord, I hear you calling!

Deuteronomy 33:26: "There is no one like the God of Israel! He rides on the clouds in his divine greatness. He comes riding through the skies to help you." (ERV)

"There is none like the God of Jerusalem. He descends from the heavens. In majestic splendor to help you." (TLB)

There is no one like you!

Day 61

THOUGHT OF THE DAY: What do they see? What do they hear?

Let's be honest! How many times have we seen Christians we know act in such a way that we're embarrassed? We get angry, saying to ourselves, "That person doesn't represent the Jesus I know." Haven't we all seen believers being rude, obnoxious, full of pride, offensive, and acting inappropriately? How many times have we heard other Christians say things with which we don't want to be identified?

It's probably a good thing we don't live our lives surrounded by mirrors. Why do I say this? Because all of us have been guilty of the things we see in others.

What do they (people) see when they see you and me? What do they hear?

Paul writes in Second Corinthians 6:3-4: "We try to live in such a way that no one will ever be offended or kept back from finding the Lord by the way we act, so that no one can find fault with us and blame it on the Lord. In fact, in everything we do we try to show that we are true ministers of God." (TLB)

Oh Lord – HELP US!

What do they see? What do they hear?

Day 62

THOUGHT OF THE DAY: Believe that I love you

Yesterday in the early morning hours I'd come across a prophetic word in Brennan Manning's book Ragamuffin Gospel that I'd planned to use and did use yesterday morning in service. The amazing thing is that during worship one of our precious ladies came to me shaking and saying that she had something to share. I handed her the microphone, and the theme of what she said was, "Please believe how much I love you." Seemingly a simple statement, yet very profound.

Here is why it's so amazing. On page 117 we read that a thirty-four-year-old widow named Marjory Kempe from Lynn, Massachusetts gave this prophetic word in 1667. The word was that it was "More pleasing to me than all your prayers, works, and penances is that you would believe I love you."

It's not about our performance. It's not about us proving our love for him. It's about simply receiving His love for us. This is such a profound reality – Lord, please work this word into us!

Day 63

THOUGHT OF THE DAY: Why should people follow?

Nine times in the gospels Jesus says, "Come follow me." When we look at these verses, he says:

• "If anyone desires to come after Me, let him deny himself, and take up his cross, and follow Me." (Matthew 16:24; Mark 8:34: Luke 9:23)

• "If you want to be perfect, go, sell what you have and give to the poor, and you will have treasure in heaven; and come, follow Me." (Matthew 19:21: Mark 10:21; Luke 18:21)

• When Jesus speaks to Peter about his future, Peter asks about John's future. John 21:21-23: "Peter, seeing him (John), said to Jesus, 'But Lord, what about this man?' Jesus said to him, 'If I will that he remain till I come, what is that to you? You follow Me.' "

• "Then He said to them, 'Follow Me, and I will make you fishers of men.' " (Matthew 4:19: Mark 1:17)

These are not feel-good, casual statements but incredibly challenging. So what caused people to follow Jesus? What would cause people to follow us?

Why don't we all take some time today and list the reasons we think people followed Jesus. Then after we compile the list, do two things: 1. Look and see if those characteristics are a part of our lives and 2. Place the reasons people would follow in the comments section.

Just a little more food for consideration: not everyone who started following Jesus continued following Him. After hearing Jesus in John six, it's written in verse 66, "From that time many of His disciples went back and walked with Him no more."

Why should people follow us?

Day 64

THOUGHT OF THE DAY: Thomas Merton, Thoughts in Solitude (p. 293)
My Lord God, I have no idea where I am going. I do not see the road ahead of me. I cannot know for certain where it will end. Nor do I really know myself, and the fact that I think that I am following your will does not mean that I am actually doing so. But I believe that the desire to please you does in fact please you. And I hope I have that desire in all that I am doing. I hope that I will never do anything apart from that desire. And I know that if I do this you will lead me by the right road though I may know nothing about it. Therefore will I trust you always though I may seem to be lost and in the shadow of death. I will not fear, for you are ever with me, and you will never leave me to face my perils alone.

Day 65

THOUGHT OF THE DAY: I wish I had more money
I can't tell you the countless times I /we have said this – I wish I had more money. I would give it to the needy, I would give it to missions, I would give it to _____.

Here is our reality; we often spend money on things that are really meant for the kingdom. In Luke 15:13 it says the prodigal "wasted all his money." It's hard to admit that each of us has spent money on "stuff" that was really intended for the kingdom. Is there a voice here?

Then to make matters worse, we actually spend money to avoid what the Holy Spirit is showing/telling us to do. Remember Jonah? He's instructed to go to Joppa, but he doesn't want to go. In fact, it says that Jonah ran from the presence of God – Jonah 1:3: "But Jonah arose to flee to Tarshish from the presence of the Lord."

It goes on to say that he "went down to Joppa, and found a ship going to Tarshish; so he paid the fare, and went down into it, to go with them to Tarshish from the presence of the Lord."

The point is that we're willing to spend money going in a wrong direction and doing what we want and then dare to wonder where the presence of God is. Is there a voice here?

I wish I had more money...

Day 66

THOUGHT OF THE DAY: "I don't see anything."
Over the last week or so I've been frustrated trying to "see" what the Holy Spirit is doing. This morning I was up at 4:15 and started praying and pacing the floor. I was asking the Lord what He was doing. What do

you want me to see? What do you want me to understand? What do you want me (the church) to do? The more I prayed, the more frustrated I became. I continued to pray and pace.

Then the story of Elijah and his servant on Mt. Carmel "just" came into my mind. In 1 Kings 18:43 Elijah is praying for rain and sends his servant to look over the sea. His servant comes back and says, "I don't see anything." There it was in four words, God summarizing exactly where I was at. In fact, I believe many of you are saying it's where you're at too: "I DON'T SEE ANYTHING."

Okay, so this brought some comfort. The Holy Spirit was saying, "I know exactly where you're at." This was good, but I was still unable to see. So now what?

Then I read on: "Seven times Elijah said, 'Go again.' " The Holy Spirit was saying, "Be persistent." It's when we stop looking that our inability to see will persist. Finally, Elijah's servant sees and comes to Elijah and says in verse 44: "Oh yes, a cloud! But very small, no bigger than someone's hand, rising out of the sea." (MSG)

Immediately Elijah's servant falls into the mindset we often default to – we minimize the potential of what we see. "The natural man cannot perceive the things of the Spirit." (1 Corinthians 2:14) But Elijah says in so many words, "You better warn Ahab that it's going to really rain and he better leave now. Quickly then, on your way. Tell Ahab, 'Saddle up and get down from the mountain before the rain stops you.' "

The spiritually-minded man sees the potential and has confidence that God is up to something big. Zechariah 4:10: "Do not despise these small beginnings, for the Lord rejoices to see the work begin." (NLT)

I still don't see what God is up to, but it's big so I can rejoice knowing that "It's going to rain."

Day 67

THOUGHT OF THE DAY: The need is great, and the laborers are few!

It's 2:30 a.m. and I'm blessed to be helping in one of the two overflow shelters here in Fall River. Have you been outside tonight? It's really cold.

Here in this shelter men and woman are all sleeping on cots in the same room. They don't mind the conditions; they don't mind the snoring; they don't mind that the beds are very close to one another; they don't mind that there are no showers!

They are thankful for a place to sleep safe from the cold temperatures in the teens. They're thankful that there are heat and bathrooms. They're thankful to have a cup of coffee and cereal in the morning before they walk the streets waiting until evening so they can get a meal and be warm for another night. The need is great, and the laborers are few!

There are shelters here in the city, but they're filled to capacity. So what's being done? There are four churches which have opened their doors to house what's called the overflow. Originally there was supposed to be one overflow church per night which was staffed by volunteers. Well, there are so many people in need that a second overflow church was opened for the same night. This has created a problem, as they do not have enough volunteers. The need is great, and the laborers are few!

Do you have four hours you can give? Shifts are 7:00 – 11:00, 11:00 – 3:00, and 3:00 – 7:00. You can always work a double. I am here 11:00 – 7:00.

Through the years I've seen people travel to foreign nations to love and serve people in need, but let me suggest that there's a mission field right where you live. Perhaps the town or a city near you has shelters that need volunteers. It isn't every night. I serve once every two weeks. Others serve less, while others serve more.

Can you serve? If we don't have enough volunteers, then the overflow shelters can't be open. The need is great, and the laborers are few!

The overflow shelters will close at the end of March. So there are two more months. The need is great, and the laborers are few!

If you can help here in Fall River, contact me, and I'll give you a phone number to call. If you don't live nearby, then perhaps you can help where you live. If you're wondering if you'll be alone; the answer is no – you'll always be teamed up with at least one person.

The need is great, and the laborers are few!

Day 68

THOUGHT OF THE DAY: I didn't do it

How many times in your life have you been misunderstood? How many times have people drawn false conclusions? How many times have people presumed? How many times have people been unwilling to hear your perspective? How many times that no matter what you've said, they didn't hear you?

Often the more we try and explain what really happened or what the truth really is, it only makes matters worse, leading to frustration and emotional pain. Sadly, we too have been guilty of the same unwillingness to listen. Often our own disappointment, hurt, and pain create an inability to want to hear. Yes, we too have been just as guilty.

How often did we just want the truth to be known and embraced? "I didn't do it!" we want to cry. Through the years I've had to cling to Psalm 17:2: "Let my vindication come from Your presence."

In the end only God knows the truth. Only God can make things right, and yes, sometimes things never get right. But I have learned to cling to the fact that true vindication can only come from the presence of God.

I didn't do it! Be at peace. Vindication comes from the presence of God.

Day 69

THOUGHT OF THE DAY: Words

The last three days teams from our church along with a number of agencies have been on the streets of Fall River looking for people to answer questions on homelessness. The last two days we've been concentrating on young people ages 18-25. We're asking the big question: "Are you homeless, and if so, why?"

For those who answer yes to the first question, perhaps the most frequent answer we get to the second, is conflict between them and their parents, the breakdown of their relationships. The breakdown is in communication – WORDS.

Words that wound, words that create pain, words that separate, words that cause anger, bitterness, and resentment. Wounds from these are carried into marriages, and can and do affect children and jobs.

We're seeing so many young people live from couch to couch. They call it couch surfing, when in reality, they're homeless. So many of these young people are doing this because of the breakdown in the family, a breakdown often centered around words. It's made me evaluate what I say.

Yes, we can quote James 3:8-12: "But no man can tame the tongue. It's an unruly evil, full of deadly poison. With it we bless our God and Father, and with it we curse men, who have been made in the similitude of God. Out of the same mouth proceed blessing and cursing. My brethren, these things ought not to be so. Does a spring send forth fresh water and bitter from the same opening? Can a fig tree, my brethren, bear olives, or a grapevine bear figs? Thus no spring yields both salt water and fresh."

There is quoting, however, and then living out what we quote. Proverbs 18:21 says that, "Death and life are in the power of the tongue." It's often a mere one or two words that can change a life. What words are we speaking?

Many are homeless because of words.

Day 70

THOUGHT OF THE DAY: In spite of

In spite of our continual sin, in spite of our continual judgmental attitudes, in spite of our pride, moodiness, anger, responses, reactions, hidden thoughts, jealousies, contentions, selfishness, envy, twisting the truth or leaving things out, our impure thoughts, idolatry (putting other things before God), our unfaithfulness in giving, our compromising truth, our disobedience, and yes, the list goes on.

In spite of all these things, we are loved unconditionally! In spite of all these, He has and will never leave or forsake us. He is always present, always ready to forgive, full of compassion and mercy. In spite of all these things He leads us, guides us, teaches us, and gives us beauty for ashes and peace for strife and fear. He is the faithful shepherd of Psalm 23 who restores our souls and leads us in paths of righteousness for His name's sake. He protects and delivers us from the evil one, and He will not listen to the evil one's accusations. He has gone and prepared a place for us. He walks with us and talks with us as he has done since Adam.

In spite of our failings He delights in us and has plans for us. When we miss one plan, He has another. He does not remember our sin but frees us from guilt and shame. When we are self-righteous, He clothes us with His righteousness. When we walk away, He looks for us and calls us by name. He is with us in the fire. He will not allow us to be tried beyond what we're able to handle. When we are weak, He gives us strength. He goes before us making the crooked places straight and removing stumbling blocks. He calls us by name and has revealed the secrets of the kingdom to us, giving us the keys.

Yes, in spite of our carnal nature, He gives us a new one. He's preparing us to rule and reign with Him forever. Yes, you and I will be kings and priests forever. We will and we do sing with the angels and the 24 elders.

Can we all declare that OUR GOD IS FAITHFUL? In spite of us, He's given us His Spirit as a guarantee and has empowered us with supernatural gifts. He picks us up when we stumble and fall. He heals us from the scars and wounds of yesterday and those that will come in our tomorrows.

Yes, in spite of us, we are the most treasured and valued people on earth. He has personally selected and appointed us to represent Him on the earth. Let your heart sing, let us declare that "It is the goodness of God that leads us to repentance." (Romans 2) We did not find Him, but

He found us. In spite of us, He will perfect/complete everything that concerns us.

What words can we possibly utter or write to even begin to describe our God who loves us "in spite of" so very many things?!

Day 71

THOUGHT OF THE DAY: Take all of me!

There is no greater joy than that of knowing you and being known by you. To comprehend your unconditional and unfailing love which surrounds and encompasses us every moment of our lives. To know you searched for us and still to this day are calling us to walk with you in ways we don't yet understand.

You're calling us to abandon all; saying we have nothing to really lose and everything to gain. A new day has dawned and as yet we don't recognize it because we're living, walking, thinking, and perceiving through what we've known. The joy and revelation of yesterday is not our provision for tomorrow.

I hear you say that you know that we don't know how to get to our tomorrow. With a smile on your face you say it's because we're trying to get there on our own using old road maps and methodology. As it's said in Joshua 3:4 "For you have not passed this way before."

Father, we don't know how to get to the place to which you're calling us. Yet we're crying out Psalm 57:2: "I will call to God Most High, to God who accomplishes things concerning me." (Lexham English Bible) And from the New King James Version: "He will "perfect everything that concerns me." Yes, we know that your love for us will bring us to the place of your desire.

Father, we cry out, "Take all of me!"

Day 72

THOUGHT OF THE DAY: "Then God blessed them."

In Genesis chapter one God (Hebrew Elohim – Father, Son and Spirit) created everything. There was no big bang. There was no evolutionary process whereby one thing changed into another. Everything that was made was uniquely designed and created – how unfathomable is this? Every cell formed and fashioned into His entire creation. When I begin to ponder this, my breath is literally taken away, and I am speechless.

For a moment try and comprehend the first thing that God did after He created man. It says in verse 28: "Then God blessed them." We were created and then immediately received His divine blessing. This was not a mere formality or some meaningless gesture. We were created to carry not just some religious blessing but to carry the blessing of the Lord.

When I think of this, I have two immediate reactions: 1) I am incredibly excited; 2) I am angry because I realize that the evil one has stolen this truth from our hearts and lives. Even still I can see that we don't comprehend or understand that we were created to have and to carry "The Blessing." This was not a temporal blessing but an eternal one. From the beginning it was and is Elohim's eternal gift to us as His children.

What is this blessing? The rest of verse 28 says, "God said to them, 'Be fruitful and multiply; fill the earth and subdue it; have dominion over the fish of the sea, over the birds of the air, and over every living thing that moves on the earth.' " The Douay-Rheims 1899 American Edition Bible says, "And God blessed them, saying: Increase and multiply, and fill the earth, and subdue it, and rule over the fishes of the sea, and the fowls of the air, and all living creatures that move upon the earth."

We were created to be successful; we were created to govern; and we were created to have divine, delegated authority.

When we hear about the principle of God restoring us to His original intent, this is it – that we were created to be His children and to have and walk in His Blessing.

Think on this - "Then God blessed them."

Day 73

THOUGHT OF THE DAY: Feeling left alone – part one

There are times when we've all felt like Elijah – that we're all alone. We feel isolated, that no one else can understand what we're going through. We have no one to relate to, no one who can identify with us, and we don't get the support we feel we need from people.

In 1 Kings 19:14 we hear how Elijah is feeling: "And he said, 'I have been very zealous for the Lord God of hosts; because the children of Israel have forsaken Your covenant, torn down Your altars, and killed Your prophets with the sword. I alone am left; and they seek to take my life.' "

In verse 18 God tells Elijah that he isn't alone in being obedient. In fact, there are seven thousand other people who haven't bowed their knees to Baal.

Interestingly, Elijah after hearing from God and having a supernatural encounter, obeys God yet remains the same – depressed and discouraged. We can all be doing the right things, but our emotions stay unmoved even after having an encounter with the Holy Spirit. Here's a question we need to ask - what was the root of Elijah's loneliness?

To find the root we must go back to 1 Kings 18 where Elijah defeats the prophets of Baal, prays for rain, and then gets it. Since Elijah has had this success, he's confident that the next move of God will be certain - that both Ahab and Jezebel will be overthrown as leaders of Israel. He's so confident this will happen that he runs in the rain all the way to Jerusalem to confront Jezebel. When he arrives, his expectations are not met. In fact, just the opposite happens as Jezebel threatens his life, and he runs away. I also believe that he's disappointed that the people of Israel weren't there to show support for a national uprising.

I believe there were two keys to Elijah feeling alone: 1) Elijah felt that he had obeyed God, that he'd followed through on what he was instructed to do, but God didn't do what Elijah thought he would do – Elijah felt let down and disappointed by God; 2) Elijah then felt let down and disappointed by the people, because they weren't there to support him. He thus believes, "I am left alone."

We can relate, can't we?

It's a lonely place when we feel unsupported by God and unsupported by people. We have to be aware that we can become depressed like Elijah and afflicted with the spiritual virus called "poor me."

Are you feeling like you're alone? God will bring you out of this place. You're in a place where there are things the Holy Spirit wants to teach you. How blessed we are that the Holy Spirit will not leave us feeling lonely and will redeem the time for the purposes of His kingdom!

In part two we'll learn more about being alone. But for today I'm asking, are you feeling left alone?

Day 74

THOUGHT OF THE DAY: Left alone - part two

Welcome to the place where some of God's greatest work is accomplished in us! Being left alone is one of the most important keys to our being changed. It's a place of DIVINE APPOINTMENT. Without going to the place of being alone we won't reach our greatest potential.

In Genesis 32:23 it says, "Then Jacob was left alone; and a Man wrestled with him until the breaking of day." Jacob purposely left his two wives and all of his children behind in anticipation that he would meet Esau after not seeing him for years.

Jacob is expecting one kind of encounter, but God set him up for another. The Holy Spirit will set us to be alone with him because he knows that what has to be accomplished in our lives cannot transpire with others involved. The Holy Spirit has to isolate us where we can't be distracted or influenced by other people.

Welcome to "Peniel!" It's here that you and I will have a divine encounter that will change us forever. In fact, we'll visit Peniel several times in our journey. In Genesis 32:30 it says, "So Jacob called the name of the place Peniel: 'For I have seen God face to face, and my life is preserved.' " The phrase "my life is preserved" is translated "and I am still alive," meaning that he saw God and lived.

Peniel is a place of divine revelation where God will reveal himself to us in new ways. This place of being alone is the place where God wants to change us permanently. It is the place for which we yearn.

We will be so altered by the Spirit, that as with Jacob, He'll want to change our name and our identity! In verses 27-28 it's written, "So He said to him, 'What is your name?' He said, 'Jacob.' And He said, 'Your name shall no longer be called Jacob, but Israel.' " God changed his name from Jacob (meaning "supplanter") to Israel (meaning "ruling with God"). Think about this. God met with a man, and the outcome was a permanent, physical limp for the rest of his life!

Haven't we all wrestled with God? Don't we all want to have our character and our identity changed? The place that this happens is Peniel; the place of great struggle, the place where we're left alone!

Day 75

THOUGHT OF THE DAY: Overcoming Gideon mentality

In Judges chapter six an Angel of the Lord shows up. This is what is known as a theophany; a manifestation or appearance of God in human form. So the angel says to Gideon, "The Lord is with you, you mighty man of valor!" (verse 12) Gideon says to Him, "O my lord, if the Lord is with us, why then has all this happened to us? And where are all His miracles which our fathers told us about."

First of all, Gideon didn't recognize that this was the Lord speaking to him. Sound familiar? He didn't have the capacity to hear, "The Lord is with you" nor could he hear "you (yes YOU) mighty man of valor." Gideon was looking, as we all do, at his present conditions. He was looking at what God had done, not what God wanted to do. He didn't hear (as we don't), "the Lord is (note IS) with YOU"... Gideon saw himself through his own lenses (eyes). We see this again in Judges 6:15: "O my Lord, how can I save Israel? Indeed my clan is the weakest in Manasseh, and I am the least in my father's house."

He says to the angel, in case you didn't know, I come from a family of "nobodies" and by the way, I am the biggest "nobody" in my family.

Just prior to Gideon replying to the angel, the angel said to him, "And the Angel of the Lord appeared to him, and said to him, 'The Lord is with you, you might man of valor!' " (Judges 6:12)

Gideon wasn't able to hear or receive what the Lord had just said to him. "Then the Lord turned to him and said, 'Go in this might of yours, and you shall save Israel from the hand of the Midianites. Have I not sent you?' " (verse 14) When we see ourselves as "nobodies," it inhibits us from hearing how God sees us and wants to use us.

Hasn't God sent all of us? You know those Great Commission verses in Matthew 28? Aren't we already anointed? Yes, but we are a nobody from a family and church of nobodies. Here is God's response, "And the Lord said to him, 'Surely I will be with you.' " (verse 16)

If in God's love for Gideon, He helped Gideon fulfill his calling, then He'll help us.

• Philippians 1:6: "Being confident of this very thing, that He who has begun a good work in you will complete it until the day of Jesus Christ."

• Ephesians 2:10: "For we are His workmanship, created in Christ Jesus for good works, which God prepared beforehand that we should walk in them."

To overcome Gideon-mentality we have to stop relying/looking to what we can do. As God spoke to Joshua, He is speaking to us. Joshua 1:5: "I was with Moses, so I will be with you. I will not leave you nor forsake you." Again, in Joshua 3:7: "As I was with Moses, so I will be with you."

As I was with Gideon (Mr. Nobody), "I WILL BE WITH YOU."

Day 76

THOUGHT OF THE DAY: The season of waiting

Are you in a season of waiting? What do I mean? I mean are you in a period of time where there is nothing you can do except wait for God to act? You can pray, fast, beg, plead, and attempt everything you know and yet nothing changes.

I feel like Noah who was shut up in the ark. Do you feel like God has you shut up? This is where we're in "our ark," and we're waiting for God. Imagine for a moment that Noah had to wait inside the ark either 375 or 365 days, depending on the commentary you use. There was nothing Noah could do but wait.

The ark finally comes to rest on top of the mountain after 150 days, or five months. Think of five full months of seeing no land and having no idea how long it's going to be until God is going to release you. How long have you been waiting for God? It says in Genesis 8:5: "The waters decreased continually until the tenth month. In the tenth month, on the first day of the month, the tops of the mountains were seen."

Noah had to wait two months before he could even start to have hope. That's how long Noah had to wait to see the top of the mountains after the ark had rested on them. If you're doing the math with me, you'll know it's been seven months that Noah has been in the ark. It was five months later that he was finally released.

Though we might be in a season of waiting, God is working on our behalf!

If I could pass along one thing I've learned in my seasons of waiting, it would be to learn how to enjoy where you are.

Day 77

THOUGHT OF THE DAY: Who am I?

This is the question Moses asks God when He tells him to go to Pharaoh and deliver Israel from captivity. Exodus 3:11: "But Moses said to God, 'Who am I that I should go to Pharaoh, and that I should bring the children of Israel out of Egypt?' "

Can we identify with Moses? For so long we've looked at who we're not. We've only looked at what we can do in our own ability, spending so much of our lives examining what we're capable of. As of yet we still haven't comprehended who we are, but that's changing. Though we might have natural abilities, those natural abilities are not the supernatural abilities that are in each of us. We cannot advance the kingdom by the natural man.

I love the response God gives Moses in verse 11: "Who am I that I should go to Pharaoh, and that I should bring the children of Israel out of Egypt?" The response: "So He said, 'I will certainly be with you.' " (Exodus 3:12) Simple but profound – I WILL CERTAINLY BE WITH YOU.

Let that sink in for a moment. Repeatedly we see God saying to those He calls, "I will be with you." Please take the time and let the following words God speaks be written in your heart and mind. If you just read the verses, you won't hear the voice of God!

·   To Joseph - Genesis 39:2: "The Lord was with Joseph, and he was a successful man."

·   To Jacob - Genesis 28:15: "Behold, I am with you and will keep you wherever you go, and will bring you back to this land; for I will not leave you until I have done what I have spoken to you."

·   To Joshua - Deuteronomy 31:23: "Then He inaugurated Joshua the son of Nun, and said, 'Be strong and of good courage; for you shall bring the children of Israel into the land of which I swore to them, and I will be with you.' "

· To Gideon - Judges 6:16: "And the Lord said to him, 'Surely I will be with you, and you shall defeat the Midianites as one man.' "

· To Jehoshaphat and his people - 2 Chronicles 20:17: "You will not need to fight in this battle. Position yourselves, stand still and see the salvation of the Lord, who is with you, O Judah and Jerusalem! Do not fear or be dismayed; tomorrow go out against them, for the Lord is with you."

Whatever the Lord asks you to do, you can say to yourself what God told Moses to say to the children of Israel. Exodus 3:14: "Thus you shall say to the children of Israel, 'I AM has sent me to you.' " Hear that? I AM HAS SENT ME...

Lastly, here is a word we declared yesterday over our community (church). It was not only a word to us but the word of the Lord to HIS CHURCH. Exodus 34:10: "And He said: 'Behold, I make a covenant. Before all your people I will do marvels such as have not been done in all the earth, nor in any nation; and all the people among whom you are shall see the work of the Lord. For it is an awesome thing that I will do with you.' "

Who am I? I am everything God declares I am!

Day 78

THOUGHT OF THE DAY: I hope they see Jesus in me today

I can remember like it was yesterday. It was 1967, and I had just entered my freshman year in college. I knew I wasn't ready to go, though, because I had no idea who I was. My parents ran a family restaurant and hotel in New Hampshire, so there wasn't a lot of time to discover who we were; everyone worked to support the family business. As I look back, I can see how God used all of that just as He uses everything. What an awesome Father we have.

In 1967 it was either college or Vietnam. I was about to join Special Forces when I was given a football scholarship to a Baptist College in Canada. In the years I was there I can say I never met one person who talked about Jesus, and I never met one person who reflected his life. I don't in any way blame anyone for my choices during those years, BUT, HONESTLY, THERE WAS NOT ONE!

I knew some students who talked about being Baptist, but I never heard or saw Jesus reflected in them. At one point during a major crisis in my life, I made a deal with God that if He got me out of the mess I was in, I promised that I would figure out if He was real. In fact, I remember kneeling and saying, "I don't know if you exist, and frankly I don't care, but if you get me out of this mess in 24 hours, I promise to investigate whether you're real."

Literally and exactly at the 24th hour to the minute, I was out of my mess. But did I keep my promise? No! For the next two weeks, however, I heard a voice say to me, "You promised." Every day and several times a day, I heard, "You promised."

There was a young man there who was so afraid of me that when he saw me coming, he would either cross the street or retreat up the stairs to avoid me. From that you realize that I was not a nice person but instead an angry and lost young man who played football. This young man and I lived on the same floor of the dorm, and I'd known him since my freshman year. I knew he was receiving a religious magazine in the mail, and when I knocked on his door to ask him for a copy, he turned white, like Casper the Friendly Ghost. Though I never saw or heard Jesus in him, God used the magazines he was getting to change my life forever.

We can be reading all the right material but never reflect the truth of it. I know, because for years afterwards I read the Bible, but I didn't reflect Jesus. Instead I was the Pharisee Jesus spoke about.

So that brings me to a prayer I pray often – "I hope they see Jesus in me today!"

P.S. I came home from college and lived in a paneled garage with a bed and a toilet. I bought a bible with no references, no notes, just the word of God. I didn't want anyone's opinion. I knew that if God was real, He would reveal Himself to me. That's exactly what He did in 1970, and He's still doing it today!

Day 79

THOUGHT OF THE DAY: The anointing you carry

Twenty times in the gospels we see the word touched. Either Jesus touched a person or people touched him. Here is Matthew's account.

- Matthew 8:3 - He touched the leper, and he was healed.
- Matthew 8:15 - He touched the hand of Peter's mother-in-law, and she was healed.
- Matthew 9:20 - He was touched by the woman with the issue of blood, and she was healed.
- Matthew 9:29 - He touched the eyes of two blind men, and they were healed.
- Matthew 14:36 - As many people that touched his clothes were healed.

- Matthew 17:7 - He touched his disciples and dealt with their fear.
- Matthew 20:34 - Being moved by compassion, he touched two more blind men, and they were healed.

It didn't say Jesus prayed! It says he touched or was touched.

- 2 Kings 13:21 - It is written that when a dead man touched the dead body of Elisha, he came back to life!
- 1 Corinthians 4:20 - "For the kingdom of God is not in word but in power."
- 2 Corinthians 4:7 - "We are like clay jars in which this treasure is stored. The real power comes from God and not from us." (CEV)

We are clay jars that carry an anointing.

Day 80

THOUGHT OF THE DAY: The power of one word

This morning I went to the Travel Clinic in Providence to make sure all my shots were up to date for my upcoming trip to Haiti. As I often do, I said hello to everyone I passed on the sidewalk, people who were sitting in the waiting room, and of course, the medical staff. I'm continually amazed to see how people respond to one word – hello.

The next time you go out, watch people's response to you when you say hello. There are different types of hellos. There are the casual hellos that are said as a pleasantry, hellos said out of obligation, and then there are hellos that communicate that you care about the person. These have the sound of love, empathy, compassion, and hope. One word can cause a person to open up and change a life. One word can be a supernatural seed.

In Acts 11:15 Peter began speaking to the people who had gathered at Cornelius' house. It says, "And as I began to speak, the Holy Spirit fell upon them." Imagine that when you and I speak, the Holy Spirit can and does fall on people. In 1 Corinthians 3 it says that one man plants, another man waters, and that God produces the increase. Your hello spoken with a genuine and compassionate spirit can be a supernatural seed or living water.

"And as I began to speak, the Holy Spirit fell upon them."

Day 81

THOUGHT OF THE DAY: Our good ideas can lead to disaster

There have been times in all of our lives that we've made decisions because it seemed like the right thing to do. Often we seek out other people to get their perspective, and they too think it's a great idea. We even feel the Lord will be pleased and honored with the decision we've made, especially when the decision is being made to honor Him. Even with all this, however, we can make the decision and discover it was wrong because we made the same error as they did in 1 Chronicles 13:4. Even though "the thing was right in the eyes of all the people," it was still wrong in the eyes of God.

We have good ideas and God ideas; what separates them is an "o". So off we go to do something filled with good intentions. We THINK our decision will be pleasing to the Lord. We can even spend time in worship, but worship doesn't change the consequences of a bad decision.

First Chronicles 13 is the perfect example of what I'm referring to. David wants to bring the ark of God back to Jerusalem. Everyone he talks to says it's a great idea. David has the whole worship team preceding the ark as they head towards Jerusalem. Everything is going fine; everyone is excited.

Then everything goes wrong. The ark of God begins to slide, and it's very possible that it will slide off the cart unless someone prevents it from happening. In verse nine it says Uzza put out his hand to hold the ark. Good idea, right? No, it was a terrible idea, because the moment he touched the ark, he died. David's response is seen in verse 11: "He became angry at God."

Why did all this happen? In 1 Chronicles 14:13 it says David failed to consult with God about moving the ark. His good idea was not a God idea. David assumed – we assume. First, the ark is not supposed to be on a cart. Secondly, Uzza probably had grown familiar with the ark because it sat for years in his father's field. The warning to us is - don't become familiar with God's presence. Also, just because something seems right, we still need to inquire of the Lord as to His heart and desire on the matter. There's a right way and a wrong way. We'll only know by asking the Lord.

I have my hand raised concerning all the times I've made decisions that seemed right but turned into disasters. Praise God that He gives us new opportunities to do things differently.

Before we make even the smallest decisions, inquire of the Lord, because good ideas aren't always God ideas.

Day 82

THOUGHT OF THE DAY: Why churches don't cancel services during bad weather

Have you ever wondered what goes into making the decision to canceling a church service? I'm kind of an expert in this area.

Here comes the truth. Yes, we want to gather and worship the Lord together, to enjoy the Lord's presence, and enjoy each other's company. Yes, we'll miss what God wants to do supernaturally as a corporate group but still know that He wants to work supernaturally no matter where people are. We want everyone to be safe.

With all that said, the number one reason pastors are reluctant to cancel church is "THE BUDGET." You mean money? Yup! You're probably saying, well, pastors just need to trust God. This is true! Pastors can trust God; it's trusting God's people that's the problem.

Here's the reality of things. Most churches are just making it financially. You know; there are mortgages or rents to be paid, utilities, insurance, all the church budget items for the various ministries, and staff salaries. Plus the missionaries who are often waiting for every penny to be sent. You're probably nodding your head saying, "I know that."

What you might or might not know is that there's a very large portion of the church population that will keep this week's tithe or offering. Though we all believe the tithe and offering belongs to the Lord, it's a sad reality that a good majority will spend the Lord's money somewhere else this week. This is also true when people miss a regular service for whatever reason. Holidays and vacations are often funded by the Lord's money. Pastors can trust God; it's God's people who can't be trusted. It's very difficult to maintain a church budget. Once you fall behind, it often becomes a struggle for the rest of the year.

Now I do want to say that this is not true of everyone. Thank God for all of you who are faithful. Sincerely, THANK YOU!

There is so much work to be done in our Father's kingdom. Please be faithful in your giving. Did you know that under the Law eight times in the book of Leviticus it's written that for any reason you use the tithe, it's required to add an additional one fifth. Now if the law was a shadow of things to come, what would the Spirit say now about us using the Lord's tithe or offering? I will throw this out there: tithing was something the people of God did before the law. In Genesis we clearly see both Abraham (Hebrews 7) and Jacob tithing. We read in Genesis 28:22 that Jacob said, "Of all that You give me I will surely give a tenth to You." They tithed under the covenant of promise. The law was given much later. So yes, tithing is a principle we should be following. Here is what Malachi 3:10 has to say, and please read this slowly: " 'Bring the whole tenth into the storehouse, so that there will be food in my house, and put me to the test,' says Adonai-Tzva'ot." (CJB)

"See if I won't open for you the floodgates of heaven and pour out for you a blessing far beyond your needs." Tithing opens floodgates of heaven. Yes, there will be lean times, but I have seen God's incredible and undeniable faithfulness in finances for 44 years.

Why don't churches cancel services during bad weather?

Day 83

THOUGHT OF THE DAY: I need to thank you again

When I awoke this morning, I was immediately overwhelmed with joy, which then led to tears. In that moment I thought how blessed and honored I've been to have known so many people I've had the privilege of calling a brother or sister in Christ. I've often thought that at my funeral I wanted to have a continuous tape playing as people approached the casket. One of the things I wanted to have playing was this thought I'm writing today.

I want to say THANK YOU! Thank you that you have allowed me to be part of your lives; thank you for allowing me - no matter how long or how briefly - to have walked with you. Whether it's been one step, one mile, or several miles, my life was made richer, fuller, and more complete because I've known you.

In our journey each of us at times has lost our way, stumbled, and yes, even fallen. Each of us has gone through multiple seasons in our lives. Each of us have missed the mark. Yet in spite of all these failings and shortcomings, we've loved each other though at times we didn't understand one another.

The one common thread that linked our lives together was and is Jesus. I've given up my seat of judgment because I've had Isaiah 53:6 written on my heart. Here is how it reads in the Message Bible - "We're all like sheep who've wandered off and gotten lost. We've all done our own thing, gone our own way. And God has piled all our sins, everything we've done wrong, on him, on him."

Yes, we've all missed the mark (sinned), messed up, blown it, stumbled, and fell. We've disappointed Him and at times each other. But here's the "BUT" – from the Voice Bible; "The Eternal One laid on him, this silent sufferer, the sins of us all."

Thank you for sharing your lives with me! Thank you for the gift you've been. I decided not to wait until my funeral to say, "THANK YOU!"

Day 84

THOUGHT OF THE DAY: Looking back

Remember Lot's wife in Genesis 19:26? It says, "But Lot's wife looked back. When she did, she became a pillar made out of salt." (NIRV)

Why did she look back? Was she longing for the life she was leaving behind? Was she mourning the past? Was her heart fixated on her past and unable to look ahead to her future?

How we view our past will have a lot to do with how we view our future. Unlike Lot's wife, who died quickly. we can die a slow death by always recounting the past, becoming prisoners of our yesterdays. I'm not suggesting we don't deal with our past issues at all, because if we don't deal with them, they'll most certainly deal with us. But taking a peak at our past is different from living there or even yearning for it. Yesterday's hurt, pain, abuse, disappointments, and even all the wonderful times, will either positively or negatively affect our tomorrows. Our past can distort the reality of what once was and what is to be.

Often there's a voice coming from our past which says, "You could've and should've done this or done that." We become prisoners of it. We allow our faults and failures to keep us from having hope or a new beginning. The expression "If we don't learn from the past, we're doomed to repeat it" is so true.

Our past has layers to it. You peel off one layer and yes, there's another. I continue to recognize that there are areas in which I still need healing. Often our healing is tied to forgiveness. There are so many biblical examples of this.

Praise God that one of the reasons Jesus was beaten and died was to heal our past. He died that we might be free from our yesterdays. In writing this I can't help but feel that there are many of you who are stuck. You're stuck emotionally as well as spiritually. These are often indicators that it's time to ask the Holy Spirit if there's something we need to see from our past that can enable us to fulfill our potential. Don't reject the little thoughts that come to your mind, but be discerning.

I have things come to mind, but feel a check inside of me. The check is the Holy Spirit telling me that it wasn't Him speaking, but instead, the enemy of our souls. If you're unsure, ask someone who's walked with the Lord for awhile and is qualified to help you. Then there are those who've walked with the Lord for many years but are stuck themselves.

· Philippians 3:13 - "Brethren, I do not count myself to have apprehended; but one thing I do, forgetting those things which are behind and reaching forward to those things which are ahead." The idea is that of a runner using all of his/her strength, every muscle working, and leaning forward with everything they have to cross the finish line.

· Isaiah 53:4 - "Surely He has borne our griefs and carried our sorrows."

Don't sit around an emotional campfire endlessly roasting marshmallows and examining your past. Ask the Lord how to deal with unresolved matters and then move on in freedom.

Day 85

THOUGHT OF THE DAY: Help is on the way

For a moment think of all the times we were in need of help. We needed help emotionally, physically, spiritually, and financially - help to deal with relationships, help to deal with circumstances, help to deal with demonic oppression, etcetera.

We've been brought to a place where we have no options. Unless the Lord works on our behalf, nothing will happen. We have trusted in so many things, but the hour has arrived when our help is only in the Lord. Human help is worthless.

• Psalm 108:12 - "Help us against the enemy; human help is worthless." (GNT)

• 2 Chronicles 14:11 - "Asa cried to the Lord his God, 'O Lord, there is none besides You to help, and it makes no difference to You whether the one You help is mighty or powerless. Help us, O Lord our God! For we rely on You.' " (AMP)

• Deuteronomy 33:26 says, "There is no one like the God of Israel, who rides through the skies to help you." (NCV) Can we picture The Lord riding through the heaven to help us? HELP IS ON THE WAY...

Help is coming from His throne room just for us.

• Psalm 20:1-2 - "May the Lord answer you in the day of trouble; May the name of the God of Jacob defend you; May He send you help from the sanctuary, And strengthen you out of Zion." Not only will He help and defend us; He WILL STRENGTHEN US...

We will declare.

• Psalm 46:1 - "God is our refuge and strength, A very present help in trouble."

• Psalm 54:4 - "Behold, God is my helper."

• Psalm 121:2 - "My help comes from the Lord, Who made heaven and earth."

• Isaiah 50:9 - "Surely the Lord God will help Me."

• Isaiah 41:10 -"Fear not, for I am with you; Be not dismayed, for I am your God. I will strengthen you, Yes, I will help you, I will uphold you with My righteous right hand."

It says, I AM YOUR GOD, I WILL STRENGTHEN YOU – YES, I WILL HELP YOU!

Let's declare - HELP IS ON THE WAY...

What should we do? Hebrews 4:16 says, "Let us therefore come boldly to the throne of grace, that we may obtain mercy and find grace to help in time of need." We also need to have the heart of three young Jewish men (in their teens) - Daniel 3:16-18: "Shadrach, Meshach, and Abed-Nego answered and said to the king, 'O Nebuchadnezzar, we have no need to answer you in this matter. If that is the case, our God whom we serve is able to deliver us from the burning fiery furnace, and He will deliver us from your hand, O king. But if not, let it be known to you, O king, that we do not serve your gods, nor will we worship the gold image which you have set up.' "

Over and over again, God helped Israel! There were many times they hadn't deserved His help, but He helped them because they were His children.

I know we're all in some difficult situations. I also know that HELP IS ON THE WAY!

Day 86

THOUGHT OF THE DAY: Don't lose heart – the glory of God is on the way

For months now my heart has been filled with the absolute conviction that God is going to do something. It's His desire to glorify His name and to cause a revival that the world has never seen.

Here is just one verse that makes me want to shout:

Haggai 2:6-9:

For thus says the Lord of hosts: "Once more (it is a little while) I will shake heaven and earth, the sea and dry land; and I will shake all nations, and they shall come to the Desire of All Nations, and I will fill this temple with glory," says the Lord of hosts. "The silver is Mine, and the gold is Mine," says the Lord of hosts. "The glory of this latter temple shall be greater than the former," says the Lord of hosts. "And in this place I will give peace," says the Lord of hosts.

Yes, once more in a little while, God is going to shake everything. We see this promise again in the book of Hebrews. Hebrews 12: 26-29:

...whose voice then shook the earth; but now He has promised, saying, "Yet once more I shake not only the earth, but also heaven." Now this, "Yet once more," indicates the removal of those things that are being shaken, as of things that are made, that the things which cannot be shaken may remain. Therefore, since we are receiving a kingdom which cannot be shaken, let us have grace, by which we may serve God acceptably with reverence and godly fear. For our God is a consuming fire.

Don't lose heart - THE GLORY OF GOD IS ON THE WAY...

Day 87

THOUGHT OF THE DAY: The wind is blowing

Can't you feel it? Isn't there something that's causing your spirit to jump inside of you? Isn't there a sense of anticipation? Okay; God's up to something!

John 3:8 (CEB): "God's Spirit blows wherever it wishes." Perhaps we should all ask what the Lord is up to.

I can hear these verses:

• Ephesians 5:14-16 - "Wake up from your sleep, Climb out of your coffins; Christ will show you the light! So watch your step. Use your head. Make the most of every chance you get. These are desperate times!" (Message Bible)

• Joel 2:1- "Blow the trumpet in Zion, And sound an alarm in My holy mountain!"

• Joel 3:9-10 - "Proclaim this among the nations: 'Prepare for war! Let all the men of war draw near Let them come up. Beat your plowshares into swords And your pruning hooks into spears; Let the weak say, "I am strong." ' "

What is this saying to you?

Day 88

THOUGHT OF THE DAY: Limiting God through our perceptions

In 2 Kings 5 we find that Naaman, a great general of Syria, has leprosy. He hears that if he goes to Israel he'll be healed. It would be good to read the story for yourself.

We pick up the story where Naaman comes to the house of Elisha. Elisha doesn't even come out to talk to Naaman but instead sends a messenger. The messenger tells Naaman to wash himself in the Jordan seven times. Here is Naaman's response "But Naaman became furious, and went away and said, 'Indeed, I said to myself,' "He will surely come out to me, and stand and call on the name of the Lord his God, and wave his hand over the place, and heal the leprosy." ' " (verse 11)

Naaman had a preconceived idea of how he would be healed. Can't we see ourselves? We pray and have preconceived ideas of how God is going to answer our prayer. More often than not we look for answers in the natural and not in the supernatural, like here where the answer was to go wash seven times in the Jordan.

Naaman thought that Elisha would simply come out and wave his hand over him, and when it didn't happen his way, he became angry. If it wasn't for his servants who convinced him to do the unusual and be willing to look for answers in supernatural places, where would he be?

Often when God doesn't do it our way/the way we perceived He would, we become disappointed. Like Naaman who became furious, his response/attitude would have kept him from receiving his healing. Think for a moment about how Jesus heals the blind man by putting mud in his eyes. The mute is healed when he touches his tongue, and the deaf person is healed when Jesus sticks his finger in his ear. The dead boy is raised to life by Elisha only after he lays on the boy twice. The widow's debt is canceled, and she has money to live on for the rest of her life, as she borrows jars and shuts the door, and then God fills those jars with oil.

We've all severely limited God or haven't been able to see the answers because we're looking through our natural minds. Let's stop having naturally-minded perceptions. Our God is bigger than our finite minds. Jehoshaphat wants to know if he should go to war; God tells him to dig ditches. We have to get God out of the box.

I believe we'll start seeing God move more when we stop looking in natural places. Yes, it's time we stop "limiting God through our perceptions."

Day 89

THOUGHT OF THE DAY: "Nothing is too hard."

I was sitting here at my computer musing over what the Lord had just spoken to me. I heard the Lord say, "Today your life will change forever! Then I immediately began to ponder what He'd said. This is a huge word!!! Then I heard "NOTHING IS TOO HARD FOR ME!" WOW...

Here's the verse this word comes from - Jeremiah 32:17: "Ah, Lord God! Behold, You have made the heavens and the earth by Your great power and outstretched arm. There is nothing too hard for You." This word was given to Jeremiah while he was under house arrest by King Zedekiah. Not only was he a prisoner, but Israel was under siege by Nebuchadnezzar, and soon all of Israel would be under his control.

The word came to him to buy a field. Not only was he to buy the field, but his cousin would come to him while he was in prison and ask him to buy the field. Sure enough, he does come, and Jeremiah buys the field without understanding why he's buying it. You see, it didn't make sense.

Here is Jeremiah's prayer: "Look, the siege mounds! They have come to the city to take it; and the city has been given into the hand of the Chaldeans who fight against it, because of the sword and famine and pestilence. What You have spoken has happened; there You see it! (verse

24) And You have said to me, O Lord God, 'Buy the field for money, and take witnesses!'—yet the city has been given into the hand of the Chaldeans." (verse 25)

Then God answers, "Then the word of the Lord came to Jeremiah, saying, 'Behold, I am the Lord, the God of all flesh. Is there anything too hard for Me?' Therefore thus says the Lord: 'Behold, I will give this city into the hand of the Chaldeans, into the hand of Nebuchadnezzar king of Babylon, and he shall take it. And the Chaldeans who fight against this city shall come and set fire to this city and burn it.' " (verses 26-29) Later in this chapter God tells Jeremiah that the people taken into captivity will return to their land. Oh, and it isn't until later that God tells Jeremiah that it would be seventy years before they'd come back.

So get this: Jeremiah buys a field while in prison; his cousin comes to him all during Nebuchadnezzar's siege, and he does this without knowing why. What he does know is that "nothing is too hard for God." God affirms this in verse 27: "Behold, I am the Lord, the God of all flesh. Is there anything too hard for Me?"

So wherever we are today, whatever our circumstances - "NOTHING IS TOO HARD FOR GOD!" Yes, it might take time. We simply need to do what He shows us to do and leave the rest to Him.

Day 90

THOUGHT OF THE DAY: Oh Lord...

As I sit here this morning, my heart is broken! Oh Lord, look at our nation! Oh Lord, look at this world and all those who you've created. Oh Lord, look at all the hurting and broken. Oh Lord, look down and see our desperate need for YOU!!

This is the Christmas season, and Lord, we need you to come again! Look down and see the hurting, the broken, and those in need of healing and deliverance. Isaiah cried out "Oh, that You would rend the heavens and that You would come down, that the mountains might quake and flow down at Your presence." (Isaiah 64:1)

I haven't written this week, because I had no idea what was on our Father's heart. I did hear, "Can you hear the angels sing?" I pondered and pondered. I listened and listened, but I could not hear them. It was silent!

But what I have heard all week was the groaning of brokenness. How I wanted to hear the joy of angels singing, but it was silent. I have heard the groaning of the broken. Oh Lord, look down and come! We are desperate for YOU!

Why were the angels singing in Luke 2:14? Because they were rejoicing that a savior was born. Luke 2:10-11: "Then the angel said to them, 'Do not be afraid, for behold, I bring you good tidings of great joy which will be to all people. For there is born to you this day in the city of David a Savior, who is Christ the Lord.' "

Wait a minute; I can faintly hear singing. All week I've listened, and finally I can hear them rejoicing - "He has come and He is coming."

Oh Lord, come! WE ARE DESPERATE FOR YOU!

Day 91

THOUGHT OF THE DAY: Ready or not

When we were growing up, we all played the game Hide and Seek. Part of the game is when the person who has to find and touch the other players counts and then says, "Ready or not, here I come."

For the past few years the Lord has been speaking to us to "Get ready." Over the last six months or so I've been hearing "Ready or not, here I come."

How exciting to think that the Holy Spirit is about to invade our lives and invade our churches. Here is what Zechariah 2:10 says: "Shout and celebrate, Daughter of Zion. I'm on my way. I'm moving into your neighborhood! God's Decree." (MSG)

I just love the way the Message Bible puts it - "I'm moving into YOUR NEIGHBORHOOD! At the end of this verse God says, I'm decreeing this - it's GOING TO HAPPEN.

We're out of options. Frankly the only option we desire is the Holy Spirit. "READY OR NOT, HERE I COME!"

Day 92

THOUGHT OF THE DAY: The voice of discouragement

Today I awoke to a familiar voice which has become louder in the last year or so. It's the voice of discouragement. This voice doesn't have to make things up; it simply points out our circumstances. This voice tells us that things are bad, and they are. This voice gives little or no hope that things will change. It doesn't tell us to quit because that's too obvious. This voice steals our hope. This voice at times causes us to go from disappointment to depression. It tells us that we don't matter. It makes us feel that we shouldn't even bother. It causes us to be silent. Today I awoke to this voice. "Why bother writing! Why bother speaking!" it shouted. "WHY BOTHER!"

These are real thoughts and real feelings! Why bother! Then I sat with my head bowed and heard the verse from Isaiah 58:1: "Cry aloud, spare not; Lift up your voice like a trumpet!" The feeling of why bother is still here, but I'm reading and rereading "Cry aloud, spare not; Lift up your voice like a trumpet!"

I've begun to hear another voice. Though it's still faint; I know it's the voice of the Lord. I keep listening, hoping the voice will get louder, and then I realize there's a war taking place in the spirit. "Hold on, I'm coming!" Oh, how I hate these times when there's a battle within me. My feelings and my natural mind are discouraged, but there's a voice that says, "Choose. Don't live by your feelings, but live from the place of faith."

I remember part of a verse in Ephesians six which says "having done all, to stand." So I'm choosing to stand and wait for my feelings to change. Yet I hear this voice getting louder, and it's saying, "Tell them they matter! Tell them they're making a difference!" I can hear "Cry aloud, spare not; Lift up your voice like a trumpet!"

Go ahead - "Cry aloud, spare not; Lift up your voice like a trumpet!"

Day 93

THOUGHT OF THE DAY: Have we lost our awe of God?

During this Christmas season as I've gone back and re-read the accounts in Luke two and Matthew two, one thing that's jumped out at me is the awe, wonder, and majesty that the shepherds and the magi had. I've been praying, "Oh Lord, cause me to once again be filled with wonder and awe!"

In Matthew two we read, "Now after Jesus was born in Bethlehem of Judea in the days of Herod the king, behold, wise men from the East came to Jerusalem, saying, 'Where is He who has been born King of the Jews? For we have seen His star in the East and have come to worship Him.' "

The primary reason the magi came was to worship the Lord. We're told they traveled 1000 miles, and it took two years to get there. Think - it took two years, and when they finally reached their destination, what did they do? "And when they had come into the house, they saw the young Child with Mary His mother, and fell down and worshiped Him. And when they had opened their treasures, they presented gifts to Him: gold, frankincense, and myrrh." (verse 11)

When they saw the Lord, they FELL DOWN AND WORSHIPED! Oh, what awe, what splendor, what majesty! We cry out for Him to fill us again with awe and wonder!

The shepherds in the field were in awe and wonder as innumerable angels filled the night sky with worship. The shepherds couldn't get there fast enough. Matthew 2:20 says, "Then the shepherds returned, glorifying and praising God for all the things that they had heard and seen, as it was told them." Oh, and they were filled with awe and wonder!

Lord fill us with awe and wonder.

Day 94

THOUGHT OF THE DAY: If today was my last day on earth

It's a little after 5:00 a.m. and I'm pondering what I'd say if this was my last day on earth. What would you say?

Perhaps I would whisper about the greatness of our God. How His love is truly unconditional, that nothing has separated or could separate me from His love. That I had learned He was always with me, always encouraging even when my heart was hard. I would tell you of my many failures so that you could learn about His abounding mercy and constant willingness to forgive and cleanse my conscience.

I would speak about His ability to mold and shape our hearts to be more like His. I would speak of my regret that I didn't love the way He loves. I would say to be ready to forgive and quick to pardon. Not to keep record of faults or times I was hurt. I would speak about the brief time I had here on earth and how I'd like another chance to do it differently.

I would spend more time with my family and know that it's okay with God not to be at every church event. I would spend less time pointing out the faults of my children and more time making them feel safe to tell me anything. I would overlook faults as God continually overlooked mine. I would plead with everyone who heard my voice about the intimacy of worship, that it was one of my deepest regrets that it took me forty years to know as reality what God spoke to Moses in Exodus 33: that His presence "would go with him and that God would give him rest."

I regret also not realizing sooner that I was simply His son and that He enjoyed/delighted in being with me. That if I had learned to be still sooner in life, I would've heard him rejoicing over me with singing.

I would tell people how He whispers even in the midst of our storms. I would tell them to love people where they're at, not where we think they should be. I would speak on loving people even when you're disappointed in them and when they continue to have some of the same weaknesses.

I would tell people that my body language and facial expressions communicated more than my words. I would speak of the joy of laying down my life for others and to do all that you can do to have others surpass anything you might have done in the kingdom.

There is so much more I could say, but I will allow my Master to teach me what that is before my time is up some 30 plus years from now. You see, I have so much more to learn, and I look forward to the day that He'll allow me to write it.

I guess it's already been summarized: "Love God with all your heart, soul, and strength, and love others the way you love yourselves." Sounds simple, doesn't it?

If today was my last day on earth, I'd say... I love you!!!

Day 95

THOUGHT OF THE DAY: I had a dream

Early this morning I awoke to a dream I had last night where I'd traveled to another church where there was some sort of difference with our ministry philosophies. Then out of nowhere and without permission, they searched my car and found an empty beer bottle in the back under the front seat. They immediately convened a meeting which they left me out of, and sat around and discussed the matter, drawing all kinds of conclusions without once asking me a question.

Then they asked me to come to their meeting where they delivered their conclusion. It was harsh and unfounded. After they finished speaking to me, I quoted Proverbs 18:13: "Let people finish speaking before you try to answer them. That way you will not embarrass yourself and look foolish; or "Spouting off before listening to the facts" (NLT) is both shameful and foolish." (ERV)

I awoke from the dream angry, because this has happened to me - people sitting in judgement without hearing "the rest of the story," as Paul Harvey was famous for saying. James 4:12 says: "There is one lawgiver and judge[a] who is able to save and to destroy. But who are you to judge your neighbor?" (HCSB)

So here I am musing about this injustice when I hear, "You've done the same thing." Immediately, I recalled times when I'd jumped to conclusions about people, and when they did speak, I didn't really listen because my mind was already made up. I stopped what I was doing and asked the Lord to forgive me, and prayed healing for those I had hurt. Then I asked the Lord to not allow me to do this again.

Oh, and the beer bottle wasn't mine. Someone had borrowed the car and had a passenger in the rear seat. The passenger had brought an open bottle into the car, and the driver was unaware of it.

"Let people finish speaking before you try to answer them."

Day 96

THOUGHT OF THE DAY: How long will He ask?

As I'm sitting here this morning in worship, God tells me to stop looking for the ram in the thicket.

He's showing me that while I'm looking for answers, I'm not looking at Him for them. Funny how we can be looking but not looking in the right place. As I'm sitting here in worship, I hear Him say, "How long will I call and my people will not answer?" The call is to be alone with Him. To come and sit at His feet.

Mary sat at his feet, and Martha was busy serving. If we would sit at Jesus' feet, he would overshadow and overwhelm us. Matthew 11:28: "Come to Me, all you who labor and are heavy-laden and overburdened, and I will cause you to rest. {I will ease and relieve and refresh your souls.}" (AMPC)

Could we have imagined that in April of 1906 in a home of Afro-Americans that God would pour out His Spirit, which in turn would lead to the Azusa Street Revival?

Remember the culture of 1906? Black people were still being treated as less than white people. They didn't vote; they rode the back of buses and weren't allowed into many restaurants. Yet in God's eternal plan He used the despised and rejected, He used the nobodies to turn the world upside down. In this small house, people gathered to simply worship the Lord. Then suddenly everything changed.

There is no doubt God is about to do this again. He's looking for people who will put away their agendas and their clever plans and simply come and worship. John 4:23-24: "But the time is coming — indeed, it's here now — when the true worshippers will worship the Father spiritually and truly, for these are the kind of people the Father wants worshipping him. God is spirit; and worshippers must worship him spiritually and truly."

Our Father is looking for worshippers. Did we really hear that? He is looking for worshippers. Can we hear Him calling us to come? Can we believe that once again God will pour His Spirit out like he did in 1906 and once again CHANGE THE WORLD BECAUSE WE ARE WORSHIPPERS?

HOW LONG WILL HE ASK?

Day 97

THOUGHT OF THE DAY: The new wine skin

Little did I understand that in order for the Lord to pour in a new wine, it would require a new wine skin.

That means that there has to be some radical changes in us. Even though we've had an awareness of areas in our lives that need to change, we've been okay living with them - character flaws, wrong attitudes, "little" areas of weakness that we allow to exist in our lives. Yet new wine requires new wine skins. We're so desperate for NEW!

So here we are in the Valley of Decision (Joel 3). New or old - our choice.

I was sitting and musing about where I needed a new wine skin and heard, "First Corinthians 13." My reaction was to think that I know first Corinthians already - don't you? I heard, "Go look it up, for this is your beginning." So here is first Corinthians 13:1-8 in the Jewish Complete Bible. Please read it slowly as if you're reading it for the first time.

What if I could speak all languages of humans and of angels? If I did not love others, I would be nothing more than a noisy gong or a clanging cymbal. What if I could prophesy and understand all secrets and all knowledge? And what if I had faith that moved mountains? I would be nothing, unless I loved others. What if I gave away all that I owned and let myself be burned alive? I would gain nothing, unless I loved others. Love is kind and patient, never jealous, boastful, proud, or rude. Love isn't selfish or quick tempered. It doesn't keep a record of wrongs that others do. Love rejoices in the truth, but not in evil. Love is always supportive, loyal, hopeful, and trusting. Love never fails!

I must admit that I don't love this way. Do you? Yet this is what the new wine skin is made from. Oh Lord, we give ourselves to you not for small changes, but with the same fervor as the day we first committed our lives to you.

Galatians 5:6 does a great job of summarizing why we need to begin with love: Faith works through love: "If you are a follower of Christ Jesus, it makes no difference whether you are circumcised or not. All that matters is your faith that makes you love others."

Oh Lord, pour in the new!!!

Day 98

THOUGHT OF THE DAY: God attended a funeral yesterday

Yesterday, I spent a good part of my day supporting a close friend I've had for close to thirty years. His mother had died on Christmas Eve. There are a couple of things I wish to share about it this morning.

Yesterday the Holy Spirit was at the funeral mass.

I'm a former Catholic "basher," but I'll say that the Holy Spirit dealt with that in the late seventies. The scripture says, "Wherever two or three are gathered in MY NAME I WILL BE THERE." If God's presence depended on correct theology, He'd never show up.

As we entered the church, there was a young lady singing "Be not afraid; I go before you always." This song has to be close to 40 years old. I'm telling you that the presence of God fell on me, and my eyes began to puddle, the voice of God saying, "BE NOT AFRAID; I GO BEFORE YOU ALWAYS."

Can you hear that this morning? I can hear His voice so clearly in that this morning. In fact, here would be a good place to stop and "muse" to see what the Holy Spirit wants to say to us about those eight words. The next part of the song says, "Come follow me, and I will give you rest." Can you hear His voice? Hasn't God been speaking about rest? Will we find rest the more we follow Him?

So here I am sitting in a funeral mass, and God is present and speaking. The mass continues and another song is sung. I just had to raise both of my hands in worship. You see, if we're open to the working of the Holy Spirit He'll show up in the most unusual places. Yes, He's omnipresent!

One of the deacons gets up to do a reading, and he read from Revelation 21:1-8. If you have a chance, take a peek at it. It's so full of hope. The beginning of verse three says, "And I heard a loud voice from heaven saying..." At that moment it was if God's voice began to thunder as the deacon continued, "Behold, the tabernacle of God is with men, and He will dwell with them, and they shall be His people. God Himself will be with them and be their God." I heard the Spirit say, "I am coming soon to be among you and my people will be used in unique and powerful ways." Then verse five was read, and it so confirmed that God has been speaking about "doing a new thing." Revelations 3:5: "Then He who sat on the throne said, 'Behold, I make all things new.' And He said to me, 'Write, for these words are true and faithful.' "

God is saying, "Write it down. I'm not a liar; I'm about to do something new. Write it down. I will do it!"

I was sitting drinking in all that God was doing, and then He tells me what to share on Sunday morning and how He wants to continue to speak about the need for a new wine skin so He can pour in new wine. If that wasn't enough, when the priest took the incense near the end of the service and was waving it toward the people sitting in the pews, I was hit in my chest as if a soft lighting bolt had struck me. I'm not kidding! When it hit me, I was actually pushed backwards in the pew. I felt the presence of God as amazing and overwhelming. There was such peace, joy, and a sense of hope. I had just been touched by God.

Yes, at a Catholic funeral mass God was present. My life is richer because of yesterday. My life was changed because of yesterday.

Our God is among us, and He is doing great things. Are we open to hear and receive from God in places we might not expect? Remember Naaman? He limited how God could speak because of his preconceived ideas of how God was going to move. Part of the new is just that - God speaking and moving outside of our past experiences, that He is and will move outside of our current mindset.

I believe we're going to be shocked at how God is going to shatter our little paradigms.

God went to a funeral mass yesterday!

Day 99

THOUGHT OF THE DAY: We cry out

Father, I lift my hands to you this morning. I know you're listening, but at times it feels like you're not.

In Habakkuk 1:2 I see Habakkuk pleading with you as he asks, "How long must I cry, O Eternal One, and get no answer from You?" (VB)

When David was in the wilderness of Judah he writes in Psalm 63:1: "O True God, You are my God, the One whom I trust. I seek You with every fiber of my being. In this dry and weary land with no water in sight, my soul is dry and longs for You. My body aches for You, for Your presence." (VOICE)

Father, this morning we cry out. We need you! The world is in chaos, and the only answer is You. Oh, if you would allow each of us to carry your manifest presence, that when we walk into a room the entire room fills with you, that people would feel and sense that God walked into the room, that the air would be filled with love, compassion, grace, mercy, and healing, that without a word being spoken, people would have a divine encounter with you.

Father, with my hands lifted to You I utter part of Habakkuk's prayer from chapter three, verse two: "Lord, I have heard the news about you. I am amazed, Lord, at the powerful things you did in the past. Now I pray that you will do great things in our time. Please make these things happen in our own days." (ERV)

We cry out...

Day 100

THOUGHT OF THE DAY: Cherish your friendships

As I told you yesterday, I attended a funeral of a friend's mother. I went to the funeral to support him, even though I'd never met his mother. It was all about honoring him and our relationship.

For some people relationships come easy, but not so for me. I grew up active in sports and other school activities, and even though I was seen as popular and was even voted "Most Popular" by my fellow seniors, I was a loner. Circumstances within my immediate family caused me to be friendly, but you can be friendly without having friends.

Several years ago in the early 1980s, the Lord told me to go away. I had no idea where I was supposed to go, but two supernatural events made it clear it was necessary, as out of nowhere two people approached me and gave the same message.

The first person was our babysitter. Donna and I had just returned from a vacation, and this woman told me that every time she passed the brown chair in our basement, she felt the presence of God. This chair, by the way, was where I would go every day to pray.

While she was praying at my chair, she heard that she was to tell me to "go away by myself." Almost immediately upon our return from the trip she came and told me that I was to go away alone.

The second person spoke to me at church on that Sunday morning. A strange-looking lady approached me, and at first glance I thought she was a witch. She said simply, "You're supposed to go away," and then disappeared, simply vanished.

It took me 3 months to arrange my schedule so I could obey what I was told.

The long and short of it is that I ended up outside of the home where I had committed my life to Christ. After that was the home of a very close college friend. The Lord said simply, "Call him." There were no cell phones back then, so off to a pay phone I went. For over two hours I called everyone with his first and last name. Finally the Lord prompted me to call his father, who, by the way, was still living in the same house some 14 years later. From him, I got Jeff's number.

Jeff had moved to western Massachusetts and unbelievably had also become a minister. We talked briefly, but to be honest, there was no true connection. He had become a stranger. I asked the Lord what it was all about. Here was his reply:

He told me that I had failed to honor and cherish my relationship with Jeff just as I was also not honoring and cherishing the relationships I had now. Wow! I was floored. You see, it all comes down to one of the reasons we were created – for relationships. Since that time I've been working on it. (Notice that the phrase "working on it" implies process.)

Sadly, in our lifetime, we've moved on from three churches. The loss of relationships has been very difficult. With the loss of each came the resistance to make new ones. I didn't want to be hurt again.

Then I was reminded that Jesus did say, "Turn the other cheek;" in other words, be willing to become vulnerable and be hurt again.

Let me say that whatever friendships you have today, cherish them.

Day 101

THOUGHT OF THE DAY: Appearances

It was several years ago that I went to a home group dressed very shabbily. My hair was uncombed; I wore a plaid shirt that belonged in the trash, an old pair of paints full of paint stains, and sneakers that matched my pants, dirty and paint-stained as they were.

I arrived at the home group late on purpose; they had started the meeting without me. I came and sat down on one of the unoccupied chairs and after a few minutes began to teach. There were new people there that night as well as some who always had an opinion about how things should be. I handed out index cards and asked people what they thought about me when I first sat down.

At least three or four people said they felt uncomfortable and then shocked that I was the teacher; another person was disappointed I would arrive in that condition to the small group, and several more believed that if I was going to come dressed like that, I shouldn't have come at all.

Aren't we all guilty of judging by appearances?

I was the assistant pastor in a church for eleven years, and there was a woman there who was overweight, loud, and extremely talkative - she would talk and talk and then talk some more. Each time I saw her I had an opinion. In fact, I wished she attended another church. Then one day she came up to me and handed me a folded piece of paper and walked away.

Later that day I read what she'd written. It was a prophetic word that was right on, even down to the smallest detail. For about four years she wrote these amazing prophetic words that I still have to this day. Again, I was guilty of judging by appearance.

I met a man some forty years ago who didn't have a place to live. He would travel and live from house to house. Today we call that "couch surfing," a term used for the homeless. In listening to him, it was clear that his theology was really different from what I was accustomed to.

Several of the ministers I knew disagreed with most of what he said. They didn't like the fact that he hadn't been to bible college or seminary, and yet he spoke with such authority it would irritate them.

There were many things he said that I didn't like at all and many things I just couldn't understand and was even confused by. As much as I didn't like the things he said, though, what he did say would resonate in my heart. Then finally, after studying his message, I decided to commit my life to him.

By now you've figured out.... I'm talking about Jesus.

We judge not only by outward appearances but based on how people think. If people think differently than we do, it's often hard for us. We close off, believing we know better and thus become unteachable. For years I had this attitude.

Perhaps I'm the only one who's been guilty of judging by appearances?

Day 102

THOUGHT OF THE DAY: Taking an honest look

It was last Monday during early morning worship that the Lord told me I was to share about the rich young ruler mentioned in three of the four gospels.

My first response was, "Sure, I can do that." Little did I know that this story would impact my life. You know how scripture can get too familiar, how we can have the "I know that already" attitude? In the process we can read and study scripture and form opinions about the person in the story and meanwhile never see that the person in the story could easily be us.

This is exactly what happened to me this week. I saw how the rich young ruler ran and knelt before Jesus, and Jesus spoke to him about keeping the six relational commandments with man. He responded that since his youth he had done this very thing. Often when the Holy Spirit asks us to examine ourselves, like the rich young ruler, we can't see the truth either, because we're blind to our condition or haven't taken the time to ask the Holy Spirit to show us the truth.

In Mark 10:21 Jesus responds to him. It says, "Then Jesus, looking at him, loved him." Only Jesus can look at a person and see their true nature in all of its pride, self-righteousness, and blindness and still have the will and desire to love them where they are. I must admit that I haven't arrived at this place of loving someone unconditionally, especially when they have a wrong attitude. Thank God that He loves us all of the time even when our attitudes and character are far from where they need to be.

Verse 21 continues with Jesus saying to him, "One thing you lack: Go your way, sell whatever you have and give to the poor, and you will have treasure in heaven; and come, take up the cross, and follow Me." I had always read this story without recognizing the possibility that the Holy Spirit could turn to me and say, "Brian, I want you to sell everything you have – EVERYTHING, and give it AWAY to the poor."

It hit me this week that the Lord could ask me to do this. Even with the promise "of having treasure in heaven," if I'm honest. I don't think I would do it. Perhaps the only way I would is if Jesus appeared in bodily form and asked me.

Think about it: give away everything you have and follow the Lord. Would you give EVERYTHING away?

(Then even if we DO comply, we still have to pick up a cross and follow Him...)

Jesus is described in scripture as having "nowhere to lay his head," so in essence we could say he was homeless. Truly, Jesus trusted his Father for his daily bread plus everything else, and yes, it got him "killed."

May God honor all the people who've abandoned everything to follow Him. When I put this out to our congregation today, only two people raised their hands to accept Jesus' conditions.

This week I saw that I'm very much like the young rich young ruler with areas in my life that the Holy Spirit still needs to work in! But thank God I know that when He looks at me, He LOVES me right where I am!

Taking an honest look!

Day 103

THOUGHT OF THE DAY: It's more than an overflow shelter for the homeless

There's a homeless shelter in the city of Fall River which unfortunately has too few beds to meet the needs of those who don't have a place to sleep – hence the need for other places for people to go. We are one of those places.

Tonight we reached capacity in the overflow shelter - 15 people. In fact, we had 17 people, but two were able to go to the main shelter, which is called The First Step Inn. (What a great name – one which signifies a person's first step toward a new life!) After we reach capacity, a second overflow shelter will be opened. Even then, that might not be enough to meet the needs of people who require a place to be warm, to sleep, get a meal, a cup of coffee, and some love.

You don't realize how blessed you are until you begin chatting with these wonderful people who find themselves homeless. Each story is different, and if it wasn't for the grace of God, many of us could be in the identical situation. The bottom line is that they're real people with real emotions, real hope, real dreams, and they, like us, want to be loved and respected. For the next ten weeks we can give them shelter from 6:00 p.m. until 7:00 a.m., and then most of them will spend their day walking, trying to stay warm, and hoping that they can get into a program, find a job, get something to eat - just survive another day.

The very first night, a woman who had major surgery found herself with no place to live on New Year's Day. She was considering that life wasn't worth living when she heard about the overflow shelter, and it gave her hope. Her first night was Sunday, and a woman volunteer went to sit with her. She listened, loved, and encouraged. To see the look of hope on this woman's face had us saying that all the work to this point was worth it all.

The second night, the woman who'd spent time with her sent word to say hello and to ask for her. When the woman was given the message, her eyes teared up. She couldn't believe that someone would care enough to ask for her. She asked at least three times, "Did she really ask for me?" Tonight this same woman looked discouraged, so someone went to her and said, "You look like you could use a hug." She just melted as she received it.

Last night a man shared that he hadn't seen his daughter in five years, and so one of the workers was able to encourage him by sharing the various programs that could help him. With that inspiration, he was able to set the goal of having a home for his daughter to visit the following year.

Hope is being birthed in a homeless shelter.

It's only been three nights, but something is happening in this overflow shelter. You see, Jesus is walking around the shelter and touching lives through ordinary people sacrificing some time to offer love, hope, and encouragement.

It's much more than an overflow shelter for the homeless...

Day 104

THOUGHT OF THE DAY: Oh Lord, I am looking for you
Since yesterday I've been looking for you. In fact, I can hear the heart cry of multitudes of your children. They're also looking for you.

All are desperate to see you; desperate to be near you and literally abide in your presence. It's there we find peace, rest, and hope, gaining wisdom and understanding. It's there we capture your heart and are filled with joy because we know that you hear us and that you quiet our soul.

Psalm 63:1-3 captures our cry. This is a psalm of David birthed while hiding in the wilderness of Judea. Please read it slowly! "O God, my God! How I search for you! How I thirst for you in this parched and weary land where there is no water. How I long to find you! How I wish I could go into your sanctuary to see your strength and glory, for your love and kindness are better to me than life itself." (Living Bible)

What happened when you read this slowly? My experience was to be put instantly in His presence where I felt that everything was going to be okay. Then I was asked, "What do you want?" Immediately I began to speak in tongues, because I didn't want my natural mind and voice to limit what really needed to be said. I had such an urge to replay the worship music I'd had on, instrumental worship by Ruth Fazal. I didn't want words from a song to clutter or interfere with the cry of my heart. (Let me say this - Don't let the voices in the songs of others speak for you. Yes, there are times when worship with words is exactly what we need, but there are others when we can't let others' words speak for us.)

Oh Lord, see our desperation. As much as I would want to mention my own personal needs, desires, and wants, they seem so small here in your presence. Oh Lord, see your people! Oh Lord, see the needs and desperation of those who are lost and homeless, those who are confused, broken, and deceived. Hear the cry of your people that you would come and fill us with your love, your mind, heart, and presence. Oh Lord, look down, oh Lord, come down and be among us. FOR ONLY YOU CAN DELIVER! ONLY YOU CAN HEAL. ONLY YOU CAN SATISFY! YES, IT IS YOU WHO WE SEEK. Continue to teach us to seek you and not your hand. If twelve men could change the world; what about us?

Oh Lord, I was looking for you, and I found you. Yes, it took two days, but you are indeed faithful when you say, "And you will seek Me and find Me, when you search for Me with all your heart." (Jeremiah 29:13)

Hear this: my circumstances have not changed, but my heart has. He has an appointed time for everything. He has satisfied my soul!

Oh Lord I am looking for you...

Day 105

THOUGHT OF THE DAY: Writing from Jerusalem

It's 4:00 a.m. and I'm sitting in the overflow shelter. I had to come back tonight to train the 3:00 a.m. to 7:00 a.m. team. We're so thankful that so many people have agreed to come and help. If you'd like to volunteer, you can go online and type in www.TCshelter.com where there's an application you can fill out.

I can't begin to tell you how rewarding it is to sit and listen to people's stories of how they ended up here. Tonight I was speaking to a man who for multiple years had a serious drug habit. He was living a secret life when the day finally came that a family member discovered the truth. The entire family was devastated.

As painful as it is to be away from his family, the man is thanking God that he's no longer taking drugs, sharing that for 23 years he had this habit. Once it was discovered, he turned himself in to get "clean." The first day he was in the clinic he prayed and asked God to take away his dependence and deep craving for the drug. What did God do but immediately deliver him from any desire. As he told me this story, tears ran down his checks.

With his voice quivering, he went on to share his pain of not being with his family. Tears flowed like a faucet. As I listened, like so many other volunteers, I simply put my arm around him. After a few minutes he said, "THANK YOU."

Tonight I see how the people serving here sit, listen, and truly care for people. One man was in another shelter in another town and heard about this overflow shelter so had someone bring him. He told me tonight how wonderful it was to be here. He said that all the volunteers sincerely care and treat him like a real person and so was thankful to feel safe and cared for. He said that by being here, it gave him hope. Wow!

In Acts 1:8 it says, "But you shall receive power when the Holy Spirit has come upon you; and you shall be witnesses to Me in Jerusalem, and in all Judea and Samaria, and to the end of the earth." We are to be witnesses in our personal Jerusalems. Where is your's?

To be a witness in the Greek means "to be one who testifies as in a court of law." Often our witness is not with words but through loving, caring, and listening. What might seem insignificant can change a life. I've written before that I've discovered the power of hello. A simple hello is often the key to reaching a person's heart.

You don't have to go on a missions trip to Africa, Haiti, or some other faraway place. Just look around where you live and work and see your own personal Jerusalem.

Writing with joy from Jerusalem!

Day 106

THOUGHT OF THE DAY: "It's not about me."

Haven't we all had days where we can't figure out why we're out of sorts? What do I mean by that? There are days like today when I can't seem to get a handle on my thoughts and feelings. For several hours I couldn't figure out what was going on. I felt frustrated, irritable, confused, sad, bewildered, disappointed, and a whole bunch of other emotions I couldn't define.

Ever had one of those days?

So I did my normal routine. I worshipped - it didn't help. I read scripture - it didn't help. I asked myself the why question. I asked if it was the enemy, was it this or was it that? The more I asked, the more bewildered I became. I tried worship again, but I continued to be bewildered and frustrated. Ever have one of those days? I began to think about this and that, and my emotions just intensified.

Ever notice the more you strive, the worse it gets? I really dislike days like this.

Finally, after trying to get answers, I asked, "Lord what's going on?" I heard Him say, "You still haven't learned that it's not always about you!" Then I realized my connection to the body of Christ and to the Lord's heart. I closed my eyes and wanted to cry.

You see, we're connected to one another. As I closed my eyes I began realizing that I was carrying God's heart for the church, that I was and am carrying God's heart for His people. I closed my eyes again and saw people I knew and some I didn't know. They were hurting, confused, bewildered, etcetera. Again I heard, "It's not all about you."

I've caught a small glimpse of your love for people. Oh, how you love people. "Please give me your heart for people" is my cry. Yet as I pray this, I'm asking myself if I can bear that level of burden when I'm struggling with this small one.

Father, come! Reach through eternity and invade the lives of all those who are crying out. Reach out even to those who are NOT crying out!

I want this burden to lift, yet I know, "It's not all about me."

Day 107

THOUGHT OF THE DAY: They wanted to see Jesus

In the twelfth chapter of John, some Greeks had come to Jerusalem to keep the feast. They'd heard that Jesus was there, so they approached one of the disciples with their request. One disciple went to another, then another, and finally they came to Jesus and told him that there were a number of Greek converts to Judaism who wanted to see him. Jesus had a very strange answer. He said in John 12:24: "Most assuredly, I say to you, unless a grain of wheat falls into the ground and dies, it remains alone; but if it dies, it produces much grain."

Yesterday I shared an epiphany in church about Jesus' unusual response. After all, all of us want to gain a better revelation of Jesus, to see him and understand him more clearly. I realized that just as a seed/grain of wheat has an outer covering/shell, my own heart has a shell over it. If I want a deeper revelation of Jesus, then that outer shell around my heart has to be broken.

My hard shell prevents me from having the compassion that Jesus was moved by. I can either be motivated by compassion or by biblical responsibility. Yesterday I realized that I am most often motivated by biblical responsibility and not by the compassion Jesus exhibited, the kind which comes from the deep bowels of one's inner being. This has to change. I have to allow the Lord to show me how and when my shell was made. It wasn't just one experience, but several, that have served to form this shell around my heart. Before I can let people in, I have to give permission to the Holy Spirit.

Perhaps those of you reading this might consider that you too have some hard layers around your heart which not only inhibit you from having "Jesus Compassion," but a deeper revelation of Him.

They wanted to see Jesus...

Day 108

THOUGHT OF THE DAY: "You're blessed when you're at the end of your rope. With less of you there is more of God and his rule."

The verse you just read is Matthew 5:3 from the Message Bible. It usually reads "Blessed are the poor in spirit, For theirs is the kingdom of heaven." I love the very real Message Bible version.

The THOUGHT OF THE DAY (or perhaps it should be the question of the day) – Do you consider yourself "AT THE END OF YOUR ROPE"? The verse goes on to say that when there's less of us, there's more of God and his kingdom rule in our lives.

It's been awhile since I've thought about the fact that when we're broken, when we're exhausted from our efforts, when God uses circumstances in our lives that create a deeper need for him, we've arrived at exactly the right place. This is the place where we begin seeing the reality of another kingdom in our life - the place where we rule and reign. I see it as a place where I've had control, yet in order to live in His kingdom, I need to relinquish my own.

The Amplified Bible puts it this way: "Blessed (happy, to be envied, and spiritually prosperous—[with life-joy and satisfaction in God's favor and salvation, regardless of their outward conditions) are the poor in spirit (the humble, who rate themselves insignificant), for theirs is the kingdom of heaven!"

I had to go back and read this several times, because in reading it just once I couldn't grasp the depth of what the Holy Spirit was trying to not only show me, but to actually inscribe on my heart by bypassing my mind. In fact, I need to write this down on an index card or piece of paper to carry with me to read throughout the day.

Don't we all want to be blessed, happy, spiritually prosperous, and have a life of joy and satisfaction? Don't we all want God's favor? This is God's promise when we come to the end of our rope. When we come to the end of ourselves. When we relinquish our control for His kingdom. So that leads me to the question of whether the Holy Spirit is allowing us to be, as Isaiah says in Isaiah 6:5, "undone." Lord, what are you after in us?

As I consider Isaiah chapter six, I'm realizing that the things we're experiencing in our lives now are not only for the purpose of having more of God and His kingdom in our lives, but in order that we can be prepared to be sent where He wants us to go. Isaiah 5:6 says, "Woe is me, for I am undone!" Then verse eight says, "Also I heard the voice of the Lord, saying, 'Whom shall I send, and who will go for Us?' Then I said, 'Here am I! Send me.' "

We are at the end of our rope not only so we can have more of His kingdom and be blessed, happy, spiritually prosperous, joyful, satisfied, and full of favor, but also so that we may be prepared to be used! Now I'm getting excited!

As I was finishing this, I received a phone call from a solicitor. Within 30 seconds I was able to share with her - "You're blessed when you're at the end of your rope. With less of you there is more of God and His rule."

Day 109

THOUGHT OF THE DAY: Having a midlife crisis

I haven't written a thought in a number of days because I was and still am going through a spiritual midlife crisis. Like Isaiah, I am feeling "undone." I said yesterday in church that something is wrong with my Christianity. I'm seeing that I haven't fully grasped or lived out 1 Corinthians 13, the "Love is..." verses we hear at every wedding.

I'm realizing that I don't love the way Jesus loved or how the Father loves us. I'm recognizing that my love is often conditional and that I withhold my love and affection when someone disappoints me or they exhibit a wrong attitude or behavior. Jesus, by contrast, in hearing the excuses and attitude of the rich young ruler, "loved him."

Yesterday during my morning musing with the Lord, I saw the prodigal son's father day after day sitting on a porch peering out for any sign of his son's return. He wasn't thinking about him wasting inheritance. He wasn't fuming in anger. He was waiting for his son to come home, longing to embrace him and throw a party and restore him.

The day finally came. The father violated every Jewish custom as he saw his son coming, yet ran to him and kissed him over and over again. You can be sure that I have not loved like that.

While serving in the overflow homeless shelters this past week, I've seen something different. By God's grace, I saw people as hidden treasure. I saw how valuable and precious these people were and realized that this is how the Father sees us – as treasure that has been buried under all kinds of rubble. Even today I recognize God's relentless pursuit of me. Here I thought that I was pursuing Him, when in reality He is the one pursuing me.

I'm beginning to identify with Saint Thomas Aquinas, a famous and well-known theologian who wrote volumes and volumes on various theological topics. Toward the later years of his life, however, he just stopped writing. A close companion came and asked him why. He said that after an encounter with Jesus, his view of what he'd written had changed. Looking back, he realized that what he'd written was "like straw." Not only did it have no real value, but it was going to burn.

Yes, I'm seeing that there has to be a radical change.

Here is a prayer you might be hesitant about. "Search me, oh God!" To be honest I haven't really prayed that yet, because I'm still coming to some sort of awareness that I don't love like the one I'm called to reflect. I have this sense that the Holy Spirit is unearthing the buried treasure - me... He is not mad or disappointed. In fact, I can see him smiling as a tear is running down His cheek. I can feel and I can hear this whisper, "I LOVE YOU!"

After all of these years I'm having a midlife crisis because of the treasure He sees.

Day 110

THOUGHT OF THE DAY: We're silly people
I wonder if God sometimes looks at us and laughs?

We are indeed peculiar people and yes, some of us more peculiar than others. We're silly because we've all felt at times better than someone else. Our opinions and perspectives happen to be better than someone else's. Our theology is better. In fact, I would suggest that we've all felt at one time or another that the world would be a better place if people were more like us. We're silly people.

We're silly because we form opinions about others without really knowing them. We're quick to speak and slow to listen. We too often pass on tidbits about others for no real reason at all. We call it "sharing" instead of gossip. Why is it that we subtly elevate ourselves at the expense of putting someone else down? We're silly people.

We're ecstatic that we're embraced by grace, yet while celebrating grace for ourselves, we see and respond to others through the law. We have one set of standards for ourselves and another set of standards for others. We're silly people.

I wonder if God sometimes looks at us and just laughs? We're silly people.

Day 111

THOUGHT OF THE DAY: Affection

Over the past few years the Holy Spirit has been showing us that God's love for us is not a sterile love devoid of deep affection. In fact, the opposite is true.

Our own expressions of love to people are sincere. They communicate that we care for them, we appreciate the relationship, we want them to be happy, we want the best for them, and so on. Even so, we can say, "I love you" to a person and still lack a deep sense of genuine affection for them. It's a feeling that's mostly mechanical, neutered, and ultimately devoid of any real emotion.

For most of my walk with God I knew He loved me because it says in 1 John 4:8 that "God is love." I felt that God had to love me, that His very nature was such that he was obligated to. Up until a few years ago, however, I didn't understand this love or even feel His affection for me.

When I hear the word "love," it generates certain thoughts and emotions, but the effect of the word "affection" is very different. Oh, how I yearn to be fully enveloped in His affection. If I can, and if it is key to receive His affection, then it seems to follow that I'll be better able to pour affection on others.

Don't we all want to surpass love and move to affection?

A number of years ago I read Brennan Manning's book called Ragamuffin Gospel, and on page 188 he writes that when he moved from

Clearwater Florida to New Orleans, he did some research on the Christian faith in that area. He writes, "One hundred years ago in the Deep South, a phrase so common in our culture today, 'born again,' was seldom or never used. Rather the phrase used to describe the breakthrough into a personal relationship with Jesus Christ was "I WAS SEIZED BY THE POWER OF A GREAT AFFECTION.' "

Oh, how I love that phrase! "I WAS SEIZED BY THE POWER OF A GREAT AFFECTION." You and I were taken captive not by some ordinary affection, but by a powerful, supernatural, divine affection. Just writing this I can feel that sense of affection touching me.

Yet I can also feel a blockage. My heart breaks that there's something in me, and I believe in most of us, that hinders us from fully receiving His affection. Oh Lord, we cry out for you to take down the walls and bring healing so that when we awake every day and we're greeted by your affection, that we're able to not only receive it but also embrace it. We cry out that we might be carriers of your affection so that when people are around us, they can feel your love...

Father, I'm realizing that carrying your presence is also carrying your AFFECTION.

Day 112

THOUGHT OF THE DAY: If we could only encourage one another

Yesterday in church, I asked people who among them liked to be encouraged. Everyone raised their hands.

I don't know about you, but I'm all too familiar with my faults and weaknesses and honestly, don't need to be reminded of them. It made me think about the likelihood that if we aren't encouraging people, then we're probably discouraging them.

Barnabas we know as one of the apostles after the original twelve; his name means son of encouragement, and that is who he was. He had the ability to see what people could become, and he encouraged people not only by his words, but by his actions.

The church is desperate to have this spirit. Paul in writing the church of Thessalonica says in chapter five, "Therefore comfort each other and edify one another, just as you also are doing." (verse 11 – NKJV) The Living Bible says: "So encourage each other to build each other up, just as you are already doing," and the Phillips Bible says to "Go on cheering and strengthening each other." Such a simple admonition.

Let's become spiritual cheerleaders!

Most of us would like to prophesy. I know that in the strict biblical sense prophecy is "speaking for God secrets of the heart" (1 Corinthians

14:26), but I'd like to expand its intent. Let's read 1 Corinthians 14:3: "But he who prophesies speaks edification and exhortation and comfort to men." (NKJV) The CEB Bible says, "Those who prophesy speak to people, building them up, and giving them encouragement and comfort." Prophesying is breathing life. In Ezekiel 37 we see that as Ezekiel prophesies to the bones, there's a loud noise as the bones rattle and come together.

Get ready for a loud sound as we speak life: encouragement, edification, and comfort. This could be the beginning of revival. As we continue reading Ezekiel 37, we see that he then speaks to the sinews and he speaks a breath, and the result is that a vast army is brought to life. Imagine that a great army can be brought to life if we'd only encourage, edify (build up), and comfort people. As Paul writes in 1 Corinthians 14:1: "Pursue love, and desire spiritual gifts, but especially that you may prophesy."

Off in the distance I can hear the sound of a mighty army rising because we've learned to ENCOURAGE ONE ANOTHER.

GET READY! THERE'S AN ARMY RISING!

If we could only encourage one another.

Day 113

THOUGHT OF THE DAY: Discerning the subtleties of the Holy Spirit

I awoke this morning thanking God that I'm home and safe with my family. After spending three days in a factory during the blizzard of 1978, it's always a joy to be home. As I put on the tv to see what's happening with the storm, tears come to my eyes and a deep sense of concern fills my heart. So I pray, asking God what's going on.

I immediately thought of all the people who we've been serving at the homeless overflow shelters. Where are they? Are they okay? Are they being cared for? What about all the homeless people who are living in the woods or by the railroad tracks? Oh God!!!

I continued to pray, not being able to identify exactly what I was feeling or why I was feeling it. After an hour or so I heard, "My eye is on the sparrow." With that came a deep sense that God was in fact aware of all the people I've grown to care for. My feelings for these people in the shelters, the ones I've come to call "buried treasures," are more than trite concern or obligation. I'm realizing that God is using my time in the shelters to do a work in me.

For years I've recognized my need to love people the way God loves them. Even though I saw my need, I was still unable to change. I know Philippians 1:6 says, "And I am sure that God who began the good work within you will keep right on helping you grow in his grace until his task within you is finally finished on that day when Jesus Christ returns." Imagine: God is using homeless shelters to help mold me more into His likeness.

What is God using in your life to bring about true change? It's funny that my purpose in serving in the overflow shelters was to bring about change in the lives of others (these buried treasures) when God had all along determined that He would use this time to change me.

This is such a remarkable time in our lives. I pray that we're all able to discern the subtleties of the Holy Spirit.

Day 114

THOUGHT OF THE DAY: Do you know Mr. Nobody?

Every home has a Mr. Nobody. Perhaps he doesn't go by that name in your home or life, but we all know him. Mr. Nobody takes the blame for so many things. When something disappears, something is broken; when something happens, and no one did it, it gets blamed on the invisible Mr. Nobody.

Mr. Nobody has a good friend, and his name is I-Know-Nothing. We all know Mr. I-Know-Nothing all too well. He's also an invisible character surfacing just when we need him. When posed with an issue for which we don't want to take responsibility, we say we didn't do it or "I know nothing."

Both of these invisible people rob us of telling the truth. They cause us to stumble and miss out on the blessing of accountability. This problem of not being accountable hinders our growth as men and women of God and robs us of promotion into deeper things of the Spirit, and ultimately, reaching our destiny.

Mr. Nobody and Mr. I-Know-Nothing have been around since man was first created. In fact, both of these characters have another friend called Mr. Blame-Shift. All three of these characters we see all too often in our lives. We even read about them in the bible. In Genesis 3:11 when God asks the piercing question, "Who told you?" Adam's reply shifts the blame from himself to God and his wife. We read Genesis 3:12: "The woman whom You gave to be with me." Yup, you read it right: God and Eve's fault.

Sadly, because neither Adam nor Eve took accountability or responsibility, they were expelled from the garden and brought a curse on mankind. Praise God that the curse was broken when Jesus was crucified. Galatians 3:13: "Christ has redeemed us from the curse of the law, having become a curse for us." When we allow these three characters to influence our lives, it not only affects us, but everyone around us.

Taking accountability /responsibility takes maturity and courage. Even King David had a hard time taking responsibility for the sin of having Uriah killed. Nathan said to David in 2 Samuel 12:7: "You are the man!" It wasn't until David understood that he was responsible that he repented.

The way to our growth and destiny is through taking responsibility. There are three steps to accountability which I call the three Rs: 1. Recognize there's a problem; 2. Take responsibility for the problem; 3. Repent.

I would encourage all of us to kick Mr. Nobody, Mr. I-Know-Nothing, and Mr. Blame Shift straight out of our lives!

Day 115

THOUGHT OF THE DAY: Our Father reaches out to the broken

He was 20 years old in college and knew he was on empty. He had worked full-time since he was twelve. His father drank too much and his mother had a breakdown and was in and out of sanitariums.

It all started one night around 1:30 in the morning when he was suddenly awoken by a voice telling him that his father would come home drunk and beat his mother. Sure enough, 10 minutes later this occurred. Over the next few years he was fathering four children. There were many occasions when his mother would have breakdowns and would need to return to the hospital.

Then in the eighth grade, his father bought a restaurant and hotel. He went to work as a busboy three nights a week during school and then on weekends to support his family. In the ninth grade he moved and starting working for his father in the restaurant and hotel. Before and after school he waited on tables, all the tips going to his father to help pay the bills. He worked during the summer from 6:00 in the morning until 1:00 in the morning the next day. Once a week he went swimming in the afternoon, and when he was old enough to drive, once a week he'd go dancing. Freshman through senior year of high school he played football. As graduation approached, he knew he had no money so planned to join the Special Forces and go to Vietnam. Then a letter came in the mail offering him a football scholarship, so having no clue who he was, he went off to college.

When he arrived there, he had no structure and a lot of freedom. He was angry, hurt, confused, and very empty on the inside, and over the next three years drank and partied daily. Finally, out of a feeling of sheer emptiness, during his junior year he went to the chapel and started reading the Book of Revelation about how people go to hell.

He became angry at this kind of God and stood up and cursed Him. A few weeks later he was in trouble. Daily he would smoke pot in order to anesthetize his pain, and occasionally he would take a pill as a means of escape. Sure enough, one night he took a drug which caused him to hallucinate for hours. He'd gone outside to be alone when he sat down and saw a dragon in the sky laughing at him. He knew it was Satan, because he had just read about him in Revelation.

After about 17 hours he was still hallucinating and grew tired of watching images in his room. Someone came in who told him that the effects of the drug would last 72 hours. As the person left, he got on his knees and said, "I don't know if you exist and frankly, I don't care, but if you get me out of this in 24 hours, I promise to seek you." Well at exactly the 24-hour point, like someone had thrown a light switch - he was totally normal. This kind of thing just doesn't happen.

The promise was of course, not followed. Then a few weeks later he began to hear a voice say, "You promised!" This went on daily for weeks until this voice told him to leave college. To make a long story short, he left college, got on a plane, and as the plane took off, his arm went up in the air, and he started waving at no one in particular. He had no control over this waving.

As he sat there wondering what was going on, he heard, "You're waving goodbye to your old life." That was 45 years ago, and the 12-year-old boy was now 20. He was lost, broken, confused, and angry, but God reached out to him and still reaches out to him daily. You see, that 12-year-old boy was me.

P.S. My father stopped drinking, my mother recovered, and they spent the next 50 years of their lives loving each other.

Day 116

THOUGHT OF THE DAY: Jesus, what are you doing?

All day yesterday, this morning, and even last night at the River of Life Church in Dighton, the scripture that was and is still burning in my Spirit is from John 21:18: "When you were young, you were able to do as you liked and go wherever you wanted to; but when you are old, you will stretch out your hands and others will direct you and take you where you don't want to go." (Living Bible)

I think we'd all agree that over the last year or so we've found ourselves in places both spiritually and emotionally where we're uncomfortable. There's a deeper work that the Holy Spirit wants to do in us and we've known it. Previously, and for many of us even beginning recently, we were being led (and some of us dragged) to examine things in and around our lives. We've had a new and deeper yearning for change! We've come or are coming to realize that we've been stuck.

For too long we've been comfortable, and I will even say, lazy. There's been a complacency. The fire that once burned within us is now smoldering, the enemy and even our own flesh causing us to become lethargic. We find it takes a lot of effort to participate in any church event, and even getting up for church on Sunday has been a struggle. We go out of obedience, but there's little burning desire to "run to the House of the Lord."

So is there any wonder that in order to do the work in us, in order to rekindle our fire, in order to provoke us towards our destiny, that the Lord is allowing and is in some cases actually leading us to places that we don't want to be? The Holy Spirit has us looking at our character, our attitudes, our true spiritual state. We're avoiding areas that still need healing from our past because the process is either too much work, or we just don't want to relive the pain of what occurred.

At this juncture you might suggest that you don't need healing, but I strongly beg to differ. I can see it!

Why are we being taken places we don't want to go? Because something is about to break out! I believe it's going to stagger our imaginations! New wine is on the way, and it can't be placed in an old wineskin. There's a cry from the throne of God - "Rise up and fulfill your destiny!" We're like athletes out of shape, and the Lord has provided a private instructor (the Holy Spirit) to provoke us to get ready to be used in the very way we've all dreamed about. It's time to dust off the dream book that so many have put away. This I know: God hasn't forgotten the dreams He gave to us.

Jesus, what are you doing?

With a piercing smile and a voice that resonates with encouragement, He's taking us places we don't want to go. As I'm concluding this THOUGHT OF THE DAY, I'm reminded of how the majority of people in captivity in Babylon stayed in Babylon when the time came to leave. Why did they stay behind? Would we be willing to leave everything we'd built, all the comfort and familiarity of our surroundings, and literally abandon everything in order to fulfill the purposes of God?

You see, they were being challenged to go where they didn't want to go. Please do not settle for an almost-destiny, like the song with the lyrics, "We almost had it all!"

Perhaps an appropriate prayer would be, "Lord, I can see that you're trying to take me to places I'm really not fond of. Would you seize my heart and compel me to go to the places that will propel me into my destiny?"

Jesus, what are you doing? His answer: I am taking you places you don't want to go BECAUSE I LOVE YOU!

Day 117

THOUGHT OF THE DAY: Are we in need of a heart transplant?

Over the past few weeks I've become aware that we can do the right thing out of biblical responsibility and at the same time not have the same compassion that compelled Jesus. During these times we've task-orientated rather than moved by love and affection.

What I'm saying is that we can do the right thing but not have the heart of Jesus.

How many times does scripture say that Jesus was moved by compassion? In Luke 19:41 it says, "Now as He drew near, He saw the city and wept over it." Jesus arrived in the city at the time known as the "triumphal entry" just before his crucifixion. His focus was not on his own emotions, knowing he shortly would be scourged and crucified; his focus was on the people of Jerusalem. He literally broke down and wept audibly for others with no regard for his own emotions. He didn't just pray for the city; he wept over it.

So I ask myself if I've actually ever wept over a city? Have I ever wept over people's lives? I can reach out, serve, do the biblical thing because it's the right thing to do, and all the while not have the compassion that compelled Christ.

Here is a question: are we motivated by law or by grace? As I was musing about this yesterday morning, I came across Acts 18:10: "For I have many people in this city." It hit me like a ton of bricks that God declared that He had many people in the city He wanted to reach. I immediately felt that somehow we needed to reach out even more to our community, but I also saw that compassion and tears were far from me. I was biblical but didn't have the heart that was in Jesus.

I need a heart transplant!

In Luke 10:33 we find that the Samaritan stopped and ministered to the man in the road. Why? It said he had compassion. Then there's the parable of the prodigal son. Luke 15:20 says of the father, "But when he was still a great way off, his father saw him and had compassion, and ran and fell on his neck and kissed him." The father was motivated by compassion, which enabled him to greet his son affectionately instead of peppering him with accusatory questions.

Heart transplant?

When Jesus saw the multitude in Matthew 9:36, it says, "But when He saw the multitudes, He was moved with compassion for them, because they were weary and scattered, like sheep having no shepherd."

When we see a number of people gathered, what is our response? Mine would be that the majority I'm seeing need to be saved. Jesus' response was to have compassion. I have the right biblical mind set, but I lack the heart of Jesus.

Heart transplant?

You can look up compassion and see that often when Jesus healed people, he did so because of compassion. Here's a question: when we pray for those who are sick, do we do so because it's the biblical thing to do, or because we're motivated by compassion? Is it possible that we don't see more results when we pray for people because we're praying because of the law and not because of grace?

Is it possible that we need a heart transplant?

Day 118

THOUGHT OF THE DAY: Lessons from Job and others

How does Job and all that he went through fit into your theology?

God is the one who initiated the conversation with Satan about Job, and then short of killing him, God gave Satan permission to do anything. Job 1:8-12:

Then the Lord said to Satan, "Have you considered My servant Job, that there is none like him on the earth, a blameless and upright man, one who fears God and shuns evil?" So Satan answered the Lord and said, "Does Job fear God for nothing? Have You not made a hedge around him, around his household, and around all that he has on every side? You have blessed the work of his hands, and his possessions have increased in the land. But now, stretch out Your hand and touch all that he has, and he will surely curse You to Your face!" And the Lord said to Satan, "Behold, all that he has is in your power; only do not lay a hand on his person."

Consider what happens next and then see Job's response. Job 1:13-21:

Now there was a day when his sons and daughters were eating and drinking wine in their oldest brother's house; and a messenger came to Job and said, "The oxen were plowing and the donkeys feeding beside them, when the Sabeans raided them and took them away—indeed they have killed the servants with the edge of the sword; and I alone have escaped to tell you!" While he was still speaking, another also came and said, "The fire of God fell from heaven and burned up the sheep and the servants, and consumed them; and I alone have escaped to tell you!" While he was still speaking, another also came and said, "The Chaldeans formed three bands, raided the camels and took them away, yes, and killed the servants with the edge of the sword; and I alone have escaped to tell you!" While he was still speaking, another also came and said, "Your sons and daughters were eating and drinking wine in their oldest brother's house, and suddenly a great wind came from across the wilderness and struck the four corners of the house, and it fell on the young people, and they are dead; and I alone have escaped to tell you!" Then Job arose, tore his robe, and shaved his head; and he fell to the ground and worshiped.

Did you notice what he did? He worshipped!

Job loses everything and has three friends who come to give him their council. And...they're all wrong. Ever been there? Why is God allowing these trials in our lives? What is God up to? Remember what Paul said after going through numerous trials? He says in 2 Corinthians 4:17: "For our light affliction, which is but for a moment, is working for us a far more exceeding and eternal weight of glory, an eternal mind set."

Wow! What an eternal perspective. He says God is working for us through our "light afflictions."

Remember in the end that it says in Job 42:10: "And the Lord restored Job's losses when he prayed for his friends. Indeed, the Lord gave Job twice as much as he had before" and then verse 12: "Now the Lord blessed the latter days of Job more than his beginning." Notice that the Lord gave Job double what he had lost WHEN he prayed for his friends.

Let's consider the verses from James 1:2-4 from the Voice Bible: "Don't run from tests and hardships, brothers and sisters. As difficult as they are, you will ultimately find joy in them; if you embrace them, your faith will blossom under pressure and teach you true patience as you endure. And true patience brought on by endurance will equip you to complete the long journey and cross the finish line—mature, complete, and wanting nothing."

So much to learn and embrace from the lessons we learn from Job and others.

Day 119

THOUGHT OF THE DAY: And they worshipped

I'm still musing over the fact that after Job literally lost everything, he responded by worshipping.

We find it relativity easy to worship when things are going well, but let's look at Job again. Job 1:13-21:

Now there was a day when his sons and daughters were eating and drinking wine in their oldest brother's house; and a messenger came to Job and said, "The oxen were plowing and the donkeys feeding beside them, when the Sabeans raided them and took them away—indeed they have killed the servants with the edge of the sword; and I alone have escaped to tell you!" While he was still speaking, another also came and said, "The fire of God fell from heaven and burned up the sheep and the servants, and consumed them; and I alone have escaped to tell you!" While he was still speaking, another also came and said, "The Chaldeans formed three bands, raided the camels and took them away, yes, and killed the servants with the edge of the sword; and I alone have escaped to tell you!" While he was still speaking, another also came and said, "Your sons and daughters were eating and drinking wine in their oldest brother's house, and suddenly a great wind came from across the wilderness and struck the four corners of the house, and it fell on the young people, and they are dead; and I alone have escaped to tell you!" Then Job arose, tore his robe, and shaved his head; and he fell to the ground and worshipped.

If these things happened to us, how would we respond? Let's see - anger, disappointment in God, depression, overwhelming grief, feeling sorry for ourselves, and many etceteras. Yet Job's response was WORSHIP.

King David's son dies, and what does he do? Second Samuel 12:19-20: "When David saw that his servants were whispering, David perceived that the child was dead. Therefore David said to his servants, 'Is the child dead?' And they said, 'He is dead.' So David arose from the ground, washed and anointed himself, and changed his clothes; and he went into the house of the Lord and worshiped." What would we have done?

When Paul and Silas were arrested and beaten, what did they do? Acts 16:20-24 says,

And they brought them to the magistrates, and said, "These men, being Jews, exceedingly trouble our city; and they teach customs which are not lawful for us, being Romans, to receive or observe." Then the multitude rose up together against them; and the magistrates tore off their clothes and commanded them to be beaten with rods. And when they had laid many stripes on them, they threw them into prison, commanding the jailer to keep them securely. Having received such a charge, he put them into the inner prison.

Take a moment and put yourself in Paul and Silas' situation. They were simply preaching the gospel and casting out a demon. It's true that we can be doing the right thing and still end up in places we don't want to be, but prison and a horrific beating?? Verses 25-26 continue with the account: "But at midnight (I love that phrase "BUT AT MIDNIGHT") Paul and Silas were praying and singing hymns to God, and the prisoners were listening to them. Suddenly there was a great earthquake, so that the foundations of the prison were shaken; and immediately all the doors were opened and everyone's chains were loosed."

In their pain and suffering they worshipped. The results are simply SUPERNATURAL. Prisoners go free and salvation comes to a man and his entire family. We can assume that many, if not all of the prisoners, were saved.

Did you catch the phrase "and the prisoners were listening?" Selah - pause and reflect.

Food for thought - And they worshipped...

Day 120

THOUGHT OF THE DAY: When someone hurts you

Jesus was very clear about how to handle being hurt. Yet sadly, the instruction is rarely applied in the church. Perhaps today the Holy Spirit will convict us to a place of action.

Here's how the ERV Bible translates Matthew 18:15: "If your brother or sister in God's family does something wrong, go and tell them what they did wrong. Do this when you are alone with them. If they listen to you, then you have helped them to be your brother or sister again."

Other translations say to go to your brother in private or in secret. This implies that we need to actually go in person to the person who hurt, offended, and/or sinned against us without telling others. Normally we tell someone else or a bunch of other people and fail to tell our brother. Perhaps if we went to the person directly, they would see what they did wrong, would repent, take responsibility, and actually change so they wouldn't hurt you and others again in the same way.

There are three other things to consider :

1. That the matter was actually not a big issue but only perceived by us as such. Why? Because we may have an area in our lives that needs healing.

2. How we go and speak to our brother is critical. If we go in the wrong spirit, our words will be right, but the manner in which we say it could hinder them from hearing.

3. Timing is important. You might be ready to speak to them, but you need to discern if they're ready. For example, if they're in an angry/irritable mood; approaching them at another time would be better.

The first few words out of our mouths will go a long way in preparing the person to hear us. You can say something like, "Hey _____ do you have a minute? You're probably not aware of it, but the other day I was hurt because you did/said _____. I felt that you'd want to know because we're all trying to grow."

This is one example. In reality, there are a lot of ways to approach people. Do your best not to compound the problem.

A final word of counsel: don't try and convince the person. Our responsibility is to say it, and the Holy Spirit's job is to do the convincing. Some things are hard to hear, and it might take a while for the person to truly accept what was said. If the sin was egregious enough, Matthew 18 has a clear outline of the three steps that believers should follow.

So when someone hurts you, what are you going to do?

Day 121

THOUGHT OF THE DAY: This clay is being molded

Haven't we all discovered that when the Holy Spirit begins showing us something, we don't typically see or grasp all of it immediately?

Over the past few weeks I'm beginning to see and comprehend. For most of my walk I chose to do the right thing, though I tried and yes, failed to always do the biblical thing. As the years passed, I started to have some empathy and compassion in my decision-making. As I said before, I was a task-orientated person, where the task was often more important than the person.

One day, however, the Lord told me that "He didn't die for tasks but for people." Gotcha. Point taken. Time to switch priorities.

Even after that though, I discovered that there's a world of difference between assigning people value and having deep compassion for them. I'm asking the Holy Spirit to help me begin loving people as Jesus did. Oh my, there's such a vast difference between my love and His.

It says in John 1:14 that Jesus was "FULL OF GRACE AND TRUTH." In Psalm 85:10 it says, "Mercy and truth have met together" and Ephesians 4:15 says, "speaking the truth in love." The Amplified Bible says, "Rather, let our lives lovingly express truth [in all things, speaking truly, dealing truly, living truly]. Enfolded in love."

Did you see "enfolded in love?" I've come to realize that though I spoke the truth, it was far short of the love that was and is in Jesus. And as much as He was full of truth, He was also full of grace.

I've noticed that I have grace for some and not for others.

I wonder how over time this THOUGHT OF THE DAY will impact your life? Our clay is being molded...

Day 122

THOUGHT OF THE DAY: Do you want to carry the power of God?

I haven't met a believer yet who doesn't want to carry more of the power of God. Have you?

There are many ways in which God causes an increase in our anointing, but one we seldom think of, and frankly, are not at all fond of, is called the wilderness, or desert.

In looking at Jesus' life we see that he is baptized in water and the Spirit (Mark 1/Luke 4). God speaks from heaven (Mark 1:11 ERV): "A voice came from heaven and said, 'You are my Son, the one I love. I am very pleased with you' "

This is such a good word and one that we too like to hear. Now notice what happens next in verses 12-13: "Then the Spirit sent Jesus into the desert alone." Most translations say "Jesus was driven by the Spirit into the wilderness." He was there for 40 days, being tempted by Satan.

You read that correctly: God says you're my son. I am proud of you and I love you. Then he is driven to go into the wilderness for a month and for ten days to be purposely tempted and tried by Satan himself. One translation says that Jesus was there in the wilderness alone. While the wilderness can be a lonely place, generally it's the place where we grow in our relationship with the Lord. How can this be that He tells us He loves us and then brings us to the wilderness? It's easy to have the attitude that if God really loved us, He would protect us from trials.

An interesting thought is that the people that Moses led spent 40 years in the wilderness because of rebellion, while Jesus, led-of-the Spirit, spent only 40 days. The point is that one way or another, we will go to the wilderness. Here is what the Philips Translation says about trials: "When all kinds of trials and temptations crowd into your lives my brothers, don't resent them as intruders, but welcome them as friends! Realize that they come to test your faith and to produce in you the quality of endurance. But let the process go on until that endurance is fully developed, and you will find you have become men of mature character with the right sort of independence." (James 1: 2-4))

So here we are spending time in God's appointed wilderness, and the result is that when the trial is over, we can have confidence that we'll leave this appointed place in power. Luke 4:14: "Jesus went back to Galilee with the power of the Spirit."

Yes, we can carry more of God's power! Do you want to carry it?

Day 123

THOUGHT OF THE DAY: Hopelessness

I've been traveling to Haiti since 1995, but I've never been so impacted by its poverty as I have this last visit.

During my last two trips since the earthquake, as we landed we could smell something putrid which made everyone queasy. We passed by Tent City where three million people had come to Port Au Prince to receive aid and found none. We saw garbage piled three-feet-high for blocks on end, men and women in plain view squatting to go the bathroom, and people rummaging through the garbage to find something salvageable to eat. Others were rummaging through to find things to sell.

I've seen malnourished children by the hundreds, but never did I see the utter hopelessness that I saw on this trip. Maybe I've been so focused on all the natural things that I didn't see what is perhaps the deepest issue in Haiti - HOPELESSNESS.

Every day is literally a day of survival. When we were in the central part of Haiti, which is far more mountainous than the southern part where I typically go, we saw four and five years-old boys and girls carrying five-gallon buckets up and then down a very steep mountain road to get water. If they ate at all it was primarily rice and beans for every meal.

But their real poverty is having no hope that things will change. Unless men like Pastor Carlo and a handful of ministers like the Joseph Ministry intervene, these young people will repeat the past of their parents and grandparents, and thus the curse of the generations will persist.

There is little school for the youngsters and certainly nothing for high school students. By the hundreds they mill around all day looking to have someone love them, looking to cling to someone who cares or offers hope. The teenage girls hang out around popular gathering spots wearing mostly provocative clothing. Young men ride their motorcycles as taxis, but more often than not, they're like roosters walking around the hens on a chicken farm.

Most churches meet almost every night (as do the Voodoo priests). They hear words yet see no power, unlike in the voodoo services where sadly, power can be experienced. They're not told that God has a plan for them and that they can make a difference.

Yet...the bible is full of accounts of one person making a difference in spite of their circumstances. We too can make a difference. It begins as it did with Daniel, where it says, "Daniel purposed in his heart that he would not defile himself." (1:8)

I can hear the Holy Spirit asking, "Who will PURPOSE IN THEIR HEART TO LIVE A TOTALLY ABANDONED LIFE?" It only takes one person to change a nation, a community, a family, yes, and even friends, that Matthew 5:16 would become a frequent reality in all of our lives; "Let your light so shine before men, that they may see your good works and glorify your Father in heaven." We would see Isaiah 60:2-3 come alive "But the Lord will arise over you, And His glory will be seen upon you. The Gentiles shall come to your light, and kings to the brightness of your rising." Light are those who carry grace and truth - THEY CARRY HOPE AND THE PRESENCE OF GOD.

Yes, Haiti needs food, jobs, drinking water, education, and on and on the list goes, but their GREATEST NEED is HOPE. Somehow we have to send laborers and money to support the men and women who carry the Spirit of hope, to carry the I-can spirit of Philippians 4:13: "I can do all things through Christ who strengthens me."

Listen, we can make a difference in our own sphere; we can stand with those who are laying down their lives on a daily basis. Pray for hope, and be hope.

Father, help us to eradicate HOPELESSNESS HERE AND IN HAITI...

Day 124

THOUGHT OF THE DAY: You are valuable

Perhaps one of the most grievous things I see is that the people of God don't realize their value.

I am not mad at people, but I AM mad at the devil who continually lies to God's sons and daughters and says they aren't important. We have so many wonderful brothers and sisters in Christ who feel like they have no value and that their life doesn't matter. As I write this I could cry. Seriously! It's like the scripture in Genesis 3:11 where God asks Adam and Eve this question: "Who told you that you were naked?"

Who told you that you didn't matter? Who told you that you weren't needed? In Esther 4:14 it says, "You have come to the kingdom for such a time as this." Yes, you have come into our Father's kingdom at this very moment for a divine and supernatural purpose.

Many of you don't realize how precious are the things you do in secret. Matthew 6:3-4 says, "But when you do a charitable deed, do not let your left hand know what your right hand is doing, that your charitable deed may be in secret; and your Father who sees in secret will Himself reward you openly." Some people do things that everyone sees, but so many of you do them in secret as the verse we just read advises.

Do you realize how one simple word of encouragement can save a life and can deliver people from depression and despair - JUST ONE WORD. You may never know how your one word literally changed a life. What quickly came to mind were three occasions in my life that dramatically changed me.

One day a total stranger called me on the phone and told me that God wanted her to tell me something. (This was after I yelled at God at the top of my lungs in the middle of a field deep in the woods where I'd gone to seek Him for some answers. After hearing nothing I WENT HOME DEEPLY DISCOURAGED.) The phone rang as I entered my house, and when I picked up, a total stranger asked, "Is your name Brian Weeks?" I said, "Yes." She said, "God wants me to tell you that He's not deaf."

Two days in a row two different people told me, "God wants you to go away." Those five words led me to leave town and visit places in my past, the result of which eternally and supernaturally changed me. It was during this time of being away that I had gone to see a church in Walpole, MA. The church had a gym, and I went in to visit. The receptionist let me in and on the way out said to me, "I have only done this twice in my life, but I need to tell you something." I said, "What?" She said, "In order to go forward sometimes you need to go backwards." I was stunned. Those few words still to this day have radically change my life. That experience brought and still brings healing.

You see, I had read those exact words earlier in the day in a church I had visited that morning. I was led to pick up a book, and as I picked it up, those exact words jumped off the page: "In order to go forward sometimes you need to go backwards."

Never minimize the power of a few words or a simple gesture. I have seen how bringing soup to someone supernaturally saved their life when the person receiving it was contemplating suicide because no one cared. Who said you don't matter? Who said you aren't valuable and precious in the sight of the Lord?

In Isaiah 60:1 it says, "Arise and shine." These words in the Hebrew mean, "Arise and cast off your discouragement and depression." It goes on to say in verses two and three: "For your light has come! And the glory of the Lord is risen upon you. For behold, the darkness shall cover the earth, And deep darkness the people; But (I love this "but") the Lord will arise over you, And His glory will be seen upon you. The Gentiles shall come to your light!"

Just by living your life people will see your light, and look at the results!

If I could climb my snow-covered roof this morning, I would yell - YOU ARE VALUABLE, BECAUSE... YOU ARE!

Day 125

THOUGHT OF THE DAY: And we are - CHOSEN!

Good morning, everyone! I am still adjusting to my time in Haiti as well as trying to play catch-up with all the things I didn't do for a week.

I know what I'm about to write, and I can feel the tears welling up in my eyes. There's a sense of urgency inside of me that I can't explain.

I'm continuing to comprehend who we are - seriously! I may say some things that you might not agree with, but perhaps they're something that might plant a seed in each of you.

I came to the realization that for over forty years I was trying to persuade people to become Christians. While we are Christians, and I'm glad to be one, my message fell short of God's real identity for us. We've all replaced our true identity of being sons and daughters with the identity of being Christians.

For years when we talked to people, we'd discuss our particular church's doctrines and teachings rather than our adoption and how we're now His own special children. When I prayed as a Christian and asked something, it was meaningful, but I felt more like a beggar than a son. You see, when a son or daughter asks their Father for something, it's far more intimate and far more personal.

This past Sunday I shared that we were CHOSEN. Our video camera wasn't there, but it will be on our website soon in audio version. May I encourage you to listen to it? Because of the snow our attendance was down, but our pastoral team felt so strongly about what was said, they encouraged me to share it again.

Here are some scriptures and a few remarks I'd like us to reflect on:

John 15:16: "You have not chosen Me, but I have chosen you and I have appointed you [I have planted you], that you might go and bear fruit and keep on bearing, and that your fruit may be lasting [that it may remain, abide], so that whatever you ask the Father in My Name [as presenting all that I Am], He may give it to you." (AMP)

I want you to see that it wasn't about you and me finding or choosing God. Instead, it's all about God choosing us. Not only choosing us, but appointing/ordaining each of us to bear fruit, or as Matthew 5:16 says, "Let your light so shine before men, that they may see your good works and glorify your Father in heaven." When people see our lives they'll be compelled to glorify God. A parallel verse is found in Isaiah 60:1-3: "Arise, shine; For your light has come! And the glory of the Lord is risen upon you. For behold, the darkness shall cover the earth, And deep darkness the people; But the Lord will arise over you, And His glory will be seen upon you. The Gentiles shall come to your light."

May blessing (praise, laudation, and eulogy) be to the God and Father of our Lord Jesus Christ (the Messiah) Who has blessed us in Christ with every spiritual (given by the Holy Spirit) blessing in the heavenly realm! Even as [in His love] He chose us [actually picked us out for Himself as His own] in Christ before the foundation of the world, that we should be holy (consecrated and set apart for Him) and blameless in His sight, even above reproach, before Him in love. For He foreordained us (destined us, planned in love for us) to be adopted (revealed) as His own children through Jesus Christ, in accordance with the purpose of His will [[a]because it pleased Him and was His kind intent]. Eph. 1:3-5 (AMP)

Did you see that he "picked you out for Himself"? Our Father went into the orphanages of this world, and He said, "I want that boy. I want that little girl, because I have big plans for them."

It was our Fathers joy/delight to choose YOU! Then there is this: Please read it slowly!

1 Peter 2:9: "But you are the ones chosen by God, chosen for the high calling of priestly work, chosen to be a holy people, God's instruments to do his work and speak out for him, to tell others of the night-and-day difference he made for you—from nothing to something, from rejected to accepted." (AMP)

Did you see that "BUT YOU ARE THE ONES CHOSEN BY GOD; CHOSEN TO BE GOD'S INSTRUMENTS"? HE HAS MADE A DIFFERENCE IN OUR LIVES. WE HAVE GONE FROM BEING REJECTED TO BEING ACCEPTED!

Are we Christians - sure! But our goal is not to be Christians, but instead, SONS AND DAUGHTERS!

AND... WE ARE - CHOSEN!!

Day 126

THOUGHT OF THE DAY: Would you come home?

How many of us know friends and families who once walked with God but at this time in their lives are wandering? They still love God, but they're not fond of the church. There are too many reasons why this is, and trying to list them would take pages.

Honestly though, all the reasons don't matter! What matters is that they come home. Not come home to our old religious systems, not home to our church cultures and traditions, but home to Abba. There are church communities, including house churches, which are not like the church you once knew.

Why should you go home? So you can love and be loved. So you can fulfill the destiny, fulfill the reasons you were created. But the most important thing is so you can once again worship! Would you come home?

Let me also say that there are many people going to church who are physically there but not really present or engaged. Perhaps these will be the hardest people for God to call home. In Zechariah 10:8 we find God whistling for His people to gather and come back to him. In the Living Bible it says, "When I whistle to them, they'll come running, for I have brought them back again."

The reason God is calling is because He wants to have a new, more intimate relationship with us, not as a church member but as His son or daughter. The reality is that many of us and those who are scattered, have, as it says in Revelation 2:4, lost our first love. "Yet there is one thing wrong; you don't love me as at first!" (TLB) Ask yourself: Do you have the same passion you had when you gave your life to the Lord? Would you come home?

The story of the prodigal son is calling to us. It says in Luke 15:17 that the son "came to himself." Other translations say, "came to his senses." So the young man's conscience gripped him and said, GO HOME! Luke 15:20 tells us what happened next: "And he arose and came to his father. But when he was still a great way off, his father saw him and had compassion, and ran and fell on his neck and kissed him."

It says, "When the son was a long a long way off the father saw him." How was he able to see him so far away? Because every day he was looking for him to come home. Once they greeted each other there was no angry exchange of words, but simply a father loving his son.

Here is what the Orthodox Jewish Bible says, "And when he got up he came home to his own Abba. And while he was still a long way off, his Abba saw him, and was filled with raceme Shomayim (heavenly mercy, compassion) and tears, and fell upon his neck and kissed him." (OJB)

Oh Father, fill us with "Shomayim (heavenly mercy, compassion) and tears."

In Zechariah 10 God says he would strengthen His people. He says HE WILL – YES, HE WILL BRING THEM BACK, HE WILL - WILL HAVE MERCY. HE WILL HEAR US. HE WILL CAUSE US TO TRULY REJOICE. CAN YOU HEAR HIM WHISTLING - COME HOME? OH, AND HE WILL RESTORE AND CAUSE INCREASE IN OUR LIVES.

Zechariah 10:6-8:

I will strengthen the house of Judah, And I will save the house of Joseph. I will bring them back, Because I have mercy on them. They shall be as though I had not cast them aside; For I am the Lord their God, And I will hear them. Those of Ephraim shall be like a mighty man, And their heart shall rejoice as if with wine. Yes, their children shall see it and be glad; Their heart shall rejoice in the Lord. I will whistle for them and gather them, For I will redeem them; And they shall increase as they once increased.

Then the Message Bible says, "I'll save the people of Joseph. I know their pain and will make them good as new." DID YOU SEE: "I KNOW YOUR PAIN"? - LET IT SINK IN! They'll get a fresh start, as if nothing had ever happened. And why? "Because I am their very own God, I'll do what needs to be done for them. The people of Ephraim will be famous, their lives brimming with joy. FRESH START! FILLED WITH JOY - EVEN YOUR CHILDREN WILL SEE AND RESPOND. Their children will get in on it, too— oh, let them feel blessed by God! I'll whistle and they'll all come running."

OH FATHER, THEY WILL COME RUNNING WHEN YOU WHISTLE!

Could I suggest that all of us come home? And what about all the people we know? Could we whistle? Could we be the Father's instrument of compassion, grace, and mercy? Can we carry the message - WOULD YOU COME HOME?

Day 127

THOUGHT OF THE DAY: Thank you!

I awoke with such gratitude this morning.

I am so speechless and overwhelmed by His love for us, to know beyond any doubt that He loves each of us in spite of all our many failures and sins.

His hand, as Isaiah says, is outstretched all day - ALL DAY! To know that He forgives us because He loves us. These truths are unsearchable. To know He has not dealt with us according to our sin. That He really delights in mercy. Micah 7:18: "Where is another God like you, who pardons the guilt of the remnant, overlooking the sins of his special people? You will not stay angry with your people forever because you delight in showing unfailing love."(NLT) The Living Bible says, "For you love to be merciful," and most translations say that "He delights in mercy."

Stop and think about that: when we sin, He literally DELIGHTS IN MERCY.

I just love the question God asks Job in chapter 38, verse four. " 'Where were you when I laid the foundations of the earth?' Oh how vast and beyond comprehension is our Father." Psalm 33:12-2 in the Amplified Bible says,

Blessed (happy, fortunate, to be envied) is the nation whose God is the Lord, the people He has chosen as His heritage. The Lord looks from heaven, He beholds all the sons of men; From His dwelling place He looks [intently] upon all the inhabitants of the earth— He Who fashions the hearts of them all, who considers all their doings. No king is saved by the great size and power of his army; a mighty man is not delivered by [his] much strength. A horse is devoid of value for victory; neither does he deliver any by his great power. Behold, the Lord's eye is upon those who fear Him [who revere and worship Him with awe], who wait for Him and hope in His mercy and loving-kindness.

First Samuel 2:2 says, "No one is holy like the Lord, there is none besides You, Nor is there any rock like our God." (NKJV) Oh Father, NO ONE IS LIKE YOU! And to comprehend and understand that you THINK ABOUT US IS INCOMPREHENSIBLE! Psalm 139:16-18 in the Living Bible says, "You saw me before I was born and scheduled each day of my life before I began to breathe. Every day was recorded in your book!"

How precious it is, Lord, to realize that you are thinking about me constantly! I can't even count how many times a day your thoughts turn toward me. And when I awaken in the morning, you are still thinking of me!

Don't read on; just allow these truths to sink in deep!

There are no words I can utter this morning. I am tongue-tied. So I will let others speak for me. Here is Paul in Romans 8:31-39:

So, what do you think? With God on our side like this, how can we lose? If God didn't hesitate to put everything on the line for us, embracing our condition and exposing himself to the worst by sending his own Son, is there anything else he wouldn't gladly and freely do for us? And who would dare tangle with God by messing with one of God's chosen? Who would dare even to point a finger? The One who died for us—who was raised to life for us!—is in the presence of God at this very moment sticking up for us. Do you think anyone is going to be able to drive a wedge between us and Christ's love for us? There is no way! Not trouble, not hard times, not hatred, not hunger, not homelessness, not bullying threats, not backstabbing, not even the worst sins listed in Scripture. They kill us in cold blood because they hate you. We're sitting ducks; they pick us off one by one. (MSG)

THEN THE FOLLOWING IS MY AMEN, MY HEART OF GRATITUDE...

"None of this fazes us because Jesus loves us. I'm absolutely convinced that nothing—nothing living or dead, angelic or demonic, today or tomorrow, high or low, thinkable or unthinkable—absolutely nothing can get between us and God's love because of the way that Jesus our Master has embraced us." (MSG)

OH FATHER, THANK YOU!

Day 128

THOUGHT OF THE DAY: Is that Annie I hear singing?

Perhaps one of my greatest regrets is that I've spent a good part of my life waiting for tomorrow.

Remember Annie's song and the famous phrase: "tomorrow, tomorrow"?

While I thank God that He has a tomorrow for us, I have truly missed so many todays because my eyes and my heart were in tomorrow. I've missed so many miracles because I was focused on the future. I missed His daily provision because I was looking ahead. I missed what He wanted to show me or teach me because of my tomorrow-mentality. Then tomorrow comes and instead of gleaning the provision of that day and all that God had for me in that moment, I again fixed my eyes on tomorrow.

So I have lived day after day waiting and longing for tomorrow. The days turned to weeks and the weeks into months and so on. Sadly, many of us spend years this way. One of the reasons God didn't send an answer is because He wanted me to learn, to grow. It's like teaching your child to tie their shoes. Over and over again you see them struggle. They whine and cry only wanting one thing: for you to do the tying. But you realize that if you do it for them, they won't learn or grow. If you give in, then soon the lesson will need to be repeated.

Instead of fixing my eyes on tomorrow, I should've fixed my eyes on Jesus who is the author and finisher of faith - Hebrews 12:2: "fixing our eyes on Jesus, the author and perfecter of faith." (NASB) I spent many days staring at my circumstances and yup, they didn't go away. I fixed my eyes on people and yup, that didn't change a thing either.

If anything, I became disappointed in people. My bad! Though I knew the verse from Psalm 118: "This is the day the Lord has made; We will rejoice and be glad in it." (verse 24 – NKJV), to be honest, I hated hearing it. It seemed like some glib and trite answer. That is because my eyes weren't on Jesus, only my situation.

Jesus was at the time standing in the room, and I never saw him or heard him because I allowed my circumstances to be bigger than God. I now read the verse this way: this is the day God has appointed just for me and no matter what, I will worship.

I wrote a THOUGHT OF THE DAY on worship a while ago. I spoke about Paul and Silas in Acts 16 and how even while they were in prison after being beaten, they worshipped.

Worship creates a new atmosphere. It might not change your situation, but it will change your heart and focus.

While I praise God for tomorrow, I'm learning to find God's manna for today and rejoice in what is instead of what isn't. You see, you can hear Annie sing or you can hear Him sing. Zephaniah 3:17: "The Lord your God in your midst, The Mighty One, will save; He will rejoice over you with gladness, He will quiet you with His love, He will rejoice over you with singing."

Who is singing now?

Day 129

THOUGHT OF THE DAY: "It bred worms and stank."

For over an hour I searched YouTube to find new worship songs of intimacy but found none. As I sat and mused with the Lord, the story of Exodus 16 came to my mind, and this thought fully captured my heart.

The thought was that I won't eat manna with worms in it. Recall the story from Exodus 16 about the children of Israel eating manna for 40 years in the wilderness. They were instructed to go out every morning and gather it from the ground, and they couldn't keep it overnight except on the day before the sabbath. If they kept the manna overnight (with the exception of gathering it the night before the sabbath), it would be infested with worms and stink. Exodus 16:20 tells us that when they failed to follow God's instructions, that's exactly what happened.

You see, we cannot live on yesterday's manna. There is no way that we can live in yesterday's provision, yesterday's "presence," yesterday's grace, or yesterday's understanding. Thank God for the sabbath days where we can be wonderfully sustained by the manna (bread from heaven) from yesterday. But I have determined that we can and will rise early to see God's face and hear His voice. In Psalm 63 while David is in the wilderness without water and running and hiding from Saul, he writes, "O God, You are my God; early will I seek You; my soul thirsts for You, my flesh faints for You, in a dry and thirsty land." (verse one – MSG)

I know that in all of us now there's a yearning and thirst that can only be satisfied by being in the presence of God and fulfilling our calling. And yes, all of us have discovered that yesterday's manna is stinky and full of worms. I praise God for His promise of Isaiah 44:3 : "For I will pour water on the thirsty ground and send streams coursing through the parched earth." (MSG) It says HE WILL send heavenly bread and water to sustain us.

I know that we're all carrying the cry of Habakkuk chapter one in every fiber of our being. Habakkuk cries out, "O Lord, how long shall I cry, And You will not hear?" (verse 2) He sees all the injustice on the earth. He sees the world devoid of God and wonders if the Lord is listening. Oh Lord, when will you come?

I realize He comes every day through each of us, but there's also a day coming and even now when He's saying, "Look among the nations and watch— Be utterly astounded! For I will work a work in your days which you would not believe, though it were told you." (Habakkuk 1:5)

But until then, don't eat rotten manna.

Day 130

THOUGHT OF THE DAY: We are what?

Yesterday in church we again looked at WHO WE ARE. I am so compelled to tell myself and whomever will listen what our true identity is.

You have to read and almost laugh at the absolute truth and humor found in 1 Corinthians 1:26-31. Please read it slowly: "Take a good look, friends, at who you were when you got called into this life. I don't see many of 'the brightest and the best' among you, not many influential, not many from high-society families." (MSG)

Isn't it obvious that God deliberately chose men and women who the culture overlooked, exploited, and abused, chose these "nobodies" to expose the hollow pretensions of the "somebodies"? The Amplified Bible says "that God deliberately chose us."

In Ephesians 2:10 we are told that WE ARE, not going to be - but WE ARE! "For we are His workmanship, created in Christ Jesus for good works, which God prepared beforehand that we should walk in them." (NKJV) The OJB Version says we are his MASTERPIECE. It doesn't say we're going to be his masterpiece but that that we ARE His masterpiece, a DIVINE ORIGINAL. That we were created IN CHRIST to produce fruit. That God prepared BEFORE THE FOUNDATION OF THE WORLD that we should walk in his unique, divine, and supernatural plan.

Look at what Jeremiah 1:5 says, "Before I formed you in the womb I knew you; Before you were born I sanctified you; I ordained you a prophet to the nations." Did you see that? BEFORE YOU AND I WERE IN THE WOMB - HE KNEW US! BEFORE WE WERE BORN, HE SANCTIFIED AND SET US APART, AND IF THAT ISN'T ENOUGH, HE ORDAINED US TO FULFILL WHAT HE CREATED US TO DO! No one can take our place.

Romans 8:15-17 again tells us who we really are. It clearly states that we were adopted and we are beyond any doubt or question HIS CHILDREN and not only children, but JOINT HEIRS WITH CHRIST.

What if we could truly comprehend the depth of that verse? READ: "You received the Spirit of adoption by whom we cry out, 'Abba, Father.' The Spirit Himself bears witness with our spirit that we are children of God, and if children, then heirs—heirs of God and joint heirs with Christ."

If the devil can keep us blinded to our identity, he doesn't care how often we attend church or how many songs we sing. We will forever wander this world as vagabonds robbed of our identities.

We are what? Well, 1 Peter 1:9 states it pretty clearly: "But you are the ones chosen by God, chosen for the high calling of priestly work, chosen to be a holy people, God's instruments to do his work and speak out for him, to tell others of the night-and-day difference he made for you—from nothing to something, from rejected to accepted." (AMP)

Day 131

THOUGHT OF THE DAY: Have you heard His voice?

It was about 1:00 a.m. and I was working on paying bills when I so clearly heard, "As the Father has sent Me, I also send you." (John 20:21)

I went to bed with this on my mind, and when I awoke, it was my first thought. Could we take a moment and really ponder this? The setting is the disciples hiding in the upper room eight days after Jesus' crucifixion. Jesus walks in, and the first thing he says to them is, "Peace be with you." Jesus knows exactly what to say all the time. He says it again when he says, "As the Father has sent Me, I also send you." Wow, he doesn't go into a long dialogue, he just says, "As the Father has sent Me, I also send you."

Even now as I write this, it's burning in my heart. It's the voice of God to all of us. I hear Isaiah 6:8: "I also heard the voice of the Lord, saying, 'Whom shall I send, and who will go for us?' Then I said, 'Here am I! Send me.' " Yes, the same voice is saying - I'm sending you!! Can you hear it?

You can hear Jesus say, "By this My Father is glorified, that you bear much fruit; so you will be My disciples. As the Father loved Me, I also have loved you; abide in My love." (John 15:8 - 9) I'm sending you so you can glorify my father.

He's saying that we too can continually abide in the Father's love. In fact, verse 12 says, "This is My commandment, that you love one another as I have loved you."

I'm sitting here shaking my head, because I'M ASKING MYSELF IF I LOVE THE SAME WAY JESUS LOVES. I'm still shaking my head. Oh Lord, how can we do this? The answer is in John 15:5: "I am the vine, you are the branches. He who abides in Me, and I in him, bears much fruit; for without Me you can do nothing."

I'm still shaking my head pleading with God – Father, take us there! For we cannot do anything without you. You sent Jesus because you loved the world. (John 3:16) It's not about going out and trying to get people saved! It's about loving people the way our God loves people. Hasn't our emphasis been giving people a message, when all along they should've seen and heard the message by our simply loving them?

First Peter 3:15 says, "Be ready at all times to answer anyone who asks you to explain the hope you have in you." (GNT) Perhaps we've been giving answers before they were ready to hear them. Could it be that if we loved people the way Jesus loved people, we would hear them ask us why we're so different?

I'm convinced we're all hearing, "As the Father has sent Me, I also send you."

Have you heard His voice?

Day 132

THOUGHT OF THE DAY: Jesus, help us to be like you

This morning the woman who was caught in adultery came to my mind. (John 8:1-11) Scripture says that Jesus was in the temple (Solomon's Porch) early in the morning when the religious brothers (not us, of course) brought a woman to him who had been caught in adultery. They tell Jesus what he already knew: that the law required a consequence; her death.

My question is why we so quickly jump to the law for others but not for ourselves? Why is it that we so readily see where others are "missing the mark" (the Greek definition of sin), and we so quickly form opinions about them? We might not say it out loud, but all too often we have an opinion. Jesus, help us to be like you!

I love the way Jesus responded or maybe better put, didn't respond. He didn't say anything.

Lord, help us to be like you! For we too often utter some sort of opinion without first considering the matter. James 1:19 says, "My dear brothers and sisters, take note of this: Everyone should be quick to listen, slow to speak and slow to become angry." (NIV) Perhaps this verse speaks to you?

At any rate, Jesus doesn't say anything but simply kneels down and begins writing in the dirt with his finger. The religious crowd demands a response. John 8:7-8: "So when they continued asking Him, He raised Himself up and said to them, 'He who is without sin among you, let him throw a stone at her first.' And again He stooped down and wrote on the ground."

Jesus' response was just a few words. I admit that many of my responses are just too long, and I don't spend enough time considering what I should say. Here is a good verse for me: Ecclesiastes 5:2: "Be not rash with your mouth, nor let your heart be hasty to utter a word before God, for God is in heaven and you are on earth. Therefore, let your words be few." (ESV) Jesus, help us to be like you!

Jesus, please help us to be like you, or as Paul puts it in Romans 12:2: "Do not be conformed to this world," or as the (ERV) Bible says, "Don't change yourselves to be like the people of this world, but let God change you inside with a new way of thinking. Then you will be able to understand and accept what God wants for you. You will be able to know what is good and pleasing to him and what is perfect."

That's it; I need God to change me from the inside out, adopting a "new way of thinking."

Jesus, help us to be like you!

Day 133

THOUGHT OF THE DAY: NOTHING

When I asked the Lord what I should write for the THOUGHT OF THE DAY He asked what I was learning that "has and is revolutionizing" my life.

I didn't have to think for even a second before I realized that something so incredible; yes, even supernatural, has gripped my life. I don't know when it actually happened, but I have gone and am going from an intellectual belief to an absolute knowing belief - deep in my very being - that nothing can separate me from "OUR FATHER'S LOVE."

THERE IS NOTHING that can or will ever separate us from God's love and affection. I wake every morning to hear, "I LOVE YOU," and so often I hear, "We're going to have a great day!" When we all grasp this - LOOK OUT! No wonder why Satan continues to blind us from this this life-changing reality.

Romans 8:38-39: "Yes, I am sure that nothing can separate us from God's love—not death, life, angels, or ruling spirits. I am sure that nothing now, nothing in the future, no powers, nothing above us or nothing below us—nothing in the whole created world—will ever be able to separate us from the love God has shown us in Christ Jesus our Lord."(ERV) Did you read Paul's "I am sure"? Most translations say, "I am persuaded." Strong's says: "evidence; an inward certainty;" Barnes says: "unwavering confidence" and Robertson says: "I stand convinced."

The Message Bible captures our Father's heart for all of us. Romans 8:31-39:

So, what do you think? With God on our side like this, how can we lose? If God didn't hesitate to put everything on the line for us, embracing our condition and exposing himself to the worst by sending his own Son, is there anything else he wouldn't gladly and freely do for us? And who would dare tangle with God by messing with one of God's chosen? Who would dare even to point a finger? The One who died for us—who was raised to life for us!—is in the presence of God at this very moment sticking up for us. Do you think anyone is going to be able to drive a wedge between us and Christ's love for us? There is no way! Not trouble, not hard times, not hatred, not hunger, not homelessness, not bullying threats, not backstabbing, not even the worst sins listed in Scripture:

They kill us in cold blood because they hate you. We're sitting ducks; they pick us off one by one. None of this fazes us because Jesus loves us. I'm absolutely convinced that nothing—nothing living or dead, angelic or demonic, today or tomorrow, high or low, thinkable or unthinkable—absolutely nothing can get between us and God's love because of the way that Jesus our Master has embraced us.

Father, bring us all to the place where we can shout - NOTHING!!! Go ahead, shout it - NOTHING!

Day 134

THOUGHT OF THE DAY: "How can I?"

This quote was taken from Judges 6:15. God had just instructed Gideon to attack the Midianites. See verse 14: "Then the Lord turned to him and said, 'Go in this might of yours, and you shall save Israel from the hand of the Midianites. Have I not sent you?' "

We'll look at Gideon's response, but let's look at what God really said, and then we'll see that Gideon didn't listen. Does that sound like anyone we know? So God said, "Go in this might of yours." The problem is that Gideon doesn't see the power he has. Then God tells him, "You shall save." The problem is that he doesn't hear or believe the simple, few words "You shall." Not maybe, but "You shall." Then He doesn't hear or believe, "I have sent you."

The problem? Gideon was focused on himself and what he could do. The deadly spiritual disease of "me," our focus on us and our ability or lack thereof.

I love how God responds to Gideon. He doesn't argue with him. He doesn't debate. He doesn't dialog long to try and convince him. God simply says, "And the Lord said to him, 'Surely I will be with you, and you shall defeat the Midianites as one man.'" (verse 16) The answer; Gideon, have no doubt, "SURELY I WILL BE WITH YOU." Remember, Moses had the same problem.

Sadly, we too don't comprehend or believe that God is with us, and not only that, but that He's IN us. We're getting there, though. The Holy Spirit has determined to "divinely stick" confidence in us. Haven't we all felt that shift/stirring inside of us? There's that inner nudging that's saying - "YOU CAN DO THIS!" God goes on to again declare to Gideon; "YOU SHALL DEFEAT."

There's a wind from God that's blowing, and it has a name. It's called "YOU CAN!" Today the meteorologists name the various storms that affect the globe. I hear the Spirit saying that there's a mighty wind blowing, and it's called "YOU CAN!" Put up your spiritual sails and catch the wind. God is speaking to all of us - "YOU CAN!" I'm sending you! "I am with you! I have empowered you!"

Listen, IT'S A DONE DEAL. We need to stop saying and focusing on "How can I?"

THERE'S A MIGHTY WIND BLOWING!

Day 135

THOUGHT OF THE DAY: When, not if.

It was sometime early this morning while I was asleep but my mind was still turned on, and I kept hearing "I'll be there!"

As I awoke I remembered some of the lyrics from Michael Jackson's song, "I'll Be There." In starts out, "I'll reach out my hand to you. I'll have faith in all you do. Just call my name and I'll be there (I'll be there)." Then some of the other lyrics are "I'll be there to comfort you, I'm so glad that I found you. I'll be there with a love that's strong. I'll be your strength. I'll keep holding on. Yes I will. Yes I will. Let me fill your heart with joy and laughter."

But before Michael Jackson said it, our Father said it. In Isaiah 43:1 it says, "But now, thus says the Lord, who created you, O Jacob," (put your name here) "And He who formed you, O Israel:" God shouts "I formed YOU;" Don't be afraid because I HAVE REDEEMED YOU; "Fear not, for I have redeemed you." Listen to what He says next. "I have called you by your name; You are Mine." "I CALLED YOU BY NAME; YOU ARE MINE!"

While all these things are true, it doesn't mean that we won't go through trials! But what it does mean is that when we go through them (when, not if), He WILL be with us. Isaiah 43:2 tells us, "When you pass through the waters, I will be with you." When, not if. The verse continues to tell us, "And through the rivers, they shall not overflow you. When (*when*, not if) you walk through the fire, you shall not be burned, Nor shall the flame scorch you." Yes, the message is clear: it's when, not if!

Verse four tells us three things: our God says we are precious, that He honors us, and that He loves us! Verse four: "Since you were precious in My sight, you have been honored, and I have loved you." Take a minute to hear: YOU ARE PRECIOUS, HONORED, AND YOU ARE LOVED. JUST MUSE FOR A MOMENT. LET IT SINK IN. REMEMBER "PHL" - precious, honored, loved.

God goes on to declare, "Fear not, for I am with you." (verse five) Then verse seven: "Everyone who is called by My name, Whom I have created for My glory; I have formed him, yes, I have made him." When, not if, you go through trials. He tells us not to be afraid (because) he says, "I AM WITH YOU." HE HAS PERSONALLY CALLED EACH OF US BY NAME.

As I wrote that, I could hear my name being called. I had to stop writing and listen. Then I heard, and I need to comprehend what He just said. It was from Psalm 138:8: "The Lord will perfect that which concerns me." God will complete the work He starts in all of us!

Two final verses: 1 Peter 4:11-12: "Beloved, do not think it strange concerning the fiery trial which is to try you, as though some strange thing happened to you; but rejoice (we are to what - REJOICE) to the extent that you partake of Christ's sufferings, that when His glory is revealed, you may also be glad with exceeding joy." And 1 Corinthians 10:13: "Every test that you have experienced is the kind that normally comes to people. But God keeps his promise, and he will not allow you to be tested beyond your power to remain firm; at the time you are put to the test, he will give you the strength to endure it, and so provide you with a way out." (GNT)

Remember that it's when, not if...

Day 136

THOUGHT OF THE DAY: God remembers
When I started musing about what to write today, I heard, "And God remembered."

The first recollection that came to my mind was Genesis 8:1: "Then God remembered Noah. And every living thing, and all the animals that were with him in the ark. And God made a wind to pass over the earth, and the waters subsided."

Sometime during the forty days of rain, God remembered Noah and his family. He saw that it was time to begin bringing Noah's time in the ark to a conclusion. So it says that He "made a wind to pass over the earth."

If you recall, the other day I wrote that a wind was passing over us, and the wind's name was "I can." When we read Genesis chapter eight, we see that it was somewhere around 324 days later, according to many sources, when Noah finally left the ark. The point is that it's often a process from when the wind begins to blow, to seeing the results of the wind. Take a little time and read Genesis eight.

God saw the children of Israel groaning in Egypt after more than 400 years in captivity, and Exodus 2:24 says, "So God heard their groaning, and God remembered His covenant with Abraham, with Isaac, and with Jacob." How long was the period between when God heard and called Moses to return to Egypt and when Moses finally responded and returned? Indeed, God hears and remembers His promises to us, but it's a process that requires time.

There was Rachel who for years couldn't have children but continually cried out to the Lord about being barren. We read in Genesis 30:22: "Then God remembered Rachel, and God listened to her and opened her womb." And how long was it after God heard that she got pregnant? Well, we know for sure that the pregnancy itself was nine months.

Yes, there's a period between God remembering and the actual manifestation.

There was Samuel's mother who also was barren, and 1 Samuel 1:19 says, "And Elkanah knew Hannah his wife, and the Lord remembered her." Genesis 19:29 says: "God remembered Abraham." And then there is Psalm 103:14: "For He knows our frame; He remembers that we are dust."

Be encouraged! God sees and hears all of our struggles. All of our anguish and groaning. God has remembered us, His children, His church. He remembers all the promises He has made to us individually and corporately.

Can't you feel the wind blowing? God has remembered, and He has begun to manifest His goodness to us.

Be encouraged! "GOD REMEMBERS." GOD REMEMBERS YOU!

Day 137

THOUGHT OF THE DAY: Until we meet again

Tonight is the last night of our serving in the overflow homeless shelters in Fall River, and I am so disappointed that I can't be there. When I awoke this morning tears literally came to my eyes. I began to think about all the wonderful people I have met over the past ten weeks.

With this in mind I dedicate much of today's thought to them:

I want to thank you for allowing me to spend time with you. Thank you for teaching me so many things. Thank you for allowing me to see our God in a way that I've never seen Him. I've learned more about His unconditional love, His endless mercy and grace, and how His heart breaks for the hurting and broken. I've seen your constant daily struggles and I, along with other volunteers, felt crippled because we weren't able to help you more. I can't begin to tell you how my heart broke each time we had to tell you that you couldn't come into the shelter even for one night, never mind for seven, and on the rare occasion, we couldn't have certain people return for the entire season.

You will never know how much God has used our time together to change me.

When I was a little boy there was a television show with Roy Rodgers and Dale Evans. At the end of the show they would sing a song, and the key lyrics were "Happy trails to you until we meet again." So I say to all of you (and sadly to many who will never hear or read this post), "Happy trails to you until we meet again."

To the staff and volunteers of First Step Inn, I thank you for truly caring for the people we call guests who you see each day. Thank you for often going beyond "the job" to try and make a greater impact on their lives. Thank you for making the hard decisions to not allow guests to stay, when for whatever reason, it was in their best interest, also to convey this to certain volunteers. Thank you that each time it happened, to follow procedure, you struggled with your humanity.

Thank you that you are part of an organization that is doing all it can with limited resources to try and make a better way of life for these "buried treasures" that I like to call the guests of the overflow shelters. Thank you for your desire and ability not to overreact when one of the guests made a lousy decision or when their reactions/responses at times were difficult.

"Happy trails to you until we meet again."

To our volunteers - WOW! Thank you for your commitment and sacrifice to serve these "buried treasures." Thank you for coming in when your body and mind were saying "Stay home." Thank you for your willingness to learn and adapt to a culture to which you have never been exposed. Thank you for not overreacting when at times the situation and people around you brought up hard feelings. In the end, aren't we all thankful for the honor and privilege to love others the way Jesus loves us?

"Happy trails to you until we meet again."

A very special thank you to our captains who had to schedule and reschedule the volunteers for whom they were responsible. Thank you for answering phone calls at all hours of the night. Thank you for going in when you were short-staffed. Thank you for your leadership and for setting an example for those under you. Thank you for your sacrifice and commitment.

"Happy trails to you until we meet again."

To Pastor Tom and Lisa, there are just NO WORDS TO CAPTURE THANK YOU. Thank you for truly fulfilling John 15:13: "Greater love has no one than this, than to lay down one's life for his friends." I will see you next week as I continue to have the honor to work side-by-side with you in our Father's kingdom.

I also want to thank the pastors who opened their churches for people to stay. Thank you for the financial commitment you made to have your doors open.

Thank you Reverend Meir, Richie, Tony, and Shanna for going way beyond just serving.

May the grace and love of God continually saturate all of your lives. THANK YOU for being a part of mine.

Day 138

THOUGHT OF THE DAY: Cause us to fall down and worship

It's early Monday morning, and all I can do is worship. Oh Lord, I never want to lose my awe of you! There are no words to describe how overwhelmed I feel this morning. In fact, after almost every service I'm blessed to be a part of, I feel this way. In fact, even after personal worship time, it's almost too much to grasp! To have the privilege to be in service after service and to sense the literal presence of God filling the entire room is beyond description.

When I first became a believer, I would sing hymns, and oh, how I just loved worshipping. There was no felt presence of God, but I was so in love with Him because of the everlasting mercy and grace He had and still has for me. Then I transitioned to charismatic worship and that brought me to a more intimate place.

Sadly, the church went through a period of time when perfection and performance trumped worship, and we ended up putting style and form first. In spite of this, though, God would be in our midst. Then something happened! I'm not sure what it was, but somehow the Holy Spirit caused us to simply want to be with God. We weren't seeking a blessing or a feeling. We became desperate and still are desperate just to be with Him.

Perhaps that is the answer: the Holy Spirit created in us a desperate desire to fall down and worship Him because we love Him, and in loving him He comes and loves us.

That's it - we didn't do anything. He did and does it all. It was and is His desire to be with us. It was and is His desire to pour/lavish His affection upon us. He brought us from worship songs to worship. He desired and desires to reveal/manifest Himself to each of us individually and corporately. There is this constant wooing that causes us to want to be in His presence. Nothing else can satisfy that hunger! We are living in Song of Solomon 2:10: "My beloved spoke, and said to me: 'Rise up, my love, my fair one, And come away.' " God has placed in us the heart of Moses when in Exodus 33:15 he says to God, "If Your Presence does not go with us, do not bring us up from here."

That's it – God, we are not doing a thing without your presence. I will not worship for the sake of worship. Lord, cause us to embrace the things we read in the book of Revelation. Let these verses be the way we live and express our personal and corporate lives and worship.

Revelation 4:9-10: "Whenever the living creatures give glory and honor and thanks to Him who sits on the throne, who lives forever and ever, the twenty-four elders fall down before Him who sits on the throne and worship Him who lives forever and ever, and cast their crowns before the throne."

Revelation 5:8: 'Now when He had taken the scroll, the four living creatures and the twenty-four elders fell down before the Lamb, each having a harp, and golden bowls full of incense, which are the prayers of the saints." Verse 14: "Then the four living creatures said, 'Amen!' And the twenty-four elders fell down and worshiped Him who lives forever and ever."

Revelation 7:11: "All the angels stood around the throne and the elders and the four living creatures, and fell on their faces before the throne and worshiped God."

Revelation 11:17: "And the twenty-four elders who sat before God on their thrones fell on their faces and worshiped God."

Revelation 19:4: "And the twenty-four elders and the four living creatures fell down and worshiped God who sat on the throne, saying, 'Amen! Alleluia!' "

Why Lord? "For all nations shall come and worship before You." (Revelation 15:4)

Oh Lord, cause us to fall down and worship!

Day 139

THOUGHT OF THE DAY: Our gospel is meant to be verified by signs and wonders

It was in 2006 that I had the privilege of being on a team that went to some small villages outside of Bangalore, India. Lord willing, I hope to return there some time this year.

Of all the mission trips I've taken, this was the most amazing and supernatural. On two occasions we were taken to remote villages to preach the gospel. The first village had about 120 people, among which we were told there were two believers. When we arrived, we were greeted and adorned by the leader of the village with the most beautiful floral leis.

The pastor who took us to the village then asked me to get up and preach. I asked him why they would listen to me when they have 330 million gods in India. I told him that I would just be offering them another one.

But... if I could demonstrate the Kingdom of God, they would listen.

I got up and walked into the middle where the women and children were sitting. The men sat or stood on the outside of them. As I started to pray and lay my hands on them, the power of God came with such force that no one was able to stand. When the men saw what was happening, they tried to push the women out of their way – male-dominated culture, yes, but not the culture of the Kingdom of God. Our team held the men off, as I continued to pray for the women and children. Then I alternated between the groups, demonstrating that the Kingdom of God is about equality between men and women.

One man I prayed for was very intoxicated. When he fell under the power of God, he stayed there about 30 minutes and when he got up was sober and his breath like lilies. This went on for a few hours before it got dark. To make a long story short, of the 120 non-believers, some 60 plus people gave their lives to the Lord that night. Why? Because they could see the kingdom. They could see God's power.

In Hebrews 2:4 it says that "God verified what they said (apostles) through miraculous signs, amazing things, other powerful acts, and with other gifts from the Holy Spirit as he wanted." (NOG) First Corinthians 4:20 says, "For the kingdom of God is not in word but in power." God is wanting and waiting to work through you and will verify your message with signs and wonders.

After Peter and John were arrested, they returned to tell the other disciples what happened. After they finished, they stopped to pray. What did they pray, and what was the result? Read Acts 4:29-30 slowly, "Now, Lord, look on their threats, and grant to Your servants that with all boldness they may speak Your word, by stretching out Your hand to heal, and that signs and wonders may be done through the name of Your holy Servant Jesus." Now see how God answered - verse 31: "And when they had prayed, the place where they were assembled together was shaken; and they were all filled with the Holy Spirit, and they spoke the word of God with boldness."

They all were filled (again) and were given boldness and power. Acts 5:12 says, "And through the hands of the apostles many signs and wonders were done among the people. And they were all with one accord in Solomon's Porch."

God wants to use each of you! He wants to demonstrate His kingdom through you. We too should be praying as the apostles did - FOR POWER. PRAY FOR POWER!

Our gospel is meant to be verified by signs and wonders.

Day 140

THOUGHT OF THE DAY: God, do you hear me?

It's one of those mornings, and lately there have been a lot of these mornings.

Before I went to Michigan, I'd been praying about God making a way, and I'm still praying – Father, please make a way. There is nothing I can do, but you can. I feel like Jehoshaphat who in 2 Chronicles 20:12 prayed, "I don't know what to do but my eyes are upon you." I am fully aware that I'm powerless to do anything. I have no power or ability to cause things to change. Haven't we all have been here countless times, and somehow it doesn't seem to get easier. I know and love Psalm 120:1: "In my distress I cried to the Lord, And He heard me."

On a personal note, twice I had back injuries. The first time, for five plus years I was in and out of hospitals. I lived on a wooden floor and was out of work for three and a half years. The second back injury lasted seven years, and it really cost me. Near the end of the seven years it was taking me two hours to get dressed. Was I praying? Sure, I was. Oh God, do you hear me? And here I am again! Here we are again. God, do you hear us?

We all can so identify with Daniel who was praying for understanding and wisdom. Things were a mess for Israel. He needed an answer from God. In Daniel 10:12 we read that the Lord sends an angel to him, and the angel says, "Then he said to me, 'Do not fear, Daniel, for from the first day that you set your heart to understand, and to humble yourself before your God, your words were heard; and I have come because of your words.'"

The first thing the angel addresses is FEAR! That's great news! DON'T BE AFRAID, AND YOU NEED TO KNOW YOU'RE LOVED. (Funny, when we're going through something, we often don't feel loved; but we are.) Even though God sees our hearts, often things don't change right away.

Then verse 13 starts with that three-letter word "BUT!" The old but word. "But the prince of the kingdom of Persia withstood me twenty-one days." Now 21 days doesn't always seem like a long time, but whether it's 21 days (three weeks), three months, or three years, it does cross our mind to ask, "God, do you hear me?" Daniel couldn't do a thing. He had to wait until God fought for him. Until the appointed time.

When the enemy is warring against me, when feelings and circumstances don't change, I have to remind myself of Psalm 66:19: "But God did listen! He paid attention to my prayer." (NLT) Circumstances might not change, but I remember I'm loved and though there's a delay, that an answer is on the way. Even Jesus in the garden struggled and asked the Father if there was another way.

Know this: Our Father hears us, loves us, and though at any given time there may be a delay, HAS A PLAN!

In Genesis 35 Jacob leaves us a tremendous example to follow - learning to worship when God doesn't appear to answer us in our distress. Too often when God finally does answer, we don't build an altar but instead become jaded. Genesis 35:3: "Then let us arise and go up to Bethel; and I will make an altar there to God, who answered me in the day of my distress and has been with me in the way which I have gone."

God, do you hear me? YES, He says, I DO!

Day 141

THOUGHT OF THE DAY: Don't listen to the lie

Over the past number of months the Holy Spirit has been ministering to us about our true identity. We have listened to the lies since we can remember. Our mind, other people, and the devil continually remind us of who we're not, and we're continually barraged by thoughts and words that devalue us.

If you were asked how you see yourself, how would you answer? If you were asked how you feel about yourself, how would you answer? If you were asked on a scale from one to 10 to rate your value, what would your response be? Don't listen to the lie.

We don't recognize our true value and see ourselves as adopted sons and daughters, partly because of our emphasis on being Christians. If the focus is on being a Christian, then the weight will rest on what we need to be doing, rather than being – very simply, our Father's child.

And since we devalue ourselves, we often find it hard to assign value to others. So much of our lives we haven't valued ourselves, which has made it difficult to assign value and honor to others. We've spent years carrying the "want to be" spirit. I want to be like so and so, I wish I had so and so's gifts, talents, and personality. It's difficult to accept ourselves with all of our weaknesses, never mind seeing ourselves as having overwhelming value. Don't listen to the lie.

Just think about the idea of being overwhelmed with a true and deep sense of our value. When we look in the mirror, starring back at us is this most incredible person, valuable not because they've done anything, but because of who they are. The days of proving our worth is over. Sons and daughters of God don't go around proving their value. They realize that there's nothing to prove. Don't listen to the lie.

In Luke 12 Jesus uses a simple story/parable to try to get us to see our true value. Luke 12:24: "Think about those crows flying over there" (most translations say consider). "Do they plant and harvest crops? Do they own silos or barns? Look at them fly. It looks like God is taking pretty good care of them, doesn't it? Remember that you are more precious to God than birds!" (VOICE)

I just love the way the Voice Bible asks the question. It looks like God is taking pretty good care of them, doesn't it? Then Jesus says "REMEMBER" REMEMBER WHAT? THAT YOU/WE ARE- NOT GOING TO BE BUT ARE TODAY - MORE PRECIOUS/MORE VALUABLE THAN THE BIRDS THAT OUR FATHER TAKES CARE OF, YES, WITHOUT THEM EVEN DOING A THING.

Don't listen to the lie.

JESUS SAID, "REMEMBER" YOU ARE VALUABLE/IT'S YOU ARE, YOU ARE, YOU ARE – VALUABLE and PRECIOUS!

DON'T LISTEN TO THE LIE!

Day 142

THOUGHT OF THE DAY: Would you?

I wasn't out of bed five minutes when I started to ponder what the Lord would have me write. I heard with clarity the verse from 1 John 3:16. Do you know what it says? More importantly: are we living it?

Before I share the verse, I'll say that I was overwhelmed with a very deep emotion. I started to think of all the people who I've known who actually not only have this spirit in them, but live it. To all of you I want to say "Thank you." I want to say it again, "THANK YOU"...

My life and the lives of so many others are richer and fuller because of you. When I think of you, I say to myself, "I have seen Jesus." I feel blessed and honored to know you. Thank you for making a difference in my life and the lives of others. Not only have you said it, but more importantly, you did it. In some cases you didn't say very much, if anything, but your actions said it all.

By now I hope you're wondering what 1 John 3:16 says. I used to have this on my business card many years ago. It's one thing to have it on a business card or posted on our refrigerators, but quite another to live it. Perhaps most of us have lived it at times but at others are trapped by ourselves. We become preoccupied by our own lives, wants, desires, and yes, even our needs. Our common enemy has caused us to be trapped in the world of "me-itis." While I know that there's officially no such word, sound it out and you'll capture the meaning – ME I TIS.

It's a sad fact that very often we put ourselves first. Everything centers around what "I want" and "I need." We do this even when we see that others are in need. And their need is often greater than our own. Perhaps now you know the scripture. Before I share it, I'll say that I heard this whisper: "WOULD YOU?"

Here's what 1 John 3:16-18 says:

We know and, to some extent realize the love of God for us because Christ expressed it in laying down his life for us. We must in turn express our love by laying down our lives for those who are our brothers. But as for the well-to-do man who sees his brothers in want but shuts his eyes—and his heart—how could anyone believe that the love of God lives in him? My children, let us not love merely in theory or in words—let us love in sincerity and in practice! (Phillips Bible)

The end of this verse is just ringing in my ears. Let's sit with these words for a few moments... Then join me in praying, "Father, put this in me! Put this in us!" Listen to the tenderness that John writes with: "My children, let us not love merely in theory or in words—let us love in sincerity and in practice!"

Earlier in his writings, we see John scribe this. John 15:13: "Greater love has no one than this, than to lay down one's life for his friends."

Thank you for sacrificing yourself for the sake and benefit of others. You and even most of us have done this on occasion but only through and because of our relationship with the Father. John 10:15: "As the Father knows Me, even so I know the Father; and I lay down My life for the sheep." Our thoughts, actions, and lack of action will reflect our current relationship with the Godhead. I can hear the words of Peter, but if I'm honest, I can ALSO see me. John 13:37: "Peter said to Him, 'Lord, why can I not follow You now? I will lay down my life for Your sake.' " The good news is that as Peter became more like Jesus, he was able to fulfill "I will lay down my life for Your sake."

There's that whisper again, "WOULD YOU?"

Father, we want to be more like your Son, who said, "I lay down My life for the sheep."

WOULD YOU? AND WE ALL ANSWER, "YES!!!"

Day 143

THOUGHT OF THE DAY: The pharisee

Yesterday morning Donna asked me about the topic I was going to teach. I told her, "the Pharisee that I don't see." She asked me if I meant "the Pharisee in you," meaning the Pharisee in all of us. Yeah, that's it.

Maybe it's different for you, but I can see the Pharisee in others fairly easily, but I rarely if at all see the Pharisee in myself. I sat and listed the most obvious traits of a Pharisee, and here they are. There is no doubt you can add to the list.

Pharisees:

- Look to find and point out the faults in others but can't see or don't look at their own
- Are quick to give solutions for problems (yet are unable to give or receive counsel from others)
- Are better at preaching to others than practicing what they preach
- Criticize others for their actions and attitudes
- Own part of Ford Motor Company (they always have better ideas)
- Complain a lot about others
- Are rarely, if ever, wrong
- Tend to over-spiritualize everything

- Are full of pride and self-righteousness
- Tend to think that it's too bad people aren't more like them

I think I just did a pretty good job describing the Pharisee in me and perhaps in you. Jesus shares a parable in Luke 18:9-14. Perhaps we can see ourselves in it. There are two men in the story. Which one can we identify with the most?

Luke 18:9-14:

Also He spoke this parable to some who trusted in themselves that they were righteous, and despised others: "Two men went up to the temple to pray, one a Pharisee and the other a tax collector. The Pharisee stood and prayed thus with himself, 'God, I thank You that I am not like other men—extortioners, unjust, adulterers, or even as this tax collector. I fast twice a week; I give tithes of all that I possess.' And the tax collector, standing afar off, would not so much as raise his eyes to heaven, but beat his breast, saying, "God, be merciful to me a sinner!" I tell you, this man went down to his house justified rather than the other; for everyone who exalts himself will be humbled, and he who humbles himself will be exalted."

It's interesting that the Pharisee didn't say what he was thinking. Sound like someone you know? The Pharisee sees himself as more spiritual and believes the church would be better off if other people were like him. They rest in what they have done or are doing and fail to see that it's Christ in them who enables them, in spite of their flaws, to do/accomplish anything.

I told people to skip over the word tithe because much of the church doesn't believe in it anymore or better said, they believe it but don't practice it.

Then there is the tax collector. I like him! This man/woman depends and embraces the continual grace and mercy of God. They rejoice and live in Lamentations 3:22-24: "Through the Lord's mercies we are not consumed, Because His compassions fail not. They are new every morning; Great is Your faithfulness. 'The Lord is my portion,' says my soul, therefore I hope in Him!"

I prefer to be the tax collector rather than the Pharisee. While we're not always the Pharisee - he is allowed to exist far too much in us.

When you come across a Pharisee, how do feel about him/her? Consider this.

Day 144

THOUGHT OF THE DAY: Justified

The other day I was reading in the book of Galatians and came across the following verse - Galatians 5:4: "You have become estranged from Christ, you who attempt to be justified by law; you have fallen from grace." (NKJV) Even today that verse has simply floored me. When we attempt to be justified by works it says we become "estranged" or separated from Christ. Galatians 2:21 says, "For if righteousness comes through the law, then Christ died in vain."

I believe we all struggle with the concept of being fully justified by grace, especially after we've sinned. Somehow after we sin we want to once again earn our way back into His favor/grace. We want to show or demonstrate our sorrow. Here on planet earth when we fail someone, we look to make amends to the person we've hurt and sinned against. We want to restore our relationship.

Our relationship is restored with Christ by taking responsibility and confessing our sin and then fully embracing the reality that we're justified by what He did, not by what we do.

How can we possibly earn something that Jesus purchased for us by his blood? In Romans five it says that Christ demonstrates his love for us in that he justified us by his blood.

Easter will be here in a few weeks. Spend some time considering that we can't earn our justification, and in fact trying to earn it will actually separate us. Paul, who writes so much about justification, pens a conclusion that we all need to embrace. Romans 3:28: "Therefore we conclude that a man is justified by faith apart from the deeds of the law."

Day 145

THOUGHT OF THE DAY: What spirit do we carry?

Haven't we discovered that often our thinking/musing with the Lord is generated by the "season" we're in?

This is the Easter season, and our thoughts surround the death and resurrection of Jesus. This morning when I awoke, I had the following thought come crashing into my mind: "BUT THERE IS FORGIVENESS WITH GOD!"

Immediately I began thanking Him that He always forgives. I then wondered if I carry that same spirit with me. When people get near me, what do they sense? Do people sense that I'm approachable and want to draw near me because they sense a lack of judgement in me, an unconditional nature? Can they sense mercy and forgiveness even in my hello? Typically, when someone says hello to us, we can so readily discern what "spirit" they carry.

What spirit do people discern in us?

As I mused about the thought, "but there is forgiveness with God," I did what I normally do when I get part of a verse, I go to Bible Gateway and type it in. If a scripture doesn't come up, I modify the words in the search bar. Then normally a verse or several verses pop up. Here is one of the verses that appeared. It is Psalm 130:3-4: "If You, Lord, should mark iniquities, O Lord, who could stand? But there is forgiveness with You, That You may be feared (honored, worshiped)." (NKJV)

Oh Lord, thank you that there is "FORGIVENESS WITH YOU."

THE QUESTION THAT ENTERS MY MIND IS, IS THERE FORGIVENESS WITH ME?... if God doesn't keep record of our sins - do I?

What an unspeakable joy it is that God doesn't keep records of our wrong (sin). Oh, how I rejoice that HE DOES NOT HAVE A BOOK WHERE HE WRITES ALL OF OUR SINS. And yes, it does cause me to be in awe; it does cause me to worship! It makes me want to draw near to Him.

While musing about keeping records of wrongs, the question came to my mind about the kind of spirit I carry when it comes to forgiving. I remembered the story of Peter when he asked the Lord how many times he should forgive a brother who sins against him.

Right then and there we can see he'd put a limit on how many times he would forgive. Jewish law says that people were required to forgive three times, so Peter, wanting to show his deeper spirituality, says "How about seven times?" Oh, thank God that He doesn't put limitations on forgiveness!

Here is what Peter says and then Jesus' response to him. Matthew 18:21-23: "Then Peter came to Him and said, 'Lord, how often shall my brother sin against me, and I forgive him? Up to seven times?' Jesus said to him, 'I do not say to you, up to seven times, but up to seventy times seven.' "

Don't you want to jump up and down? Jesus says we must continually carry the spirit of forgiveness. He was saying to be like his Father. In a sense he was rephrasing Psalm 130.

Question - What spirit do we carry?

Day 146

THOUGHT OF THE DAY: I remember

When I awoke this morning I heard God speak these two words to me. He simply said, "I remember." Lately, like so many of us, I need to make some difficult decisions. Like you, many things are troubling me, and I know there's nothing I can do but express my needs to our Father.

Then I remember Matthew 6:8: "For your Father knows the things you have need of before you ask Him."

Can we hear that? Can we feel that? Our Father knows our needs BEFORE WE ASK. How can that be? Because He loves us. Because we are His children. Matthew 7:11 says this from the Voice Bible: "So if you, who are sinful, know how to give your children good gifts, how much more so does your Father in heaven, who is perfect, know how to give great gifts to His children!" Most translations translate "sinful" here as "being evil," and yes, having a carnal nature is in opposition to God.

Paul says in Romans 8:7: "Because the old sinful nature within us is against God. It never did obey God's laws and it never will." (TLB) Yet with that nature we STILL pour out our love and blessings on our children. We remember that they are "OUR KIDS." IF WE REMEMBER OUR CHILDREN AND SEE ALL THEIR FAULTS - WHAT ABOUT OUR HEAVENLY FATHER? He says, "I REMEMBER!" Listen to this from Isaiah 49:15: "Can a woman forget her nursing child, and not have compassion on the son of her womb? Surely, they may forget, Yet I will not forget you."

Did we hear that? "I WILL NOT, I WILL NOT FORGET YOU! He is saying, "I remember you."

Over and over again it says God remembered! He remembered Noah! He remembered Abraham, Rachel, Hannah, and Vashti. In the middle of their crises God said, "I remember!" In several verses it says God remembered His covenant. Psalm 105:42 says, "For He remembered His holy promise." God remembers us. Psalm 103:14: "For He knows what we are made of, He knows our frame is frail, and He remembers we came from dust." (VOICE)

Yes, God says, "I REMEMBER!"

Day 147

THOUGHT OF THE DAY: Something is happening... "COME FORTH"

What in the world is going on? For months now, just about every morning I want to cry.

There's a cry so deep within me that we, the sons and daughters of God, would take our place. That we would arise. That we would have the courage to step into our tomorrow. That we would forget the past and press into our tomorrow. That we would cry out day and night as Habakkuk 1:2: "How long must I cry, O Eternal One, and get no answer from You? Even when I yell to You, 'Violence is all around!' You do nothing to save those in distress." (VOICE)

Oh Lord, we cry out - send a mighty move of your Spirit!

I can hear it! I can feel it! Can't you? All of creation is screaming! Romans 8:19 "For [even the whole] creation (all nature) waits expectantly and longs earnestly for God's sons to be made known [waits for the revealing, the disclosing of their sonship]." (AMP)

All of creation is longing for you to take your place as a son/daughter. Take your place.

I know so many of you have been hurt and disappointed by pastors and churches. I've been guilty of hurting. But it's time to rise. Take up your post again. War with this verse in Ecclesiastes 10:4: "If the spirit of the ruler rises against you, do not leave your post."

The Spirit is crying out; Isaiah 60:1-2: "Arise [from the depression and prostration in which circumstances have kept you—rise to a new life]! Shine (be radiant with the glory of the Lord), for your light has come, and the glory of the Lord has risen upon you! For behold, darkness shall cover the earth, and dense darkness [all] peoples, but the Lord shall arise upon you [O Jerusalem], and His glory shall be seen on you." (AMP) GOD WANTS HIS GLORY TO SEEN ON YOU... Reread this: "From the depression and prostration in which circumstances have kept you—rise to a new life."

In John 11:38 Jesus goes to the tomb of Lazarus. "Then Jesus, again groaning in Himself, came to the tomb. It was a cave, and a stone lay against it." Did you see that Jesus was groaning from deep within - he saw the stone which unless removed would keep Lazarus in the tomb. He can see our stone. Look at verse 39: "Jesus said, 'Take away the stone.' " I can hear him yelling, "Take away the stone" - the stone in our heart that blocks his life from radiating through us! Verse 43 says that Jesus "cried with a loud voice, 'Lazarus, come forth!' "

I can hear His voice. _____, (put your name here) "COME FORTH!"

Something is happening... "COME FORTH."

Day 148

THOUGHT OF THE DAY: New beginnings

I arrived home last night somewhere around 10:00 p.m. Great to see my wife, Josh, and most of our dogs. It was good to be home! Hadn't really slept in over 24 hours, even during the seven-and-a-half hour flight from London. Went to bed at midnight and was up at 5:45. Did all the routines and then I sat to pray.

As I sat I felt like something was different, and then I heard, "It's the new beginning." The atmosphere is different, I feel different. I have to laugh, because we've seen that God has declared a new beginning, and here it is. Now what? How do I respond to this new beginning? Well, first I have to be consciously aware of it and ask, now what?

How strange that the words I wrote in Heathrow Airport are ringing in my ears - Now what? We are all such creatures of habit, and I'm seeing that I need to be more aware of them. It's difficult to be led by the Spirit, to see or do something new while my mind and actions are dictated by routine/habitual living. For a while now I would wake up in the morning and chat with Abba about having an awareness of living in expectation. Today I'm sitting here and something has gone off in me. I'm excited with a sense of expectation. I didn't pray about it. I'm simply already filled with expectation. Oh, this is good...

I'm saying to myself that I hope I won't miss what He wants to do today or any day. I hear "You won't." I feel like I have new eyes. There is this overwhelming affection and gratitude inside of me! Oh God, you are soooo GOOD. I hear Psalm 23 run through my mind. Please read each word slowly...

The Lord is my shepherd; I shall not want. He leads me beside the still waters. He restores my soul; He leads me in the paths of righteousness. For His name's sake. Yea, though I walk through the valley of the shadow of death, I will fear no evil; For You are with me; Your rod and Your staff, they comfort me. You prepare a table before me in the presence of my enemies; You anoint my head with oil; My cup runs over. Surely goodness and mercy shall follow me. All the days of my life; And I will dwell in the house of the Lord Forever.

I see and feel that He is our Shepherd. He leads and restores - WHY? For His name. No matter what we go through - real or unreal, He IS WITH US! In fact, we've been anointed for each moment of each day. Are we ready for this? HIS GOODNESS AND MERCY WILL SIMPLY FOLLOW ME EVERY MOMENT OF EVERY DAY. AND WE WILL DWELL WITH HIM NOW AND FOREVER.

Why write more, as this is more than enough to muse on. You see, this is a part of our new beginning. FOR HIS NAME! FOR HIS NAME!

We are at the start of our New Beginning! My love to you all!

Day 149

THOUGHT OF THE DAY: Palm Sunday

If I want to be honest, I struggle with Christian holidays. We seem to hear the same sermons over and over just so we can say we preached on the topic for the day. Tradition seems to outweigh presence. Looking at

Palm Sunday this year, I see three distinct emotions and lessons to be learned.

The first is our need to truly rejoice, not to rejoice or sing songs for the sake of rejoicing, but to rejoice with meaning for all the many works we have seen (all the great and marvelous things that God has done in our lives). Luke 19:37 says, "Then, as He was now drawing near the descent of the Mount of Olives, the whole multitude of the disciples began to rejoice and praise God with a loud voice for all the mighty works they had seen."

Too often we praise for praise's sake instead of recalling all the great things God has done for us. We seem to reflect more on what God hasn't done rather than EVERYTHING HE HAS DONE AND WILL DO FOR EACH OF US! The first lesson is to be truly and deeply thankful and to rejoice with all of our hearts rather than just mechanically sing.

The second thing to stop and consider is Jesus weeping audibly over the condition of Israel and what he saw coming. Amazing how quickly he shifted from one emotion to another. Jesus tells us in verse 42: "But now they are hidden from your eyes." To be honest, I think we like having things hidden from us. You see, once we know what's going on, it brings accountability.

Part of the word from Palm Sunday is that we need to be deeply burdened for the condition of our country and the condition of the church. We also need to be willing to see things that we perhaps don't want to see. Jesus' focus wasn't on himself but on others. Jesus wept because Israel missed the time of his visitation. Interestedly, one of the Greek meanings for visitation is "investigation." That brings a hmmm to my mind.

The second lesson is to carry the broken heart of God for others and a deep burden for the church/world, because we're missing what the Holy Spirit is trying to accomplish here and now. We seem to be preoccupied/distracted by our own personal world.

The third emotion which Jesus expressed in the later part of the day was anger. Luke 19:45-46: "Then He went into the temple and began to drive out those who bought and sold in it, saying to them, 'It is written, "My house is a house of prayer, but you have made it a 'den of thieves" ' " This was the second time in Jesus' ministry that he did this. The first time was at the beginning of his ministry (John 2).

So Jesus begins and ends his ministry by trying to stop the corruption in the church, the corruption over money and the emphasis on trying to make it. I wonder what Jesus thinks of the church today in regard to this?

Is Jesus visiting our temple and asking us to throw some things out? Am I really willing to ask him what doesn't belong in me?

I wonder if we've turned Palm Sunday into just another religious experience rather than capturing God's heart - tradition verses Spirit. Of course this is the danger we face every holiday and yes, every Sunday. So Palm Sunday is more than a tradition. It's more than about getting a palm branch that in a few days or few weeks we'll simply throw out. It's a time to reflect on the emotions and lessons of the day.

I hope you had a great Palm Sunday!

Day 150

THOUGHT OF THE DAY: God is among us

I awoke yesterday morning and heard, "God is among us."

So off to Youtube I went to find worship music that had the title or lyrics "God is among us." Then I did a scripture search for "God among us." As I was listening to worship, I read John 1:14: "So the Word became human and made his home among us. He was full of unfailing love and faithfulness." (NLT) Other translations say he was full of grace and truth.

Here it is Wednesday morning, and I'm still musing over the word, "God is among us." I'm still asking what He's trying to show me and what He means by saying, "God is among us." There's always a quick conclusion that we draw, and then there's a much deeper revelation.

If you're like me you like both the quick and the deep revelations to come fast. There is way too much Martha in me and not enough Mary - the busy us (Martha) and the one willing to sit at his feet and wait (Mary). I can't count the number of times I perceived only a portion of what God was saying to me because I was in a hurry. Sadly, I run off only knowing half of what He wanted to show me. All day yesterday, though, I was restless and wanted an answer. I wanted to perceive and receive what He was trying to show me, but hurrying the process is not an option. I really dislike this, but at the same time refuse to draw a conclusion before its time.

Here it is 24 hours later: I still haven't received the full intent/meaning "God is among us," yet I refuse to give up. I will wait until He shows me what He means by "God is among us."

I wasn't up but a few minutes when I realized that the frustration I felt yesterday has been replaced by excitement. In a way I feel like Moses in Exodus 33 when he refuses to enter the promised land unless God himself goes with him. Remember that God tells Moses that His Angel will go with him, but Moses speaks to God and says in verse 15, "If Your

Presence does not go with us, do not bring us up from here." Moses is persistent. He refuses to move unless God goes with them.

Hmmm... "refuse to move" if God is not among us...interesting thought...

There's this excitement inside, and I can hear, "Refuse to move if God is not among you." Can you hear that? "REFUSE TO MOVE!" I feel like jumping around and shouting, "REFUSE TO MOVE!" I know there's more He wants to show me in regard to "God is among us."

But I will give you this to ponder. Before I go on to seek more understanding, I want to rejoice and be fully enveloped in the idea "REFUSE TO MOVE!" It's like He's started a video in my mind, and I realize how vital this word is for where I am and I believe many of you are too. REFUSE TO MOVE!"

God is among us...

Day 151

THOUGHT OF THE DAY: Can you see me?

Close your eyes for a moment. Now what do you see? What do you sense? You have just stepped into another realm. Things are different here. You have a greater sense of confidence; your hearing from God is more acute, and there's an overwhelming sense of His presence. This is the realm of the Spirit. Can you hear - "YOU CAN LIVE HERE"?

My question is, how do I live here with my eyes still open?

It's a matter of knowing and believing that there's another realm and that not only can we see it but we've actually ALREADY entered it. It's the KINGDOM OF GOD. John 3:3: "Most assuredly, I say to you, unless one is born again, he cannot see the kingdom of God."

We've spent our entire lives seeing with our natural eyes and processing what we see by our natural mind, and now it's time to SEE in this realm of the kingdom. John 3:5 says, "Most assuredly, I say to you, unless one is born of water and the Spirit, he cannot enter the kingdom of God." Jesus is telling us that when we're born again that without any doubt, we've ENTERED THE KINGDOM.

We have read and quoted these verses and have never fully believed the simplicity of what they say. The problem is that we have two minds: the natural one and the spiritual one. What does Paul say about the natural mind? First Corinthians 2:14: "But the natural man does not receive the things of the Spirit of God, for they are foolishness to him; nor can he know them, because they are spiritually discerned." (NKJV)

The natural mind CANNOT RECEIVE OR PERCEIVE the spiritual realm. We've been living with our natural mind and trying to see and perceive the things of the Spirit (kingdom). Impossible. Paul goes on two verses later and says, in 1 Corinthians 2:16: "But we have the mind of Christ." What a simple verse, yet we've only read it and haven't fully received and embraced its overwhelming truth. WE HAVE THE MIND OF CHRIST!

So, you might ask, what does it mean to have the mind of Christ?

We read Romans 8:5-6: "For those who live according to the flesh set their minds on the things of the flesh, but those who live according to the Spirit, the things of the Spirit. For to be carnally minded is death, but to be spiritually minded is life and peace." When we open our eyes, we default to seeing and living with our natural mind. Yet it says when we live in our spiritual mind, we have "LIFE AND PEACE."

Understand this, that when we see and live in the reality of the kingdom, we recognize that "GOD IS AMONG US." We can see what the Spirit of God is doing, and likewise what Satan is doing (his methods and devices); Second Corinthians 2:12 says, "For we are not ignorant of his (Satan's) devices."

We should be staggered by these simple and yet profound truths. God is among us... We can live with our eyes open. Psalm 27:4 says, "One thing I have desired of the Lord, That will I seek: That I may dwell in the house of the Lord All the days of my life, To behold the beauty of the Lord."

God: Can you see me? For I am among you!

Day 152

THOUGHT OF THE DAY: Good Friday

It's the day after Good Friday. My life was a bit complicated yesterday, so I didn't have time to write down my thoughts.

The first question that struck me was - what was so good about Good Friday? Here are five answers that occupied my mind yesterday, so I was able to declare with a joyful and happy heart - IT IS A GOOD FRIDAY!"

Our sins were fully atoned for: John 1:29: "Behold! The Lamb of God who takes away the sin of the world!"

Our conscience was cleansed, and we are therefore free from guilt and shame: Hebrews 9:13-14: "For if the blood of bulls and goats and the ashes of a heifer, sprinkling the unclean, sanctifies for the purifying of the flesh, how much more shall the blood of Christ, who through the eternal Spirit offered Himself without spot to God, cleanse your conscience from dead works to serve the living God?"

Eternal life was fully paid for: John 19:29: "So when Jesus had received the sour wine, He said, "It is finished!" And bowing His head, He gave up His spirit."

Direct access to the Father was made available when the veil was ripped from top to bottom: Mark 15:38: "Then the veil of the temple was torn in two from top to bottom."

The proof of the resurrection for all mankind was when the graves were opened, and they were seen in Jerusalem. Matthew 27:51-53: "Then, behold, the veil of the temple was torn in two from top to bottom; and the earth quaked, and the rocks were split, and the graves were opened; and many bodies of the saints who had fallen asleep were raised; and coming out of the graves after His resurrection, they went into the holy city and appeared to many."

Good Friday? - Absolutely!!!

Day 153

THOUGHT OF THE DAY: Are you losing the battle for your mind?

Over the past several months the warfare for our minds has been unbelievable. Joyce Meyer has written a book about it called Battlefield of the Mind.

It seems like Satan has pulled out all the stops to get us to have, as Alcoholics Anonymous says, "stinking thinking." I know that several times a day I have to look beyond my circumstances and my reality. I have to put off negative thinking and thoughts. I've had to fight with the sword of Philippians 4:8 every day for weeks. It says, "Finally, brethren, whatever things are true, whatever things are noble, whatever things are just, whatever things are pure, whatever things are lovely, whatever things are of good report, if there is any virtue and if there is anything praiseworthy—meditate on these things."

The very last admonition Paul provides in that series is to think correctly. We have to force our minds to think about positive things. Isaiah 26:3 says, "You will keep in perfect peace all who trust in you, all whose thoughts are fixed on you!" (NLT)

The enemy doesn't have to lie to us; he just has us look at our circumstances. He then uses discouragement, despair, and depression. I can look at my circumstances, or I can look at God. That's why it says in Hebrews 12:2 "that we must look (fix our eyes) on Jesus who is the author and finisher of our faith." There's no option; it says we MUST. If our eyes aren't on Him, then they're on other things that will cause us to get into trouble. After Peter got out of the boat, he did fine until he looked at the waves. The longer we look at circumstances, the more despondent we become.

Go back and slowly reread Philippians 4:8. Then please tell me you won't let Satan use you to discourage others. Breathe hope instead. We certainly don't need negative words coming from others, nor do we want to be the breather of them. Sadly, Satan doesn't have to harass us; he just uses assorted people – some of them believers - to work on his behalf. Honestly, believers often spend more time discouraging, rather than encouraging their fellow brothers and sisters.

Come on now, let's put on the mind of Christ. If I think something, I can become it. Proverbs 23:7 "For as he thinks in his heart, so is he." Don't let people or Satan cause you to lose hope. In the middle of real circumstances we need to be like Abraham: "Hoping in spite of hopeless circumstances, he believed that he would become 'the father of many nations,' just as he had been told." (Romans 4:18, ISV)

Are you losing the battle for your mind? Go ahead, "put on the mind of Christ," because 1 Corinthians 1:26 says, "But we have the mind of Christ."

Day 154

THOUGHT OF THE DAY: It's time to seize what God has promised you

It's time we stood up and reminded ourselves, the devil, and God what God has promised us.

There have been countless promises God has made to all of us, and we have allowed them to be stolen. We have allowed them to dissipate and to fall by the wayside because we gave up on what God said to us. It's time we go back and retrieve what God has promised us and take back what we've allowed the devil to steal.

In Jeremiah chapter one when God speaks to Jeremiah about being a prophet, He asks him a question in verse 11 and then in verse 12 tells him He'll perform (complete, bring to pass what he has told him) it. Jeremiah 1:11-12: "And the word of the Lord came to me, saying, 'Jeremiah, what do you see?' (What do you see? What has God shown you in the past? Whether it was yesterday, last week, last month, or years ago, what did He say/show you? What promise did He make?) "And I said, 'I see an almond branch.' Then the Lord said to me, 'You have seen well, for I am watching over my word to perform it.' " (ESV) The Message Bible says, "God's Message came to me: 'What do you see, Jeremiah?' I said, 'A walking stick—that's all.' And God said, 'Good eyes! I'm sticking with you. I'll make every word I give you come true.' "

The Spirit is saying, I'M WATCHING MY WORD TO PERFORM IT. It's going to happen!

Too often we become discouraged and disheartened when we don't see what God has promised come to pass within our time frame, and the result is that we don't cling/hold on to what He told us. The whisper of the enemy, our own thoughts, and yes, even our friends and family, have all caused us to disbelieve what God has promised us. We need to declare what David wrote in Psalm 57:2: "I will cry out to God Most High, To God who performs all things for me." He says, I WILL CRY OUT TO GOD MOST HIGH, TO GOD WHO PERFORMS - READY FOR WHAT'S NEXT - PERFORMS ALL THINGS FOR ME!"

We need to have the spirit of Abraham we read about in Romans 4:20-21: "He never doubted that God would do what He promised. He never stopped believing. In fact, he grew stronger in his faith and just praised God. Abraham felt sure that God was able to do what He promised." (ERV) This passage is referring to the promise that he and Sarah would have a son. It says, "He never stopped believing." It says he continually praised God. Abraham had the confidence that, "GOD WAS ABLE TO DO WHAT HE PROMISED."

Jump up from your seat and declare, "God, I believe you're able to do what you've promised!" It's one thing to declare but quite another to live!

It's time to seize what God has promised you!

Day 155

THOUGHT OF THE DAY: Christ in you

I have been musing for a few months now about the verse, "Christ in you." I have not even begun to understand it.

Perhaps you too might want to consider this staggering thought. In John 14:23 it says, "Jesus said to him, 'If a person loves me, he will obey me. My Father also will love him. And we will come to him and will live with him.' " (WE BIBLE)

Where is God living? He's living in us now. Where is His presence? It's in you now. We have gone from meeting to meeting looking for the presence of God while all along the presence of God is already in us. Since we haven't as yet fully comprehended this, we continue to look for His presence. Can you imagine what kinds of amazing and supernatural things would take place wherever we went if we truly comprehended this?!

Paul tells us that all of creation is waiting for us. Romans 8:19: "For [even the whole] creation (all nature) waits expectantly and longs earnestly for God's sons to be made known [waits for the revealing, the disclosing of their sonship]." (Amplified Bible) Another translation says, "The whole creation waits breathless with anticipation for the revelation of God's sons and daughters."

Before all of creation can see the revealing of the sons and daughters of God, we who are the sons and daughters of God, must first understand and embrace who we are.

Now consider John 17:22: "All the glory You have given to Me, I pass on to them. May that glory unify them and make them one as We are one." (Voice Bible) B. W. Johnson calls it, "the glory of Sonship" and Adam Clarke, "the power to do miracles." Everyone agrees that one of the reasons Jesus gave his glory is so that "we would be one."

I would say we haven't yet begun to activate this word. Does the lack of unity hinder the power of God from being revealed? Does the lack of unity hinder creation from seeing the sons and daughters of God? Where is God's glory? It's in YOU!

One last verse to consider is Colossians 1:27: "God's plan is to make known his secret to his people, this rich and glorious secret which he has for all peoples. And the secret is that Christ is in you, which means that you will share in the glory of God." (GNT BIBLE)

Christ in you? What if we could comprehend this? Christ is in you!

Day 156

THOUGHT OF THE DAY: Faith is

Yesterday I encouraged everyone to watch my YouTube video, and again today I want to encourage you to take the time to watch it. Here are some highlights:

Here is pb's (my) faith summary: Living by faith is not living by circumstances or emotions: It's living from your spirit. In the process you'll have to fight your own thoughts, and your own emotions and feelings. You'll also have to fight the opinions of others. Living by faith is not living by logic or by what you see. It's living by something God has shown you, spoken to you, or put in your spirit.

One of the biggest obstacles to living by faith is our natural mind, which Paul says, "CANNOT RECEIVE/PERCEIVE THE THINGS OF THE SPIRIT." Besides the natural mind, we have our adversary the devil. Paul wrote in 1 Timothy 1:18, "This charge I commit to you, son Timothy, according to the prophecies previously made concerning you, that by them you may wage the good warfare." Whatever God has spoken, we must remind ourselves of and remind the devil of as well.

This is especially true when there's a delay/long period of time between when God spoke to you and the fulfillment of the word. I love Hebrews 11:10 which says, "He (Abraham) WAITED for the city which has foundations, whose builder and maker is God." This is such a vital key, and it's how we wait.

We can wait in the Spirit or wait in our flesh. When we wait in the flesh, we'll often make decisions that will oppose or even work against what was told to us. What happened to Saul when he didn't wait for Samuel to come and make the sacrifice? He lost the kingdom altogether. What did Abraham and Sarah do when they didn't wait? They had a son called Ishmael whom Abraham tried to convince God about, that Ishmael should be the son that God gave Abraham through a prophetic promise. Yet it was 14 years after the birth of Ishmael that Isaac was born. Think of it: God gave a word to Abraham and Sarah, and after waiting 11 years they became impatient and created a problem that the world is still facing today.

Here is how the Amplified Bible interprets Hebrews 11:1-2: "Now faith is the assurance (the confirmation, the title deed) of the things [we] hope for, being the proof of things [we] do not see and the conviction of their reality [faith perceiving as real fact what is not revealed to the senses]. For by [faith—trust and holy fervor born of faith] the men of old had divine testimony borne to them and obtained a good report."

I encourage you to read these two verses again.

Day 157

THOUGHT OF THE DAY: You want me to do what?

I want you to picture that it's a quiet and beautiful day, and yet your heart is troubled by all the corruption that you see, and you're believing that something has to change. Then all of a sudden God comes and says to you, "I want you to build an ark." A what? An Ark? Why?

Noah, it's going to rain. What's rain? Noah, it's going to rain so much that it will flood the earth.

Let me get this straight. You say it's going to rain. I don't even know what rain is, never mind raining so much that it will flood the entire earth! Huh?

Lord, don't you know that I'm 480 years old, and you want me to build an ark that is how big? You say it's 437 to 512 feet in length, and it's what - three stories high? It's going to what? Rain?

So Noah began to build the ark. He was asked to build something so far beyond human understanding because... he was asked to. He hadn't seen rain, which means he did this by faith. He couldn't see or perceive rain, but he began to build an ark by faith. What do you think people thought? What did all his neighbors say to him? Hey Noah, you're nuts. Noah, you're wasting your time.

It's said that the ark was an engineering genius, and it wasn't until the 19th century that a shipyard built a boat this large. The ark, they said, was virtually impossible to capsize. The estimated interior was 1,518,750 cubit feet. They estimated it would hold 569 standard railroad boxcars and 125,000 sheep. Noah, you're nuts.

But he was doing this by faith.

There is disagreement about how many years it took to build the ark. The estimate is a minimum of at least 60 years, and most believe it was closer to 120. Noah continued to believe what God had spoken in spite of his own emotion, his own thoughts, and the verbal comments of others. He clung to faith, but faith that was followed by action, not just for a few years, but close to 120.

Faith is more than mentally believing something. It's taking action. I want to encourage you take steps toward what God has said to you.

Day 158

THOUGHT OF THE DAY: Are you willing to move on?

It's two times in Genesis that we see Abraham being told to leave his home.

The first time he was living in Ur, and as he left there his father went with him. (Although he was told to leave everyone behind; he didn't.) He traveled to Haran, which is half way to the Promised Land. We too are often told to move on but only go part of the way.

We see a short summary in Acts 7:2-4: "Brethren and fathers, listen: The God of glory appeared to our father Abraham when was in Mesopotamia, before he dwelt in Haran, and said to him, 'Get out of your country and from your relatives, and come to a land that I will show you.' Then he came out of the land of the Chaldeans and dwelt in Haran. And from there, when his father was dead, He moved him to this land in which you now dwell."

Often we're told to move, and like Abraham, it isn't clear where we're to go. Perhaps we do know but don't move anyway. Sadly, it often takes a major event to finally get us going. In Abraham's case, it was the death of his father. Why don't we move? Let's list a few reasons.

· We wait for clarity. Where am I going? Sometimes you have to make the decision to leave/move on before you know where you're to go. Hebrews 11:8: "By faith Abraham obeyed when he was called to go out to the place which he would receive as an inheritance. And he went out, not knowing where he was going."

- We're influenced by our family.
- Yes, we're afraid. Which shows what?
- We're comfortable. The church we're in has all the perks. The place we might be called to doesn't.

- We have a position. I've seen people forgo the calling of God because they had a position in ministry.
- We don't want to travel. It's more convenient to go a short distance rather than a longer one.
- We've become complacent. We'd rather stay in a place where we know we shouldn't be rather than go to a place where we know there will be obstacles.

For many of you it's like the lepers in 2 Kings 7. They couldn't stay where they were; they couldn't go back; they could only go forward. The obstacle to going forward was facing the enemy armies. A funny thing though? They left where they were, and God defeated the enemy. Oh, and the lepers gathered up the spoils - money, food, clothing, animals, and much more.

Perhaps God's provision and blessing for you and others is in a place you don't want to go.

Why did I write this thought today? It's simple: I was told to. Are you willing to move on?

Day 159

THOUGHT OF THE DAY: I have a long way to go

One of the greatest traps we all fall into is to keep seeing all of our weaknesses. We keep on seeing who we haven't yet become. We keep on seeing our sins. We keep on seeing all of our failures. We see the same character flaws we've had for years. I hear God saying, "GET YOUR EYES FIXED."

How can I do that? I don't know how to fix them!

As I'm writing this, I'm reminded of the letter that was written to the Church of Laodicea. Perhaps you know this church? The one which is neither hot nor cold? It seems to be a popular church these days. In Revelation 3:18 the Holy Spirit says: "Here's what I want you to do: buy medicine for your eyes from me so you can see, really see." (MSG) The NOG Bible says, "Buy ointment to put on your eyes so that you may see."

Lord, this morning we come before you to anoint our eyes that we can see as you see. Though you see us where we are, you also see us as complete. If only we could embrace that you see us now as totally complete. From Colossians 2:10 "And because you belong to Christ you are complete." (ERV) Oh, let's spin around and dance - WE ARE COMPLETE BECAUSE WE BELONG TO YOU!

Yes, I'm beginning to see - I AM COMPLETE.

Are there yet things that have to change in me? Without a doubt! But I'm going to declare Philippians 3:13: "Brothers and sisters, I know that I still have a long way to go. But there is one thing I do: I forget what is in the past and try as hard as I can to reach the goal before me." (ERV) We need to have short memories!

I have a long way to go. As true as that is, it is also true that I AM COMPLETE, AND I WILL REACH TOWARD ALL THE GOALS BEFORE ME...

Day 160

THOUGHT OF THE DAY: 1 Corinthians 4:5: "Therefore judge nothing before the time."

In our desire to draw conclusions or have closure, we often make judgements well before all the facts are in. We struggle with living in the unresolved.

How many times do we wish we had waited just a little longer or maybe even a lot longer? How often have we heard one side of a situation and drawn our conclusions, only to find out that when we heard the other side of the story, everything changed? Proverbs 18:13 in the (Living Bible) says, "What a shame— yes, how stupid! — to decide before knowing the facts!" The Message Bible says, "Answering before listening is both stupid and rude."

Then there's Proverbs 18:17: "Any story sounds true until someone tells the other side and sets the record straight." (TLB) The New King James Version says, "The first one to plead his cause seems right. Until his neighbor comes and examines him," or as Paul Harvey used to say, "And now... for the rest of the story."

How many times have we said something or drawn a conclusion only to regret that we said it? Once it is out of our mouths it's too late. All of us have done this over and over again, and we continue to do it. Why? Many times we have unresolved issues in our own lives, issues where we've been hurt, issues that are still in need of healing. Sadly, we transfer these onto others. How fair is that?

Then there is the monster called fear. Fear that we'll be taken advantage of - AGAIN. Fear that something will happen because it happened before. I can't begin to tell you of all the marriages, families, and even close relationships that have been damaged because we misjudged a matter. We continue to make excuses. We throw around "I'm sorry" only to continue drawing conclusions prematurely.

This doesn't sound like the life Jesus purchased for us, does it? Let's reread 1 Corinthians 4:5. It says, "JUDGE NOTHING BEFORE THE TIME" - JUDGE NOTHING - that seems to be pretty clear. Will power and behavior modification don't work. We have to become desperate enough that we cry out for help. Lord, help! And He says, "Are you willing to forgive and release? Are you willing to be healed?"

The big question is...are we really willing to have a new identity?

Quoting this verse has no value if our lives are not dramatically changed.

"Therefore judge nothing before the time."

Day 161

THOUGHT OF THE DAY: Sandbox

I was in the bathroom, one of my favorite places to pray, or perhaps better said, to chat with my Father.

I began to consider some of the thoughts that had come to me. Thoughts like "Get Ready," "Are We Ready," and "Trials are for Training." Then I thought of the potter's wheel in Jeremiah. Haven't we all visited the potter's wheel countless times? I thought of the woodshed where at times we've gone to be disciplined by the Lord. I was considering all these thoughts and randomly chatting with the Lord about them when He interrupted me. There was a loving tone in his voice, and he said, "Come to the sandbox."

Immediately I saw a sandbox, and I saw the Lord kneeling in the sandbox playing with a Tonka Toy bulldozer. He was pushing up the sand making a sandhill. He looked at me and smiled. His smile said it all - come join me!

My mind went to my childhood, and I said out loud, "My father never played with me in the sandbox." Then He showed me that even though my natural father never played with me there, that He was always with me in the sandbox.

I started to get melancholy, but Abba interrupted my going to the "poor-me place." He said, "Come join me." There was a long pause when nothing was being said. All I could see was His smile. Then He said to me, "You have known the potter's wheel and you have known the woodshed. Now it's time you learn about My Sandbox. This is the place where you and others will learn of my delight. Yes, it will be a place where we can have fun together in the warm sun. This is a side of my nature you have not known, and since you have not known it, you cannot carry it, but all of that will change today.

Notice this was not your thought or idea; it was and is MINE. You and others talk about carrying my presence. Well, this is a part of my presence you and others will begin to carry. It is the place of my delight. It's more than my approval! It is what John knew as he leaned his head on my breast. Again, I want to say this was not your idea. But that's all it

154

will be unless you come join me in the sandbox. This will be a place where you will hear Me in ways you have never heard Me before. It is the place where a Father will speak to HIS SON AND DAUGHTER things you haven't had the capacity to hear."

What's that I hear? I hear singing, and there's also humming. I look and all I can see is a smile and tears running down His cheeks. He's saying, "How I have yearned for this day. I have called you and others so many times, but you did not hear me. BUT TODAY ALL THAT WILL CHANGE!"

The Lord continued to speak, saying that we will carry a Spirit of Delight. It's more than the Spirit of acceptance, more than the Spirit of approval, more than the Spirit of affirmation and adoption. WE WILL CARRY HIS DELIGHT!

"COME TO THE SANDBOX!"

Day 162

THOUGHT OF THE DAY: Are you uncomfortable? Is something stirring in you?

If your answer is yes, then you are in a great place. I would still encourage you to watch the YouTube message from Sunday. It's full of Holy Ghost gems.

In Deuteronomy 32:11 it says, "Just as an eagle stirs up its nest, encouraging its young to fly, and then hovers over them in case they need help, and spreads its wings and catches them if they fall, and carries them up high on its wings." It says here that the eagle stirs the nest. We're like the eaglets who've been enjoying hanging out in the nest. In many ways we've become comfortable and would rather be comfortable than challenged.

The mother eagle has to do two things when it's time for her eaglets to fly. First, she makes the nest uncomfortable for them to remain where they are. When the eaglets find another spot to be comfortable, she then goes and makes that area of the nest uncomfortable as well. Then the day comes (the appointed time) and the mother eagle literally flings the young eaglets out of the nest. There is one purpose in mind: to get the young eaglets to fly. She repeats this until they do.

Are you uncomfortable? The Spirit is trying to do one thing: to get us to exercise our faith in a new way, to soar in the Spirit like we've never soared before.

In the verse we quoted, it said the eagle stirs the nest. The Hebrew word is 'ur' meaning to stir up, awaken, arouse to action, excite, to open one's eyes. Can't we see that's what God is up to? This same Hebrew word is used in Haggai 1:13-14 where it says, "Then Haggai, the Lord's messenger, spoke the Lord's message to the people, saying, 'I am with you,' says the Lord. So the Lord stirred up the spirit of Zerubbabel, governor of Judah, and the spirit of Joshua, the high priest, and the spirit of all the remnant of the people; and they came and worked on the house of the Lord of hosts, their God." God was trying to stir and provoke the people who'd returned from exile to return to work and complete the work on the temple.

Can't we all feel a stirring inside? It's time to rise and build the Kingdom of God.

For many years we built our churches and our ministries and now it's time to build "the unshakeable kingdom." Yes, the nest has become comfortable, and we actually run the risk of dying there. The eaglets probably were thinking, "I didn't ask for this. I would rather be sitting in my safe and comfortable nest." Yet they would never learn to fly by remaining there, and neither will we reach our potential by staying where we are. What we think is an awful place to be is a place which causes God to jump up and down with great joy. Why? Because He sees what we'll become.

Are you uncomfortable? Is something stirring in you? Then you're in a good place. Get ready to soar...

Day 163

THOUGHT OF THE DAY: I'm a _____

Picture an ordinary day and we're meeting someone for the first time. We're not too far into the conversation before we inform the person we're speaking with that we're a Christian.

From that point forward if the conversation continues, we have a religious conversation. We can't help ourselves, and so begin the doctrinal tour of our theology. We tell them we're born-again and somehow imply or tell the person we're talking to that they too must be born-again. We often follow that up with some version of the Roman's Road speech. You know the one about being separated from God and the large gulf between us and God, and that only Jesus' death and resurrection can bridge the gap between God and eternal life?

If the conversation doesn't head that way, normally the first question we're asked is what church we attend. Are you Catholic, Protestant, Evangelical, Pentecostal, etcetera. We then spend the next number of minutes explaining our denominational affiliation and give a quick overview of why we are whatever we are. If our answer is nondenominational, we spend the next few minutes trying to explain what that means.

When the conversation is done, what we've had is simply another religious conversation. Is there really any wonder why we haven't been effective in spreading the gospel of the Kingdom of God? We spend more time being a witness of both our church and our doctrine than the affection and love of God.

The question we need to ask is about our identity: are we a Christian or perhaps one of the born-again variety? If you think about it, when we say born-again, it implies that there was a birth. That birth is into the family of God, which implies relationship.

We were born again not to tell people about our religious convictions, but to speak about our relationship with our Father. When we look at the ministry of Jesus, we see that he was always talking about His Father. Here are some of Jesus' comments about scriptural knowledge for its own sake. John 5:39: "Here you are scouring through the Scriptures, hoping that you will find eternal life among a pile of scrolls. What you don't seem to understand is that the Scriptures point to Me." (VOICE) Matthew 22:29: "But Jesus said, 'Your error is caused by your ignorance of the Scriptures and of God's power!' " (TLB)

Are we only a Christian or does our identity go deeper? To be clear, I am blessed to be a Christian. However, Jesus didn't come to offer just another religion, he came to offer a relationship. In fact, in John 14:23 it says, "Jesus answered and said to him, 'If anyone loves Me, he will keep My word; and My Father will love him, and We will come to him and make Our home with him.' "

He said He and his Father would come and make their home in us.

Paul summarizes the concept of sonship by saying that we've been adopted as sons, that we are His children, and because we are His children, we are His heirs. He concludes this thinking by saying that all of creation is waiting for the manifestation of the sons of God. Romans 8:15 –19:

You received the Spirit of adoption by whom we cry out, "Abba, Father." The Spirit Himself bears witness with our spirit that we are children of God, and if children, then heirs—heirs of God and joint heirs with Christ, if indeed we suffer with Him, that we may also be glorified together. For I consider that the sufferings of this present time are not worthy to be compared with the glory which shall be revealed in us. For the earnest expectation of the creation eagerly waits for the revealing of the sons of God.

Paul also writes about this in Galatians:

But when the time arrived that was set by God the Father, God sent his Son, born among us of a woman, born under the conditions of the law so that he might redeem those of us who have been kidnapped by the law. Thus we have been set free to experience our rightful heritage. You can tell for sure that you are now fully adopted as his own children because God sent the Spirit of his Son into our lives crying out, "Papa! Father!" Doesn't that privilege of intimate conversation with God make it plain that you are not a slave, but a child? And if you are a child, you're also an heir, with complete access to the inheritance. (4:4-7)

Yes, we are children, sons and daughters. What if the world could discover relationship instead of religion? (Please go back and reread these verses and focus on key words that reference relationship.)

So what are we? Yes, we are Christians, but our true identity is as sons and daughters.

Day 164

THOUGHT OF THE DAY: Perhaps you can relate?

It's Friday morning, and I'm feeling stressed, frustrated, and burdened by the weight of trying to make the decisions that you, Abba, would want me to make.

So I bow my head to pray and immediately am conflicted. I want to spend time just musing with the Lord, telling him how much I love and appreciate Him, but the pressure of my circumstances keeps filling my mind. I think of worshipping, but my heart and mind are overwhelmed. I want to ask Him what is on His heart and mind, but the weight of what is on my heart and mind comes crashing in. I really don't want to give Him my to-do list - you know, the God, fix this and that; take care of this and that.

Father, please remove this feeling of being overwhelmed, stressed, and frustrated. In the moment it's so difficult to pray. Ever been here?

I'm conflicted because I so want to just be with Abba this morning. I don't want to give Him my please-help list. I don't want to be a son who's always coming to ask God to address all of my concerns. Yet I remember Psalm 120:1: "In my distress I cried to the Lord, and He heard me." I'm conflicted because I don't want to be a son who's always asking something of his Father. Then I remember the words of Jesus in Matthew 11:28: "Come to Me, all you who labor and are heavy laden, and I will give you rest." I'm conflicted, yet I know He understands.

I'm conflicted because I'm trying to have a relationship that's not based on what He can do for me. I want Him to know that I love Him for who He is, not for what He does. Then the Lord reminds me of multiple times in scripture where people just "unload," and besides, there is Psalm 116:1: "I love the Lord, because He has heard My voice and my supplications." Somehow that verse has lifted my conflict.

Can I say this again: "I love the Lord, because He has heard My voice and my supplications." My mind is filled with relief, and then I remember Psalm 139:17-18: "How precious also are Your thoughts to me, O God! How great is the sum of them! If I should count them, they would be more in number than the sand."

OH, HE UNDERSTANDS ME!

Yes, and there is Psalms 139:1-4: "O Lord, You have searched me and known me. You know my sitting down and my rising up; You understand my thought afar off. You comprehend my path and my lying down, and are acquainted with all my ways. For there is not a word on my tongue, but behold, O Lord, You know it altogether."

The conflict is gone because He knows me. He also knows you.

As I was writing this I heard, "Just be honest with how you feel." Oh, praise God the conflict is gone. My circumstances haven't changed, yet I know He appreciated my taking the time to talk about how I was feeling. He knows us!

Perhaps you can relate?

Day 165

THOUGHT OF THE DAY: Come my child

As I sat to spend time with Abba, I heard, "Come my child."

I was impressed that I was to write this word. It's a word for all of us. Yet no word has value unless it's acted upon. Please consider the following.

Come my child!

I have been waiting all night for you to arise to come and spend some time with me. Today is not like any other day. Today marks a day of new and fresh beginnings. Today I begin to fulfill promises I made to you so long ago. You see, my child, I have been working in you. When you thought you were ready, you were not. Even my own son when he was twelve knew and confessed that he had to be about "my Father's business," (Luke 2:49) but he was not ready. It took 18 years for him to be released.

Would you come? Let me whisper. Let me hold you. Today is a day of expansion and increase. You will and must remember it is not what you have done or will do. When you thought you were ready you were not. Put off the Martha spirit (all your busyness) and come and be still. Be quiet and do not speak. Find intimate instrumental worship and sit and soak. Do not be anxious to hear. Just sit and wait, and even at times you will lay down before me. Do not draw conclusions. A piece is not a whole. Would you come?

It is new and awkward. You might think you have been here before, but you have not. Honor what I say by writing down what I say. Too often my children have not honored what I have said. I said to John, 'Write." I say to you, 'Write.'

One last thing I want to say to you this morning. Listen, meditate, and yes, even speak it. Have I not said that, "IF YOU WOULD BELIEVE YOU WOULD SEE THE GLORY OF GOD." (John 11:40)

Come my child!

Day 166

THOUGHT OF THE DAY: Hold on to what you believe

In 1 Thessalonians 5:20-21 it says, "Do not despise prophecies. Test all things; hold fast what is good."

This scripture is clear: don't reject, brush off prophecies, or as the ICB says, "Do not treat prophecy as if it were not important." Then verse 21 in the CEB says, "but examine everything carefully and hang on to what is good."

When we receive or even give a prophetic word, we need to go back and evaluate the word. We need to consider before God whether the word is true or not. Too many words given and received have never produced fruit because the word/seed was never cultivated. In Matthew 13 we read about the parable of the seeds. Some seeds are stolen. This happens too often when we allow the devil to talk us out of the word, and by not assigning value to it, it gets stolen. Some seed falls on a hard heart, and thus the seed never germinates. Then there are the cares of the world which eventually choke the word which has either been given or received.

The verse says, "HOLD ON" to the word. Sadly, however, so many words go to the prophetic rubbish pile. We often don't spend time considering/meditating on what we either said or heard. The reality is that if you and I don't believe the word, then who will? In 1 Timothy 1:18 it says, "Timothy, you are like a son to me. What I am telling you to do agrees with the prophecies that were told about you in the past. I want you to remember those prophecies and fight the good fight of faith." (ERV)

We are to fight with words spoken and received. The prophetic word given or received becomes a weapon. Have we lost our weapon?

Remember 2 Corinthians 10:4: "For the weapons of our warfare are not carnal but mighty in God for pulling down strongholds." We get to pull down strongholds with prophetic words.

Without going into detail, I had given a word to the leadership team of a church, but they didn't like the word because it didn't fit their plan. Not only did they reject the word, but at best, they believed it to be inaccurate. When I was questioned about the word I gave, I held onto what I said. I didn't fudge it, soften it, or adjust it, because I knew it to be true. I held on to what I believed. In spite of my being criticized and their saying it was a false word, I held onto it. Today I received a phone call and was told that what I had prophesied had come to pass.

Remember 1 Thessalonians 5:20 - "Hold fast to what is good." Hold on to what you believe until such time that you see that you were wrong. Romans 14:5: "Let each be fully convinced/persuaded in his own mind."

Hold on to what you believe!

Day 167

THOUGHT OF THE DAY: There is a shaking going on

Has your life been full of change, transition, and trials? Then you are in a good place. Have you been barraged by one situation after another? Then you are in a good place. Are you being stretched emotionally? Then you are in a good place. Are you being stretched financially? Then you are in a good place. Are you being challenged spiritually? Then you are in a good place.

Right about now, you might be asking, really? Says who?

You see, this is the place where God is working. He's working things in us and working things out of us. He's giving us new eyes to see differently. He's giving us new ears so we can hear differently. He's having us press into His presence more than ever before. He's provoking us to move from the outer court to the inner court.

And have you discovered that once we're there He's still not done? Why? Because He is bringing us into the "Holy of Holies" - the place where the priests would go once a year.

He's bringing us into His presence and rather than once a year or once in a while, He's bringing us in daily.

What we're all going through is not something we would choose, yet there is actually a purpose God is working in us. Philippians 2:13-14: "For God is working in you, giving you the desire and the power to do what pleases him. Do everything without complaining and arguing."

Lord, I am honored that you are working in us, but to be honest, I'm just not crazy about how you're going about it.

Here is God's response written by Paul. Second Corinthians 4:16-18:

For this reason we never become discouraged. Even though our physical being is gradually decaying, yet our spiritual being is renewed day after day. And this small and temporary trouble we suffer will bring us a tremendous and eternal glory, much greater than the trouble. For we fix our attention, not on things that are seen, but on things that are unseen. What can be seen lasts only for a time, but what cannot be seen lasts forever. (GNT)

He uses the phrase "light and temporary." Indeed, how we view the "season" we're in is everything. It allows us to go beyond just enduring and complaining to a place of thanking Him for molding us into the image of His Son. Romans 8:29 in the Message Bible says, "God knew what he was doing from the very beginning. He decided from the outset to shape the lives of those who love him along the same lines as the life of his Son." Other translations call it being "changed into his image." God is shaping us to look like and live like His son.

You see, God is shaking everything so that we can receive His kingdom, and our lives will be filled with worship and a passion to serve Him with humility and awe. See Hebrews 12:26-28:

Then [at Mount Sinai] His voice shook the earth, but now He has given a promise: Yet once more I will shake and make tremble not only the earth but also the [starry] heavens. The expression, "Yet once more" indicates the final removal and transformation of all [that can be] shaken—that is, of that which has been created—in order that what cannot be shaken may remain and continue. Let us therefore, receiving a kingdom that is firm and stable and cannot be shaken, offer to God pleasing service and acceptable worship, with modesty and pious care and godly fear and awe. (AMP)

There's a shaking going on! What a great place to be!

Day 168

THOUGHT OF THE DAY: The lie must stop

It's not who you're going to be; it's who you are now. Who is in you? The answer is simply stated in the Message Bible, Colossians 1:27: "The mystery in a nutshell is just this: Christ is in you."

Christ is in you and me now. So what's the problem?

We continue to see our deficits rather than seeing ourselves as being in Christ. We must believe John 20:21: "As the Father has sent Me, I also send you." We are waiting to be perfect/complete. Yet Colossians 2:10 says, "And because you belong to Christ you are complete, having everything you need." (ERV) Did you see that - "having everything you need"? Christ is ruler over every other power and authority.

We're frequently guilty of the "perhaps-one-day" attitude. We say to ourselves that "perhaps one day" we'll be more qualified. Colossians 1:11-12 says, "May you be strengthened with all power, according to his glorious might, for all endurance and patience with joy, giving thanks to the Father, who has qualified you to share in the inheritance of the saints in light." (ESV)

Stop and mediate on this: Christ is in you. Therefore, you are complete, qualified, and have already been sent. Stop believing the lie...

Day 169

THOUGHT OF THE DAY: It's time for healing - Part 1

I can't begin to tell you of the deep sadness in my heart. As I look back through the years, I've seen countless wonderful people who have been hurt in and by the church. Zechariah 13:6 says, "I was wounded in the house of my friends."

So many precious people can relate to the verse in Jeremiah 30:12: "Your affliction is incurable, Your wound is severe."

I wish I could write that I'm not guilty of this, but I am. What about you?

I'm here to tell you that there's a wind blowing. The name of the wind is healing. If you've been wounded – there's healing for you. Run from house to house and find your friends and family who've been wounded. Tell them that there's a wind blowing, and it's called healing. When Israel was hurt and wounded, God spoke through Jeremiah that a day was coming where the people of God would be healed. That day is now! Jeremiah 33:6: "Behold, I will bring to it (God's people) health and healing, and I will heal them and reveal to them abundance of prosperity and security." (ESV) Not only healing, but peace, security, and the discovery of God's abundance.

It's time for healing. It's time that you and people you know who've been wounded in the church step into the wind. It's time for people to be restored and for each and every person to once again serve the Lord with joy and awe. God's cry is that there's healing in His wings. Malachi 4:2: "But for you who fear my name, the Son of Righteousness will rise with healing in his wings. And you will go free, leaping with joy like calves let out to pasture." (TLB)

There's a wind blowing, and it's declaring that it's time for healing.

Day 170

THOUGHT OF THE DAY: It's time for healing - Part 2

When I awoke this morning and was taking the dogs out, I heard "You (meaning all of us) can help the wind of healing to blow." I asked Him how. He replied, "By forgiving."

Immediately I thought about the number of people who needed forgiveness but had never asked for it. He replied, "Neither did the people who mocked and crucified my son, but he forgave them anyway." Luke 22:34: "Then Jesus said, 'Father, forgive them, for they do not know what they do.' "

Almost immediately I saw us knocking on doors. This was a prophetic picture of us going to people and speaking our forgiveness. But who, Lord? I began to close my eyes, and names and faces came to my mind. I had a feeling come over me. In fact, I had several emotions flood my heart and mind. I could see that I was still wounded by the actions and words of others. Under my breath I said I wasn't ready. I became more aware of the hurt I was carrying and realized that the pain was still there and at times affected my attitude and sometimes my decisions.

It didn't take the Holy Spirit very long to speak to me about the parable of the unforgiving servant in Matthew 18. You remember the servant who was forgiven his great debt but didn't forgive the debt of another? Matthew 18:32-35:

Then his master, after he had called him, said to him, "You wicked servant! I forgave you all that debt because you begged me. Should you not also have had compassion on your fellow servant, just as I had pity on you?" And his master was angry, and delivered him to the torturers/torments (demons) until he should pay all that was due to him. So My heavenly Father also will do to you if each of you, from his heart, does not forgive his brother his trespasses.

I can feel the struggle in my heart. I don't really want to forgive. But...I realize that neither myself nor those who hurt me can be truly healed and set free until I speak these three words – I forgive you. Speaking these words is like a prophetic breath/wind, even though I end up struggling with the question of whether they'll realize how much they hurt me.

In the end, we don't ask the wind to blow; it just blows. Whether a person realizes it or not, we must breathe on them as Ezekiel did in the story of the dry bones. In Ezekiel 37:3 God asks this question - "And He said to me, 'Son of man, can these bones live?' " You see, God knew if Ezekiel would breathe/speak on the dry bones, that something supernatural would take place. If we speak, "I forgive you," watch and see what will happen.

I know some of you are thinking that you can't possibly approach the person who's hurt you. So what do you do? Write a note and say something to the effect of "It's quite possible you don't know how much you hurt me, but you did. I want you to know that I forgive you."

If the person who hurt us has died, we can speak forgiveness and release upon that person and their family. This will nullify the effects of unforgiveness on both yourself, your family, and the family you're forgiving and releasing.. If some of you are thinking that you don't want to forgive and release, then you're setting yourself up to be tormented. Here is what Matthew 18:35 says, "So My heavenly Father also will do to you if each of you, (allow us to be tormented) from his heart, does not forgive his brother his trespasses."

Think on this: we carry the wind of healing! Here is what Matthew 6:12 says, "And forgive us our debts, as we have forgiven our debtors [letting go of both the wrong and the resentment]." (Amplified Bible)

It's time for healing... Oh, and we've all been anointed to heal. Isaiah 61:1: "The Spirit of the Lord God is upon Me, Because the Lord has anointed Me to preach good tidings to the poor; He has sent Me to heal the brokenhearted."

It's time for healing... The wind of healing is blowing, and we're part of that wind.

Day 171

THOUGHT OF THE DAY: It's time for healing - Part 3
Unquestionably the wind for healing is blowing!

As I was musing about this, it came to me that there's another component to breathing the breath of God, and that we can play a major role in this wind called healing.

Yesterday we learned that we can say the three words "I forgive you" and so create a supernatural wind which will achieve supernatural results. This morning I heard five more words that we're being called to speak. After all, remember Proverbs 18:21: "Death and life are in the power of the tongue."

These five words are very powerful, but to be honest, difficult to utter. We may even ask how in the world we can do it. The answer is simple: it won't be from your own power, but from the power of the Holy Spirit.

What are the five words? They are: "I'm sorry. Please forgive me."

Let's be honest; these are very difficult to say. We've been focusing on our need for healing, but what about us bringing healing to others? Wouldn't we love if people who've hurt us said they're sorry and asked us to forgive them?

It's really clear. We want healing for our lives. Shouldn't we want healing for the lives of others? Acts 4:29 says: "Grant to Your servants that with all boldness they may speak Your word." Amazing to think that the prayer for boldness would bring us to seek people out and utter the words, "I'm sorry. Please forgive me."

In many cases doing this may seem impossible. Yet the answer we know is Luke 1:37: "For with God nothing will be impossible," and Matthew 17:20: "I say to you, if you have faith as a mustard seed, you will say to this mountain, 'Move from here to there,' and it will move; and nothing will be impossible for you."

Yes, I know: quoting scriptures is one thing; living their message is another.

My simple prayer this morning is this – "Father, help! Give us the courage and boldness to carry and speak healing to those we have hurt."

Yes, five words – I'm sorry. Please forgive me!

It's time for healing!

Day 172

THOUGHT OF THE DAY: It's time for healing - Part 4

It's funny; I was just about to write about another thought I received this morning, but as I sat down, the Lord said, "You're not done with 'It's time for healing.' What you left out was the need to forgive and release yourself."

Oh wow... How true this is. Often our inability to forgive or accept forgiveness from others is hindered and limited by the fact that we haven't forgiven ourselves, and our attitudes towards others are often a reflection of that. Hard to give grace and mercy if you're not experiencing it yourself.

Think about this: the Father has totally forgiven us through the complete and perfect atonement for our sins in Jesus' shed blood. If this is the case - that God has forgiven and released us from our sins - have we in turn, forgiven ourselves in certain areas? If we haven't, we're certainly still prisoners to our guilt and shame.

This hinders us from forgiving others. It hinders our ability to love others and yes, even ourselves. When we choose not to forgive ourselves, it becomes a form of idolatry.

Idolatry? Yes, idolatry. If God forgives us, then who are we not to forgive ourselves? What we're saying through our unforgiveness is that, in effect, our standards are greater than God's - that forgiving ourselves is greater and harder than God forgiving us. In so doing we put ourselves above God.

The concept of forgiving ourselves is often something we've never thought about. As I'm writing this, I can see the Holy Spirit asking each of us - "Have you forgiven yourself?" Perhaps we've forgiven ourselves in some areas but not in others. Just as we need to continually forgive others and be forgiven by them, we must also be consistent in forgiving ourselves.

I get a picture in my mind of the angel of the Lord opening the prison cell for Peter and him staying there until the angel gave him a "dope slap" to wake him up. Acts 12:7: "Now behold, an angel of the Lord stood by him, and a light shone in the prison; and he struck Peter on the side and raised him up, saying, 'Arise quickly!' And his chains fell off his hands." Interesting that "the chains fell off."

It's time for healing, so forgive yourself!

Day 173

THOUGHT OF THE DAY: Alone

Are there times when you try and connect with others but can't? Are there times when you're looking for comfort, and there is none? Are there times when you're looking for someone to understand or give you some insight, but no matter who you speak with there's no understanding? Are there times when you're around people but still feel lonely?

Aren't there numerous times that you just feel alone?

Often we feel this way because Abba is calling us to come away and be with Him, and it's important that we follow His promptings because it's in these moments that the Holy Spirit does some amazing stuff in us. Jesus himself purposed to be alone, as one translation puts it, "to talk with God." Matthew 14:23: "After he had sent them away (multitudes), he went up on the hill by himself to talk with God. Evening came and he was there alone." (WE Bible) Notice he sent people away for this specific purpose.

Is the Holy Spirit telling you to create some alone time?

In Genesis 32 Jacob was left alone. We have to hear that - "He was left alone." Why? Because God wanted to change him forever. In fact he was so changed that he was given a new name and a new identity... Here is Genesis 32:24-28:

Then Jacob was left alone; and a Man wrestled with him until the breaking of day. Now when He saw that He did not prevail against him, He touched the socket of his hip; and the socket of Jacob's hip was out of joint as He wrestled with him. And He said, "Let Me go, for the day breaks." But he said, "I will not let You go unless You bless me!" So He said to him, "What is your name?'" He said, "Jacob." And He said, "Your name shall no longer be called Jacob, but Israel"

Being alone is often a struggle, but if we don't give up, the reward is amazing.

Yes, there are times when we feel alone, as if we're the only ones going through something. We're weary, tired of the battle, and begin feeling sorry for ourselves. Well, we can identify with Elijah, can't we? Remember in 2 Kings 18 verses 10 and 14 when Elijah tells God, "I am left alone."

I've been there. It's the "only me" mindset, or alternatively "the poor me syndrome." It's when we feel like we're facing major things, and with Satan's help, our emotions distort the truth. In verse 18 God tells Elijah that he's wrong and that there are actually 7,000 people just like him.

I so appreciate knowing that other people have been and are going through the same things I am. It's comforting that I'm not alone.

The place of being alone is the place the Holy Spirit does work in us, a place God has ordained to change us forever... I'm thinking "Count me in," and I hear "Oh ya, you're already counted in."

Day 174

THOUGHT OF THE DAY: Pressure

Today is May ninth, and I leave for Romania on Wednesday, May 13 for two weeks. People have asked me if I've raised enough money for my trip, and with a chuckle I tell them no, not yet. I say that because I'm confident that in time, He'll supply.

In the midst of preparing for Romania, the pressure surrounding my life has been unbelievable. A number of weeks ago while sharing on a Sunday morning, I took a tube of toothpaste and squeezed it until it was empty. At the time I knew little of the extent to which this prophetic picture would capture the events of the coming weeks. You see, under pressure, what's in us comes out. God will use circumstances to help us see what's really inside.

So what's in you? What are you going through? What are the things that are coming out of your mouth? What kinds of things are you thinking? What does your body language communicate? Are you moody and cranky? Is your focus on the pressures in your life rather than looking at your God who grants us His peace in your circumstances?

We tend to want to escape our circumstances rather than placing our expectations on the Lord. I love Isaiah 43:1-4. Please read it slowly and let each word impact your heart.

But now, thus says the Lord, who created you, O Jacob, And He who formed you, O Israel: "Fear not, for I have redeemed you; I have called you by your name; You are Mine. When you pass through the waters, I will be with you; And through the rivers, they shall not overflow you. When you walk through the fire, you shall not be burned, Nor shall the flame scorch you. For I am the Lord your God, The Holy One of Israel, your Savior; I gave Egypt for your ransom, Ethiopia and Seba in your place. Since you were precious in My sight, You have been honored, And I have loved you."

You can read this over and over again. Key to this passage is the word "WHEN," not IF, but "WHEN."

Second Corinthians 4:7-9 says that we have this treasure from God, but we are only clay jars which hold it. "This is to show that the amazing power we have is from God, not from us. We have troubles all around us, but we are not defeated. We often don't know what to do, but we don't give up. We are persecuted, but God does not leave us."

Can't we all relate to having "trouble all around us?" Yet the pressure we're all under is part of a larger refining process. In Malachi three it says, "He will purify the Levites, the ministers of God, refining them like gold or silver, so that they will do their work for God with pure hearts." (TLB) Oh, praise God that it's all for a divine purpose.

The pressure is for our refinement...

Day 175

THOUGHT OF THE DAY: A day declared to be a new beginning

Yesterday was a supernatural day, yet it couldn't be seen by the natural eye or perceived by the natural mind.

Yesterday marked our first service in the new building. Interestingly, it was Mother's Day. A time of birth. The birth of something new. Yesterday morning while musing with the Lord He told me to declare that yesterday was a day of new beginnings. As I spoke that, I looked into a number of eyes and could hear people yelling inside themselves. "YES, TODAY IS MY NEW BEGINNING!"

For us as a church it was also a day to begin anew. He was telling us to step into each day and live with expectation. How exciting is this, to actually determine that going forward we'll make a conscious decision to live with expectancy.

As I was studying beginnings, I came across the following verse in the book of Job. The verse is meant to be personal as well as corporate. The Holy Spirit spoke this over us. Perhaps He's speaking this over you. Read each one slowly. Meditate on it, and let it sink deep inside:

Job 8:7 (ESV): "And though your beginning was small, your latter days will be very great."

Job 8:7 (CEB): "Although your former state was ordinary, your future will be extraordinary."

Job 8:7 (CJB): "Then, although your beginnings were small, your future will be very great indeed."

Job 8:7 (CEV): "Your future will be brighter by far than your past."

There are times we all need a new beginning and a fresh start, to wake up and find that whatever was in the past is literally gone as if it never happened. This is what Paul meant by Philippians 3:13: "Brethren, I do not count myself to have apprehended; but one thing I do, forgetting those things which are behind and reaching forward to those things which are ahead." (NKJV)

For the Lord declares this a day of NEW BEGINNINGS...

Day 176

THOUGHT OF THE DAY: Did you hear?

I have been up just a short while, awaking with a burden on my heart. As I sat to muse, the burden grew stronger and my eyes began to fill with tears. I could see an old prophet standing on a mountain shouting, "They do not hear, for the day of new beginnings has begun, and they have not heard that the winds of change are blowing."

I don't want to be critical, but something is wrong. Where is the passion I once saw? Where is the commitment and sacrifice I once saw? Where is the joy I once saw when I saw the fulfillment of Psalm 122:1: "I was glad when they said to me, 'Let us go into the house of the Lord.'"

My heart is broken! In the book of Jude he's seeing the church's condition and in his closing remarks says in chapter 20: "But you, dear friends, must build up your lives ever more strongly upon the foundation of our holy faith, learning to pray in the power and strength of the Holy Spirit."(TLB) He calls them DEAR FRIENDS, but all the same says that THEY bear the responsibility for building themselves up in the SPIRIT.

In 1 Samuel 30 David had returned from fighting only to find that his own home in the town of Ziklag had been raided and destroyed. Everything was gone - woman, children, livestock; EVERYTHING. David and his men wept until they couldn't weep any more. Finally, their weeping turned to anger, and David's own men wanted to stone him. David too was weeping and grieving, and then we find this phrase in verse six: "And David was greatly distressed, for the people spoke of stoning him because the soul of all the people was bitter, each one for his sons and for his daughters; but David encouraged himself in the LORD his God." (JUB) The key was David taking action to encourage himself.

What am I saying? The need for a new fire in the church is not only in the corporate gathering, but in each and every one of us. Our response: WELL, LET'S START OUR OWN FIRE!" Proverbs 26:20 says, "Where there is no wood, the fire goes out."

In Haggai the church was stuck, and the building of the temple stopped because people became preoccupied with their own lives. Does this sound familiar? Haggai said, "Consider your ways." Verses 7-8:"Thus says the Lord of hosts: 'Consider your ways! Go up to the mountains and bring wood and build the temple, that I may take pleasure in it and be glorified,' says the Lord."

It sounds like I'm on a rant this morning. I have such a burden that we would see the glory of God not only in the corporate church but also the fulfillment of Isaiah 60:2: "But the Lord will arise over you, And His glory will be seen upon you."

I believe that the winds of change are blowing and am convinced that our Father is doing new things - things that have been hidden and have been kept a secret...But God is about to reveal them to his children.

Isaiah 48:6-7: "You heard and saw everything that happened, so you should tell this news to others. Now I will tell you about new things, hidden things that you don't know yet. These things are happening now, not long ago; you have not heard about them before today. So you cannot say, 'We already knew about that.' " (NCV)

New means new; not a remodeling of the past. What God is about to do is going to be so radical. The church won't need more lights, smoke machines, greater and louder music, or more clever programs. It's at our door. It's not a makeover of what was; it's NEW. You might ask me, what is it? I don't really know, but I'm pursuing it. The word says, "It's created now."

Isaiah 60:1: "Arise [from the depression and prostration in which circumstances have kept you—rise to a new life]! Shine (be radiant with the glory of the Lord), for your light has come, and the glory of the Lord has risen upon you!" (AMP)

Did you hear?

Day 177

THOUGHT OF THE DAY: There is a voice speaking from heaven

As I began to muse with the Lord, I again saw an old prophet dressed in clothing common to ancient Israel. As I write this, I see that he's changed clothing and looks like one of us. He is again yelling something, and despite the fact that everyone below can hear the echo of his voice, very few are responding.

The streets are full of people going about their everyday routines, busy and preoccupied by their daily tasks. I can hear the comments of the people, "Oh it's that prophet again. What does he want now?" The old prophet, though, is the Holy Spirit declaring the word of the Lord.

Can you hear it? He's shouting Isaiah 6:8: "I heard the voice of the Lord, saying: 'Whom shall I send, And who will go for Us?' " If you close your eyes you can hear it! "Whom will I send?"

He doesn't want to send us to where we're not anointed. He wants to take each of us and send us where we're gifted. He would not send a plumber to do an electrician's job, nor send a hair dresser to pick up a trowel. However we're constructed, whatever our DNA prescribes, that is where He wants to send us. You might not be called to Haiti but are instead called to your own "sphere of influence."

There is silence, and with his hands lifted up and his eyes fixed on heaven, Isaiah says, "Here am I! Send me." What will our response be?

There's a voice speaking from heaven!! "Whom shall I send, and who will go for us?"

And we say???

Day 178

THOUGHT OF THE DAY: Get ready for radical change

This is what we'll hear in church today. The ground is shaking! Angels are being released! Can this be a form of revival?

We often evaluate ourselves by looking at what we're not instead of seeing the value of who we are and how we can help set a vision for our church community. As we all look at who we are in relationship to a church's vision, we first have to "blow up" our present and past concepts of what a church look likes.

Imagine how difficult it was to go from an old testament church and all of its rituals and traditions to a new testament church. You may have made the same kind of change yourselves and experienced the culture shock of leaving your traditional church and walking through the door of a more pentecostal/charismatic variety!

We have to be prepared to radically rethink what the church should look like. God is not looking to remodel or do a makeover! Remember that each church community will look different from another. Our heart is to discover who and what we are and not try to compare ourselves with any other church, either in the same city or elsewhere.

Is it possible that we're being realigned to fulfill Mark 16:15: "Then he said to them, 'As you go throughout the world, proclaim the Good News to all creation.' "?(CLB) Notice it says, "As you go or as you're going," implying that we learn this only AFTER we start moving.

Get ready for radical change! The church is about to be revolutionized...

Day 179

THOUGHT OF THE DAY: What is the radical new church?

For years we've been asking people to come to church. Is it time instead that the church went to the people?

The early disciples went to the people; they didn't ask them to come to a building. Something has to change!

Is it possible that we've been fishing on the wrong side of the boat for awhile now? Remember in John 21 that they'd labored all night and didn't catch anything. Is it possible that we've all been laboring and haven't seen the results we believe we should've had? Yes, we've had a measure of success in the past. Is it time for a change?

In John 21:6 look at what happened. Could this happen again? "And He said to them, 'Cast the net on the right side of the boat, and you will find some.' So they cast, and now they were not able to draw it in because of the multitude of fish."

It may be time to build the church (people) outside of the walls of the building or else restructure it to offer training in diversified areas. Who is God going to use to do this? Inside our churches are people who have incredible gifts and talents that often lie dormant. I call it buried treasure, which, in the end, is our responsibility to unearth.

We've been looking at what we don't have while all along missing what we do have. We've been looking outside of the church for help in building the kingdom while all along God's provision has been right in the house. We need to capture the Spirit of Elisha. In 2 kings 4:2 it says, " 'Tell me, what do you have in the house?' And she said, 'Your maidservant has nothing in the house but a jar of oil.' " Like the widow, we haven't seen what we do have in our churches, and God will cause increase as we present each person the opportunity to be used by Him.

What do we have in our churches? We have jars that God has and will fill to accomplish His purposes. We have done a reasonable job at teaching and training people in spiritual gifts, but we haven't done well at raising people up and assigning them value in who they are. There's the plumber who can reach people through plumbing and moms who can teach/mentor other women to be mothers/wives. The possibilities are endless.

When it came time to build the Tabernacle, who did God use? He chose men like Bezalel who not only used his natural talents to build the Tabernacle (kingdom), but also taught others. Can we follow the pattern of taking what's already inside our church communities to not only build the kingdom, but mentor others?

Take a look at the following verses: Could God be calling people like Bezalel?

Exodus 35:30-34: The Artisans Called by God

And Moses said to the children of Israel, "See, the Lord has called by name Bezalel the son of Uri, the son of Hur, of the tribe of Judah; and He has filled him with the Spirit of God, in wisdom and understanding, in knowledge and all manner of workmanship, to design artistic works, to work in gold and silver and bronze, in cutting jewels for setting, in carving wood, and to work in all manner of artistic workmanship. And He has put in his heart the ability to teach, in him and Aholiab the son of Ahisamach, of the tribe of Dan."

Is God calling His people to operate garages, florist shops, music stores, drop-in centers, and so on? We can make disciples outside of the church by using men and women like Bezalel who are filled with the Spirit of God and wisdom, understanding, and knowledge. They can use their gifts and talents to mentor and make disciples in everyday life, not only because of what's inside of them, but also because of their ability to be mechanics, painters, plumbers, florists, etcetera.

We'll be building the kingdom every day outside the walls of our building, or if possible, we'll offer these things within the diversified structure of our churches. We can host art classes, teach computer skills, and parenting. We can offer personality profiles so people can discover more about their preferences and thus choose professions better suited to their personality types. We can make disciples and preach the gospel of the kingdom through our everyday lives.

It's not about building our churches or having greater attendance, (though this will happen as a result of our kingdom approach). It's about fulfilling the great commission found in Mark 16:15: "Then he said to them, 'As you go throughout the world, proclaim the Good News to all creation.' " (CJB) Notice it says "as you go" or "as you're going."

The radical church is being empowered and released to fulfill the purposes of God.

Day 180

THOUGHT OF THE DAY: You are special

If you would take a moment and just muse on the fact that out of all the billions of people in the world, God chose YOU!

I believe that once we truly perceive and believe this, when we're rejected or devalued we can remember who we are and that we've been "accepted in the Beloved." (Ephesians 1:6) We should feel special, because we are!

In fact, that is what God says in Deuteronomy 14:2: "For you are a holy people to the Lord your God; the Lord your God has chosen you to be a people for Himself, a special treasure above all the peoples on the face of the earth." We are chosen and special! Here is what the Message Bible says about us: 1 Peter 2:9-10: "But you are the ones chosen by God, chosen for the high calling of priestly work, chosen to be a holy people, God's instruments to do his work and speak out for him, to tell others of the night-and-day difference he made for you—from nothing to something, from rejected to accepted."

We have been supernaturally changed from nothing to something. We've been called to be His instruments of grace! Hey, you are special!

God chooses and He ordains. If you've been waiting to be ordained; know that you already are. That's what's said in John 15:16: "You have not chosen me, but I have chosen you, and ordained (appointed) you, that you go and bring forth fruits, and that your fruit remain."

LISTEN, YOU ARE SPECIAL!

Day 181

THOUGHT OF THE DAY: Overwhelmed

I awoke this morning with this question on my mind. Who am I? Who am I that God would choose me? Even now it's too much to grasp. In 1 Chronicles 17:16 David goes into the tabernacle to pray a prayer of thanksgiving. I must admit it's been a while since I've done that. How about you? Here's David's prayer: "Then King David went into the Tent of the Lord's presence, sat down, and prayed, 'I am not worthy of what you have already done for me, Lord God, nor is my family.' " (GNT) He went and sat in the Lord's presence.

Stop here and let's do that.

What did you hear? I heard, "I have been waiting for you to come. To tell you how much I love you and how important you are. Stop doing things in your own strength when you can have mine." I asked what He was saying to others, and He said, "What THEY NEED TO HEAR." I need to muse a while on what He said, otherwise I'll devalue it and not fully receive it.

So before I do that, here's how the Message Bible puts it: 1 Chronicles 17:16-20:

Who am I, my Master God, and what is my family, that you have brought me to this place in life? But that's nothing compared to what's coming, for you've also spoken of my family far into the future, given me a glimpse into tomorrow and looked on me, Master God, as a Somebody. What's left for David to say to this—to your honoring your servant, even though you know me, just as I am? O God, out of the goodness of your heart, you've taken your servant to do this great thing and put your great work on display. There's none like you, God.

Did you see what David said? He sees his family as also blessed. He sees into the future and gets a glimpse of his tomorrow. He says, God, you made me to be a somebody, even though you know everything about me.

I just want to shout! It's because of God's goodness, His heart! David was right, "There is none like you."

Overwhelmed! Please go back and meditate/muse over what God said to you. Don't miss the moment.

Day 182

THOUGHT OF THE DAY: From A. W. Tozer

We are desperate to hear the prophetic voice to the church. Here is an excerpt from a book written by A. W. Tozer called Of God and Men. Tozer lived from April 21, 1897 – May 12, 1963. If he saw the need in his day, then what about now?

One of the quotes from his book is found in numerous devotionals. It says, "A prophet is one who knows his times and what God is trying to say to the people of his times."

We're all desperate to truly understand the times we're living in so we can impact those around us. Tozer goes on to say,

What God says to His church at any given period depends altogether upon her moral and spiritual condition and upon the spiritual need of the hour. Religious leaders who continue mechanically to expound the Scriptures without regard to the current religious situation are no better than the scribes and lawyers of Jesus' day who faithfully parroted the Law without the remotest notion of what was going on around them spiritually. They fed the same diet to all and seemed wholly unaware that there was such a thing as meat in due season. The prophets never made that mistake nor wasted their efforts in that manner. They invariably spoke to the condition of the people of their times.

I often say that we must understand the culture where God sends us to minister. For example, the cultures of Haiti and the Dominican Republic are different, even though they're on the same island. We can be more effective if we understand who the natives are as a people, like the sons of Issachar who were said to have "understanding of the times, to know what Israel ought to do." (1 Chronicles 12:32)

Let's seek wisdom for it. I'm confident that when we seek wisdom, our Father gives it to us.

Day 183

THOUGHT OF THE DAY: Oh, time, where have you gone?

This morning I looked on Facebook, and my son had posted a number of pictures of our family from 20 or so years back. Where has time gone? What mistakes have I made that I can share with you so that you might not make the same?

Here are a few:

- God, FAMILY...ministry
- God, FAMILY, ministry
- There is an appointed time for everything. I spent too much time trying to influence God to speed things up
- God's not in a hurry
- I didn't ask Him about timing
- I didn't appreciate the small things
- I was always looking past today looking for what wasn't instead of living in the moment
- I didn't cherish relationships as I do today, telling people how much they mean to me
- I didn't spend nearly enough time in just being with God. I always had something to say. Always telling Him what to do, how to do it, and when to do it
- I should have just enjoyed being in His presence
- I should have worshipped and listened more
- I didn't learn, and I mean learn, contentment for many years. Please learn it
- I didn't know how to simply rest

- I didn't know how to turn my mind off. Isaiah says a mind that is focused on God is a person at peace.
- I didn't realize how fast time would pass
- I preached too many sermons trying to convince people, not knowing that that is the Holy Spirit's job
- Forgive and release people and then go on to step three: BLESS THEM AND BLESS THEIR LIVES
- Learn to discern what God is doing and realize that He just wants to be with us
- Ask God what He really thinks instead of convincing Him that such and such is a great idea
- I didn't realize I was truly adopted. I was and am a SON of God
- God not only loves me but has affection for me
- Micah 6:8: "He has shown you, O man, what is good; And what does the Lord require of you but to do justly, to love mercy, and to walk humbly with your God."

About a week ago walking past our garden I heard the flowers singing the Hallelujah Chorus. I stopped to listen. Then as I walked to our steps, I could hear the rhododendrons singing the same chorus, but the bass part instead.

I want to say thank you for who you all are. I am thankful for your friendship, love, prayers, and emotional - and as you are led - financial support. THANK YOU!

The great news is that we can redeem the time, and God will restore the fields the locusts have devoured!

Oh, time, where have you gone?

Day 184

THOUGHT OF THE DAY: Consider this

For months now I've been frustrated with the majority of worship music on Youtube and have been searching for new, fresh, and intimate worship songs. But... I keep on hearing noise.

Here is what it says in Amos 5:23: "Take away from Me the noise of your songs, For I will not hear the melody of your stringed instruments." The Message Bible puts it this way, "I can't stand your religious meetings. I'm fed up with your conferences and conventions. I want nothing to do with your religion projects, your pretentious slogans and goals. I'm sick of your fund-raising schemes, your public relations and image making. I've had all I can take of your noisy ego-music. When was the last time you sang to me?"

Sadly, in most of our churches we have songs that are well presented and produced. They sound good and people enjoy them, but they do not carry the presence of God. If we want to see signs and wonders, we need the presence of God. So, if we can't find it (presence of God), then we have to create it.

Lift your hands and begin to sing and speak the things that come into your heart. Perhaps we are looking to others for something we are to do. As you do this, have a pen and paper nearby and write down the things you hear, because He's going to speak!

The time has come for each of us to cultivate our own anointing. Time for us to believe we carry the presence of God wherever we go. You're it... God's anointed son or daughter.

The question is... who's waiting for whom? I believe He's waiting for us.

Consider this.

Day 185

THOUGHT OF THE DAY: Are we listening?

In the book of Judges 2:17 it says, "Yet they would not listen to their judges." Is there anyone out there who's listening? We all have selective hearing. We hear the things we want to hear but all too often turn a deaf ear to things that challenge us or that we find difficult. We forget that as Jesus said in John 14:10: "The Father who dwells in Me does the work."

Father, help us to know you will do the work. I can hear Zechariah 8:15: "So again in these days I am determined to do good to Jerusalem and to the house of Judah. Do not fear."

Can we grasp this? The Holy Spirit is saying that he's made his mind up to do good to the people of God. Israel had just come through a period of time where God was disciplining them, but now it was time to work on the behalf of its people. God has made His mind up that He's going to work a work that will be hard for us to grasp or believe. I am fully persuaded something is up...

What are we to do? In 1 Samuel 18:14 it says, "And David behaved wisely in all his ways, and the Lord was with him." That seems so simple; whatever we do we are to as Micah 6:8 says, do it "justly," to simply do what's right. Yes, it is easier said than done, and it's time to step forward and become the people God has called, anointed, and appointed us to be. Look again at what it says, "and the Lord was WITH THEM."

Are we listening? For we are about to see Habakkuk 1:5: "Look around at the godless nations. Look long and hard. Brace yourself for a

shock. Something's about to take place and you're going to find it hard to believe."
BRACE YOURSELVES!

Day 186

Thought of the Day: So you want revival

I don't think there's one of us who doesn't want to see revival sweep through every village, town and city throughout the world. We can't wait for the manifest love and power of God to be experienced by every person. We can't wait to see people healed and delivered in untold numbers. We're yearning to see countless people commit their lives to Jesus. We're praying the prayer of Acts 4:29-30: "Grant to Your servants that with all boldness they may speak Your word, by stretching out Your hand to heal, and that signs and wonders may be done through the name of Your holy Servant Jesus."

Yes God, give us boldness, stretch your hand to heal. Yes, let signs and wonders be done through the name of Jesus. Are you excited now? Perhaps we missed the beginning of verse 29: "Now, Lord, look on their threats." With the power of God comes resistance. And from whom? Let's see what revival brings and then ask ourselves if we're ready for it.

Let's go back to Acts chapter three. The apostles had been preaching, and Christ and Peter and John are used by God to heal the man at the Gate of Beautiful. This is exciting, but look what happens next. Peter and John get arrested and spend the night in jail. Yay, jail! Acts 4:1-3: "Now as they spoke to the people, the priests, the captain of the temple, and the Sadducees came upon them, being greatly disturbed that they taught the people and preached in Jesus the resurrection from the dead. And they laid hands on them, and put them in custody until the next day, for it was already evening." Then in verse 17 it says, "Let us severely threaten them, that from now on they speak to no man in this name."

Am I saying that with revival will come problems? Yes. Are we ready for them?

This was not a new problem. We read in Matthew 14:10 that John the Baptist is beheaded. "So he sent and had John beheaded in prison." In Matthew 26:3-4 the religious leaders plot to kill Jesus and eventually do crucify him. "Then the chief priests, the scribes, and the elders of the people assembled at the palace of the high priest, who was called Caiaphas, and plotted to take Jesus by trickery and kill Him."

And in Acts 5:14-16 this is what happened after the prayer for boldness and power: "And believers were increasingly added to the Lord, multitudes of both men and women, so that they brought the sick out into the streets and laid them on beds and couches, that at least the shadow of Peter passing by might fall on some of them. Also a multitude gathered from the surrounding cities to Jerusalem, bringing sick people and those who were tormented by unclean spirits, and they were all healed." This is awesome but we have verse 33: "When they (religious leaders) heard this, they were furious and plotted to kill them." Now Verses 40-41: "And they agreed with him (high priest), and when they had called for the apostles and beaten them, they commanded that they should not speak in the name of Jesus, and let them go."

"So they departed from the presence of the council, rejoicing that they were counted worthy to suffer shame for His name." Am I suggesting that a worldwide revival could cause a reaction we might not be prepared for? Yes! Did you see how they rejoiced that they were beaten?

Wherever God moved, persecution came with it. In Acts 9:23-24 Paul's life gets threatened, "Now after many days were past, the Jews plotted to kill him (Saul/Paul)." We know Paul is in and out of prison and is eventually killed. Acts 12:2 says they killed James, "Then he killed James the brother of John with the sword."

Yes, we want revival, but I'm suggesting that we also need to be prepared for the reaction to the kind of revival we yearn to see and be part of.

So you want revival?

Day 187

THOUGHT OF THE DAY: Father, you promised!

I haven't written for a few days, because I've been struggling with a thought that I've had.

There are times when we get a thought/word from the Lord and have an initial response. Yet for me, my initial response is usually not all there is to the matter. If I had written how I was feeling a few days ago, for example, it would've lacked balance and wouldn't have reflected God's heart. Instead it would've been my knee-jerk reaction to what I'd heard. In the past I've spoken prematurely, not spending enough time musing with the Lord to gain the entire perspective on what He was saying.

If you go back and review the last few posts, you can see I was and still am carrying a burden for us as a people of God; even more than that, as sons and daughters of God. I'm yearning to see "the goodness of God in the land of the living." We are crying out for the fulfillment of Joel 2:28-29: "And it shall come to pass afterward. That I will pour out My Spirit on all flesh; Your sons and your daughters shall prophesy, Your old men shall dream dreams, Your young men shall see visions. And also on My menservants and on My maidservants. I will pour out My Spirit in those days."

I've been writing and asking us to reflect on the condition of the church and the condition of our own lives. I wrote the thought, "Consider this" where a part of Amos 5 was quoted from the Message Bible; "I can't stand your religious meetings. I'm fed up with your conferences and conventions. I want nothing to do with your religion projects, your pretentious slogans and goals. I'm sick of your fund-raising schemes, your public relations and image making. I've had all I can take of your noisy ego-music. When was the last time you sang to me?"

Then the next day I wrote, "Are we listening" and I quoted Judges 2:17 which says, "Yet they would not listen to their judges." Is there anyone out there who's listening? I wrote that I believe we all have selective hearing and that God has made his mind up to do some amazing things. The question was and is, are we listening? Next I wrote "So you want revival?" which was about accepting the persecution which inevitably comes with it.

The next day the Holy Spirit led me to Haggai where it says, "Consider your ways." My first response was to look at Haggai when the work had stopped on the temple for 15 years, and God asked the people why. He wanted them to ask themselves why the church was in that condition. Yesterday in church I asked the same question and asked the congregation to respond. What would you say?

One of the things Haggai told them was to "Climb the mountain and bring wood to build the temple." What is it that we can do to help bring about a move of God? What can we bring? I spoke to a friend of mine who's a musician, and when he heard "what can I bring," immediately God told him to "bring new songs."

What can we bring? Is God waiting for us? Proverbs says, "If you don't put wood on the fire, the fire goes out." Are we putting wood on the fire?

One thought is that perhaps we've been trying to build the church when we were called to build the kingdom. Jesus said in Matthew 16:18, "I will build My church."

We are all waiting for God to pour out His Spirit! I believe the Lord wants us to do some reflecting. Would you take the time?

Father, you did promise...

Day 188

THOUGHT OF THE DAY: It's time we stop looking at what we don't have

It was a couple weeks ago when I realized that I was looking at what our church didn't have, and because my focus was on what we didn't have, it hindered what we could do.

Then the Holy Spirit spoke to me from 2 Kings 4:2 where the widow of a prophet is in debt and is pleading with Elisha for help. I believe that far too often in our personal and corporate lives we're looking at what we don't have instead of looking at what we do. This applies to our gifts and talents. We're saying to ourselves, "I'm not that talented, not that gifted, not that anointed." I remember the disciples asking Jesus to increase their faith, and he responded by telling them to use the faith they had.

Instead we keep looking for another time or another day. We look to other people rather than looking at what's in us today. That's part of the wind of change. What's in us? It's Christ in us, the hope of glory!

It's time we stopped listening to the voice of insecurity, the belittling spirit.

Remember the story in Luke 9:13-14 where the crowd had been following Jesus all day. It was getting late, and Jesus realized that the people were hungry and needed to be fed. So he turned to his disciples and said, " 'You give them something to eat.' The disciples respond, 'Are You kidding? There are at least 5,000 men here, not to mention women and children. All we have are five loaves and two fish. The only way we could provide for them would be to go to a nearby city and buy cartloads of food. That would cost a small fortune.' " (Voice Bible, 1-14)

The disciples made the same mistake we often make when we look at the impossibility of a task. We immediately begin to assess the little we have or look at what we can put together using our own skill or ability. We look to ourselves rather than looking to the Lord. Yes, our natural mind chokes out divine possibilities.

This has to stop! Instead of focusing on what we don't have, let's recognize what we do have and how the Holy Spirit can increase it. The disciples were looking for an earthly solution. Our answer is not in the natural realm, but in the realm of the Spirit.

We have to catch the wind of change! It's the "I can" Spirit, not the "I can't." We are the Holy Spirit's greatest secret weapons!

It's time we stop looking at what we don't have!

Day 189

THOUGHT OF THE DAY: When you're overwhelmed

There are some days and even some weeks and months when we're overwhelmed, and the weight of what we're facing can cause us to be depressed, discouraged, despondent, disheartened, disappointed, disillusioned, and more. To be honest I don't like those days. In the midst of them I want a few minutes of prayer and worship to deliver me from the pit I'm in.

When prayer doesn't seem to work, then I try worship. When that doesn't work, I have a choice to stay in my mess or press in and through.

Remember in 1 Samuel 30 when David returns to his hometown of Ziklag after fighting the Philistines? He returns only to find that everyone had been taken captive and the town burned. The Amplified Bible says in verse six, "David was greatly distressed, for the men spoke of stoning him because the souls of them all were bitterly grieved, each man for his sons and daughters."

So what did David do? "David encouraged and strengthened himself in the Lord his God." This is more than a five-minute process. You literally have to press through your feelings, emotions, and even the lack of God's presence, and refuse to stay in your mess.

It says David encouraged/strengthened himself. There are times we're hoping our husband or wife will encourage us. Sometimes when that doesn't work, we look to a friend or our pastor, but that doesn't work either. In the end we find ourselves left alone to press in as Jesus did in the Garden of Gethsemane where it says he "began to be sorrowful and deeply distressed." (Matthew 26:37)

Jesus was disappointed with his disciples because when he needed their support, they fell asleep. He had to encourage HIMSELF by praying and did so more than once.

When you're overwhelmed, learn to encourage yourself in the Lord.

Day 190

THOUGHT OF THE DAY: Prayer of Jabez

Over the past two days I've been pleading with God to answer the prayer of Jabez from 1 Chronicles 4:10.

We can't help but plead with God that He'd cause each of us to have a significant increase in our anointing. Reading a newspaper, listening to the radio, or watching the news on television has to cause us to grieve. But I want to go beyond grieving and shaking my head at the condition of the world and see the Holy Spirit intervene in such a way that the world will know that there has been a heavenly invasion. YES, A HEAVENLY INVASION!

I am convinced that God has chosen His people to be the instruments of His goodness and power! The prayer of Paul in Ephesians 1:19-20 is still uttered by the Spirit of God. PLEASE FATHER, WRITE THIS IN OUR HEARTS AND THEN GRANT US THE CONFIDENCE TO SIMPLY GO DO WHAT HE PRAYED. The CEV Bible says, "I want you to know about the great and mighty power that God has for us followers. It is the same wonderful power he used when he raised Christ from death and let him sit at his right side in heaven."

See that, "I WANT YOU TO KNOW ABOUT..." ABOUT WHAT? THE GREAT AND MIGHTY POWER THAT EACH OF US HAS RIGHT NOW. It's not something that's earned; it's a GIFT given to ordinary people - HIS FOLLOWERS!

We need to have the prayer of Jabez answered without delay. What is the prayer of Jabez? It concerns increasing the anointing that affects lives and protects us from the evil one such that God is so alive in us that we won't hurt people.

Here's the Prayer of Jabez from 1 Chronicles 4:10: " 'Oh, Lord, bless me indeed and expand my territory. Keep Your hand on me, and keep evil from me, that I may not cause pain!' And God granted him what he requested."

Day 191

THOUGHT OF THE DAY: God has made a promise

In Genesis 12 God made a promise to 75-year-old Abraham that he would have a son.

What has God promised you? Like Abraham there's often a significant time period between when the promise is given and its fulfillment. The challenge is how to live our lives in the present-day reality and make the decisions which will cultivate and position us to receive the promise. Alternatively, we can make decisions that will hinder, and in some cases, actually kill the promise.

In the case of Saul, it was God's promise that he and his family would govern Israel forever. We know that didn't happen. Why? Saul made numerous decisions which he knew to be contrary to God's word and the direct instructions given to him. In 1 Samuel 13 Saul was told to wait (there's that word - wait) seven days for Samuel to come and make an offering to the Lord before he went to war, but Saul didn't. In verses 11-12 we see Saul's reasoning, "And Samuel said, 'What have you done?' Saul said, 'When I saw that the people were scattered from me, and that you did not come within the days appointed, and that the Philistines gathered together at Michmash, then I said,' "The Philistines will now come down on me at Gilgal, and I have not made supplication to the Lord." 'Therefore I felt compelled, and offered a burnt offering.' "

All too often we're compelled by our reason, emotions, and by what we see with our natural sight instead of what we see by the Spirit. The reality in the present causes the natural man not to see the promises as even a possibility. Our reaction is often to try and fulfill the promises of God through our own ability. We don't like to wait.

Abraham and Sarah are prime examples. They waited 10 years, and when they "SAW" that the promise wasn't fulfilled, they decided by their natural reasoning how they could fulfill the promise that God had made.

We tend to react in two ways – both of them extreme. We either attempt to fulfill something that only God can do, or... we forget what was promised. We forget by not cultivating the promise through our daily relationship with the Lord. Perhaps the biggest promise-killer is DISAPPOINTMENT.

How long have you been waiting? Abraham and Sarah had a son. His name was Ishmael. Sadly, our own reactions birth consequences, but thank God that He's bigger than our poor decisions.

The word in Habakkuk chapter two verse three comes to mind: "Though the vision (promise) tarries, wait for it, for it will SURELY COME."

Lord, help us make the decisions that cultivate your promises.

Day 192

THOUGHT OF THE DAY: It's time to laugh

Ok I've had it... I'm fed up with the tactics of Satan. I'm fed up with Satan using circumstances or causing circumstances in our lives to bring us discouragement, depression, or disappointment. That's it; I'm going to join Elijah!

When Elijah confronts the prophets of Baal on Mt. Carmel, he laughs at them. It's time to step back and tell him that his days of causing us to be discouraged, depressed, and disappointed are over. It's time to follow Elijah's example: "About noontime, Elijah began mocking them. 'You'll have to shout louder than that,' he scoffed, to catch the attention of your god! Perhaps he is talking to someone, or is out sitting on the toilet, or maybe he is away on a trip, or is asleep and needs to be wakened!' " (1 Kings 18:27, TLB)

Satan, we're done with your tactics!

In Ecclesiastes 3:4 it says that there is "a time to weep, and a time to laugh; a time to mourn, and a time to dance." Well, let's declare that it's time to laugh and dance. Proverbs 17:22 says, "A joyful heart is good medicine but depression drains one's strength." (GW) Over the last several months we've all been experiencing one thing after another. Honestly, I can't remember such an on-slot of Satan's attacks against us. He has stolen our joy and laughter. Well, I'm done with that.

In Job 8:21 it says, "He will yet fill your mouth with laughing, And your lips with rejoicing."

Father, fill us with laughter and cause us to rejoice. I am confident that He will do it. Why can I say that? Because I believe 1 Kings 17:22: "Then the Lord heard the voice of Elijah."

Think about it. God heard the voice of a man. Daniel 10:12: "Then he said to me, 'Do not fear, Daniel, for from the first day that you set your heart to understand, and to humble yourself before your God, your words were heard; and I have come because of your words.' "

Listen; it's time to laugh...

Day 193

THOUGHT OF THE DAY: Seeing through joy

When we read Hebrews 12:2 it tells us that Jesus' focus was not on the shame or pain of the cross, but on the joy he saw in his future.

We must never stop looking to Jesus. He is the leader of our faith and the one who makes our faith complete. He suffered death on a cross but accepted the shame of it as if it were nothing because of the joy he could see waiting for him. Do we see that? All his suffering was NOTHING because of the JOY AWAITING HIM. The joy was in his future.

This perspective is developed in 2 Corinthians 4:17-18:

For our light, momentary affliction (this slight distress of the passing hour) is ever more and more abundantly preparing and producing and achieving for us an everlasting weight of glory [beyond all measure, excessively surpassing all comparisons and all calculations, a vast and transcendent glory and blessedness never to cease!] "while we do not look at the things which are seen, but at the things which are not seen. For the things which are seen are temporary, but the things which are not seen are eternal. (AMP)

The reward is IN THE FUTURE.

The two keys are realizing that what we see with our natural eyes is only temporal; what we need to look toward is our tomorrow. This can only be done by seeing with our spiritual eyes. The second key is to think with an eternal perspective, not allowing the present reality to dictate our decisions.

I'm pretty excited. We can see and think from an eternal viewpoint, living our lives with greater joy! We can live in our present reality because we can see the joy of our tomorrow.

Day 194

THOUGHT OF THE DAY: What kind of faith do I have?

During my study time today, I came across an expression from an obscure Bible commentary which floored me. In one of the verses I was studying, it posed the idea that many of us have what the author called "educational faith," a faith based on education, study, and mental ascent.

I had to stop and ask myself what my faith was. Is it in my spirit or does it originate in my mind?

What kind of faith do you have?

Day 195

THOUGHT OF THE DAY: God is preparing us

I awoke this morning with such a hunger to see the glory of God fill the earth. Then I remembered the prophetic words of Isaiah 43:6-7: "I will tell the north, 'Give them up!' and tell the south, 'Don't hold them back! Bring my sons from far, and my daughters from the ends of the earth—everyone who is called by my name, and whom I have created for my glory, whom I have formed. Yes, whom I have made.' "

God is whispering, and soon it will be a shout: "I created you for the purpose of carrying MY GLORY"...

Get ready! He's getting us ready. Peter 4:12-13: "Friends, when life gets really difficult, don't jump to the conclusion that God isn't on the job. Instead, be glad that you are in the very thick of what Christ experienced. This is a spiritual refining process, with glory just around the corner." (MSG)

It's a time of God refining us.

Know this from Habakkuk 2:14: "But [the time is coming when] the earth shall be filled with the knowledge of the glory of the Lord as the waters cover the sea." (AMP)

Yes, we'll be a part of carrying his Glory throughout the whole earth. God is getting us ready!

Father "Don't hold back!"

Close your eyes and lift your hands...

Day 196

THOUGHT OF THE DAY: Erosion

When I awoke this morning I saw a picture of a beautiful shore which reminded me of Nauset National Sea Shore.

Nauset is one of the most beautiful places in the world. When you arrive, you have to walk hundreds of feet to reach the beach, and all you can see for miles is the most incredible shore line. Literally the beauty of the beaches will take your breath away.

A number of years ago when I went back to visit, I noticed that the beaches had eroded tremendously. It was during this same time that a number of homes in Plymouth, Massachusetts which had been built overlooking the Atlantic, literally fell into the water.

Think of it: something so beautiful, so breathtaking, and so amazing eroding to the degree that homes built on it just fell into the ocean.

This morning when I awoke, I heard, "You must discern the danger of erosion." Erosion is something that while invisible to the eye, does happen over time. Slowly, steadily, consistently the elements of the ocean wear away the beautiful cliffs. Storm after storm, and these beautiful homes eventually fall into the ocean.

This is exactly what Satan does. We have the most incredible lives to live. We have the most beautiful lives and yet slowly, consistently, and over time, Satan uses the process of erosion to destroy lives. I remember reading that engineers would visit the homes on the shoreline and warn the homeowners of what was coming, yet many of them did nothing because of the vast cost to protect them.

Thank God that the cost for us has already been paid by the death of Jesus. This morning I have a deep sense of warning that once again, Satan has slowly, steadily, and without notice been eroding many of our lives. He's been eroding our faith. He's been eroding our hope, and I say it's time to take a stand, to once again reestablish our vision and our hope and to reestablish our lives on a solid foundation called "the rock."

It's time to take a survey of our lives. It's time to see where Satan has been subtly and consistently eroding our very foundation. Matthew tells us that if we build our homes on sand they will most certainly collapse, but he also says that if we build our houses on our rock, they'll stand.

Matthew 7:24-27:

Therefore whoever hears these sayings of Mine, and does them, I will liken him to a wise man who built his house on the rock: and the rain descended, the floods came, and the winds blew and beat on that house;

and it did not fall, for it was founded on the rock. But everyone who hears these sayings of Mine, and does not do them, will be like a foolish man who built his house on the sand: and the rain descended, the floods came, and the winds blew and beat on that house; and it fell. And great was its fall.

I believe that over time we've been unaware of the erosion taking place in parts of our lives, but this morning the Holy Spirit has given us eyes to see and ears to hear so that we will once again reestablish our lives on the solid rock.

Let's take a walk around our lives and see where Satan has been slowly eroding the foundation. In a quiet moment just now I could hear the sound of the heavy equipment coming to shore up our lives so we will not fall.

This subtle erosion will no longer affect our lives! Can you hear the sound of the heavy equipment? I can see cranes, bulldozers, and trucks full of rocks. They are coming and in fact are here now to ensure that our homes and lives will not fall. As I look, I see that each one of these pieces of equipment are being driven by angels who are all smiling and singing with loud voices. They're declaring that the day of erosion is over.

Come on, let's join them and sing that the day of erosion is over!

Day 197

THOUGHT OF THE DAY: Let's prophesy
Sound the alarm! Gather the sons and daughters of God. Let's take our place. Let's position ourselves. Let's shed the lies.

Who said we were nobodies? Who said we're insignificant?

We're the mighty men and women of valor. We are our Father's best. This is the day we declare to every living thing that "We are who we are by the grace of God."

Go ahead and declare Deuteronomy 28:13: "And the Lord will make you the head and not the tail."

Go ahead; prophesy!

Joel 3:10: "Announce this to the godless nations: Prepare for battle! Soldiers at attention! Present arms! Advance! Turn your shovels into swords, turn your hoes into spears. Let the weak one throw out his chest and say, 'I'm tough, I'm a fighter.' " (MSG)

"Let the weak say, 'I AM STRONG!' "

Day 198

THOUGHT OF THE DAY: Today is your tomorrow
It's time to stop singing the song from Annie called "Tomorrow."

Day after day we wake up and not too long after, begin thinking about tomorrow. Thinking about tomorrow cripples the potential of today. In actuality our tomorrow starts today by simply taking one step. Our mind tells us that one step is not enough, and since the one step is not enough, we don't bother taking it. Think about it - just one step!

It's much like a person who wants to lose 20 pounds. They look at the goal and believe it's overwhelming and impossible, but if that person lost just half a pound a day, over time it would change their tomorrow. But because we can't notice a half pound, our mind says it's not enough. You can't see the result of a half-pound, but today is the beginning of our tomorrow.

I can see Jesus walking on the water. He's calling us to get out of the boat and come. It just takes one step. I can hear Jesus say, "Come on; you can do it." Our tomorrow starts today.

If you ever saw the movie Forrest Gump, you'll remember that he wore braces on both of his legs. Day after day he was crippled because of his braces, but one day, (I want to say that again), one day, he began to run. Yes, it was the circumstances that caused him to begin to run. It started with just one step. He ran, and he ran, and he ran, and the braces broke off, and he was no longer crippled.

Today is a great day to take the step which will break off the braces that cripple all of us. Today's circumstances will propel us to take just one step - FORWARD.

Refuse to sing Annie's song of "Tomorrow" any longer, because today is your tomorrow!

Day 199

THOUGHT OF THE DAY: Today will not be like any other day

As I'm sitting here musing with the Lord, the question that comes into my mind is whether this day will be ordinary or extraordinary.

In just a few hours we'll be in church. Will it be just another ordinary Sunday? Or will today be something very different?

There's a new television program show called The Last Ship, which is a story about a vessel that's carrying the only cure for a worldwide epidemic. In spite of severe obstacles, they've determined that they'll manufacture, carry, and distribute the cure throughout the world. In this television program the men and women dedicate and give themselves fully to the one purpose of carrying the antidote for this deadly virus that's spreading across the whole globe.

Isn't that a prophetic picture of us? Each of us carry the anointing. This anointing is the only cure for the deadly disease called sin. You and I have been given the privilege and the mandate to be carriers of an anointing that will give life. There's no other cure for sin than the goodness of God.

Mark 3:3-5 records the story of Jesus being in the synagogue on the Sabbath and seeing a man with a withered hand. Here is what Mark says about the story: "And He said to the man who had the withered hand, 'Step forward.' Then He said to them, 'Is it lawful on the Sabbath to do good or to do evil, to save life or to kill?' But they kept silent. And when He had looked around at them with anger, being grieved by the hardness of their hearts, He said to the man, 'Stretch out your hand.' And he stretched it out, and his hand was restored as whole as the other."

There are two prophetic keys that we must initiate today and every day. The first is the concept of stepping forward. The majority of the time we wait and wait, and the Spirit is telling us to stop waiting. Step forward; do something. The second prophetic key is initiated once we step forward. We need to be willing to take action, and that will include being stretched. Both of these keys require action.

Today in our little community we're going to act out this prophetic picture. We're going to step out of our chairs/pews and together take a step forward. Then we'll stretch out our hand as a prophetic picture that we'll no longer wait but will activate/provoke a moving of the Holy Spirit. Today we'll release something in the Spirit!

Today will not be like any other day!

Day 200

THOUGHT OF THE DAY: Jesus asked, "Do you believe?"

In Matthew 9:28 we read the following; "And when He had come into the house, the blind men came to Him. And Jesus said to them, 'Do you believe that I am able to do this?' "

We can read this verse with our mind, but it's important that we gain an emotional perspective of what it's saying. There are two blind men who for years have groped around in the dark unable to see, their lives crippled physically, emotionally, and psychologically. Then they hear about a man - I'll say that again – then they hear about a man who could change their lives forever.

Imagine... Jesus walks into the room, and the overwhelming presence of God walks in too. In the midst of our trials, our tragedies, our disappointments, our depression, our blindness, our sin, and our hopelessness, there's a question that's in the spirit this morning. No matter how long we've waited, no matter how long we've struggled, no matter what has occurred or what hasn't, do we believe that Jesus is able to do something about the circumstances in our lives?

Our belief is demonstrated in how we live our lives in the process of waiting. Here is what Proverbs 12:4 says, "People will be rewarded for what they say (the fruit of their mouth), and they will also be rewarded for what they do (the work of their hands)." (EXB) What we say and do demonstrates what we really believe.

Jesus asked the two blind men if they believed that he was able to heal them. This morning I can hear Jesus asking us that same question: do you really believe? The men answered in unison, "Yes, Lord."

As I look into the eyes of the Lord, with tears running down my face and joy leaping in my heart, I say, "Yes Lord, I believe."

Today is our day to declare what we believe and then watch for what the Lord is about to do!

Day 201

THOUGHT OF THE DAY: My heart breaks

I know that I've written about this before. Yet this morning as I sit before the Lord, I can see all that He wants to do. Can we dare to dream? Can we dare to believe? If not, what's stopping us?

Stop for a moment and really consider Jesus' prayer in John 17:11 when he asks that "They may be one as we are." I know that inside each of us there's a deep desire and yearning that we your sons and daughters, Father, might truly be one.

We can read Scripture day in and day out. We can see what God has done. The cry of my heart is that we actually become what we read. Below are a number of verses, and I pray that each of us will take the time and ask the Holy Spirit to write these things in our hearts. And once they've been written, that we would find the grace and enabling power to live what we've read.

ACTS 2:1-4: "When the Day of Pentecost had fully come, they were all with one accord in one place. And suddenly there came a sound from heaven, as of a rushing mighty wind, and it filled the whole house where they were sitting. Then there appeared to them divided tongues, as of fire, and one sat upon each of them. And they were all filled with the Holy Spirit and began to speak with other tongues, as the Spirit gave them utterance."

ACTS 4:23: "They raised their voice to God with one accord" and verse 31: "And when they had prayed, the place where they were assembled together was shaken; and they were all filled with the Holy Spirit, and they spoke the word of God with boldness."

2 CHRONICLES 5:13: "Indeed it came to pass, when the trumpeters and singers were as one, to make one sound to be heard in praising and thanking the Lord, and when they lifted up their voice with the trumpets and cymbals and instruments of music, and praised the Lord, saying: 'For He is good, For His mercy endures forever,' that the house, the house of the Lord, was filled with a cloud."

GENESIS 6:11, ERV: "The Lord said, 'These people all speak the same language. And I see that they are joined together to do this work. This is only the beginning of what they can do. Soon they will be able to do anything they want.' "

BRG: "And the Lord said, 'Behold, the people is one, and they have all one language; and this they begin to do: and now nothing will be restrained from them, which they have imagined to do.' "

CEB: "And the Lord said, 'There is now one people and they all have one language. This is what they have begun to do, and now all that they plan to do will be possible for them.' "

CJB: "Adonai said, 'Look, the people are united, they all have a single language, and see what they're starting to do! At this rate, nothing they set out to accomplish will be impossible for them!' "

CEV: "He said: 'These people are working together because they all speak the same language. This is just the beginning. Soon they will be able to do anything they want.' "

ESV: "And the Lord said, 'Behold, they are one people, and they have all one language, and this is only the beginning of what they will do. And nothing that they propose to do will now be impossible for them.' "

AMP: "And the Lord said, 'Behold, they are one people and they have all one language; and this is only the beginning of what they will do, and now nothing they have imagined they can do will be impossible for them.' "

WITH TEARS I WRITE - NOTHING, NOTHING, WOULD BE IMPOSSIBLE. Does your heart break?

Day 202

THOUGHT OF THE DAY: Musing

This morning as I sit before the Lord, the thought that comes to mind is that there are some things I don't understand. I'm even having a very difficult time dictating this thought, and I'm dictating because my right hand is still injured. I'm having such a difficult time holding back the tears. My mind and my heart are flooded with so many thoughts and feelings.

I'm thinking of all the brothers and sisters in Christ that I've known. I want to say to all of us that we are it. We are the ones that God is counting on. We are the ones that carry His presence. We are the ones to carry His passion.

Admittedly there are innumerable things that have transpired in all of our lives that I don't understand. There have been countless disappointments. Countless days when we were all so depressed it was hard to put one foot in front of another. Countless days that we all tried to recover from pain inflicted by others. Yes, even pain that we've inflicted upon ourselves. Numerous times when the church hurt us. Numerous times when pastors such as myself let people down. (Not feeling guilt, just stating truth.)

Then there were numerous times when tragedies and circumstances came crashing into our lives like ocean waves crashing onto the shoreline. Sometimes I just shake my head and tell the Lord I don't get it. And though He doesn't always answer me, I know that He is perfect in all of his ways. I know that one day whether here or whether with Him in heaven, He will let me understand. Like you, I have learned to live in the unresolved.

Today I have the honor of performing a wedding, the third in a family that I've been privileged to know for years. In fact, I knew Ricky and Mc before some of their children were born. Today Ricky will not be there physically but will be there in so many other ways. You see just over a year ago I lost one of my closest friends, as Ricky went to be with the Lord on his 55th birthday. I continue to shake my head and say, "Lord, I don't understand."

I look at the body of Christ and shake my head and say," Lord, where is our passion? Where is the fire that once burned in all of our lives? Lord, I don't understand. I don't understand why so many people who have known you personally no longer walk with you. I don't understand why so many churches have split and split and have even closed their doors. I don't understand why the same people who couldn't wait to be in church find it difficult to get out of bed on a Sunday morning. I don't understand why so many who sacrificed and sacrificed and sacrificed, have a fire that is not burning, but instead smoldering.

Though I don't understand, I know the days are coming when there will be a rekindling of the passion of the fire. Yes, even a rekindling of the gifts that God has supernaturally placed in each of our lives. That day is coming. I believe that the day is upon us. This Sunday at the Porch we'll have God rekindle the fire, passion, and gifts in us. You're invited to come.

As I sat considering all these things and more, a song came to my mind that I haven't thought of in years. The song is "Worth It All"... You see the Holy Spirit is telling us that it's going to be worth it. Yes, even though we don't understand, and the passion and the fire are not what they once were. Though there have been countless tragedies and circumstances that have invaded our lives, I know that I know that we will and can sing, "It's going to be worth it all."

The wind of God is blowing and soon will touch all of our lives and will change us from the inside out, and we'll be transformed into another man. In 1 Samuel 10:6 it says, "Then the Spirit of the Lord will come upon you, and you will prophesy with them and be turned into another man."

Though I don't understand so many things, I can sing, "It's going to be worth it all."

Day 203

THOUGHT OF THE DAY: The day after

You might recall my THOUGHT OF THE DAY from yesterday. It was a day I was struggling to understand a number of things. My answer was that God is perfect in all of His ways and that I would be content in whatever state I was in.

Today when I awoke, I distinctly heard, "My grace it is sufficient for you." I couldn't wait to get out of bed to read 2 Corinthians 12:9: "But the Lord said, 'My grace is all you need. Only when you are weak can everything be done completely by my power.' " (ERV)

In Gill's Commentary he writes, " 'and he said unto me,' meaning that Paul heard a voice from heaven or that he heard an audible voice." This morning I heard that same voice. "Brian, my grace is sufficient for you." Clark's Commentary states "We will not sink under afflictions, and that our enemies will not prevail against us." The ERV Bible states it beautifully, "Only when you are weak can everything be done completely by my power."

It's almost impossible to articulate what I want to put into words. As soon as I heard "My grace is sufficient," my heart, my mind, my soul, and my very being were overwhelmed with a deep and fulfilling sense of great peace and great joy – what I can only call a SUPERNATURAL GRACE.

Imagine, the day after my struggling, the Holy Spirit came and flooded me, and He'll flood you too with an overwhelming sense of heavenly grace. As with Paul, the circumstances of your life may not change; they didn't for Paul even after he asked the Lord three times to remove his affliction. The point is that while circumstances and situations may often not change, there is an endless supply of grace that is freely available to us at all times.

This morning my focus has dramatically changed away from questioning. I am no longer looking for answers to the question of why, because He's told me not to look to the whys but instead to His grace. When I find this grace, my enemy will not prevail against me, and Satan will no longer be able to take advantage of my weakness. For at the very moment of my weakness, my struggle, and my questioning, I will have available to me the very power of God for whatever I need.

Grace gives us a heavenly and eternal perspective. Grace will cause us to see and respond differently. In all of our questioning, in all of our struggles and troubles, at the moments of our greatest weakness, we have available a grace that can't be defined by words. None of us will need to look for grace; the grace will simply be there! Why? Because He really loves us, always seeing our needs, our afflictions, and our troubles, and His heavenly grace never runs dry. It's almost like the healing pools of water that were at Jericho. People would come from hundreds of miles to dip in its pools, and the properties of that water somehow healed them.

This morning I feel that I have been dipped in the oasis pools of Jericho. My questions and my struggles have been eliminated, and I'm overwhelmed with a sense of peace, joy, and contentment. He's whispering, "My grace will always be sufficient for whatever you need."

Can you hear the voice from heaven? Listen. It's saying, "My grace is sufficient."

Day 204

THOUGHT OF THE DAY: Oh, happy day

This morning as I sat before the Lord, I was quiet. I was wondering what He wanted to say to me, to say to us. Within moments I heard, "I will never leave you."

I will NEVER forsake you even when your life is upside down. In all of your imperfections, in all of your sin, He declares that I WILL NEVER, NEVER leave you. Not only did I call you from before the foundation of the world, I knew you in your mother's womb. My love is greater than all your weaknesses; you are my son. My blood that I shed on Calvary thoroughly cleanses each of you from all of your unrighteousness.

Not only does his blood cover our sin, his blood thoroughly and completely eradicates our sin; even our consciences are free from every form of guilt and failure. It's not because we earned it. It's not because we deserve it. It's all because he loves us unconditionally.

As these thoughts and words filled my heart and my mind, I was overwhelmed with such a sense of peace, joy, and contentment. Then the thought came, "Oh Lord, if we could only believe and embrace not just truth, but your love, your affection, and how you really feel about us." Two verses come to my mind, the first Matthew 28:20: "Look, I myself will be with you every day until the end of this present age." (CEB) And the second is from Hebrews 13:5: "I will never leave you; I will always be by your side." (VOICE)

I just love Matthew's account. He said, "I'll be with you every day," and then Hebrews where God says, "I will never, never, never leave you." Some translations say, "I will never abandon you."

There's a very affectionate voice this morning coming from heaven, and I can see a smile on our Father's face. There's an intense pleading I'm hearing - He is saying, "I will always be by your side." "My love is greater than any failure, any thought, any action."

Search and see. It's the perfection of one man, and his name is Jesus, for he was the only one who was perfect. It says in Romans that "We all have sinned and fallen short of the glory of God." I love that it says "all." We were never called to establish our own perfection! For our Father knew that even with our very best efforts we couldn't live a sinless life. The Father sent His Son that we may live in His perfection.

If you close your eyes and are still, you will have a sense, an overwhelming sense that He's not only near you, but He's in you. There's that smile again, and He's beckoning us to come. I can see His hand motioning for us to come close, and He's pointing to the ground. He's saying, "Sit and find rest for your souls." He's saying "Come and learn of me," for it is when we learn of Him that we learn "who we are."

It's funny that as I sit here with my eyes closed, I can hear a choir singing, "Oh happy day." Get ready to jump up, clap and shout – https ://youtu.be/a37bBm8pXSk or Ray Charles https: // youtu.be / wv5n_eCGkvM

Day 205

THOUGHT OF THE DAY: Not saying good-bye

This afternoon I went to see an old friend who's in intensive care at the VA Hospital in Providence, Rhode Island. I hadn't seen Rod in a number of years. The natural Rod had no idea I was in the room, but his spirit knew I was there.

Rod is a gentle soul who's loved the Lord for many years. As he laid there unresponsive, I began to recall so many fond memories. As I stood nearby, I asked the Lord how I should pray, and the words had just finished coming out of my mouth when I heard angels singing, "Coming Home." The presence of God filled the room, and I saw a door open and angels standing there smiling and singing. I saw the lamb's book of life, and one of the angels pointed to his name. At that moment I knew Rod's journey was coming to the end.

I began to pray and release Rod to be with the Lord. I reminded him that he had a reservation, and that there was a place there just for him. I reminded him that he was about to enter into eternity not because he was perfect, but because he worshipped Jesus who IS perfect.

Soon Rod will have a new body, for the one he's in now is not doing a good job supporting him. (There had to be eight to ten IV bags connected to him.) I commented to the nurse about how many bags there were, and she said that when he was first admitted, Rod had even more.

I told her that Rod's journey was nearing an end and that I was praying to have the Lord come and get his "little" boy (though Rod is anything but little). She said that Rod's sister (Hope) was praying the same thing.

I quoted 1 Corinthians 15:55 from the Voice Bible; "Hey, Death! What happened to your big win? Hey, Death! What happened to your sting?" There was such joy in the room because we knew that in one brief moment he would be changed and in the glorious presence of God.

What an unfathomable truth that Jesus has gone to prepare a place for us, that our sin and our carnality will not keep us from spending eternity with him.

As I left the room, I wasn't saying good-bye. I told Rod that I'd see him later.

Day 206

THOUGHT OF THE DAY: Come follow me

Can you see him? Can you hear him? He's standing on the shores of our lives and motioning with his right hand to come and follow him. There's something different this morning. Are those tears running down his cheeks? Can you hear him? He's saying, "Follow me. I want to take you places that you've never seen or perceived."

How many times have we heard him call us?

Jesus said that he's inviting us to follow him. It's an invitation that has somehow become distorted. Perhaps we forgot that he's truly alive and still speaks to people today. With our theology and religious lifestyle, we replaced a relationship with a religious system, in many ways "depersonalizing" Jesus.

Jesus became an historic person. He was the God of yesterday and is the God of tomorrow, yet somehow we forgot he is the God of TODAY. By depersonalizing him, if we're honest, it becomes easier to compromise. It's easier to sin against a system than against a living person. Sin becomes more personal when the person is alive and a part of your life. Psalm 51:4 has to become more of a reality in our lives: "Against You, You only, have I sinned, And done this evil in Your sight."

Our future is only limited by the capacity of our mind to believe Luke 12:32: "Do not fear, little flock, for it is your Father's good pleasure to give you the kingdom." (NKJV) Look at the ISV: "Stop being afraid, little flock, because your Father is pleased to give you the kingdom."

Our Father delights in giving us the fullness and totality of His kingdom. I love the ISV that says, "STOP BEING AFRAID!" Can't you hear Him saying this to each of us?

Wait a minute; He wants to give us His kingdom NOW... Let's abandon everything to follow Jesus. Let's say yes to Matthew 16:24: "Then Jesus said to his disciples, 'All who want to come after me must say no to themselves, take up their cross, and follow me.' " (CEB)

I can hear him even now, and he's saying - Come follow me!

Day 207

THOUGHT OF THE DAY: We are

For months now I've written in one way or another about who we are. We (the church) have allowed the enemy, our own natural thinking, our church doctrine, and our traditions to overemphasize who we're not rather than who we are.

It's been the culture of the church to train and train and train, and after that still make people feel that they need more training before they're qualified to be sent to preach and share the gospel. How much training did the disciples have before Jesus sent them out – weeks / a few months? Out of fear that people will make mistakes, we often hold them back.

The reality is that I'm still making mistakes. And Jesus never worried about the disciples' mistakes. He'd send them out and then upon their return sit with them and talk about what happened. It was in sitting with them that he'd seek to adjust their attitudes, and whatever mistakes they were making, he'd point them out. We, the church need to follow this example.

The fear of making mistakes has crippled many of us, causing us to be afraid to say anything to people. The key is being willing to be taught by our mentors. We've felt inadequate, when all along the Holy Spirit has been reminding us that he lives inside of us and therefore we have everything we need.

I've written this verse before, but I want to share it again. It's Ephesians 2:10: "For we are His workmanship, created in Christ Jesus for good works, which God prepared beforehand that we should walk in them." (NKJV) The NLT says, "For we are God's masterpiece."

We need to say it out loud and often. Say, "I am now (not in the future but right now), God's masterpiece! I've been created and ordained to do good works." When the enemy or well-meaning people try and hold us back from doing what we're called to do, we need the spirit of Nehemiah. Nehemiah 6:3 says that he sent messengers to his distractors, "So I sent messengers to them, saying, 'I am doing a great work, so that I cannot come down. Why should the work cease while I leave it and go down to you?'"

It's vital that we assign value to what we're doing. Listen - DON'T LET THE ENEMY BELITTLE WHAT YOU'RE DOING. Remember, we grow, and our capacity to do more grows as we do.

I'm pleading that we comprehend the meaning of Genesis 11:6: if we're unified, we'll be unstoppable. Here's the verse, "And the Lord said, 'Indeed the people are one and they all have one language, and this is what they begin to do; now nothing that they propose to do will be withheld from them.'"

Paul warns us in Colossians 2:8 that we can be cheated, misled, and robbed from fulfilling our calling/destiny. Read this slowly, "Beware lest anyone cheat you through philosophy and empty deceit, according to the tradition of men, according to the basic principles of the world, and not according to Christ." Now see how the Amplified Bible expands the depth of what Paul wrote; "See to it that no one carries you off as spoil or makes you yourselves captive by his so-called philosophy and intellectualism and vain deceit (idle fancies and plain nonsense), following human tradition (men's ideas of the material rather than the spiritual world), just crude notions following the rudimentary and elemental teachings of the universe and disregarding [the teachings of] Christ (the Messiah)."

There's no need for me to explain what we just read, but do ask the Holy Spirit to show you if you're being "cheated."

Remember to recognize who we are - now, today, at this very moment. I declare - WE ARE!

Day 208

THOUGHT OF THE DAY: Empathy or compassion?

This morning while at my chiropractor, Dr. Jan remarked on how much I'd been through physically during the last year or so. For six to eight months I suffered from a double concussion, and now I've ruptured the tendon on the baby finger of my right hand.

Out of nowhere she then asked me what God was trying to show me.

This doctor and I have had numerous exchanges about life and faith. She has also been the recipient of prophetic ministry. Like all of us who've seen prophetic ministry or been blessed by it, it has a profound effect.

As soon as she asked me the question, without hesitation I told her that I'm learning the difference between compassion and empathy. I'd never thought about or considered this before that moment, nor have I ever considered the difference between compassion and empathy, or furthermore, if there even is a difference.

Compassion is defined as a feeling of deep sympathy and sorrow for another who is stricken by misfortune, accompanied by a strong desire to alleviate their suffering. (Dictionary.com)

Empathy, however, goes deeper, as empathy is not only the feeling of sympathy for someone, but the realization that you actually understand and share that person's experiences and emotions. (Dictionary.com)

It's fully possible for me to have compassion without being able to deeply identify with a person emotionally.

During the past month I've had very limited use of my right hand and have been thinking about our veterans who've lost arms and also those who've lost capacity through strokes. I know the two do not begin to compare, but still, something has gone off inside of me, and I just want to weep.

In some very minute way, I understand. For years I can say I've had compassion for people, but I can't say that I've had empathy. I'm realizing that I need empathy, a feeling that seems to spring from the "bowels." There's a yearning deep within me to be a man who has more than compassion. I want to be a person of deep feeling and emotion for the broken and hurting. I want empathy deep in my "bowels," because when we truly feel something deeply, our prayer is far more personal and seems to come from the very core of our being.

I guess what I'm saying is that I want to be more like Jesus. You see, as I've been writing this, I've been reminded of what Isaiah writes as one of the characteristics of the coming Messiah, that he would be "a man of sorrows and acquainted with grief." (Isaiah 53:3)

I want to love more deeply. Don't you?

Jesus, what we're saying is that we want to be more like you. We want to have your compassion and empathy!

Day 209

THOUGHT OF THE DAY: Having a bad day?

When I'm having a bad day, I often consider Hebrews 11:35-38: "Others were tortured, not accepting deliverance, that they might obtain a better resurrection. Still others had trial of mockings and scourgings, yes, and of chains and imprisonment. They were stoned, they were sawn in two, were tempted, and were slain with the sword. They wandered about in sheepskins and goatskins, being destitute, afflicted, tormented— of whom the world was not worthy. They wandered in deserts and mountains, in dens and caves of the earth."

Now that's having a bad day!

Day 210

THOUGHT OF THE DAY: First love

On Thursday night we had our once-a-month prayer meeting. I just love this night, as the presence of God is there to show us how to pray and worship.

It was early in the meeting when Lisa introduced a new worship song called "Simplicity" by Rend Collective. Essentially, it's about returning to our first love. We read about this in Revelation chapter two in the letter to the Church of Ephesus.

In this letter, the Holy Spirit commends the church for all their labor and fervency in dealing with false doctrine and false teachers. Yet in spite of these attributes, the church has a serious problem; they have, as it says in verse five, "left" their "first love." The Spirit goes on to say, "Remember therefore from where you have fallen; repent and do the first works, or else I will come to you quickly and remove your lamp stand from its place—unless you repent."

As we worshipped, I became silent and said, "Lord, bring me back to when I first loved you." That first season of faith is perhaps a lot like in your marriage, at the beginning of your relationship when your love compels you to be with the other person as often as you can. Each time you see one another, there are these emotions/feelings that are akin to fireworks. Then after a time the fireworks don't detonate as often.

I could remember as I sat there the desire to know and be with the Lord. Every waking moment I just wanted to be with him. I remember waking in the morning and I just couldn't wait to study and pray. My heart was so filled with excitement and joy. I just wanted to be with him. Yet sadly as in marriage, as time goes on, that overwhelming, compelling desire fades.

Can you relate to this? We can be doing all the right things. We can pray, study, uphold doctrine, serve and so on, but can do so mechanically or as a lifestyle choice without really being head-over-heals in love with the Lord. Sadly, we can often recognize this problem in other people's lives but fail to see it in our own. As we read in verse five, the Holy Spirit tells them to repent and if they fail, there are eternal consequences. Remember that the Spirit was writing to a church, to people like us.

Here it is Saturday morning and something is stirring inside of me. I can begin to feel a fresh and captivating affection. Oh Lord, we want more. Bring us back each day to our first love for you. When I say emotion/feelings, you know what I mean. Father, bring us back to where it all began, when we were totally overwhelmed by our love for you.

I'm reminded of Zechariah 10:8 where it says, "I will whistle for them and gather them." I'm realizing that it was and is the Lord reaching out to us. It's his love calling to us! It almost takes your breath away to realize that he so desires to be with us.

I don't want a mechanical relationship, which I often refer to as habitual living. Do you?

Father, continue to bring us back to our FIRST LOVE!

Day 211

THOUGHT OF THE DAY: He will not

I don't know about you, but it seems like we've all been in a season where we're being barraged by every kind of trial imaginable. It's like being at the ocean in the middle of a storm where wave after wave crashes the shoreline. The waves have names like finances, sickness, relationships, attitudes, temptations, thoughts, feelings, and oh yes, the wave that Satan rides.

Have you ever said, "Okay, enough already!?" Ever decided you're going to take a stand against this? Ever declare that it's all over? Yet as soon as one wave ends, another one is right behind it. So what do you do?

Well, I'm running and holding onto 1 Corinthians 10:13: "No test or temptation that comes your way is beyond the course of what others have had to face. All you need to remember is that God will never let you down; he'll never let you be pushed past your limit; he'll always be there to help you come through it." (MSG) The NKJV says, "But God is faithful, who will not allow you to be tempted beyond what you are able."

There's an expression which applies here. It says, "Take that to the bank."

God is faithful; He'll never let us down. We won't be pushed beyond our limit, though at times we've all told Him we're surely coming close to approaching it. Funny thing is, we always seem to go further. Why is that? It's because of Him living and working in us. It's by His strength and not ours that we overcome.

The bottom line is... God is not a liar! He has made this promise to us and He will keep it.

I never knew the story behind the song "I Have Decided to Follow Jesus." It was sent to me by a pastor I chat with in India and hope to visit later this year. It spoke to me, and I trust it will speak to you.

"I Have Decided to Follow Jesus" is a Christian hymn which originated from India.

The lyrics are based on the last words of a man in Garo, Assam, northeast India.

About 150 years ago, there was a great revival in Wales, England. As a result of this, many missionaries came from England and Germany to northeast India to spread the Gospel. At the time, northeast India was not divided into many states as it is today.

The region was known as Assam and was comprised of hundreds of tribes which were quite primitive and aggressive by nature.

The tribals were also called head-hunters because of a social custom which required the male members of the community to collect as many heads as possible.

A man's strength and ability to protect his wife was assessed by the number of heads he had collected. Therefore, a youth of marriageable age would try and collect as many heads as possible and hang them on the walls of his house. The more heads a man had, the more eligible he was considered.

Into this hostile and aggressive community came a group of Welsh missionaries spreading the message of love, peace, and hope in Jesus Christ. Naturally, they were not welcomed.

One Welsh missionary shared the gospel, and a man, his wife, and two children believed in Jesus. This man's faith proved contagious, and many villagers began to accept Christ.

Angry, the village chief summoned all the villagers. He then called the family who had first converted and demanded that they renounce their faith in public or face execution.

Moved by the Holy Spirit, the man instantly composed a song which became famous through the years. He said, "I have decided to follow Jesus. No turning back, no turning back."

Enraged at the refusal of the man, the chief ordered his archers to arrow down the two children. As both boys lay twitching on the floor, the chief asked, "Will you deny your faith? You have lost both your children. You will lose your wife too."

But the man said these words in reply: "Though no one joins me, still I will follow. No turning back, no turning back."

The chief was beside himself with fury and ordered his wife to be arrowed down.

In a moment she joined her two children in death.

Now he asked for the last time, "I will give you one more opportunity to deny your faith and live."

In the face of death, the man said the final memorable lines: "The cross before me, the world behind me. No turning back, no turning back."

He was shot dead like the rest of his family. But with their deaths, a miracle took place.

The chief who had ordered the killings was moved by the faith of the man. He wondered, "Why should this man, his wife and two children die for a man who lived in a far-away land on another continent some 2,000 years ago? There must be some remarkable power behind the family's faith, and I too want to taste that faith."

In a spontaneous confession, he declared, "I too belong to Jesus Christ!"

When the crowd heard this from the mouth of their chief, the whole village accepted Christ as their Lord and Savior.

The tune for the song was given by Sadhu Sundar Singh a few years later when he stumbled upon some historical literature and read about this incident during one of his travels to the North East.

This powerful song was composed by a man who forsook everything to give his life for Christ, which in turn led to the salvation of the whole tribe. The combination of these two testimonies fills this song with a vitality which generates more followers of Christ, even today.

I know we all face discouragement, but hold on and remember...you've decided to follow Jesus...

Day 212

THOUGHT OF THE DAY: Prophetic words and failure

Has the Holy Spirit spoken to you? Has he given you a prophetic word about your future? Does it seem like that prophetic word will never come to pass? Have our failures seemed to cancel out how God sees our future?

Sadly, there are times when our decisions will profoundly affect God's plan for our lives. If for some reason our decision has affected plan "A," let's rejoice that God still has, as Jeremiah says, "plans for us."

Yes, through the redemptive nature of God, there isn't a situation that He can't redeem. When I read Psalm 103, I can't help but put my hands up and thank Him. Here's a peak at some of the verses in Psalm 103; "The Lord is merciful and gracious, Slow to anger, and abounding in mercy. He has not dealt with us according to our sins, Nor punished us according to our iniquities. For as the heavens are high above the earth, So great is His mercy toward those who fear Him; As far as the east is from the west, so far has He removed our transgressions from us."

Now doesn't that just make you want to shout?!

I thank God that my failures do not define me. I thank God that Jesus specializes in transforming our failures from tragedy to triumph. Remember Jesus' prophetic word to Peter in Matthew 16:18-19 where we read, "And I also say to you that you are Peter, and on this rock I will build My church, and the gates of Hades shall not prevail against it. And I will give you the keys of the kingdom of heaven."

He said this to him even while knowing Peter would deny him not just once, but three times. In Matthew 26:73-74, not only does Peter deny him, but he also ends up cursing and swearing: "And a little later those who stood by came up and said to Peter, 'Surely you also are one of them, for your speech betrays you.' Then he began to curse and swear, saying, 'I do not know the Man!' "

Jesus, knowing Peter would deny him, gives Peter a second prophetic word which is in Luke 22:32: "But I have prayed for you. I have prayed that your faith will hold firm and that you will recover from your failure and become a source of strength for your brothers here." Jesus tells Peter that after he repents (an important step), he wants him to take his failures and use them to help and encourage others in their walk.

Don't allow your own thinking or what others say (including Satan), to cause you to live in your failures when Jesus redeems us from them. Our failures do not define us.

Which is greater: your prophetic word or your failures?

Day 213

THOUGHT OF THE DAY: Moving into the new

Are you groaning? Are you travailing? Are you dissatisfied? Are you troubled? Are you restless? Is there a burden in your soul? Is there a deep yearning within you? Well, if there is, (and I believe it to be so); then you are in transition! You are at a place of birthing!

The concept of birthing is that we first need to be pregnant. My observation of pregnancy (my wife's and other women's) is how uncomfortable expectant women became and how near the end they just want to have the baby. For many of us that's where we are. Yet having a child is a process. Often we can relate to Genesis 35:17: "Now it came to pass, when she was in hard labor, that the midwife said to her, 'Do not fear; you will have this son also.' "

The labor is hard; there is pain involved, and yes, during the process, fear is one of the giants we face.

As we enter the new season, we need to be aware that trouble and trials await us, yet we can rejoice that the following verse is true. Psalm 46:1: "God is our refuge and strength, A very present help in trouble."

Our God is not concerned or afraid of trouble, because He is greater than our troubles. Whatever trouble we're in, I believe Isaiah 43:1-2: "But now, thus says the Lord, who created you, O Jacob, And He who formed you, O Israel: 'Fear not, for I have redeemed you; I have called you by your name; You are Mine. When you pass through the waters, I will be with you; And through the rivers, they shall not overflow you. When you walk through the fire, you shall not be burned, Nor shall the flame scorch you.' "

Yes, He has purchased us! He knows you and me by name. Can't you hear Him calling to you even now?

We often love the idea of new but are faced with fear - fear of the unknown, fear of failing, fear that we've made a mistake. It's vital to remember Genesis 28:15: "Behold, I am with you and will keep you wherever you go, and will bring you back to this land; for I will not leave you until I have done what I have spoken to you."

Please don't just read over this. Take a minute and meditate on what it's saying. It says, "I WILL," not I might!

The Holy Spirit has made us pregnant. We are in a place of transition, a place of birthing. It's time to move into the new.

Don't fear - OUR GOD IS WITH US!

It's time to move into the new...

Day 214

THOUGHT OF THE DAY: SHKR

I haven't written a THOUGHT OF THE DAY in a while. Why? Because I didn't have any clear thought to write about.

There are times we feel like heaven is shut up. Several times in scripture it says, "Heaven was shut up and there was no rain." I really dislike those times. You're seeking God, yet you feel God isn't speaking.

What I discovered while ministering yesterday, however, was that it wasn't that God wasn't speaking; it was that He wasn't speaking about the things I wanted Him to.

I don't know about you, but when I'm not hearing with clarity, I tend to get the "boo-hoos." This is not a good path to go down, because then the giant called DISCOURAGEMENT comes into the fields of our lives and wants to take us to a place of darkness and depression. And when we get to this place, there are no magic wands to wave. There are no abracadabras, or at least I've never found one. There are no "Simon says" either. As each day passes, we can become engulfed in a sea of emotions.

When we arrive at this place, though, we can be assured of the truth that our God is the God of "SHKR." Let's read Exodus 3:7: "And the Lord said, 'I have surely seen the oppression of My people who are in Egypt, and have heard their cry because of their taskmasters, for I know their sorrows.' " (NKJV)

S – I've already (I like that) SEEN where you are;

H - I have HEARD - God's already heard our crying and groaning

K - God KNOWS our sorrow...

GOD SEES, HEARS, AND KNOWS!

After He sees, hears, and knows, He responds, "So I have come down to deliver them out of the hand of the Egyptians, and to bring them up from that land to a good and large land, to a land flowing with milk and honey, to the place of the Canaanites and the Hittites and the Amorites and the Perizzites and the Hivites and the Jebusites." (verse eight)

God invades earth. He invades each of our lives to deliver us from where we are, and He again reaffirms His promise to each of us. What is His promise? I WILL (not I might). I WILL take you out of where you are, and I WILL take you to the place(s) I have promised you. Then there's a subtle P.S. - the place I'm taking you is truly amazing, but you need to know there are a bunch of "ites" there.

What are "ites?"

They're the giants that we'll face and will defeat. Read Exodus 2:24: "So God heard their groaning, and God remembered His covenant with Abraham, with Isaac, and with Jacob."

R - God REMEMBERS His covenant.

Praise God that He is the God that - SHKRs!

Day 215

THOUGHT OF THE DAY: Keeping your heart right

One of the greatest challenges we all face is to keep a right heart when our flesh says it's okay to be angry, bitter, and resentful. We end up giving ourselves permission to be just as miserable and ornery as the person who's acting this way towards us. How do we live with an attitude of grace and forgiveness? Is it possible for the bitterness to not affect you?

Such is the challenge of refraining from acting towards a person the way they're acting towards you. It says in 1 Thessalonians 5:15: "Make sure that nobody pays back wrong for wrong, but always strive to do what is good for each other and for everyone else," (NIV) or the Message Bible: "And be careful that when you get on each other's nerves you don't snap at each other. Look for the best in each other, and always do your best to bring it out." Then there is Proverbs 26:4: "Don't give a foolish person a foolish answer. If you do, you will be just like him." (ISB)

All too often we settle for "tit for tat." In other words, we treat the other person the way they treat us. We give ourselves liberty to be unforgiving when people don't ask for forgiveness or when the person is unwilling to see where they're wrong. I'm so grateful that Jesus didn't respond this way, that he didn't wait to forgive those who spoke to him with vile comments or those who mocked and spit on him, tortured and ultimately crucified him. The scripture says both in Isaiah 53:7 and in Acts 8:32: "He was beaten, he was tortured, but he didn't say a word. Like a lamb taken to be slaughtered and like a sheep being sheared, he took it all in silence." (MSG)

Selah- pause and mediate.

I think of Ruth who suffered the tragedy of the loss of her husband, and day after day she listened to the bitterness of Naomi. Imagine how hard this was. Yet Ruth honored her mother-in-law. In fact, when Ruth asked Boaz why she had found favor in his eyes, he responded, "It has been fully reported to me, all that you have done for your mother-in-law since the death of your husband, and how you have left your father and your mother and the land of your birth, and have come to a people whom you did not know before." (Ruth 2:11) I'm wondering if we have the same sort of reputation?

Then there's Joseph who was hated and rejected by his brothers, falsely accused of misconduct, and put in prison for something he didn't do. Joseph had to suffer all he suffered so he could be in the right place at the right time with the right spirit. When he saw his brothers again after many years, he forgave them and ended up being God's provision for an entire nation.

Perhaps this will give us something to muse on today.

Father, even under difficult and trying circumstances, help us to always have the right heart!

Day 216

THOUGHT OF THE DAY: Why don't you believe and think the way I do?

I just have to laugh. As I look back on my journey with the Lord, I can see to what extent I wanted people to conform to the image of what I thought a believer should be. Little did I understand Romans 8:29: "For whom He foreknew, He also predestined to be conformed to the image of His Son."

Yes, we're called to be conformed to Christ, not the image of our fleshly imaginations. I can remember how I had strong opinions of what people wore to church. If I saw someone wearing jeans, I would think that in reality they should be dressed more like me. Now it's me who wears jeans to church. Again, laughable.

We can look at the conflicts that existed between Jews and Gentiles with the Jewish brothers wanting the Gentile brothers to be circumcised, to not eat shrimp, lobster, clams, bacon, ham, etcetera. They also wanted the Gentile brothers to keep the Sabbath from sundown Friday to sundown Saturday. Boy, can I relate!

In reality we still have conflict between people and denominations. Can I suggest that in all of us there are still opinions that we believe others should adopt? The people who don't drink believe that no one else should either. By contrast those who do drink think that those who don't, should, because they themselves have found liberty and others should be free to experience the same liberty they have. And both sides stand strongly and resolutely on their own side of the matter.

The ultimate goal is for all of us to live Ephesians 5:10: "trying to learn what is pleasing to the Lord." (NET) Embracing and following the example of Jesus who said in John 8:29: "for I always do those things that please Him." What I thought was pleasing to the Lord in 1970 is far different than what I believe is pleasing to the Lord today. People are called to follow Christ, not my conception of what I think they should be following.

Romans chapter 14 speaks of a controversy in the church over what people should or shouldn't eat. Paul gives an instruction that applies across many situations. In Romans 14:22 we read, "Cultivate your own relationship with God, but don't impose it on others." (MSG)

For many years I was convinced that what I believed was the ONLY way to believe. Then a funny thing happened: what I once believed, I didn't believe anymore. Finally I realized that I was called to love and not impose my convictions on another person. I can share the truth in love and can sincerely love and care for people with whom I disagree. And sadly, when we have a wrong attitude, people can discern it.

You've experienced this before: the person whose disapproval you sense even though they're smiling at you? Why the disapproval? Because we're not living our lives according to their standards and convictions. What comes to mind is this verse: "Who are you to judge another's servant?" (Romans 14:4). Then there's 1 Corinthians 10:29: "For why is my liberty judged by another man's conscience?" Great questions.

How many times have I been guilty of imposing this?

So Lord, search me. Search us. Please eradicate the spirt that asks, "Why don't you believe and think the way I do?"

Day 217

THOUGHT OF THE DAY: "And He said, 'Hagar, Sarai's maid, where have you come from, and where are you going?' " (Genesis 16:8)

The Angel of the Lord asked Hagar this question as she was fleeing from Sarah the first time. It's a question that we need to ask ourselves when we're trying to make big decisions. You see, if we don't know where we've been and why we've been there, then we can easily repeat the same mistakes. We may not have fully gleaned all that God was doing, therefore we'll most likely repeat what we didn't learn the first time. How can we truly go forward when we don't know where we've been?

In this story the angel sent her back to be under Sarah. Often we're looking to move on at the wrong time or for the wrong reasons – we're uncomfortable or struggling with our relationships. A later time might be the right time.

Years later, for example, Hagar again flees from Sarah, and this time she's told not to go back. Many of us are contemplating big decisions and moving on. My advice in this is to be sure you know where you came from so it will be clear where you're going.

Time for assessment and inventory. "Where have you come from, and where are you going?"

Day 218

THOUGHT OF THE DAY: Waiting

So tell me, when God has you in a place of waiting, how does it go? Are you irritable, frustrated, moody? Do you get angry or become difficult to be around?

More often than not, as for the children of Israel, waiting produces people who complain. Before you know it, people start grumbling about everything. Like cancer, the complaining seeps into everything. This is because our focus becomes what God has not done rather than what He has. This leads me to question the kind of atmosphere we're creating. In Proverbs 14:12 we read, "A man will be satisfied with good by the fruit of his mouth."

Paul gives us great counsel in Philippians 4:8-9: "Finally, brethren, whatever things are true, whatever things are noble, whatever things are just, whatever things are pure, whatever things are lovely, whatever things are of good report, if there is any virtue and if there is anything praiseworthy—meditate on these things." "Meditate" meaning having your mind and heart fully occupied. In verse eight Paul tells us the result of thinking this way. "The things which you learned and received and heard and saw in me, these do, and the God of peace will be with you."

Imagine God's presence with us and peace therefore overflowing our lives?

So how should we wait? Psalms 40:1-3 gives us this insight. "I waited patiently for the Lord; And He inclined to me, and heard my cry. He also brought me up out of a horrible pit, Out of the miry clay, And set my feet upon a rock, And established my steps, has put a new song in my mouth— Praise to our God; Many will see it and fear And will trust in the Lord."

Let's see what these verses are telling us:

The phrase "waited patiently for the Lord" in the Hebrew means that waiting is active, not passive.

To wait means to delay action in an expectant manner as you hope for God's promises to be fulfilled on your behalf.

It goes on to say that "He inclined to me, and heard my cry. He also brought me up out of a horrible pit, Out of the miry clay."

When we have God's attention, not only does He hear, but takes us "out of a HORRIBLE PIT."

He will set us on the Rock (Jesus).

He will order our steps.

He will put a new song in our mouth.

Can we say He WILL?

Oh, and people will see what God is doing in our lives and they'll be in awe.

So here's our choice: we can wait and complain, or we can wait with expectation as we hope and trust in all the promises He's made us. He will and does remember His covenant.

So how do you want to wait?

Day 219

THOUGHT OF THE DAY: Sharing my broken heart

Each day when I awake, thankfully I'm greeted by our Father who knows everything. I'm not awake for even a few moments when my heart is filled with brokenness for those who I know are in desperate need. Often when I pray, I'll say, "Father you know everything." I'm aware that the scriptures say "to cast your burden on the Lord." With that being said, there are countless days and even weeks and months, where needs go unmet.

On a daily basis I'm made aware by pastors, missionaries, and others I know and have known for years, of real crisis situations. They pour out their hearts, needing someone to talk to, someone who'll listen. It's great to pray with them and for them, perhaps offer some encouragement and counsel, but frankly, this is so often not enough.

On a daily basis, ministers I know contact me (and even some who hear about our ministry), and I listen to their turmoil and real-life problems. Often, it's the lack of financial support from God's children that causes such overwhelming problems and pressures. Daily I hear from missionaries from India, Romania, Africa, and Haiti. They're faced with difficulties that literally crush your heart. They're in need of food for themselves as well as for the people God has entrusted to them. There's great need for medical supplies, oil to cook rice and beans, and even clothing.

Often the things that are collected and designated for shipment will sit in containers, unable be distributed for months at a time, because the shipping costs are unaffordable. Pastors often go without so they can feed others and give them medical supplies and provide for other simple needs. I know pastors who've been unable to pay their own rent here in America because people who once gave don't give anymore or have drastically cut back. Lately people (as well as pastors) who've promised to send support don't send the support they promised. Day in and day out I listen to the pain and disappointment of these men and women. Some of them are close to emotional breakdown.

I'm sharing this with all of you so you can pray. Perhaps you have people in your lives who can send support. Perhaps some of you can send some support. If 50 people sent $50 each, it would amount to $2,500. Perhaps pastors who read this can approach their congregations and ask for help. In reality $25 or $50 is likely not going to change their circumstances, but it would dramatically help a missionary you might know. Perhaps instead you need to sow that money into your local church, because they're also in great need.

I could quote a number of scriptures, but I believe that the Holy Spirit has already spoken to hearts. So now what? Send help. Send it through your church. Send it directly to someone you know. Mail it, use PayPal, or Western Union. If you send it to my Paypal account I promise to send every penny on. My Paypal is brianweeksministiees@gmail.com. Click friends and family to avoid fees.

Sharing my broken heart...

Day 220

THOUGHT OF THE DAY: My difficulties haven't changed, but...

Our God is unfathomable, unsearchable, and is unable to be comprehended by either our natural or spiritual minds. He is beyond description, or as the old song says, "too marvelous for words." Yes, our God sits between the seraphim and not only see us, hears us, knows us, and remembers us, but are you ready for this... LOVES US.

Can we sit for a minute or even two and let His love (His presence) overflow us? His name is Emmanuel (God who is WITH US), the God who has made a promise that He WILL NEVER, NEVER, YES, NEVER, LEAVE OR FORSAKE US!

Take a moment – He's drawing near.

Though I might not see you or feel you, I know you are here. Psalms 63:3: "For your love and kindness are better to me than life itself. How I praise you!" (TLB) "So here I am in the place of worship, eyes open, drinking in your strength and glory. In your generous love I am really living at last! My lips brim praises like fountains. I bless you every time I take a breath; My arms wave like banners of praise to you." (MSG)

Take a minute right now; lift your arms and wave them like a "grain offering" and begin to sing. "Great is our God and greatly to be praised."

I can see the angels gathering, and I wonder why. I hear they've come because they've heard worship. There's a chorus of voices singing and cherubim flying in the heavens singing, "Holy, Holy." Let's join them...

My difficulties have not changed, but my perspective has!

Day 221

THOUGHT OF THE DAY: I'm speechless

Imagine this morning and every morning and at any moment of the day for that matter, that we know where God is.

Yes, He's in heaven; yes, He rides the clouds and has numbered all the stars. Yes, even the stars that the greatest telescopes can't begin to see. There are millions, no trillions of stars that exist, and He knows them all by name. He keeps the universes under His authority. He knows the reportedly 150,000 strands of hair on our head and the 37 trillion cells in our body; they too are numbered.

He knows us - Psalm 139:1-6:

You have looked deep into my heart, Lord, and you know all about me. You know when I am resting or when I am working, and from heaven you discover my thoughts. You notice everything I do and everywhere I go. Before I even speak a word, you know what I will say, and with your powerful arm you protect me from every side. I can't understand all of this! Such wonderful knowledge is far above me. Yes, such knowledge overwhelming. (CEV)

As I write this I can feel His presence growing not only around me, but in me. Perhaps one of the most profound truths is that God is in us. Just stop reading and think about it - God is in us. So many people are searching for the deep things of God, yet in all their searching they overlook the mystery they're looking for. Colossians 1:27: "Christ in you." I believe once we get a true revelation of this we'll begin fulfilling John 14:12: "Most assuredly, I say to you, he who believes in Me, the works that I do he will do also; and greater works than these he will do, because I go to My Father."

No matter a person's earthly status, whether rich or poor, black, white, Hispanic, Chinese, or a combination of all of them, God will use them in ways that are beyond their dreams or imagination. The entire creation is groaning, yes, waiting for the manifestation of the sons of God. Romans 8:19: "The whole creation waits breathless with anticipation for the revelation of God's sons and daughters." (CEB)

WOW!!!!

We're called to and can live in the reality of 1 Corinthians 2:4: "And my speech and my preaching were not with persuasive words of human wisdom, but in demonstration of the Spirit and of power." We won't have to try and convince or persuade people that Jesus is who He said He was. People will knock on our door where we live asking/begging for us to pray for them. People won't necessarily go to church (where we congregate) but people will seek out the church (us) because they'll recognize that we're carrying what Jesus was carrying - the ANOINTING!

I wonder how the governments of the world will respond? I wonder how we'll answer them. How will we answer NBC, CNN, CBS, FOX and others? When they do a little research into our lives, what will they find? When we're asked, what will we say about these things? My mind is flooded with numerous answers, "I am who I am by the grace of God," or as Peter and John did in Acts 3:12: "Why look so intently at us, as though by our own power or godliness we had made this man walk?" Then verse 16: "And His name, through faith in His name, has made this man strong, whom you see and know. Yes, the faith which comes through Him has given him this perfect soundness in the presence of you all."

Oh, there is so much more. Those days are coming.

Is it possible that these are the days of "getting ready" and "positioning" ourselves?

I am speechless...

Day 222

THOUGHT OF THE DAY: Our waiting is about to end

For days and even weeks and months now I've been like Habakkuk who prays in chapter one, verse one: "O Lord, how long shall I cry, and You will not hear?" This is the way I've felt, that I was crying out, and He wasn't listening. I know what the Word says and I knew He heard, but feelings, while wonderful to have, can be the devil's playground.

I've been crying out for literally everyone. Over and over again I've been praying; please Lord, release the dreams and visions we've all been carrying. Release clarity, power, and resources so these dreams and visions can become a reality. This morning I experienced a lengthy time of groaning - where I had no words but my spirit prayed.

If you haven't recognized it by now, my perspectives, burdens, and thoughts are not the norm. I'm always asking questions, often having us consider and contemplate issues of our heart and where we are and what we're thinking. Sometimes I wish I could be normal. I constantly live with burdens. I often cry, and when I'm around people, I usually don't talk much. Often I can appear moody and unfriendly. I constantly live with and at times am overwhelmed by deep yearnings and burdens. I can see some of you laughing, saying, "You've always been that way."

Anyway, as I sat and mused this morning, I saw a vision of the Lord. He had a closed fist, and then he opened his hand, and wind came out of it. I knew it meant that this was the beginning of him releasing the dreams and visions we've been agonizing over. As much as I was filled with joy and hope, I had another question enter my mind. Yes, another question! The question was, "Am I ready? Do I have the character and wisdom to know what to do and when to do it?"

I don't want to blow it. I don't want to be like the prodigal son who wasted his inheritance. Father, keep us, guide us, show us what to do and when to do it.

Ask the Holy Spirit to lead you, teach you, and guide you. He will. Do not lead yourself!

What's coming is out of the box. It's possible that some of us might miss this wind, but the good news is that there's more wind on the way. We've become so ingrained with certain ways of thinking and doing, and yet I know that "new wine CANNOT be put in old wine skins!" There's such joy in this wind but also great accountability. The wind carries with it the concept found in the parable of talents. If we use the portion He sends now and if we use it well, He'll send more.

Our Father isn't going to send everything He has for us all at once. He wants to see how we steward what is sent and monitor our heart-attitude. We could do everything else, but if our heart gets filled with pride and arrogance, the wind will stop until adjustments are made.

Get ready... Our waiting is about to end!

Day 223

THOUGHT OF THE DAY: Have you written your vision?

Here are some notes from Sunday:

Write the Vision

Habakkuk says to write down our vision. How many of us have done that?

Habakkuk 2:1:" I will stand upon my watch, and set me upon the tower, and will watch to see what he will say unto me, and what I shall answer when I am reproved."

1:2: "And the Lord answered me, and said, 'Write the vision, and make it plain upon tables, that he may run that reads it.' "

MSG – "Write it out in big block letters so that it can be read on the run."

AMP – "And the Lord answered me and said, 'Write the vision and engrave it so plainly upon tablets that everyone who passes may [be able to] read [it easily and quickly] as he hastens by.' "

Does your mate know your vision? Do your children?

Amos 3:3: Do two walk together unless they've agreed to do so?

"For the vision is yet for an appointed time, but at the end it shall speak, and not lie: though it tarry, wait for it; because it will surely come, it will not tarry."

By writing it down you can go back to it and add or delete from it. It's a lot like with house plans where it's easier to erase one part of it than to build and later have to dismantle it.

MORE ON VISION:

Where are we going? Life has been shifting, and we're unsure of our future.

Perhaps it's time to chart a new course for your life or go back and revisit the things that God has spoken to you.

It's a time of a new beginning. Without a vision, Proverbs 29:18 says, "the people perish."

GW - "Without prophetic vision people run wild."

CWJ - "Without a prophetic vision, the people throw off all restraint."

Without vision we live aimless lives. It is like sailing without a map or having no true course. We're unsure of where we're going.

Decisions made can be difficult to undo. They can imprison us or propel us into our tomorrow.

Where are you going and why?

When you have a vision, your decisions are not independent of one another but instead harmonious, with a single goal in mind. With each one, I ask, does the decision I'm making propel me closer to the fulfillment of my vision for my life?

When we don't have a spiritual vision then we allow fleshly goals to direct our lives.

What's your vision?

Day 224

THOUGHT OF THE DAY: It's almost midnight

When our lives are upside down, we need to pray and worship. When we're in great pain and suffering, we need to pray and worship. When we're in a place of hopelessness, we need to pray and worship. When it appears there's no way out, we need to pray and worship. When we feel like we're a prisoner to our circumstances, we need to pray and worship.

Why should we pray and worship? Because we'll create our MIDNIGHT! There will be a great shaking, and the chains that bind us will just drop off. Doors that have been locked will be open. How can this be? Because in the midst of our despair, we prayed and worshipped. Yes, we'll be loosed from shackles and from the things that have kept us captive, and beyond all this, we'll be able to free others! How can this be?

It's because we prayed and worshipped.

Sitting here I can hear the sound of rumblings. Our prayer and worship will cause a great shift. As in Acts 16, people are watching and listening to see what we'll do in the midst of our struggles and trials. As we lift up our voices to pray and worship, we'll effect and release a new spirit of freedom. It will cause people to want to know the God we worship. Yes, it will release a desire and a hunger in people because they will have seen and heard our steadfast love and dependence on our God. As we pray and worship in the times of trouble, we'll release something new. In the days ahead and even now there's the beginning of a rumbling, because we've learned to pray and worship in the times of trouble.

We must stop our grumbling and complaining. We must stop the negative speech. It's time people hear the sound of men and women who've been praying and worshipping in the midst of their struggles and trials. It's almost midnight.

Our midnight is not a specific time of day. It's a time when God will shake the very foundations of our lives and the lives of others because we've prayed and worshipped.

There are so many examples of a single person causing a great move of God, (and tomorrow I will write of one). In Acts 16 there were two men, who in the midst of suffering few have experienced, lifted up their voices and prayed and worshipped. Then at midnight God moved.

God is looking for people who will cause midnight to happen.

Is it possible that we can cause an event like in Acts 16:25-26? This is what is written, "But at midnight Paul and Silas were praying and singing hymns to God, and the prisoners were listening to them. Suddenly there was a great earthquake, so that the foundations of the prison were shaken; and immediately all the doors were opened and everyone's chains were loosed." Read the rest of the story and see what else happened.

For us who will pray and worship in times of struggles and trials - It's almost midnight!

Day 225

THOUGHT OF THE DAY: You can be a Daniel. Can't you?

Let's be honest; there are trials and then there are trials. Too often we make the smallest of problems and difficulties sound like we're facing Goliath.

The funny thing is that Goliath is a great example of what I'm talking about. Here's what Wikipedia says, "Goliath's stature grew at the hand of narrators or scribes: the oldest manuscripts—the Dead Sea Scrolls text of Samuel, the 1st century historian Josephus, and the 4th century Septuagint manuscripts—all give his height as "four cubits and a span" (6 feet 9 inches or 2.06 meters) whereas the Masoretic Text gives this as "six cubits and a span" (9 feet 9 inches or 2.97 meters."

To break this down, Goliath was only 6'9," yet they made him out to be 9'6," which tells us that we make our trials bigger than they really are. Sure, he was big like several situations we face, but it just goes to show us that we often make matters bigger than they really are.

When we're in a trial it's important to be honest about how big the problem is. We often "make mountains out of molehills." Either way, no matter the trial, God is looking for us to carry the spirit that was in Daniel. Daniel was given great authority because he was a man of character. Daniel 6:3: "Daniel distinguished himself above the governors and satraps, because an excellent spirit was in him; and the king gave thought to setting him over the whole realm."

Notice that he "distinguished himself" because he had "an excellent spirit." Daniels don't just come from the womb; they're formed through trials and harsh circumstances, by an unwillingness to compromise, and yes, by hard work. When the men under Daniel grew jealous, they looked for faults so they could accuse him. In verse four we read, "So the governors and satraps sought to find some charge against Daniel concerning the kingdom; but they could find no charge or fault, because he was faithful; nor was there any error or fault found in him." Oh, how much we all want to be like Daniel. Well, we can!

Even when we're doing everything right, we often find ourselves in situations that are unfair and unjust. Here in Daniel six, those opposing Daniel created a law that everyone had to obey, but since obeying this new law would violate Daniel's convictions, he refused to yield to the pressure even though it would cost him his life. Surely that's something for us to contemplate.

Sounds like what Jesus did and left us an example to do. Our problem is that sometimes we don't want to die.

To make a great story short, Daniel ends up in a lion's den. Can we give that some thought? King Darius stands outside of the lion's den and yells to see if Daniel is alive. We read in verse 20, "And when he came to the den, he cried out with a lamenting voice to Daniel. The king spoke, saying to Daniel, 'Daniel, servant of the living God, has your God, whom you serve continually, been able to deliver you from the lions?' "

People want to know that our God is real. Notice that Darius recognized Daniel as a servant of the living God. Notice that he acknowledged that Daniel served God continually, witnessing Daniel's consistent life style. What do people see when they see us?

God is not only looking for Daniels but is molding new Daniels through circumstances and trials. In the end we want people who see us and watch us and will declare what King Darius decreed in his kingdom.

Daniel 6:25-27:

Then King Darius wrote: To all peoples, nations, and languages that dwell in all the earth: Peace be multiplied to you. I make a decree that in every dominion of my kingdom men must tremble and fear before the God of Daniel. For He is the living God, And steadfast forever; His kingdom is the one which shall not be destroyed, And His dominion shall endure to the end He delivers and rescues, And He works signs and wonders In heaven and on earth, Who has delivered Daniel from the power of the lions.

You can be a Daniel!

Day 226

THOUGHT OF THE DAY: Hope - Part 1

On Saturday night I went to bed about 10:30, which is very early for me. I was tired because I had spent the last two days repairing the waterline coming from the well into our house. As I went to bed I had no idea what I was to share Sunday morning. This is not unusual. So I was sound asleep and at 1:22 a.m. awoke and heard these words, "He who promised is faithful."

Now while I knew that there's a verse in the bible that says this, other than somewhere in the new testament, I had no idea exactly where. I got up and went to my computer to do a search for this phrase. Here is what I found.

The verse "He who promised is faithful" is found in Hebrews 10:23. Now I know that this verse is directly related to our salvation, but for greater depth, context is critical: "Let us hold fast the confession of our hope without wavering, for He who promised is faithful." (NKJV)

We're encouraged to hold onto what we've been told by God about the promises He's made each one of us and to do so without wavering. I know that if I'm honest, I can share that there have been numerous times when I've become discouraged, disappointed, and disheartened, feeling that the things God had promised me would not come to pass.

Why have I felt this way? I've looked at the circumstances that have surrounded my life and looked at my own decisions - two major mistakes. First, I looked through my natural eyes and thus saw natural things, and two: I didn't really believe that "He who promised is faithful," that God's promises are bigger than my circumstances and my choices.

The WE Bible says, "We must hold onto God's promise that we have said we believed. And we must never let go. He has promised and He will do it." The encouragement is we "must hold on to" what God has promised us and what we've believed and even told others that God promised us, the two key points being 1. "We must NEVER let go of what He promised and 2. "What He promises HE WILL DO." It doesn't say He MIGHT do; it says He WILL do. It's similar to the verse, "He will perfect everything that concerns me."

Then there is the Amplified Bible: "Let us seize and hold tightly the confession of our hope without wavering, for He who promised is reliable and trustworthy and faithful [to His word]" I really like the phrase "let us seize," and once we seize it, to hold on tightly to our HOPE. WHY? BECAUSE WE CAN ALWAYS TRUST GOD.

I sat at my computer and began to recall all the promises that God had made me. I soon realized that a promise is like a seed that needs to be nurtured and cared for. It needs to be watered and even weeded. As I sat there early in the morning, I recalled two distinct promises God made me in May of 1970 on the very day that I committed my life to Christ. At the time my life was an absolute mess. (You will be able to hear this story when it's posted in a day or so.) The first promise was that one day I would have my own church. This was crazy because at the time I was 20 years old, and my life had been an absolute disaster. The second thing He said I've never really told anybody until yesterday, not even my wife.

The first promise was fulfilled in 1992! It took 22 years for God to ready me to walk in this promise. Now 23 more years, and only for five or six of them have I begun to walk in what He told me in 1970. More years of preparation.

I haven't always been faithful but instead disappointed, disheartened, discouraged, depressed, etcetera. Yet through all these years something inside of me has clung to the hope that one day I would walk in what He promised. Thankfully during the 43 years there were numerous times when God reminded me.

Remember that this THOUGHT OF THE DAY started with God waking me out of a dead sleep to say to me (and through me to you), "He who promised is faithful."

The spirit of Hope is in the air. God is faithful to YOU!

P.S. More to come on this.

Day 227

THOUGHT OF THE DAY: Hope - Part 2

The Living Bible translation of Proverbs 13:12 says, "Hope deferred makes the heart sick; but when dreams come true at last, there is life and joy."

All too often we walk around disappointed and discouraged because the hopes and dreams that the Lord has given us have not come to pass.

But look what happens when God fulfills His promises to us - "There is life and joy." There is a similar verse in Proverbs 28:18: "Where there is no vision, the people perish." Yet when God does fulfill His promises to us, our lives are filled with incredible gladness and delight.

A few weeks ago I was feeling the opposite of this – very discouraged and sorry for myself. It was on a Friday morning during my musing (or boo-hoo) time before the Lord that He told me to read Joel chapter two. I told Him that I knew what it said. He told me to read it anyway. I started in verse one and began saying to myself and then even out loud, "I know that. I know that."

In my mind I was saying that the whole thing was boring. God told me to keep on reading. Then I came to verse 25, and it was and is still now a life-changing word for me and for you. Here it is in four different translations. Notice what God has already begun to do:

BRG: "And I will restore to you the years that the locust hath eaten, the cankerworm, and the caterpillar, and the palmerworm," Notice God says, "I WILL (HE WILL, not MAY) RESTORE THE YEARS THAT HAVE BEEN EATEN.

CEV: "I, the Lord your God, will make up for the losses caused by those swarms and swarms of locusts I sent to attack you."

GNT: "I will give you back what you lost in the years when swarms of locusts ate your crops."

MSG: "I'll make up for the years of the locust, the great locust devastation."

WRITING THIS AGAIN, I'M PRETTY EXCITED!!!!

Remember that when Joseph had a dream, it took 13 years for it to come to pass. Joseph went from the pit, to prison, to the palace... Hold on to your dream. Hold on to your HOPE. For God is about to fulfill it.

Day 228

THOUGHT OF THE DAY: Stir up your hope

All of us have had countless days of discouragement. By our natural observation and through our natural senses, it's easy to be disheartened and discouraged and be dissatisfied about where we are in our lives.

Unfortunately, we seem to put fuel on our circumstances by continually allowing ourselves to see things in a negative light. And after we see it; we speak it. Thus we put, as Proverbs says, "wood on the fire." It goes on to say that if you don't put wood on the fire, the fire goes out. Seems simple enough.

One of the ways to stop the discouragement is to build another fire. The fire we have to build is the fire called hope. We must encourage ourselves and others to rekindle hope in the things God has promised. We can hear people say, "Well, I don't feel hopeful."

There we go! We are held captive because we don't feel hopeful. If we wait to feel hopeful, we'll spend the majority of our time in hopelessness. We have to get sick and tired of "feeling" discouraged, and then we can activate what Paul says in:

Romans 12;12: "Rejoicing in hope." Yes, even when we don't feel like it.

Romans 4:18 : "Hoping in spite of hopeless circumstances, he believed that he would become 'the father of many nations,' just as he had been told." (ISV)

The Message Bible puts it this way: "We call Abraham 'father' not because he got God's attention by living like a saint, but because God made something out of Abraham when he was a nobody." Isn't that what we've always read in Scripture, God saying to Abraham, "I set you up as father of many peoples"? Abraham was first named "father" and then became a father, because he dared to trust God to do what only God could do: raise the dead to life, with a word that made something out of nothing. When everything was hopeless, Abraham believed anyway, deciding to live not on the basis of what he recognized he couldn't do, but on what God said He would do.

We have to do what Hebrews 10:24, 2 Peter 1:13, and 2 Peter 3:1 all encourage us to do; that is, stir up. Then there is Jude 1:20: "But you, beloved, building yourselves up on your most holy faith, praying in the Holy Spirit."

Let's not wait until we have a feeling, but instead let's stir up; meaning "provoke, arouse, to excite, to urge, shake up, and to rekindle."

Okay; let's start now - let's not wait another moment. Stir up your hope!

Day 229

THOUGHT OF THE DAY: Where and who is our hope?

As I awoke this morning, I felt that the Lord was watching over me as a shepherd watches over his sheep. He spoke to me about trust and led me to Psalms 146:5. The Voice Bible reads this way: "Blessed/happy are those whose help comes from the God of Jacob, whose hope is centered in the Eternal their God." Then I recalled Jeremiah 17:5: "Cursed is the man who trusts in man and make flesh his strength" and Jeremiah 17:7: "Blessed is the man who trusts in the Lord, and whose hope is the Lord."

As I paused for a moment to consider these verses, and with a deep desire to have all my hope centered in the Lord, I closed my eyes. Then I had and still have this wonderful sense that I'm safe, as a child feels when their father holds them in his arms. I then got that picture - a father holding his child.

It was and is overwhelming. He's looking down with a smile on his face that says, "I love you and will always be here for you." I can see and hear the father speaking to his child and a tear coming from the corner of his eye joining other tears running down his cheek. He says as he holds the child to his breast,

I know you will go through all kinds of trials. I know the hurt, pain and disappointment that you will experience. But know this: I will always be there for you. There will be nothing that will happen in your life that I will not know about. Remember, my little one, I am always watching over you. Always put your hope and trust in me, because you see, my dear one, I AM YOUR HOPE! I know you will wander, but what you don't know is that I will right there beside you, I will always be there. There is nothing you can do that will cause me to love you any less. There is no where you will go that I won't be. Nothing, absolutely nothing you do or say will cause us to be separated. You see, my dear one, I will always hold you in my arms. You see, my child, hope is not merely a word; HOPE IS ME!

There is nothing more to say! This says it all – "HOPE IS ME..."

Day 230

THOUGHT OF THE DAY: Did you hear what the angel is saying?

This morning as I sat before the Lord to inquire about the THOUGHT OF THE DAY, I saw an angel being sent out from the throne of God.

He was saying as he flew through the atmosphere, "Do your portion." There was a pleading in his voice yet no sense of pressure or guilt. It was like he was saying that there's so much to be done. When he saw certain people, he said to them, "Stay and rest; it's not your time. Get well so one day you'll be able to come."

I saw as he flew through the atmosphere that some people were unwilling to hear. They had grown complacent. I can hear the angel say that there's so much to do. I am reminded of Ephesians 4:15-16 where Paul speaks about how the body of Christ grows by each person doing their portion. This principle can likewise be applied to the growth and the advancement of the kingdom We are simply called to do our portion.

Here is what Ephesians 4:15-16 says, "but, speaking the truth in love, may grow up in all things into Him who is the head—Christ from whom the whole body, joined and knit together by what every joint supplies, according to the effective working by which every part does its share, causes growth of the body for the edifying of itself in love." Fulfilling our calling must be done in love, not obligation, with each of us doing only our "share."

I will let the words of Isaiah 6:6-8 be the final voice of the day: "Then one of the seraphim flew to me, having in his hand a live coal which he had taken with the tongs from the altar. Also, I heard the voice of the Lord, saying: 'Whom shall I send, and who will go for Us?' Then I said, 'Here am I! Send me.'"

Lord, let this be our answer.

You are needed! Did you hear what the angel is saying?

Day 231

THOUGHT OF THE DAY: It's time to say

I have spent the last 24 hours going through all my files. I have gone through financial files going back to 2004. I have shredded (not just thrown away) old warranties on items I purchased years ago.

Boy, does that ring a prophetic note. Perhaps it's time we discard/shred warranties that were made between people, friends, ministries, family members, former employers and pastors, elders, deacons, etcetera.

I am a documentation person. I keep copies of things I have sent and things I have received. I do this in order to have necessary proof in case of...

Well, it was time to shred the past. As I was doing this, I recalled a lot of painful moments. As I shredded the documents and letters, I could see the subtle desire to keep a record of wrongs or perceived wrongs. I came across certain documentation that I still wanted to hold onto. I realized it's not possible to step into the new while remnants of the past were not only sitting in a file drawer, but sitting in the bigger file of my heart.

While wrestling with numerous emotions, I realized I only had one choice and that was to consider and apply the words of Jesus in Luke 23:34: "Then Jesus said, 'Father, forgive them, for they do not know what they do.'" As I was forgiving, releasing, and blessing people whose letters I was keeping, I soon realized that I too had said and done things that have deeply hurt people. I became aware while musing about these matters, that I didn't fully understand some of the things I had said and done. In all honesty, in many circumstances I didn't know what I was doing.

I wish I could tell you how much better I feel, but for now I've let go of things I wasn't aware I needed to. You see, it's time to say, "Father, forgive them, for they do not know what they do."

Maybe even "Father, forgive me, for I didn't know either."

Day 232

THOUGHT OF THE DAY: Are you a whoever?

This morning I was in the hospital for a scheduled medical procedure - in at 7:30, out by 10:45.

While I was waiting for my procedure, I had the opportunity to chat with one of the RNs. She had the same first name as my grandmother, so she already had a special place in my heart. After she took all my information, she left me and I waited for my procedure. During the time I was waiting, the nurse who checked me in was checking in other patients.

Rather than just lay there, I asked the Holy Spirit who I should pray for. Earlier I had learned that the RN had two daughters, one 14 and the other eight, so I was led to pray for the RN's oldest daughter. When she returned, I told her what I'd been doing and began to share with her what I believed the Lord had shown me about her daughter, who was (by the way) very much like her. As I shared, she began to cry.

Once again, I realized just how hungry and thirsty people are. People everywhere want to be loved and cared for. John 7:38 says, "Whoever believes in me, as the Scripture has said, 'Out of his heart will flow rivers of living water.' " You are a whoever! Today that could've been you in the hospital and not me. You could do what I did.

First, I asked the Holy Spirit what He wanted me to do. He said, "Pray for the 14- year-old girl." You can do that. Then what happened to me can and will happen to you. Because we're all whoevers who believe in Jesus. When a whoever who believes in Jesus prays, then "out of YOU will FLOW, FLOW, FLOW rivers (not a trickle but a river) of living (life-giving) water." Life will flow from YOU!

The attitude that God only works through a chosen few HAS TO STOP. You see, the reality is that God DOES work through HIS CHOSEN, but we are all CHOSEN! Since you are a "whoever" who believes in Jesus, then there's a river inside of you. We have allowed our rivers to be dammed up. When it says in scripture that we shall receive power, the word power is often translated as dynamite. So let's take the dynamite that God has put in and on our lives and go blow up some dams.

As I wrote this, I heard several explosions. Somebody got it! Look - there are a number of torrential rivers that have just been released. Go ahead, blow up whatever dam that restricts the flow of God's Spirit from your life. Since you are a whoever who believes, then let the river flow.

Are you a whoever? Then let the River FLOW!

Day 233

THOUGHT OF THE DAY: The joy of sowing

Is it possible that we're addicted to reaping? Have we yet learned to rejoice in our seasons of sowing?

To be honest I've always enjoyed the season of reaping but not so much the season of sowing. What a sad commentary on my spiritual condition. Think of all the countless days, weeks, months, etcetera that the Lord had me in this time and season, yet while there, I simply didn't want to be. Thus, I always wanted to be in a place I wasn't and was perpetually dissatisfied.

I'm beginning to understand that there was and is a presence and provision available during the seasons of sowing that I couldn't see or discern because I simply didn't want to be there. I want to go beyond the attitude of contentment. Remember Paul wrote that he "learned to be content in all things." (Phil. 4:12)

Part of the word he gave last week was "He would restore the fields that the locusts have devoured." The Lord wants to bring us to a place of rejoicing in our seasons of sowing. Imagine the joy that He's already planned for us.

There's a joy of sowing we're about to enter...

Day 234

THOUGHT OF THE DAY: Living beyond discouragement

I was just thinking about the other morning when I so wanted to find a new and intimate worship song. I searched YouTube for over an hour and a half and didn't find what I was looking for.

There in front of me was a very common trap called discouragement.

There are some days when negotiating life is like walking through a spiritual mine field. In the mine fields of our lives, discouragement is everywhere. I'm learning to refuse to get discouraged. I often say out loud, "I'm not going there." Like David at Ziklag in 1 Samuel 30:6, "David strengthened and encouraged himself in the Lord his God."

This I know and declare, OUR GOD IS FAITHFUL! I'm here writing this thought and am listening to some new worship music. It's not so much the words I'm hearing but the "Spirit," and He's singing to me "encouragement!" Where did these new songs come from?

Yesterday afternoon my nephew sent me two new songs in an e-mail. I can't remember the last time he's done this. Two days ago I unsuccessfully searched for new worship songs, and then an e-mail showed up yesterday. It wasn't the words of the song but the Spirit.

I can be listening to a sermon and though I might be familiar with the content, I can hear in the sermon the "Spirit." There have been countless times I've been engaged in conversations, and the person speaking is struggling with trying to find the "right words to express themselves," but by God's grace I can hear the "spirit" of their words.

Can you? Yes, you can! Don't respond to people's words but hear the spirit of their heart and respond to that.

As I'm writing, I can hear the Spirit say, "Tell them to be the voice of encouragement today." The Lord will show you someone today who needs just one or two words that will breathe encouragement into their lives. In 1 Corinthians 14:1 it says, "Pursue love, and desire spiritual gifts, but especially that you may prophesy." What a great word for today! Pursue someone you can love today; have a desire for God to work through you, and then when you find that person, "prophesy," or breathe life as God did into Adam in Genesis and Ezekiel to the dry bones. The result will be life.

Some of us will say that we just don't feel like it, but who said feelings had anything to do with it?

Haven't we all discovered that when God uses us, we're so deeply encouraged. One of the keys of living beyond discouragement is to encourage others. We've also read of two others; determine not to be discouraged, and encourage yourself. The fourth key is worship and prayer. If one key doesn't work, try another.

Now close your eyes and be encouraged:

Day 235

THOUGHT OF THE DAY: Why did David dance before the Lord with all of his might?

In 2 Samuel 6:14 we find King David dancing before the ark of God with total abandon, whirling around so much that his wife felt he was undignified. Indeed, he wasn't acting like a king, but a worshipper.

Why was David so overwhelmed with joy?

David was rejoicing because the ark of God had been brought back to Jerusalem. The ark was more than just a religious fixture. The ark literally carried within it the presence of God. When the presence of God enters a church, it should cause all of us to have a response that so grips us we can't help but respond. Some people will dance, some will lie prostrate on the floor, others will sit so overwhelmed they can't stand, still others will stand and lift their hands and voices. Some will shout, and some will be silent. No matter the response we should be like Isaiah, who was "undone."

Since Solomon's Porch was birthed in 2009, we've never had a meeting where the presence of God was not with us. We don't take it for granted, but are always confident that God Himself will be among us. We don't have to go to a particular building to be in the presence of God but should experience the presence of God wherever we are. Why? Because we are now the ark of God, and the ones to carry His presence. Indeed, wherever we are - GOD IS PRESENT.

It's such a humbling place to be.

Yes, you carry the presence of God, His kingdom wherever you go. What is the kingdom? Romans 14:17 calls it "righteousness and peace and joy in the Holy Spirit." When you walk into a room, a vehicle, or wherever, you bring the presence of God. You bring the king and the kingdom. The more we believe this, the more we see the manifest presence of God wherever we go. I am fully persuaded that we will see Habakkuk: "The time will come when all the earth is filled, as the waters fill the sea, with an awareness of the glory of the Lord." (2:14, TLB) Why? Because of who you are!

Before this can take place, we have to become like David! We need to so desire the presence of God.

Lord, it's YOU who will change the world one life at a time. Oh Lord, I'm not praying for your presence; I'm asking that we become aware of your presence and so would live our lives in awe. If people see our awe and sensed your presence, I can't even imagine what could happen.

If only the world could see us dance!

Day 236

THOUGHT OF THE DAY: Today

This morning as I closed my eyes and asked the Holy Spirit to lead me and show me what he wanted me to see, I could hear him encouraging me to have all of you do likewise.

Luke 12:32: "Do not fear, little flock, for it is your Father's good pleasure to give you the kingdom"(NKJV) or the (CJB): "Have no fear, little flock, for your Father has resolved to give you the Kingdom!" Did we hear that? Our Father has RESOLVED TO GIVE US THE KINGDOM! Then there is the (ERV): "Don't fear, little flock. Your Father wants to share his kingdom with you."

If only we could embrace this overwhelming reality. Our Father so loves us that He's made his mind up to give us His kingdom. For this very reason man was created. Listen to the VERY FIRST words God spoke to man: "And God blessed them [granting them certain authority] and said to them, 'Be fruitful, multiply, and fill the earth, and subjugate it [putting it under your power]; and rule over (dominate) the fish of the sea, the birds of the air, and every living thing that moves upon the earth.' " (the Amplified Bible)

We were created to govern His kingdom, not to spend eternity in heaven. Remember, heaven is coming to earth; Revelations 21:1-3: "Now I saw a new heaven and a new earth, for the first heaven, and the first earth had passed away. Also, there was no more sea. Then I, John, saw the holy city, New Jerusalem, coming down out of heaven from God, prepared as a bride adorned for her husband. And I heard a loud voice from heaven saying, 'Behold, the tabernacle of God is with men, and He will dwell with them, and they shall be His people. God Himself will be with them and be their God.' " Then there is Revelations 1:6: "He lets us rule as kings and serve God his Father as priests. To him be glory and power forever and ever! Amen."

We will "RULE AS KINGS."

Be encouraged. God has called you to be used TODAY!

Day 237

THOUGHT OF THE DAY: Once you say it

I just hate it when I violate principles I believe in. Why does this happen?

There are a number of reasons, and for the sake of time I'll share a couple. Why am I even writing about this? The simple truth is that even those of us who pride ourselves in applying principles, still fall prey to stupidity. Perhaps you might've picked up one major flaw already - pride. Pride is a many-tentacled monster.

Rule number one: always attempt to walk in humility, to approach people with love and honor. Recently I'd been sharing that on the night of the last supper, Jesus loved and honored Judas by giving him one of the two seats of honor at the dinner table, John getting the other one. Jesus washed Judas' feet and had communion with him. Sadly, I missed the depth of what the Holy Spirit was trying to show me. Not that I've been betrayed, but I do fail at times to love and honor.

I can now see something else that Jesus had to be experiencing the night of the last supper. It's called disappointment, a common topic for me of late.

I talked about being disappointed with Peter. Here is how the night of the last supper went. Peter is jealous that Judas is sitting where he feels he should be sitting and thus fails to complete his assignment, which was to wash the feet of those attending dinner. So Jesus does his job, and Peter says things that reveal the condition of his heart and his misunderstanding of the big picture and what Jesus was trying to demonstrate.

I have my hand raised. We say and do "stupid things" when we don't UNDERSTAND... Peter is involved in the who-is-the-greatest-among-us discussion at the dinner table, another flaw I certainly fall into periodically and perhaps more often than I think. After dinner Peter tells Jesus three times that he won't deny him, but he does. Jesus knows of course, and so prophecies that the cock would crow three times. Peter falls asleep just when Jesus could have used the prayer support or at least an arm around him. Next Peter cuts off the soldier's ear. All in all, not a very good night for Peter, and with all of it, Jesus had to have been disappointed, but he didn't stop loving, honoring, and setting the right example.

Disappointment can be real and can come from drawing wrong conclusions. This can happen when we totally misread a situation, not understanding why people make certain decisions. In the process we don't wait for the explanation. We instead say things that are hurtful, wrong, damaging, and painful, which can have a long-term negative effect on the relationship - the once-you've-said-it nightmare.

Another cause for misunderstanding is often birthed from a need for closure before its time. The problem may be, however, that one person's need for closure is not shared by the other person. One person needs closure, the other needs more time. Premature closure is not closure at all.

One of the things I've learned and am still learning is to recognize that I've said things that were hurtful or said things at the wrong time. What the Lord has had me do with this is to take responsibility for what I've said and go to the person and apologize. I struggle with knowing what is MY timing and what is the Holy Spirit's.

Today is definitely one of those mornings when I wish I could turn back the clock. I'm hopeful that by writing this I can remind myself to weigh my words and not put my needs above the Lord's timing. I'm also hoping that some of you could glean something from my faults.

Once we say something we shouldn't, it's important that we ask the Holy Spirit to show us how we can redeem the situation. There's a sad truth we read in Proverbs 18:10: "It is easier to conquer a strong city than to win back a friend whom you've offended. Their walls go up, making it nearly impossible to win them back." (TPT)

Thankfully we can rely on our Father's ability to redeem and restore. One of the most powerful tools of the Holy Spirit is saying, "I'm sorry."

Praying that perhaps you can learn from my mistakes...

Day 238

THOUGHT OF THE DAY: Willing to teach

One of the stated qualifications of a minister in 1 Timothy 3:2 is the ability to teach. More often than not this translates to a person having the ability to teach the word of God in a formal setting such as a Sunday service, classroom, home group, mission field, etcetera.

I'd like to take it to another level, however, and that is the ability to teach with our lives. I love sharing things that I've done well that I believe can help others in their walk. The more difficult things to teach are the things I haven't done well but still need to be taught.

A critical thing to teach is accountability. We're accountable first to the Lord, then to those over us, and then to one another as brothers and sisters in Christ. The danger of accountability to one another is that it can lead to people who are always seeing faults in others but never seeing their own. These are those who've become self-appointed judges of everyone, and in particular those with a public ministry. Yet if we perceive something wrong with what a brother or sister might be doing, we must approach them with love and humility.

That brings me to today. While I was in Michigan there were three occasions where I either said or did something in jest. My "kidding" and poor choice of words were not intended to be offensive, though I've since discovered that they did bother and offend a few people, which was brought to my attention in love. I'm reminded as I write this that my wife at times has said that my occasional "jesting" can be misunderstood. With that being said, I do apologize to anyone who was bothered, upset, or offended by my actions or words while in Michigan and beyond.

Paul writes in 2 Corinthians 6:3 in the New Living Translation: "We live in such a way that no one will stumble because of us, and no one will find fault with our ministry." I will ask the Lord to help me be more mindful of the way in which I communicate so as to be able to fulfill this verse.

Willing to teach when it's not always easy!

Day 239

THOUGHT OF THE DAY: Time to ponder

This morning as I sat to spend some time with the Lord, I got a picture in my mind of Jesus in his typical clothing. A number of us were sitting and listening to him on the side of a mountain. While I could see His lips move, I couldn't hear what He was saying.

The thought that came into my mind was - preconceived ideas. I believe the Holy Spirit is trying to show me that when we spend time with Him but are unable to hear what He's saying at times, it's because we have preconceived ideas of what He'll say or even still, what we want Him to say.

What I'm hearing is that when we pray, we go with our agenda. Rarely do we go and just sit. It's almost like we want to fulfill our need to pray, get our instructions, give Him our to-do list, and then go off to our daily grind.

Then I hear, "Didn't I say 'rest'? " I can see that even our prayer time is filled with the need to hurry up and say what we need to, in the end forgetting what was said. I can hear Him say, "Why don't we just spend time together?" He is showing me that it's okay not to hear anything, that just our being together is important because He wants to simply hang out with us.

Hmmm - isn't this a part of every relationship? A question comes to my mind. Can't we just be together without us wanting something?

As I stop typing, my heart is filled with sadness. I can see that the majority of our time together is me talking and looking for answers. Funny, I can hear, "I am the answer, and your mind is often too cluttered to truly hear." He goes on to say, "I understand, and I answer you because I love you, but let's go to a new place." I can almost hear the sounds of waves slapping the shore line, and He's suggesting that we spend some time here.

In this moment I can see Jesus in John 21 when Jesus has cooked fish and in verse 12 Jesus says to his disciples, "Come and eat breakfast." Yes, come over and let's have breakfast. Then the big question is asked in verse 14: "So when they had eaten breakfast, Jesus said to Simon Peter, 'Simon, son of Jonah, do you love Me more than these?' " Wow, big question.

I'm going to stop here and read the rest of John 21. Immediately I wonder what God is going to show me and what He's going to show you. All of a sudden, the following verses in John 21(20-22) came to my mind. "Then Peter, turning around, saw the disciple whom Jesus loved following, who also had leaned on His breast at the supper, and said, 'Lord, who is the one who betrays You?' Peter, seeing him, said to Jesus, 'But Lord, what about this man?' Jesus said to him, 'If I will that he remain till I come, what is that to you? You follow Me.' "

Great place to stop. Do you see what He was saying to me? Yes, it's time to ponder.

Day 240

THOUGHT OF THE DAY: Familiarity

On my recent trip to Michigan I learned a number of things. One of them was that being overfamiliar with people and their culture will cause you to be less effective with them. This holds true with those closest to us.

They can be family members, friends, co-workers, etcetera. In our approach we often can't see beyond the person we think we know, and so default to seeing the old man, their flesh, and behavior patterns. Our first response is to see what they are and have been. It becomes difficult to approach them with different eyes, as we've become too familiar. It becomes difficult to see them in the Spirit because we have known them in the flesh.

Our old thoughts about people can keep them prisoner to who they once were, and not who they're becoming.

Even the way we say hello or look at a person sends them a message. There's often no new beginning and little or no encouragement. So in reality we're living in our flesh and not living by the Spirit. Paul writes in 1 Corinthians 2:2, "For I determined not to know anything among you except Jesus Christ and Him crucified." (NKJV) The Amplified Bible says, "for I made the decision to know nothing [that is, to forego philosophical or theological discussions regarding inconsequential things and opinions while] among you except Jesus Christ, and Him crucified [and the meaning of His redemptive, substitutionary death and His resurrection]."

Somehow we have to start determining that we're going to see each other differently. We need to determine to approach everyone the way Jesus would approach them and in the way we would like to be approached. We must stop seeing people as who they're not instead of who they're becoming.

When I returned from Michigan, I realized that because I've been there a number of times, I assumed I could "kid" and even be a little relaxed in my general approach to people. I forgot that each night the people the Holy Spirit brings are uniquely different from who might've been there the previous night or even the last time I visited.

Each time we minister, we need to understand the culture of the area we're in. We need to, as I like to say, "read the room." Reading the room is about discerning who's there and the spiritual atmosphere. When we become familiar with an area and its culture, there's the potential of hindering the Lord's plans. We have entered our flesh. God in His grace will still move, yet we want our own flesh to be minimized and for the Holy Spirit to be unhindered. We also don't want people to be offended or for there to be a stumbling block.

Lord, help me to see people with YOUR eyes. I don't want to miss seeing them the way you do. Everyone will miss out.

Day 241

THOUGHT OF THE DAY: What's our message?

I woke up this morning asking myself, "What's my message?"

Is my message to people that they need to be in a church, to think and act like a church member, or that they must be born again, an idea mentioned numerous times in the bible? But born again into what and for what purpose, I ask? Is our speaking to people about a church or church culture? Is our Christian belief system about theology, or is it about our Christian culture? What should our message be?

This country needs a radical change, a cultural revolution. We do not necessarily need change in Washington, a new president, or new laws (though some are desperately needed, to be sure). What we need is for this world to be turned upside down. That's what happened in Acts 17 when Paul and Silas visited Thessalonica where it's said about them in verse 6, "These who have turned the world upside down have come here too."

What was Paul's message? It was about God's kingdom culture. What was Jesus' purpose for coming to earth? Answer Luke 4:43: "I must preach the kingdom of God to the other cities also, because for this purpose I have been sent." Okay, so what is our purpose?

I've been preaching about the Kingdom of God for over 40 years, but it wasn't until seven years ago that I began to truly understand the reality of the Kingdom of God and how we can enter it now, not just after we die. Actually, we enter the kingdom right when we give our lives to the Lord.

- John 3:5: "Jesus answered, 'Most assuredly, I say to you, unless one is born of water and the Spirit, he cannot enter the kingdom of God."

The message of the kingdom is not optional. It must be our message, not one about the church or a particular church's doctrine. We must be speaking something that will literally turn the world upside down. We read the beatitudes as a how-to-behave list, but quite literally, it should be seen as the "be attitudes," the attitudes that should be pouring forth from our lives.

I urge you to reread them. Moses went up the mountain and brought down the law. Jesus goes up the mountain and reveals the kingdom. Matthew 5:1-2: "And seeing the multitudes, He went up on a mountain, and when He was seated His disciples came to Him. Then He opened His mouth and taught them, saying: 'Blessed are the poor in spirit, for theirs is the kingdom of heaven.' " Notice Jesus said, "theirs IS the kingdom of heaven." It's remarkable how we haven't really seen that Jesus' entire life was all about His Father's kingdom.

Not only can we enter the kingdom, but we can also see it.

• John 3:3: "Jesus answered and said to him, "Most assuredly, I say to you, unless one is born again, he cannot see the kingdom of God."

Jesus tells us to seek the kingdom:

• Matthew 6:33: "But seek first the kingdom of God and His righteousness, and all these things shall be added to you."

Then right before his ascension into heaven he spends 40 days taking the kingdom:

Acts 1:1-3: "The former account I made, O Theophilus, of all that Jesus began to do and teach, until the day in which he was taken up, after He through the Holy Spirit had given commandments to the apostles whom He had chosen, to whom He also presented Himself alive after His suffering by many infallible proofs, being seen by them during forty days and speaking of the things pertaining to the 'Kingdom of God.' "

If Paul's message was the Kingdom of God and Jesus' message was the Kingdom of God, I have to ask the question, "What's my message? What's your message?"

Day 242

THOUGHT OF THE DAY: Can you hear Him calling?

As I awoke this morning, I was so aware of God's presence. There's a song we sing, and one of the lines is, "Bring me a little closer, I want to know your heart."

I had to take the dogs out, and His presence was and is so encompassing. I came back in the house, put the coffee on, and could hear Him say, "Come be with me."

As I sat at the computer, two verses came into my mind. The sense of His calling me to come is indeed getting stronger. He was saying for me to write and tell you that He's calling you. Two more verses come to mind.

Revelations 4:1: "After these things I looked, and behold, a door standing open in heaven. And the first voice which I heard was like a trumpet speaking with me, saying, 'Come up here, and I will show you things which must take place after this.' "

The door is open; leave your flesh. He says if we do this, He'll reveal things to us. Then the verses in Matthew chapter 13 came into my mind: "And the disciples came and said to Him, 'Why do You speak to them in parables?' He answered and said to them, 'Because it has been given to you to know the mysteries of the kingdom of heaven, but to them it has not been given.' " (verses 10-11)

Can you hear that He wants to show us the hidden things, both for the sake of the kingdom and to also provide insight into our lives?

The two verses that came to my mind earlier were James 4:8: "Come close to God [with a contrite heart] and He will come close to you." (Amplified Bible) and Joel 2:1: " 'Now, therefore,' says the Lord, 'Turn to me with all your heart.' " He's saying that He has so many things to show us, but we're TOO BUSY.

Then there is God's voice to us in Luke 10:39-41: "And she had a sister called Mary, who also sat at Jesus' feet and heard His word." (NKJV) Did we see that? Do you feel that? Mary sat (similar to King David), and the result/reward of her sitting was that "she heard His word." This was because she put herself in a position to simply LISTEN.

By contrast we read that Martha was "distracted with much serving" and was even annoyed with Mary for leaving her "to serve alone." "Therefore," she continues, "tell her to help me." (Verse 41) Jesus' answer? "Martha, Martha, you are worried and troubled about many things." How many of us are raising our hands right now because we can totally relate to Martha?!

I can hear Him saying, "I will show you things A LITTLE AT A TIME." So now what? We have just received a word from the Lord. How will we respond? My desire is to just be with Him; my focus is not on getting divine insight. I know He will show me things, but honestly, I just want to sit with Him.

Song of Solomon 2:10: "My beloved spoke, and said to me: 'Rise up, my love, my fair one, And come away.' "

Can you hear Him calling?

Day 243

THOUGHT OF THE DAY: This is your time

I'm so excited today. In the Spirit I can hear, "It's time. They can do it. The shackles have been broken. It only takes one step. All of heaven is behind you. 'The kingdom of God is not in word but power.' Stand up. Declare who you are son/daughter; declare that you were created for this moment. You're a joint heir. Jesus made the ultimate investment in you. Stop looking at yesterday; it killed Lot's wife: it will kill you, your dreams, and your destiny."

As in Esther 4:14: "You have come to the kingdom for such a time as this." Interesting that it says, "kingdom." We're the head and not the tail; Satan has already been defeated; live accordingly. Stop living in your natural mind because you can't receive from the Spirit. Stop your whining. Stop your complaining. It creates an atmosphere in opposition to the kingdom, which is righteousness, peace, and joy. Stop making excuses. (It didn't work for Adam.) Go to your yard, find a stone, and throw it at your giant.

Wait a minute. I can hear a faint chanting, and it's getting louder - RISE UP, RISE UP. Can you hear it? It's a day of declaration! Your tomorrow is here today!

THIS IS YOUR TIME...

Day 244

THOUGHT OF THE DAY: Hearing, seeing, doing

Perhaps the question I'm asked the most and the source of people's greatest frustration is why they can't hear God.

There are multiple books written on this question and countless thoughts and opinions as well. A number of them are legitimate. Perhaps in my little mind, though, the biggest reason is that we live the majority of our lives being naturally-minded. Every day we tend to wake up and commence living in the natural realm instead of in the spiritual one. Even if we pray or study it tends to be a religious exercise rather than a relational one. We study to study and we pray too often to tell God what He should do with His day. We tend to pray our will and not concern ourselves with His will/what's on His mind.

When asked by His disciples how to pray, Jesus responds in Matthew 6:8-11: "Therefore do not be like them. For your Father knows the things you have need of before you ask Him. In this manner, therefore, pray: Our Father in heaven, Hallowed be Your name. Your kingdom come. Your will be done." Notice he says that He knows our needs, yet we still pray what we believe our needs are.

Add to this 1 Corinthians 2:14: "Now the natural man does not receive the things from the Spirit of God — to him they are nonsense! Moreover, he is unable to grasp them, because they are evaluated through the Spirit." (CJB) Simply stated: our natural mind cannot understand the things of the Spirit. (For more on this, read what Paul says about the carnal mind in Romans 8:6-7.)

This takes me to the Apostle John as a prisoner on the island of Patmos. (Think about that.) Revelation chapter one starting in verse 10 says, "I was in the Spirit on the Lord's Day, and I heard behind me a loud voice, as of a trumpet," (NKJV) Notice that "HE WAS IN THE SPIRIT" when he heard. Then verse 11 says, "I am the Alpha and the Omega, the First and the Last," and, "What you see, write in a book and send it to the seven churches which are in Asia: to Ephesus, to Smyrna, to Pergamos, to Thyatira, to Sardis, to Philadelphia, and to Laodicea."

So he tells them to write what they see, to TAKE ACTION. Verse 12 says, "Then I turned to see the voice that spoke with me. And having turned I saw seven golden lamp stands." HE HEARD AND SAW. Go read through verse 18.

By being in the Spirit (not living with a natural and carnal mindset) we will hear, see, and hopefully do.

And why hear or see if we're not willing to do?

Day 245

THOUGHT OF THE DAY: A prophetic word

As I started to pray and muse with the Lord, I was told to write the following. Consider and ponder.

"You are clean, you are clean, you are forgiven. Take your hands and put them on your head and say 'I am free, no more guilt or shame, I am who I am by the grace of God, I have been created and called to live an extraordinary and supernatural life. Look out world; here WE come.' You're not alone in this."

Yes, it says,

I WILL NEVER LEAVE OR FORSAKE YOU. Today and tomorrow and every day after that I will walk in the Kingdom of God. I will carry His presence wherever I go. Once again, I tell you, IT'S TIME. MY KINGDOM is a place of joy. Enter this joy no matter your circumstances, because it is through joy that you will find strength. Go ahead and choose my kingdom. I am here yearning and desiring to walk more intimately with you; grab my hand and SEE. Oh, what an adventure, oh what joy, oh what power, and the boldness that you will have will astound you, as you open your mouth and I will fill it (yes, such is in my word). Read my word as if I am talking to you. There are so many things I want to show you, teach you. Will you let me teach and lead you? Surrender your kingdom (your ways) for my kingdom. You are governing in the natural. Imagine if you governed your life by the Spirit. A NEW DAY HAS ARRIVED. YOUR TODAY IS ALSO YOUR TOMORROW. I AM WAITING FOR YOU.

Read this again and declare it. Speak, announce, and proclaim these things! One last thing: "I LOVE YOU!"

Day 246

THOUGHT OF THE DAY: Change

Don't you just love change, that season when God decides to turn your world upside down? Now why would He do that, especially without your permission?

There is no one simple answer, but some of the following are possibilities: We've grown complacent. We've settled into a comfortable routine where we don't have to trust God because we have everything under control. He wants to answer our prayer to have more of Him, to be used more, to increase our anointing, to show us what He wants us to do.

I can just see God smiling because all of those desires that you thought originated with you were actually desires He put in you! It's one of His ways to bring us to a different place, a different level. Remember the verse that says, "I have plans for you"? Well, welcome to the unfolding of a new plan.

That's great, you might say, but I didn't want to be confused. I didn't want to have to struggle. I didn't want blah, blah, blah...

If God did it our way, we'd never reach the next level. We wouldn't need to be earnest in our seeking Him or drawing closer to Him. We'd never gain the wisdom or depth of character we're going to need in the next place He's bringing us to. Do you want to go there ill-equipped?

Remember that it was the Spirit who led Jesus into the wilderness. And we think that that was a picnic?! So if Jesus had to go to the wilderness, what makes us think we won't have to go there? If you read the account, it says that the Spirit drove him there. Go back and see what he had to face and then notice his responses. There's a lot to glean.

You see, I like jumping to the end of his time in the wilderness and just glancing over it. I haven't taken enough time to truly put myself in his shoes. To consider the length of time, to truly consider each challenge Satan gave him. Perhaps some of the things we're facing are Satan's subtle ways of challenging us. Have we really recognized the true root of what we're going through? Are we complaining... or praying? Are we pointing fingers instead of folding our hands?

And we think the problem is the person or persons we're dealing with, when in reality, they're only pawns in Satan's scheme. Yet if the truth be told, who is allowing it? Who asked Satan if he had considered

Job? Job 1:8: "Then the Lord said to Satan, 'Have you considered My servant Job, that there is none like him on the earth, a blameless and upright man, one who fears God and shuns evil?' "

Go back and finish reading at least chapter one. So who might be the one behind everything you're going through? But why? So we can be like Jesus.

We are brought to Luke 4:13-14: "Now when the devil had ended every temptation, he departed from Him until an opportune time. Then Jesus returned in the power of the Spirit to Galilee, and news of Him went out through all the surrounding region."

Did you see that it says Satan left Jesus alone but waited for another opportunity? It also says that "Jesus returned in power." I like the power part but am not fond of how Jesus was empowered. It was after Jesus was empowered, by the way, that he started his ministry.

Yes, it's time for a change so that you can be empowered for the next phase of your ministry. Yesterday's anointing may be insufficient for where God is taking you.

Day 247

THOUGHT OF THE DAY: Stumbling

I love the verse in Jude 24 where it says, "Now to Him who is able to keep you from stumbling, and to present you faultless." This verse contextually applies to the part of the book where he addresses false teachers and people who are being led astray into false doctrine.

While God can and does keep us and nothing can separate us from His love or take us out of His hand, a person can, in fact, decide to abandon God.

Even while this gift of salvation is free, we can give up or renounce the gift. I give you a gift and you in turn give the gift back. Jude says that God can keep us from falling, stumbling, and apostatizing so as to present us faultless and without sin. The full sanctification and justification of Christ is completely ours as long as we don't deny our belief in Jesus.

I feel like jumping up and down knowing that only the blood of Jesus and the atoning work of the cross can save me. I can do all kinds of works; I can serve, not serve, give, or not give, and Jesus will present me faultless/as without sin to the Father. I'm not suggesting that we live like "hell" and do whatever we please, because if that's our lifestyle then there's a good chance we have and are denying the Lord, and thus as it says he'll deny us. (I don't know how I got off on that tangent, other than believing that people probably needed to hear it.)

But what I want to say is that in everyday life with all of its trials and temptations, God can keep us from stumbling. I wish that meant that every time I'm tempted to sin, I can just pray, "Lord keep me from stumbling" and abracadabra, God will swoop down and stop me. That would be great, or would it?

When it says He can keep us from stumbling, it means He'll empower us to make the right choice and give us clarity as to what is right and wrong. He'll be there showing us the truth, empowering and encouraging us to choose, but He won't make the choice for us. I wish I could say that I've always made the right choices. I haven't. However, even so, I rejoice that regardless, I'll be presented faultless before our Father.

I'm also realizing more and more that although my sin displeases our Father, it doesn't in any way cause Him to love me any less. His love is TOTALLY UNCONDITIONAL. He is still proud of us simply because we're His sons and daughters. I pray that we can all grasp this so that the voice of that liar Satan will have no effect in our lives. We'll always simply know that we're forgiven.

Stumbling? The Holy Spirit will empower us not to stumble, but if we do, we have an advocate with the Son, the one who declares our innocence before the Father. Can you hear Him shout, "NOT GUILTY!"

Day 248

THOUGHT OF THE DAY: Oh, wretched man

The longer I'm honored and blessed to walk with God, the more I begin to grasp the incomprehensible love, grace, and power of our Father. (Notice that, "begin" is emphasized.)

How is it that we're so blind to our own sin, self-righteousness, and subtle but ever-so-deadly and putrid, pride? I'm unsure when this work of the Holy Spirit started in me, and I'm frightened that I'll lose grasp of the work He's already done. It may have been my last trip to Haiti where I began to see brothers and sisters in Christ so entrenched in seeing themselves as slaves to sin - as worthless, and full of guilt and shame which they'd never be free from.

Perhaps it was my reflecting on the people of Romania who've been freed from communism for 25 years yet behave as if they're still under the regime. They're free, but not really. Maybe it was our starting to organize this year's homeless overflow shelters in Fall River. God showed me that while these people are "hidden treasures," so many of them are trapped by life, circumstances, and by their own and others' choices and by the same sin nature that we have. They, like us, make choices because they're trapped by the old man. Don't we all just hate having the old man make decisions for us?

I'm realizing that all of us are trapped somewhere. That all of us fall short. Paul in Romans seven says, "The things I want to do I don't do and the things I don't want to do I do." Don't we all face that struggle? Yes, there's an inner war going on inside of us, the war between the spiritual man and the carnal man. How many times do we know what we should do or not do and just don't get it right?

There are great people trapped by their sin nature crying out and screaming, "HELP!" What Paul writes in Romans 7:24-25 we can fully relate to. It says in the Amplified Bible, "Wretched and miserable man that I am! Who will [rescue me and] set me free from this body of death [this corrupt, mortal existence]? Thanks be to God [for my deliverance] through Jesus Christ our Lord!"

So many people feel wretched and miserable but have no idea that Jesus can and does deliver us. When you're feeling wretched and miserable, it's similar to the ancient custom for law-breaking that involved attaching or binding a dead person to the body of the law-breaker. The person would carry the corpse around until it eventually consumed the person's life. What a hopeless and horrific experience that must've been. But that's what it's like when we want freedom from the old man that corrupts the new man and causes us to experience death. We just want to be free from it.

The incomprehensible reality is that Jesus can and does deliver all of us from that old, wretched man. Praise God! Jesus is our deliverer, and John 8:36 says, "Therefore if the Son makes you free, you shall be free indeed."

Oh, wretched man, move over, for freedom and joy are my inheritance!

Day 249

THOUGHT OF THE DAY: A morning of tears

Oh, it's one of those mornings that I'm having to sort through my thoughts and emotions. My mind has been flooded by scriptures, and then with each thought comes a different emotion. I liken it to the process of putting a puzzle together. I'm trying to see how it all fits without drawing a conclusion before I have all the pieces.

I'm sitting here asking, "Oh Lord, oh Lord. What are you saying?" I then hear Matthew 5:6, "Blessed are those who hunger and thirst." The (ICB) says, "Those who want to do right more than anything else are happy. God will fully satisfy them." Then I hear the voice of Jesus in John

6:38: "And here's the reason: I have come down from heaven not to pursue My own agenda but to do what He desires. I am here on behalf of the Father who sent Me." (Voice Bible)

Father, I cry out for your church, for your sons and daughters. We're hungry and thirsty desiring to do your will. I'm unable to find the words to pray. My words fail to capture the depth of my emotions, and there's a deep yearning inside of me to try and make sense of all of this. Then comes Romans 8:26: "If we don't know how or what to pray, it doesn't matter. He does our praying in and for us, making prayer out of our wordless sighs, our aching groans. He knows us far better than we know ourselves, knows our pregnant condition, and keeps us present before God." (MSG)

Yes, I feel pregnant.

Then I can see this smile and I believe, some tears running down His cheeks. I can see His head nodding, and he turns to a host of angels as He instructs them to come. I can see Hebrews 1:14, that God is sending angels to help us. You might be thinking, "Seriously?" Yet from the Amplified Bible, Classic Edition we read, "Are not the angels all ministering spirits (servants) sent out in the service [of God for the assistance] of those who are to inherit salvation?"

I'm still a mess, but I know that our Father has sent angels to help, He has given us His Spirit. I can recall Psalm 139:1-6:

O Eternal One, You have explored my heart and know exactly who I am; You even know the small details like when I take a seat and when I stand up again. You observe my wanderings and my sleeping, my waking and my dreaming, and You know everything I do in more detail than even I know. Even when I am far away, You know what I'm thinking. You know what I'm going to say long before I say it. It is true, Eternal One, that You know everything and everyone. You have surrounded me on every side, behind me and before me and You have placed Your hand gently on my shoulder. It is the most amazing feeling to know how deeply You know me, inside and out; the realization of it is so great that I cannot comprehend it. (Voice Bible)

Oh, you know us. You know everything about us. You smile and I hear you say, "I know what you're thinking and feeling because I put have put each of those thoughts in your heart and mind this morning. I so enjoy seeing you struggle to know and understand. I know you love me. I know everyone who loves me and I love all of you. You see, your tears have compelled you to spend some time with me. Don't make the mistake of trying to draw conclusions before you have all the facts. Continue to learn to live in the unresolved. Come grab my hand, and let's go for a walk.

His arm comes around me; He wipes my tears away and says, "Let's go over here for a while."

Hey, will join me? Come let's go for a walk.

Day 250

THOUGHT OF THE DAY: An open prayer

When I awoke this morning, I felt a weight in my chest. Immediately I wondered what in the world it was.

Occasionally I have to ask, "Are these my feelings or someone else's?" As members one of another, at different times we can feel what others are feeling. As I sat before the Lord, my heart was heavy; I had all these negative thoughts and feelings. I was struggling because I felt hopeless.

As I continued to pray, I saw a person, yet it was as if this person was a reflection of countless others. There was a sea of faces. Each person had their heads hung down, and they were clutching their hearts. I got this sense that I was to pray for the church because of its condition and the pain in people's hearts over it. While I don't have the gift of intercession, even so there are times when I can feel the pain and discouragement of others. I want to say, God bless those of you who are called to be intercessors. You truly carry others' burdens.

With that in mind, here's an open prayer:

Good morning, Father, it's been a while since we talked. I've missed being with you and hearing your voice. I know you know everything that is going on in my life, but I just needed to talk to you this morning. You have seemed so far away and I know this is not true, but that's how I feel. If I'm honest this morning, I have to admit that I'm feeling discouraged.

It seems I'm stuck and I don't know what to do. I've tried praying, but I'm not comforted. Everything seems to be the same. I can identify with the Psalmist who asks, "Why are you so far from my groaning?" (Psalm 22:1) I go to bed with a heavy heart and wake the same way because nothing has changed, neither my circumstances nor anything else.

Where are you? Why haven't you answered my past prayers? To be honest, that's one of the reasons I don't pray, because it doesn't seem to matter. Things stay the same. I hear about all the things you're doing in other people's lives. While I'm happy for them, I wonder what's wrong with me? To be honest I get angry when I read how others are hearing your voice. Why don't you hear mine? Sure, I know you hear, but that's not enough.

I feel like a child lost in the woods. I'm wondering why you haven't come to rescue me. I feel that the only time you're happy with me is when I'm doing something in the church. Even that is not satisfying. Growing up, the only time I got approval was when I was performing. I rarely heard encouragement. I rarely heard, "I love you." Gee, I am hurt that my life doesn't seem to matter to you. My prayers hit the ceiling and quickly fall to the floor. What can I do?

Then it hits me that it's not what I can do; it's what YOU can do. There's a faint whisper, and I hear, "You have been believing a lie." I feel like Jeremiah who was lowered down by ropes into a dried-out well. Jeremiah 38:6: "So they took Jeremiah and cast him into the dungeon of Malchiah, the king's son, which was in the court of the prison, and they let Jeremiah down with ropes. And in the dungeon there was no water, but mire. So Jeremiah sank in the mire."

That's it! That's how I feel. I'm in a pit, and I can't get out. Somehow, I'm beginning to feel encouraged, and I have a word that I'm praying for all of you. Sometimes just to be able to identify one's feelings helps a lot.

I can hear God say, "Tell them to continue to read Jeremiah 38:7-13:

Now Ebed-Melech the Ethiopian, one of the eunuchs, who was in the king's house, heard that they had put Jeremiah in the dungeon. When the king was sitting at the Gate of Benjamin, Ebed-Melech went out of the king's house and spoke to the king, saying: "My lord the king, these men have done evil in all that they have done to Jeremiah the prophet, whom they have cast into the dungeon, and he is likely to die from hunger in the place where he is. For there is no more bread in the city." Then the king commanded Ebed-Melech the Ethiopian, saying, "Take from here thirty men with you, and lift Jeremiah the prophet out of the dungeon before he dies." So Ebed-Melech took the men with him and went into the house of the king under the treasury, and took from there old clothes and old rags, and let them down by ropes into the dungeon to Jeremiah. Then Ebed-Melech the Ethiopian said to Jeremiah, "Please put these old clothes and rags under your armpits, under the ropes." And Jeremiah did so. So they pulled Jeremiah up with ropes and lifted him out of the dungeon.

I can see a bunch of old clothes and rags tied together and being lowered into your "pit." When the rope arrives, please put it around yourself. You're being lifted out.

Writing this has caused me to see how important it is to pray for others and how when you're in the pit yourself, to ask some praying people to intercede for you.

Father, I need to say thank you...

Day 251

THOUGHT OF THE DAY: More on the kingdom

Yesterday morning as I opened our Sunday gathering on the Porch, I began sharing on the Kingdom of God. It reached a point where I was trying to compose myself as I wiped away tears from my eyes. It was at that moment that something went off inside me.

I've been preaching since I was 22 years old and have preached thousands of sermons, but yesterday as I was sharing, I realized Jesus didn't preach a bunch of sermons. He talked about His Father. He came for the purpose of preaching (announcing) the Kingdom of God. Luke 4:43: "He said to them, 'I must preach the kingdom of God to the other cities also, because for this purpose I have been sent.' "

When Moses went up the mountain, he brought down the law. When Jesus went up, he sat down and started declaring the kingdom. For a moment, just imagine Jesus, who was man but also the embodiment of God, actually sitting down and sharing about the kingdom. We have taken Matthew chapters five and six and turned them into sermons, which misses altogether the true meaning of what Jesus was saying.

When Jesus was asked by His disciples how they should pray, he gave them what we call The Lord's Prayer, which we've gone so far as to avoid praying due to "vain repetition."

In so doing we've missed the very intent of Jesus' answer to his disciples. First and foremost, when we pray we're to remember that we're talking/praying to our Father, a fact which points to the relationship. While we're to approach Him as our Father, our approach should be one of deep reverence. It isn't our opportunity to approach Him with His daily "to do list."

So as I sat yesterday morning before going to hang out with a bunch of other children of God – what we call church - I read Matthew 6:10: "Your kingdom come. Your will be done. On earth as it is in heaven." As I read it, I heard that I needed to go beyond praying it to also living it, that I was called to both live and demonstrate the kingdom wherever I go. You are too. It's time we go beyond words, and as Jesus embodied the kingdom, so should we.

That brings us to the question of what we should embody. You see, it's us who need to be the answer to that prayer. Thy kingdom come in us, and His will be done in us and through us. In Luke 9: 8-9 when Jesus was sending out his disciples (us), He told them to tell people that the Kingdom of God was near. He instructed to not only tell them, but to demonstrate the kingdom; "Whatever city you enter, and they receive you, eat such things as are set before you. And heal the sick there, and say to them, 'The kingdom of God has come near to you.' "

Please don't just skim over that like we normally do. Actually see that it says, that we are to "heal" the sick. For too long not only have we misunderstood our purpose, but we have offered Christianity and not the kingdom. We aren't just to talk about it; we're to demonstrate it. Both our words and our works should proclaim the reality of the kingdom.

God's kingdom (His rule and reign) need to impact our actions, thoughts, relationships, families, our places of work - EVERYWHERE. For we are carriers of a kingdom, and as Paul wrote in 1 Corinthians 4:20, "The kingdom of God is not in word but in power."

There has to be a radical change. My tears reflected the sad fact that although I have deeply loved the Lord, I've offered a religion (Christianity) and not our Father's kingdom.

Day 252

THOUGHT OF THE DAY: Fireside chat

The expression "Fireside Chat" was birthed on March 12, 1933 when President Teddy Roosevelt used the medium of radio to explain his policies.

The following video is my own fireside chat talking about the Kingdom of God. In this video you hear about who started the crusades in 1095 and their purpose in doing so. (A hint is that they were started by a French pope to eliminate all non-Christians, and in particular, Muslims.)

I'm not trying to promote my ministry; I'm "crying out" that we must understand the Kingdom of God. I feel like John the Baptist who was the voice crying out in the wilderness. I believe if you watch a few minutes of this video, that the Spirit of God will compel you to watch the whole thing. I believe the Holy Spirit will use this video to provoke all of us to consider what the Holy Spirit is saying.

https://youtu.be/Tp4quL1M-MA

Day 253

THOUGHT OF THE DAY: Is your heart/spirit being stirred?

To be honest, at times I feel like Elijah where he says in 1 Kings 19:14: "I alone am left."

Now I know it's not true, because many of you also burn with a passion for the Lord! Being a prophetic person, however, is like living in the mind of a "crazy man." I often awake and feel instantly burdened, the burning in my heart and spirit constant.

Yes, it's a blessing, but it also causes me to continually live in the realm of the unresolved. I need to find contentment while in the midst of it, everything in me crying out to the Lord. Eight times in scripture we read the phrase, "The Lord stirred up the spirit."

I know the Lord is stirring yours. I know HE IS! What if we all followed through with this supernatural stirring? Do you think we could dramatically impact our churches or even the people around us? Imagine what the Holy Spirit could do. It would take our breath away.

This morning I'm praying that the Holy Spirit will continually provoke us to be like Elijah on Mount Carmel after he'd confronted the prophets of Baal. It says in 1 Kings 18:42: "And Elijah went up to the top of Carmel; then he bowed down on the ground, and put his face between his knees." After defeating the prophets of Baal, he went higher up the mountain to pray.

What God is calling us to do will require us to go higher. We can't live in what God did yesterday. It's a difficult place to be - to learn how to be thankful for what He's already done yet remain hungry for Him to do more. I'm praying that the Holy Spirit would provoke us, stir us, and put the cry of Isaiah in us: "SEND ME!"

Matthew 5:6 says, "Blessed are those who hunger and thirst for righteousness, For they shall be filled," (NKJV) and from the (GNT): "Happy are those whose greatest desire is to do what God requires; God will satisfy them fully!"

Lord, make it our greatest desire! This is what the Kingdom of God is like: people whose greatest desire is to do what is on Father's heart. The Kingdom of God is a new culture; it's meant to replace the one we're in, our church culture. What if we all went to church on Sunday and everyone there was filled with this desire? They would have to call every available fire department to come and PUT THE FIRE OUT, the overwhelming presence of God spurring us to action.

May we see the fulfillment of Haggai 1:14: "So the Lord stirred up the spirit of Zerubbabel the son of Shealtiel, governor of Judah, and the spirit of Joshua the son of Jehozadak, the high priest, and the spirit of all the remnant of the people; and they came and worked on the house of the Lord of hosts, their God." (NKJV)

The remnant (YOU) was/were provoked to ACTION.

Are your heart and spirit being stirred?

Day 254

THOUGHT OF THE DAY: Good morning, child

I opened my eyes and heard, "Good Morning, child. I'll always be there."

Funny thing is that I immediately recalled one of the lyrics from Michael Jackson's song "I'll Be There." Clearly there was a loving and compassionate voice saying, no matter what you do, "I'LL BE THERE." No matter your sin and struggles "I'll be there." Wherever you go or whatever you do "I'll be there." Whether you're joyful or depressed, "I'll be there." Whether you're failing or succeeding, "I'll be there." When you're angry and depressed, "I'll be there." When you're tired and weary, "I'll be there."

"You see, you are my child. I have called you, yes, YOU. I HAVE CALLED YOU BY NAME. YOU ARE MINE." From Isaiah 43:1: "Fear not, for I have redeemed you; I have called you by your name; You are mine." Can I/we hear this? Fear not. I have personally redeemed YOU. Nothing again, NOTHING can separate us from HIS LOVE."

In trying to somehow capture His love, I'm led to the Message Bible, and I will let the verses in Romans 8:31-39 speak for themselves. Oh, one last thought crashes into my mind: "I HAVE ADOPTED YOU! YOU'LL ALWAYS BE MY PRECIOUS CHILD!"

Romans 8:31-39:

So, what do you think? With God on our side like this, how can we lose? If God didn't hesitate to put everything on the line for us, embracing our condition and exposing himself to the worst by sending his own Son, is there anything else he wouldn't gladly and freely do for us? And who would dare tangle with God by messing with one of God's chosen? Who would dare even to point a finger? The One who died for us—who was raised to life for us!—is in the presence of God at this very moment sticking up for us. Do you think anyone is going to be able to drive a wedge between us and Christ's love for us? There is no way! Not trouble, not hard times, not hatred, not hunger, not homelessness, not bullying threats, not backstabbing, not even the worst sins listed in Scripture:

They kill us in cold blood because they hate you. We're sitting ducks; they pick us off one by one. None of this fazes us because Jesus loves us. I'm absolutely convinced that nothing—nothing living or dead, angelic or demonic, today or tomorrow, high or low, thinkable or unthinkable—absolutely nothing can get between us and God's love because of the way that Jesus our Master has embraced us.

GOOD MORNING, CHILD!

Day 255

THOUGHT OF THE DAY: What would you do if you moved to a foreign country?

If you moved to a foreign country wouldn't you be curious about a million different things - who was the head of the government, what are the laws, the customs, the culture, etcetera?

Well, in reality we have been transferred to a different country. We've moved from the power of darkness (kingdom of this world) to the Kingdom of God. Colossians 1:13 says, "God rescued us from the dark power of Satan and brought us into the kingdom of his dear Son."

I'd like to suggest that we haven't really grasped that reality but have instead encouraged people to know the church of which they've become members. We introduce people to the pastor and various leaders, offer classes so the people will understand the government and doctrine of the church. We want people to know our traditions, our culture, and customs. While this is not wrong, we haven't done a good job helping people see that they've actually come to live in a foreign country or kingdom. We've offered them church living, not kingdom living.

I believe one of the greatest reasons we don't see the power of God is because we don't see ourselves in the kingdom. The power of God is not found in the natural realm, but instead its source is the kingdom. Paul writes in 1 Corinthians 4:20: "For the Kingdom of God is not a matter of words but of power." (GNT)

We've been trying to operate in power while living in a church mentality rather than a kingdom mentality. We offer the church while Jesus offered a kingdom. If we see ourselves in our Father's kingdom, we'll discover the inheritance that we already have!

Isn't it time we understood that we've MOVED?

Day 256

THOUGHT OF THE DAY: When you walk into the room

Good morning. Once again, I have such an urgency in me and a cry in my heart to have the Lord help us know WHO WE REALLY ARE.

I've been listening to the song, "When You Walk into the Room" by Jon Thurlow, and below are some of the lyrics. Can you comprehend what happens when YOU, YES, YOU, WALK INTO A ROOM - EVERYTHING CHANGES... EVERYTHING CHANGES BECAUSE OF YOU!

Here are some of the lyrics:

"When you walk into the room. Everything changes. Darkness starts to tremble. At the light that you bring. When you walk into the room. Sickness starts to vanish."

Dear Jesus, help us to KNOW WHO WE ARE NOW... NOT TOMORROW!

Jesus said in Luke 11:20: "If I drive out demons by the finger of God, then the kingdom of God has come to you." The verb "has come" (ephthasen) means "has arrived, "is "now present." Can we comprehend that the kingdom has arrived. The KINGDOM IS IN YOU...

WHEN YOU WALK INTO THE ROOM - EVERYTHING CHANGES!

https://youtu.be/DOniY2ZTs4g

Day 257

THOUGHT OF THE DAY: What if we understood our value?

Jesus was standing on what is known as the Mount of Beatitudes (also known as Mount Eremos), when he began speaking about the nature of His Father's kingdom. As birds flew overhead, Jesus used them as an illustration to say something very profound, yet because it was shared in such simplicity, I believe we've altogether missed one of the most vital and critical statements in the entire Bible.

In Matthew 6:26 Jesus said, "Look at the birds of the air, for they neither sow nor reap nor gather into barns; yet your heavenly Father feeds them. Are you not of more value than they?" (NKJV) Did we hear that? You are valued! Again in Matthew, Jesus says, "Do not fear therefore; you are of more value than many sparrows." (10:31) Jesus was and is saying to us that we have value. Understanding this will help eradicate fear in our lives.

There's a deep cry of our hearts that often goes unsatisfied. We want and need to feel valued. If we could only comprehend that our Heavenly Father has assigned us the greatest value we could ever want or need, we wouldn't seek our value in what we do or what others think about us. We're often like little birds in a nest, craving to be fed. Without knowing it, we set people up to fail and disappoint us, becoming prisoners to them because we want their approval and want them to assign us value.

This is such a trap. We're often in a state of offense or hurt as people fail to meet this need of ours. Combine that with many of us not receiving a sense of value from our own parents, and the result is a huge emotional, psychological, and spiritual void deep within. In some ways we've become like addicts always looking for "VALUE," and despite our search for it, we'll never be truly satisfied, because what we're looking for can only be found in knowing and receiving VALUE FROM HEAVEN.

Jesus' simple and yet life-changing statement has been overlooked for far too long. Listen; hear the voice from heaven - YOU ARE VALUED! Let the healing begin. Let the chains and shackles be broken and the prison doors be open, as the words, or void of words from others, no longer causes you to be driven to and fro emotionally.

The lie must end. What lie is that? That we are not valued! Please hear Isaiah 43:4 as our Father declares our value once and for all. Listen, it's not based on our performance; it's based solely on who we are as adopted children. You have to hear the cry of our Father's heart as He declares, "You are precious to me, and I have given you a special place of honor. I love you." (ERV)

What if we could truly understand our value?

Day 258

THOUGHT OF THE DAY: You're it

When we were children, we would play the game Hide and Seek. The point was to search for those who were hiding and when we found them, to tag them, yelling, "YOU'RE IT!" Some of us thought we were pretty clever in our hiding spots.

Many of us are playing the same game today without realizing it.

I've seen a gleeful smile on the Lord's face. In fact, He's chuckling. He knows where each and every one of us are. I get the picture that many of us have simply sat down. We haven't wanted to participate anymore. Others of us are halfhearted, while others are just tired and discouraged.

Well, ready or not, He's pursuing us. Get ready to be tagged and to hear "YOU'RE IT! "You see, the Father has called and chosen you before the foundation. He has need of you. We're "it" - the ones He'll work through.

Hear this... YOU'RE IT!

Day 259

THOUGHT OF THE DAY: Can you hear it?

It's 4:42 a.m. and I was awoken out of a deep sleep. I got up and asked the Lord why I was up, yet there was no answer. I took the dogs out and asked the same question again.

I came into my office where I write from, and then the Spirit of God came on me. As I sat to write I could hear God calling very faintly. It was like being in the mountains in Israel where I could see the early morning mist rolling through the valley. Here in Rehoboth it's still very dark. Through the morning mist I could hear a faint voice off in the distance growing louder and louder. I heard, "I am calling my children to come." Can you hear him? He's still calling.

"Awake my beloved and come. Come sit here at my feet and listen. I want to replace your thoughts with my thoughts. I can see you are all so busy. I am asking you to come. There are many things I wish to show you, but you must come and sit. It has begun and you have not known it. Are you ready for radical ideas? Radical ways of thinking and doing? It will be outside of you. Outside of your gifts and talents, that way you cannot take any credit." He's still calling and is asking, "Will you come?"

In Second Kings chapter three we see Jehoshaphat summon a prophet when he wants to hear from God, and the prophet Elisha call for a musician, both creating an atmosphere to better hear God and receive His instructions.

So off to Youtube I go to find some worship. We must create a personal atmosphere in which we can hear the Spirit better. Second Kings 3:15-18 says, "But now bring me a musician. Then it happened, when the musician played, that the hand of the Lord came upon him. And he said, 'Thus says the Lord, 'Make this valley full of ditches.' For thus says the Lord: 'You shall not see wind, nor shall you see rain; yet that valley shall be filled with water, so that you, your cattle, and your animals may drink.' And this is a simple matter in the sight of the Lord."

You see, the answer from God was out of the box - go dig ditches! Stop living by what you see. God is calling us. He has always had unusual, creative thoughts and ideas, but we've been unable to perceive them. But that's changing because we'll come and sit at His feet and we'll listen in a new way. Again, I can hear His voice echoing from the mountains "Awake my beloved and come. Come sit here at my feet and listen. I want to replace your thoughts with my thoughts."

The day has come! The day is here! God has appointed us to be His watchmen and to tell people what we hear. Ezekiel 33:7: "Son of man, I have appointed you as a watchman for the people of Israel. Listen to what I say, and warn them for me." (GW)

Can you hear it?

Day 260

THOUGHT OF THE DAY: Lessons learned from the homeless shelter

I just love how God uses everything to form and fashion us into His likeness.

I remember when I first volunteered to serve in the overflow homeless shelter, the first lesson I learned is that the guests were people, not homeless people. My attitude was wrong, as sadly, inside I saw myself as better than them. Although my life wasn't perfect, I found myself talking down to them.

Lesson two was the discovery that I had the dread disease of self-righteousness and false humility. Yes, I was going to help these "poor people." In Galatians 6:1 Paul instructs the Galatians in how they are to help restore a person. He writes, "You who are spiritual should restore someone like this with a spirit of gentleness."

If you and I really want to help someone, then the first thing we need is to recognize our self-righteousness and allow a spirit of humility and meekness to guide us.

Yes, I know the verse is talking about someone who's sinning, but it's easy to see the concept/principle applied here too. It's with humility, gentleness, kindness, compassion, and remembrance of the words of Isaiah. In Isaiah 51:1 it says, "Look to the rock from which you were hewn, And to the hole of the pit from which you were dug." (NKJV) In other words, we have to always remember where we came and are still being cut from.

What spurred this thought today was our first training session for this year's overflow homeless shelter. My THOUGHT OF THE DAY came from my opening remarks last night. God is calling us to put our arms around these wonderful people and to do all we can to help restore their lives. You don't have to serve in a homeless shelter to participate in helping someone put their life back together. We ARE, however, looking for people who would like to give four hours each week or every other week, to be a part of restoring lives.

You can go to the website: fallriveroverflowshelter.com and register online. We could use your help.

Yes, there are lessons we can learn....

Day 261

THOUGHT OF THE DAY: Ever wonder if you're bipolar?

Are your emotions out of whack? One day you're seized by one emotion, and the next day you're seized by another? It's crazy how you can experience so many seasons in just a few days or even within a few hours. It's like an emotional, psychological, mental, and spiritual roller coaster ride, and sometimes all of them simultaneously. One minute or one hour or one day you're feeling one way, and moments later another way. Does this resonate?

There are multiple reasons for this to be happen, and there's no way I can tackle them all. All I can say is that for me it's been draining.

Trigger points are part of it, circumstances which activate a "roller coaster" of emotions.

For me at least, the Christmas season is one of these. It seems to open up Pandora's Box. This year I recognized unresolved issues from past Christmases of my life that I didn't know were there, and if I don't take the time to ask the Holy Spirit to help me deal with them, they will deal with me. As I write this, in fact, I recall one particular Christmas when I received a train set. I had totally forgotten the joy and the trauma of that day until just now.

Over the past few months also, I've had two friends die and another who came close. While I rejoice in the first two being with Jesus, it's opened up a can of worms, bringing me back to a situation where another close friend died on his birthday as did another friend a few days ago and another who's in danger of passing on his birthday as well. If I could have only seen them one last time and told them how much they meant to me. Thankfully, I was able to do that last night, as Donna and I said good bye to yet another friend.

Throw into the mix our everyday relationships and the conflict which encompasses the lives around us, and yes, there's ample opportunity to experience a vast variety of emotions. Add to that financial circumstances and our spiritual journey. There's after all what God is doing in our lives and what Satan is trying to do. There's our age and how we're viewing life through the lens of time. There's our health and the health of those around us. Then there's the matter of our children, whether they're toddlers, teenagers, adults, or we have a combination of all three. There are our jobs or lack of them. Feeling bipolor yet?

Lately many of these things are crashing into my life. What about you? It's like standing in the ocean and having one after another wave hit us. Okay, I'm ready to get off of this roller coaster. Are you?

At times like this morning, I'm just shaking my head. Then the grace of God appears, and I'm reminded of Ecclesiastes 3:1: "To everything there is a season, A time for every purpose under heaven." (NKJV) Oh, I see – THERE'S A PURPOSE! Okay, I might not know what the purpose is right now, but it gives me a place to stand. I'm not bipolar. There's a divine plan. God is working in all of us. Often I don't like the process, but I do like the results.

It's that in the end we're a little more like Jesus. Thankfully it says in Philippians 2:13 that God is at work in us so that we can live lives that will cause Him to smile, because He's working in us to do the things that please Him. Again, I'm not fond of the process, but I do love the end result.

A P.S. here: I'm in no way minimizing people who are struggling with actual bipolar disorder. I know that God is capable of redeeming everything.

If you're struggling, you're not alone. God has a purpose. I pray that although your circumstances may not have changed, may God shift something inside of you as you read this THOUGHT OF THE DAY.

Day 262

THOUGHT OF THE DAY: The need to say thank you

For a number of days I've been reflecting on the true blessing of having so many of you as part of my life.

With some I've had the privilege of serving. Others of you I've met in church or in meetings we've hosted. Many of you have sent messages or e-mails to say hello, some to offer encouragement, and others to express your appreciation for a THOUGHT OF THE DAY that touched something inside of you.

I realize that my life would not be what it is without you. Though I've not met some of you, I know that we share a common purpose.

Over the past few years the Lord has been showing me that I need to appreciate each person for who they are and not who they're not. To be honest I used to do the opposite. Perhaps that stemmed from my not seeing who I was myself. I would live each day failing to accept myself for who I was. Some of it came from my childhood where I was rarely appreciated unless I was "doing some kind of work," you know, the whole performance thing. I wasn't encouraged unless I was working or performing.

Thankfully, however, over the last few years I've come to know that I'm loved and accepted for who I am and not for what I do. It's because of this that I know I'm beginning to see people through different lenses.

I'm working on trying to say thank you a lot more. Learning to offer encouragement and to express how much I appreciate who each of you are TODAY. Please note that I said I'm learning. I haven't arrived yet, by any means.

One of the gifts of the Holy Spirit is the gift of encouragement. Can you imagine for a minute what kind of profound influence and impact we could have by simply encouraging others? What if we all lived out Ephesians 4:32 from the Amplified Bible: "Be kind and helpful to one another, tender-hearted [compassionate, understanding], forgiving one another [readily and freely], just as God in Christ also forgave you." The Phillips Bible expands it by saying, "Let there be no more resentment, no more anger or temper, no more violent self-assertiveness, no more slander and no more malicious remarks, be kind to each other, be understanding. Be as ready to forgive others as God for Christ's sake has forgiven you."

What if we could truly live this out?

Then there is 1 Thessalonians 5:11 from the Amplified Bible, Classic Edition (AMPC) "Therefore encourage (admonish, exhort) one another and edify (strengthen and build up) one another, just as you are doing."

So thank you for being a part of my life! Thank you for your caring, thank you for your encouragement, thank you for your sacrificial giving to my apostolic mission trips, thank you for all the times you've prayed for me and the trips I've taken. I wish you could see all the lives you've touched.

But most of all, thank you for being you. The scripture that says, "You are fearfully and wonderfully made" really summarizes it. Yes, all of you are AMAZING!

THANK YOU!

Day 263

THOUGHT OF THE DAY: Christmas pondering

In pondering the whole Christmas scene, the following comes to mind:

Shepherds were hanging out in the field (even though shepherds in Israel don't actually hang out in fields in December, as it's too cold). The people were meanwhile unhappy with the political system, and the Pharisees and Sadducees didn't make going to church very enjoyable. Caesar Augustus had recently decreed that a registration be carried out in the land, and people had to travel to their town of origin in order to comply. Mary was very pregnant and had very little understanding of what and who she was carrying.

I think we can relate to some of these things and especially to Mary. Mary had received a prophetic word that she was carrying a savior, a king. Do you really think she could grasp the magnitude of what was spoken to her? Do we really grasp our prophetic tomorrows, of how God will accomplish what He's spoken?

When I read Matthew 13:11 which says, "It has been given to you to know the mysteries of the kingdom of heaven," I sit and say to myself, "Father, I know very little about the mysteries of your kingdom. I've spent the majority of my walk preaching atonement theology and not kingdom theology."

I read that Jesus sends his disciples out to preach the Kingdom of God, which makes me wonder what we're spending our time doing. He gives them authority to heal, cast out demons, and raise the dead, and I wonder if we truly understand that we've been given this same authority.

In Luke's account we read about the shepherds going about their normal routine when all of a sudden, the sky lights up as if it was day time. Before them were a multitude of angels WORSHIPPING. The shepherds inquire what all this means, and they're told that a savior has been born, and they run to see for themselves. Then in Matthew's account the Magi travel a thousand miles with certain goals in mind.

Among them are the desire to find the King, worship him, and present gifts to honor him. These magi had a hunger and a desire to find a king. Perhaps that speaks as much to you as it does to me about the need to not only seek my savior, but to seek my King.

Worship must be at the very center of my life. I am convinced that we're transitioning from a place of singing worship songs to actual WORSHIP. Our number one goal on a Sunday morning is not going to be what we can get, but what we can GIVE.

And what we can give is our worship. Then we can give ourselves.

Jesus, Savior, and King. Perhaps you and I can go back and reread Luke two and Matthew two and ask the Holy Spirit to help us consider and ponder a fresh perspective of Christmas.

Day 264

THOUGHT OF THE DAY: I'm searching for you

As I write the words I'm searching for you, my mind is filled with scripture, and then there's a voice. I know it to be the voice of my Father. He's smiling and saying, "Who do you think put that desire in your heart to seek me? You see, my child, it's me who wants to be with you. It's been awhile since we've spent time together. I've missed you. Your strength is fading because I am its source."

You tell me to write and extend your invitation to come.

Yes, you're calling to us, saying, "Would you come? For I can see that you are tired and weary. Would you simply come? You want to know so many things, but I want you to know me."

I can see the scene in Luke 10 where Martha has invited Jesus into her home, and she's running around trying to be a good hostess. Martha wants Jesus to tell Mary to get up and help her. I've been guilty of this same thing: I wanted the Lord to have other people serve, because that's what I was doing.

Jesus, looking at Martha says, "But Martha was distracted with much serving." (verse 40) How interesting that we can get distracted because we're serving and not seeking. We can be serving our family and occupied by our job. We can also be busy serving in our church - been there, done that. How about you? Jesus says to her in verse 41: "Martha, Martha, you are worried and distracted by many things." (NRSV) I can see the Lord nodding his head as he looks at so many of us. We're worried and distracted because of our preoccupation with doing.

Much of the time we'll say to ourselves: I'll just do this or finish that and then I'll sit with the Lord. The problem is that we never do seem to find the time to sit. We're too busy. Here it is the Christmas season, and we're very busy and distracted by our getting ready to celebrate Christmas. I know we all agree, but still we continue in the cycle. I hear His voice again, and He's saying, "COME."

We're a lot like our children when we call them to come, yet are then barraged with replies like: "Okay, I'll be there in a minute, I'm busy, I'll be there soon." I can remember a number of times when I had wonderful surprises for my wife or my kids, yet when I called them to come, they didn't respond as quickly as I would have liked – so disappointing.

Oh, we are so good at excuses.

Lord, where are you; I'm searching for you. His answer? "I'm right here searching for you!"

Day 265

THOUGHT OF THE DAY: Growing in confidence

In 1 Samuel 10:7 Samuel is prophesying to Saul. If you remember, his father's donkeys are lost so Saul goes out with a servant to find them. After searching for a number of days, the servant suggests that instead of returning home, Saul should seek out a prophet named Samuel.

Here is what's written in 1 Samuel 9:6: "And he said to him, 'Look now, there is in this city a man of God, and he is an honorable man; all that he says surely comes to pass. So let us go there; perhaps he can show us the way that we should go.' "

Three things strike me about this verse. The first is that it was said of Samuel that he was a man of God, secondly that he was an honorable man, and lastly, that what he said came to pass. In 1 Samuel 3:19 it says, "So Samuel grew, and the Lord was with him and let none of his words fall to the ground."

"Samuel grew, the Lord was with him, and whatever he spoke came to pass." Lord, provoke us to be like Samuel!

When Saul finds Samuel, Samuel prophesies and anoints him to be the first king of Israel. Imagine that you're looking for donkeys and in the meanwhile have a divine encounter. Perhaps we too often miss everyday divine encounters because we're not expecting them.

Here as they're meeting each other for the first time, Samuel not only prophesies that the donkeys are home, but shockingly that Saul will be the King of Israel. Samuel goes on to tell him that "when the Spirit of the Lord comes on him that he will prophesy and he will be changed into another man." (1 Samuel 10:6) Then in verse seven it says, "And let it be, when these signs come to you, that you do as the occasion demands; for God is with you."

Did you notice God spoke to both men and said "I AM WITH YOU"? I pray we too can daily hear that same message. He wants us to do whatever our circumstances require because He's with us. If we had the confidence that God was really with us (in us), we would live our lives fulfilling His purposes in a more spontaneous way.

Go for it, because GOD IS WITH YOU!

I want to encourage you to daily declare - GOD IS WITH ME. If we do this, we will grow in confidence.

Go ahead; say it out loud: "GOD IS, IS, IS, IS WITH ME!"

Day 266

THOUGHT OF THE DAY: We're called to make a difference TODAY!

The truth is declared: YOU ARE LOVED AND YOU ARE NEEDED! No more will we listen to the lies of our enemy who wants to keep us from who we were created to be.

You see, the truth is that we have the power and authority to bind demons and prevent them from harassing anyone else. The truth is that they're afraid of us. You are sons and daughters of God, and God has placed within you "HIS POWER."

In multiple translations it says in 1 John 4:17, "As He is, so are we in this world." If you're waiting for "some magic moment," you've been waiting too long already. If you're waiting to be more sanctified or more holy, then you've once again bought into the lie.

Take another glimpse at Jesus' first disciples. None of them were qualified, but Jesus is masterful at qualifying the unqualified. Colossians 1:12 says, "giving thanks to the Father who has qualified us to be partakers of the inheritance of the saints in the light."

What in the world made us think we could ever qualify ourselves?

Take another look at Peter and Thomas... They were empowered even before they had the Holy Spirit and were baptized in him. Read Luke 9:1-2: "Then He called His twelve disciples together and gave them power and authority over all demons, and to cure diseases. He sent them to preach the kingdom of God and to heal the sick." This is before the Spirit lived in them and before they were baptized in the Spirit. Then in Acts

1:8: "But you shall receive power when the Holy Spirit has come upon you." Acts 3:11-12: "Now as the lame man who was healed held on to Peter and John, all the people ran together to them in the porch which is called Solomon's, greatly amazed. So when Peter saw it, he responded to the people: 'Men of Israel, why do you marvel at this? Or why look so intently at us, as though by our own power or godliness we had made this man walk?' "

I know I write a lot about who we are. Why? Because over and over again I'm told to. It is who you are now, not who you'll be later. We're literally called to turn the world upside down. Acts 17:6: "These who have turned the world upside down have come here too." This was in reference to Paul and Silas arriving in Thessalonica.

We are called to make a difference TODAY!

Day 267

THOUGHT OF THE DAY: Will this Christmas be different?

Over the last week or so there's been a stirring in me, and I have to believe there's a stirring in you that you want this Christmas to be different.

Last Sunday I spoke about Mary being pregnant and how I know that the majority, if not all of us, are feeling pregnant. We're pregnant with expectation and hope, and like a woman who's about to give birth, we're feeling uncomfortable. There's a sense of frustration and anxious anticipation, similar to times during Donna's pregnancies when she got irritable.

Christmas is only two days away, and I somehow want it to be different. Donna and I have already sent money to help Pastor Carlo with the five hundred children whose families can be blessed with rice, beans, and oil for Christmas. I speak with Pastor Carlo almost daily, and it breaks my heart to hear how so few people have responded. Donna has also purchased food for one of her former bosses she worked with for years at Bradlees. Yet something is still missing.

I took some time this morning to research Christmas stories for some insight as to what God would have me do or not do. I wondered whether there was a voice that called out from one of them. I somehow want this Christmas to be different. Don't you?

I have to be careful, though, that my "spiritual" frustration doesn't cause me to be irritable towards people. I can relate to the frustration of Mary and Joseph who had to travel to Bethlehem for taxation purposes. They didn't jump into a BMW and take the newest highway to Bethlehem.

When they finally arrived in Bethlehem, there wasn't a hotel room available. Could things get any worse? I know I kind of feel this way. Like what else can go wrong? The past few years for so many of us have been the most difficult times we've faced in a while. It seems like we're pregnant, and the Lord has taken us to Bethlehem (even though we really don't want to be here), to birth whatever is in us.

The anticipation is huge. Two days ago I was at the doctor's, because I realized I was bitten by a tick. This January I'll need more surgery on the ruptured tendon in my baby finger. I still have symptoms of a concussion that stems back to a car accident on June 7, 2014. Throughout all this we have water damage in our two bathrooms and are experiencing several spiritual transitions. Yup. I want to have this baby. I want this Christmas to be different.

So as I was musing with the Lord, He gave me an idea. I will share it after Christmas Eve. Perhaps you too can spend some time musing with the Lord, and He could show you how this Christmas can be different. How do the two ideas -- being pregnant and having a different Christmas – tie together?

The picture in my mind is that doing something different will induce labor.

Day 268

Christmas Eve 2015: IT HAPPENED AGAIN
Last night was one of those unforgettable nights. We started the service with prayer, and God said He would come and heal memories, in particular, hurtful and painful memories of Christmas' past, which He actually did! He said He was going to birth something in us!

Truly the King was among us. Rece and Lisa led us in worship with Christmas carols and our normal worship songs, which were amazing. All was extraordinary - the King was among us. Pastor Steve got up and prophesied to three people. All his words were accurate and powerful. The King was among us. I shared very briefly about how God fulfilled 354 prophecies that directly pertained to Jesus. And if he could fulfill those prophetic words, He could and wants to fulfill His promises to us.

He encouraged us to have the kind of confidence He speaks of in Philippians 1:6: "being confident of this very thing, that He who has begun a good work in you will complete it until the day of Jesus Christ." I want to say to all of you: HE WILL FULFILL WHAT HE'S SPOKEN TO YOU" for He who promises is faithful!"

Honestly, do take that in.

Before communion God did something amazing that I'll perhaps write about at another time. Truly the King was among us, and He touched and healed many lives during communion and throughout the entire service. It was a Christmas Eve I will never forget. Oh, and there were many of us who had something birthed. It was an amazing hour and ten minutes. The King was among us.

Then it HAPPENED...

I left the building, and Pastor Tom was locking up. As I was driving down Mason Street, he called me and told me to come back.

My heart began to race as I turned my car around. As I came in the building, Pastor Tom told me to follow him and then led me to the elevated altar area. He said, "Look up." I looked, and it seemed that the entire ceiling was enveloped with a foggy mist. I then asked him what he saw, to which he asked, "Can't you see the cloud?"

I took my glasses off, and sure enough, the entire ceiling was enveloped with a misty fog. It wasn't a thick cloud, yet it covered the cathedral ceilings and was 10 or 15 feet deep. It was like driving at night when your headlights catch the fog and mist rolling in. Lisa also came in to look.

Pastor Tom said that he was locking up when the Lord told him to turn around and look up. Not only did he want to share what he saw, but he wanted someone to confirm it. Sure enough, the presence of God was there in the fog and mist. We stood and prayed. I was there at least 15 minutes or longer. I didn't want to leave, because the King was among us. I had to meet my wife however, and go to a Christmas fellowship.

Indeed, I'll never forget Christmas Eve 2015!

This was the second time I've seen a cloud in a church. The first was at Jericho when a bluish cloud set off the fire alarm. The fire department came, saw, and investigated the smoke, and said they'd never seen anything like it. I told them it was the presence of God, and they replied that "whatever it was" it was "safe to come back in." When we returned to the sanctuary, we worshipped for the rest of the service. The cloud remained there for a few days. A contractor even saw it as he walked through the sanctuary the following day.

YES, IT HAPPENED AGAIN, AND I KNOW IT WILL HAPPEN AGAIN AND AGAIN. The King was and will be among us!

I want to take this time to not only say Merry Christmas but pray the blessing of the Lord upon you and your family. I pray that His presence and goodness will overtake and envelop you always.

MERRY CHRISTMAS!

Day 269

THOUGHT OF THE DAY: "The Father loves the Son and includes him in everything he is doing." (John 5:20, Message Bible)

Other translations say He shows him what He's doing. As I sat here musing this morning after Christmas, I was asking myself, "Now what?"

The holiday was really different this year (answered prayer), and we even had an incredible Christmas Eve Service. If you haven't read about it yet (yesterday's THOUGHT OF THE DAY), after service a foggy/misty cloud filled the ceiling of the sanctuary at the end of the night, or at least that's when we noticed it.

After that we actually went to a friend's house to enjoy fellowship and didn't have to rush home to wrap presents. The family slept in late Christmas Day, and after we went to our friends' home for brunch and then just hung out. Yesterday we had our Christmas dinner and then again, just hung out! This was a stress-free Christmas!

I will enjoy today's service wondering what God will do, for I'm learning to live with greater expectation. The problem I've discovered is that I've been working and straining to try and see and discern what the Father is doing. I want to know and perceive what the Holy Spirit is doing and what I should be doing in response. If that sounds like work, it is. I'm supposed to be resting, but really, I'm striving.

Then this morning I was reading John 5:19: "Jesus replied, 'The Son can do nothing by himself. He does only what he sees the Father doing.' " (TLB) I believe we all yearn to see the way Jesus saw. Then I saw it! In verse 20 it says, "The Father loves the Son and includes him in everything he is doing." It's because the Father loves us that He'll show us what He's doing. I do not have to strive! I just need to abide in our Father's love.

That in turn reminded me of John 15:4 - 5: "Abide in Me, and I in you. As the branch cannot bear fruit of itself, unless it abides in the vine, neither can you, unless you abide in Me. I am the vine, you are the branches. He who abides in Me, and I in him, bears much fruit; for without Me you can do nothing."

While that seems pretty clear, I confess that I still have a must-do mentality. Praise God that I'm learning to rest/abide in His love.

"The Father loves the Son and includes him in everything he is doing."

Day 270

THOUGHT OF THE DAY: Learning to live outside the box

Without question we're creatures of habit and have trained our minds to think a certain way. By doing this we're limited in seeing and perceiving things in ways we would've never considered or have had the capacity to even be open to. It's therefore hard to be led by the Spirit, because we have so many preconceived ideas and built-in responses.

For example, I was talking to Pastor Carlo last night about how God supplied the money for the rice, beans, and oil for Christmas for the Haitian children and their families. We were sharing how God always surprises us with regard to the ways He ends up providing. In our natural mind we think, well, so and so will send support, and they don't, or church "xyz" will send support, and they don't, and so on.

I experience this very thing when I raise funds for the trips God sends me on. The mistake involves looking to people to help us. We put expectations on so and so that they'll help, or on so and so that they'll be our source of comfort or encouragement. The expectations that we need to place on God, are instead placed on people.

What if we smash our box-thinking mentality?

In Matthew 17 the question arose when Jesus went to Capernaum if he'd pay the temple tax. Jesus prophetically knew Peter was going to speak to him about this. Verses 24-26 say, "When they had come to Capernaum, those who received the temple tax came to Peter and said, 'Does your Teacher not pay the temple tax?' He said, 'Yes.' And when he had come into the house, Jesus anticipated him, saying, 'What do you think, Simon? From whom do the kings of the earth take customs or taxes, from their sons or from strangers?' Peter said to Him, 'From strangers.' "

Jesus in the following verse says he doesn't want to offend them, so the question follows about where they'll get the money to pay the tax. Our natural mind and thinking would say that it would come from the money they carried or from some other natural source. Not so. In verse 27 we read "Nevertheless, lest we offend them, go to the sea, cast in a hook, and take the fish that comes up first. And when you have opened its mouth, you will find a piece of money; take that and give it to them for Me and you."

God's answer (provision) was from inside a fish's mouth. We need to smash our boxes and be willing to hear and do what seems outside our habitual and natural thinking. A whole new way of living is at our doorstep. Today I declare that I will live outside my box. I break off habitual thinking and living.

A whole new way of living awaits us. Go find your fish...

Day 271

THOUGHT OF THE DAY: If we could believe that we're valued

If we could only perceive in the depths of our hearts that God assigns us high value. We've all struggled with the sense that we are of little or no value. The devil enjoys telling us that and sadly many people in our lives have told us this as well.

This is where the parables come in – Jesus' simple stories which communicate valuable lessons.

In Luke 12:6-7 he said, "Are not five sparrows sold for two copper coins? And not one of them is forgotten before God. But the very hairs of your head are all numbered. Do not fear therefore; you are of more value than many sparrows."

If God doesn't forget about a sparrow, why worry? According to David Guzik's Commentaries on the Bible, a redheaded person has 90,000 hairs, a dark-haired person 120,000, and a blond, 145,000.

Matthew 12:11-12: "Then He said to them, 'What man is there among you who has one sheep, and if it falls into a pit on the Sabbath, will not lay hold of it and lift it out? Of how much more value than is a man than a sheep?' "

If God can pull a sheep out of the pit, He'll pull us out of our pits, because He values us.

This was part of what I shared yesterday in church. Afterwards, when chatting with three people, this is what they said. A woman said that all week she was telling God that she'd be happy to be a sparrow in God's temple. His word to her – "You're more valuable." One of our pastors said that all during worship he kept on hearing "If people only could understand their value." A third person was about to take a test which would put him in the company (if he passed) of only 500 other people who had this particular expertise. He was struggling with being able to receive the recognition and honor that comes with the award – the struggle of feeling valued.

Before I went to church yesterday, the Lord said he was going to break the chains off our lives and in particular, the chain of feeling unvalued. The first song the worship team sang was "Break Every Chain" by Jesus Culture.

Know this: you are VALUED, and the Holy Spirit intends to break off every chain that binds you.

Day 272

THOUGHT OF THE DAY: It has started

It has begun, so get ready for an incredible year. Why? Because September 23, 2015 was the start of the Year of Jubilee.

Jubilee happened in Israel every 50 years and was a time when all debt was canceled. Property that was sold was returned to the original owner, which in turn secured the inheritance of every family. All slaves, including all lifetime slaves, were freed. People had their property returned to them, even all that they had sold or lost through debt; slaves were freed and returned to their families.

Imagine counting the years, months, weeks, and days until God would restore, redeem and release. Yet there was one more "r" - for every 50 years they were not to plant or harvest the fields. They could pick and eat what grew on its own but were to cease from labor and to REST. For a number of years now God has been telling us to "REST."

This is the year we must learn to rest. It's the year that God wants to restore what we have lost, a year of redemption and release. The key to this is not to interfere with how God wants to do it and to be able to see what the Holy Spirit is doing. I had shared a while ago from John 5:20: "For the Father loves the Son, and shows Him all things that He Himself does." It is because of the Father's love for us that He'll show us what to do. No more striving, just resting.

The Year of Jubilee is found in Leviticus 25:10: "When the 50th year arrives, sanctify it and declare liberty throughout the land for all who live there—dramatic, radical liberty for all. It is to be your jubilee year. Each of you is allowed to go back to the land that belonged to your ancestors; and each of you may return to your own family." (VOICE)

It says, "Declare liberty throughout the land for all who live there—dramatic, radical liberty for all." So declare it! Radical, dramatic - for everyone!

From the Living Bible: "For the fiftieth year shall be holy, a time to proclaim liberty throughout the land to all enslaved debtors, and a time for the canceling of all public and private debts. It shall be a year when all the family estates sold to others shall be returned to the original owners or their heirs."

It says, "a time to proclaim liberty throughout the land to all enslaved debtors, and a time for the canceling of all public and private debts."

Here's an amazing fact. Jesus started his ministry on September 11, 26 A.D, the Day of Atonement, which always marks the beginning of the

Year of Jubilee every 50 Years. So the foundation of the ministry of Jesus was all about Jubilee. The first message He preached was from Isaiah 61: 1-2: "The Spirit of the Lord God is upon Me, Because the Lord has anointed Me; To preach good tidings to the poor; He has sent Me to heal the brokenhearted, To proclaim liberty to the captives, And the opening of the prison to those who are bound; To proclaim the acceptable year of the Lord."

Another interesting fact is that when the Liberty Bell was initially cast in 1752, they inscribed Leviticus 25 on the bell. Can you hear it ringing?

It has started - YOUR YEAR OF JUBILEE!

Day 273

THOUGHT OF THE DAY: Beyond

I haven't written in a while because I've had so many thoughts flooding my mind that it's been difficult to get clarity. It's been similar to going to the ocean where the shore line has no beach, only rocks, and as far as you can see, you're watching waves crash against them. So without clarity I didn't want to write.

I was up at 5:00 a.m. after going to bed at midnight, and as I was asking the Lord about the many thoughts, He told me to share this one.

"This is a year of change beyond your rational thinking. It will be like an adventure which will require risk. As we have heard, without risk there is no reward. It is time that you actively pursue the promises He has made you."

Know this: Hebrews 10:23 says, "He who promised is faithful," and Proverbs 26:20 "Without wood, a fire goes out." We need to gather some spiritual wood to throw on the fading fire of the dreams and promises He's given us. In Haggai 1:8 it says, "Go up to the mountains and bring wood." Gathering wood will take effort, but the reward will be great.

For too long we've been living in disappointment! Proverbs 13:12 in the Living Bible says, "Hope deferred makes the heart sick," and the Message Bible: "Unrelenting disappointment leaves you heartsick." Those days are ending, because this is a year of change beyond our rational thinking.

I'll see you on the mountain... gathering some wood.

Day 274

THOUGHT OF THE DAY: Perspective

I didn't sleep well Friday night and spent the entire day Saturday walking. I was trying to find a place to get out of the weather and simply rest. It's so hard to find a place to rest. I was exhausted and wanted to take a nap, but that was impossible. I couldn't wait for 6:00 p.m. because I knew that I would be able to get out of the weather, have a warm meal, and once again, feel safe. This is my home for a while.

Finally it's 6:00 p.m. and I'm waiting with 21 other people in a small area. We all have to go through a vigorous screening process. I go into a private room and remove everything except my shirt and pants. My pockets and backpack are checked, and I blow into a breathalyzer to test me for alcohol. Then they make sure I'm emotionally stable and not overmedicated. I can't wait to sign the sheet acknowledging that I have given them my cigarettes, my medications, and oh yes, even my cell phone. I turn in everything for the night and will get it back in the morning just before I leave. Finally, I eat a hot meal, and I can sit and rest.

Now, the night. I can have two cigarettes - one at 8:00 and one at 9:30. I get my medications at 9:00. Nine thirty is quiet time, and in 30 minutes lights will be turned out. I am lying on my cot hoping the heat will be working tonight so I can get the chill out of my bones. I couldn't wait to sleep but that was virtually impossible because the snoring was so loud that my ear plugs were useless. I laid there all night, and now it's 6:00 a.m. - time to get up. Off to the bathroom that I share with 16 other men. At 6:15 I go outside to have a cigarette. I come back inside, and I'm exhausted, because I haven't gotten any sleep. There is coffee (thank God) but no cereal or muffins. (Normally we go upstairs where we can get coffee, cereal, juice, and donuts, but today is Sunday and the center is closed.) I go into my bedroom that I share with 16 men, and on the other side of the partition five women sleep. I put my sheet and two blankets in a large garbage bag, stack my cot in the corner. and then look at the clock to see that it's almost 7:00, when my backpack will be returned to me. It has all my clothes. I look outside and see that to my dismay, it's raining hard.

It's Sunday, and the YMCA is closed so I can't get a shower. The warming center that's open every day for an hour and a half is closed because it's Sunday morning, so no coffee, cereal, or muffin. I have tried several times to call the check-in center to reserve a cot for the night. If I don't call, I don't get a cot, and if I don't call early enough, there's a chance too many people have already signed in, and so I won't have a bed for the night and will have to sleep outside. There is no answer, but thank God, I finally get through.

It's pouring outside, and the library I usually go to is closed. There is nowhere to go. The other warming center that's open during the winter on Sundays has closed down permanently. There is nothing to do except walk in the rain and find a business doorway I can stand in. Even the coffee shop we usually visit to get a coffee with the gift card we were given, today asked us to leave after an hour. Some of us were fortunate to find a church that invited us in and let us stay there all day until it was time to head back to our temporary home. Sadly, I didn't know that a church had opened its doors, so I walked all day in the rain. I am soaked and praying for the time to pass quickly. I couldn't wait for 6:00 so I could be safe, warm, have a hot meal, change my clothes, and then hopefully get some sleep.

This is my life for the next ten weeks unless a bed opens up or I can find an apartment that I can afford. By now you've realized that I'm homeless. I lost my job, had no savings, and have no family to help me. I thank God for those who volunteer their time. I have a whole new perspective about life.

One last thing: could you pray for me?

Day 275

THOUGHT OF THE DAY: That was me yesterday

I was recounting the story in John chapter eight where the woman who was caught in adultery was taken by the religious leaders to Jesus to see what he would say and do about this violation of the law. What's interesting is that the man wasn't taken to Jesus, only the woman.

How many times in our lives have we felt that certain standards are applied to some people and not others? How many times have we felt that life was not equitable? How many times have we felt that we were being judged by others yet they themselves were unwilling to be accountable for their actions?

Though these thoughts do enter our minds, they're thoughts we can't dwell on. We must simply be accountable for ourselves. Galatians 6:4 puts it this way: "He should not compare himself with others. Each person should judge his own actions." (ICB)

As we look at the story in John 8:7, Jesus offers this challenge to those who bring the woman to Jesus: "He who is without sin among you, let him throw a stone at her first." Their response was to all walk away, realizing that they too had sin in their lives. Wouldn't it be wonderful if the people who are pointing out our faults would recognize their own? Then again, shouldn't we apply that same standard to ourselves? The reality is that we too are often guilty of pointing out the faults of others.

We're a funny people, continuing to see the faults in others and yet not in ourselves. Focusing on the faults of others is often a coping mechanism or something we do to avoid our own personal issues.

Getting back to John chapter eight, as everyone left and Jesus and the woman were alone, Jesus asked the woman, "Woman, where are those accusers of yours? Where are those that were condemning you?" (verse 10) They had all left, seeing their own faults and realizing they had no right to bring accusations against her. Jesus went on to say that neither would he condemn her.

When people saw the woman in the days following, I wonder how they viewed her? Did they see her as the woman caught in adultery, or did they see her as the woman who'd been given a new beginning? Did they see her past or someone who had a fresh start? Did they see her through her yesterday or through her today? Those are the same questions we should be asking ourselves as we take a look at our own lives and the people we know.

There's no doubt in my mind that when Jesus saw the woman caught in adultery, in the day and days that followed, he didn't think, "Oh, there's the woman who was brought to me because of adultery." I believe instead, that when he saw her, he wasn't thinking about her past but instead of the great potential for her future.

How is it possible not to see people's past? Jesus knew it wasn't his place to accuse her (that is what Satan does; he accuses), but to encourage her not to repeat her actions. Reading John 8:10-11: "Woman, where are those accusers of yours? Has no one condemned you?" She said, "No one, Lord." And Jesus said to her, "Neither do I condemn you; go and sin no more." Then there is Romans 14:4: "Who are you to judge someone else's servants?" (CEB)

While I don't want to be judged or criticized for my past, I must not judge or criticize others for their past (their yesterday). Perhaps one of the most difficult things is to not imprison ourselves by always looking backward. If we continue to look at our past, it will blind us from seeing our potential. How can I see my tomorrow when all that's in my view is my past? Philippians 3:13 gives us some insight into this: "But there is one thing I do: I forget what is in the past and try as hard as I can to reach the goal before me." (ERV)

I'm not saying to ignore our issues, but they're not to hold us prisoner from seeing and obtaining our future.

We have to be able to say, "That was me yesterday."

Day 276

THOUGHT OF THE DAY: Graveyard

I can't begin to recount the number of times that my heart sinks when I drive past a graveyard. I see the countless gravestones and think of the thousands of people who are buried who never came close to their potential. They missed the supernatural purpose for their lives.

Each day I see and chat with people who don't see or comprehend who they really are. I know many of you who read my THOUGHT OF THE DAY are also amazing people who as of yet don't see the incredible potential that lies within you. Yet you are so close to the very reason you were born!

What's happened? There are numerous reasons why people don't reach their potential. Here are just a few:

- We can't believe how much God loves and values us.
- We can't believe that there's a divine plan for our lives. Jeremiah 29:11: "I know the plans I have in mind for you, declares the Lord; they are plans for peace, not disaster, to give you a future filled with hope." (CEB) Did you see that God knows and has plans? Notice that He uses the word "plans."
- We've been hurt and as of yet haven't been healed. Our healing awaits!
- We don't know we can be healed. Now you've heard that you can!
- We haven't asked the Holy Spirit what he's planned for us.
- We allow our emotional needs to cloud and distort our thinking. The Holy Spirit can give us a new way of thinking.
- We believe what people have said about us rather than what God says about us. We don't have to believe the lie anymore.
- We have made some bad decisions. God is bigger than all of them.

The list can go on and on! But I'm here to declare that this is the time for your breakthrough! This is the time that your life is about to change forever!

Imagine for a moment that the very first thing that Jesus read in church (actually, in temple) is found in Luke 4:18: "The Spirit of the Lord is upon me; he has appointed me to preach Good News to the poor; he has sent me to heal the brokenhearted and to announce that captives shall be released and the blind shall see, that the downtrodden shall be freed from their oppressors, and that God is ready to give blessings to all who come to him." (TLB)

Think about it: Jesus declares that one of the main purposes he was sent to earth was to heal us physically, mentally, emotionally, and psychologically. He came to heal our brokenness. To free us from oppression and depression. That we could discover the purpose for our lives. Even when we stumble, he will be there to forgive us and help us to once again live the life we were created for.

I plead with you to find someone who believes that they too carry this same anointing - someone who believes that they too have been appointed to continue the ministry of Jesus. To be honest, every person who believes (has committed their lives to Jesus), has this ability. Yet if the truth be told, the majority of people who've committed their lives to Jesus don't comprehend that they too have this ability to heal, liberate, and bless a person's life. If you find yourself in need of a breakthrough - FIND SOMEONE WHO WILL PRAY FOR YOU. THEN GET READY TO SEE GOD DRAMATICALLY STEP INTO YOUR LIFE.

We weren't created to go to the graveyard having never reached our created purpose/potential. Psalm 139:14 says that we are "fearfully and wonderfully made." In Isaiah 43:3 here is what God says about us: "You are precious to me, and I have given you a special place of honor. I love you." (ERV)

It says, YOU ARE, not you will be. We are special; we have a place of honor in His eyes, and HE LOVES US!

God is waiting to turn your life upside down. Get ready!

Day 277

THOUGHT OF THE DAY: I'm in a mess, but...

Jeremiah 29 is one of those good news/bad news stories in the Bible. For many years Israel decided (as we all have at times) to live their lives the way they wanted to. They disregarded what they knew was right.

We can all admit that regardless of whether we've had an understanding of the Bible, we have a conscience that speaks to us clearly about what's right and wrong. God speaks to everyone through their conscience, yet every one of us has ignored this voice. We simply wanted to do what we wanted to do.

When speaking to his disciples, Jesus said that while he'd soon be leaving, he would send the Holy Spirit to take his place. He tells them that one of the purposes of the Holy Spirit is to speak to us about right and wrong. We see this in John 16:8: "And He, when He comes, will convict the world about [the guilt of] sin [and the need for a Savior], and about righteousness, and about judgment."

God is always trying to help us live fuller and happier lives. The choice is ours!

The good news / bad news in Jeremiah 29 is that after years of trying to reach the people He (God) loved, He realized that there had to be a consequence for their decisions. It came time to discipline His children in the same way we must at times discipline our own children, though we may not want to. The discipline is not to hurt them but to try and reach them and help them to see that obedience and living within boundaries will make them and everyone around them much happier. So here in Jeremiah 29 God tells Israel that because of their choices, their consequence will be 70 years of captivity in Babylon.

It may seem like a long time, just as in our lives the consequence of our choices seems unfair and way too lengthy. Why is the consequence usually so lengthy? It's because if the discipline is too short, we'll most likely fail to learn what we need to. In the case of the Israelites, even before the discipline begins, God already has plans for them, and the plans He offers are incredible plans of hope.

Though for a time everything is a mess, God still has these mind-blowing plans for our lives. In Jeremiah 29:11 it says in the Message Bible: "This is God's Word on the subject: 'As soon as Babylon's seventy years are up and not a day before, I'll show up and take care of you as I promised and bring you back home. I know what I'm doing. I have it all planned out—plans to take care of you, not abandon you, plans to give you the future you hope for.' " The (ERV) says, "I say this because I know the plans that I have for you." This message is from the Lord. 'I have good plans for you. I don't plan to hurt you. I plan to give you hope and a good future.' "

Here's what's being said: though for a while you'll be in a place you don't want to be, God promises that He HAS PLANS FOR YOUR LIVES. I love the fact that it says, "plans" (plural), because sometimes we'll miss the first plan, and if we do, He has another plan equally as good. It's like missing the bus, but finding that another one is coming along to bring us to our destination.

If you're in a mess, if you're in a place you don't want to be, the good news is that God has a plan for your future. It's a great plan. Oh, there's a condition: you have to choose what's right. If you're ready to make that choice and follow through, then you're probably close to entering your FUTURE!

Day 278

THOUGHT OF THE DAY: Pebble in the pond

One of the things I enjoyed doing when I was young and still enjoy, is throwing rocks into a pond. As the rock hits the water, it creates ripples that eventually come to where the land and water meet, the pond's edge. Like you, I can recall that the bigger the rock I threw in, the larger the ripples in the water.

Let's say for a moment that the rocks we throw are analogous to the decisions we make. The bigger the decision, the greater impact it will have in our lives. Just as it takes time for the waves to hit the edge of the pond, it will take a while before we see the results of our decisions.

The reality is that when we throw the pebble (make a decision), the wave we create will without question come to the edge of the pond where we're standing. The scripture puts it this way: "Whatever a man sows, that he will also reap." A pastor I knew for years would often use the expression "If you plant corn, you won't get peas."

I believe God has brought everyone to a place where He's asking us to make decisions that will affect our future. He's asking and showing us that the decisions we make now will have an incredible impact. The two key words are decisions and future. Some decisions we make have immediate results, but I believe the decisions He's asking us to make are for our future. I also believe He's asking us to make decisions that may really not make sense now.

It's like Jeremiah in Jeremiah 32 when Israel was about to be captured and removed to Babylon where they'd stay for 70 years. Picture this: Jeremiah has been arrested and is in jail. The Babylon army has surrounded Jerusalem, and within a very short period of time they'll capture the city and take everyone to a foreign land 900 miles away. During this period of time God speaks to Jeremiah (in jail) and tells him that he is to buy a field that belongs to a relative. Now does that make sense? He's in jail and he is to buy a field that's in a war zone. He is to buy a field that he'll never personally occupy because by the end of 70 years when it's time to return to Israel, Jeremiah will have died. Does this make any sense?

I know God is speaking to us about making decisions that at the moment don't make sense. Why? Because the decisions are for our future.

Why did Jeremiah buy this field? God wanted to use Jeremiah to demonstrate that there was a bright future for Israel. You have a bright future. He wanted to say to Israel, "I will bring to an end the horrific place you are in. I will take you out of the circumstances you're in. I want you to have hope for your future. What seems to be impossible is not impossible."

Everything God was saying to Israel He's saying to us. No matter the circumstances we're in, God has an incredible plan for our future. The decision(s) we're being asked to make will not yield an immediate result, yet we have to make a decision that will affect our future. It will affect not only us, but our families. Remember that Jeremiah bought a field he himself wouldn't occupy but instead, one of his relatives. He was leaving a legacy. Our decisions will affect our legacy.

Are you in a place you don't want to be? Then it's time to make decisions that will dramatically affect your future. In most cases you won't see an immediate result, but oh, what a future you're creating -- a future for you and a future for others. As with Israel, God is saying, "I want you to have hope! Make the right decision(s) and watch what I will do."

You are at the edge of the pond. Throw the pebble and watch what will happen.

Day 279

THOUGHT OF THE DAY: Waiting by the phone

For the last two days I've once again felt like crying. It's taken me a few days to understand why. Over the next few days I'll share with you what I heard.

What is the Holy Spirit saying by using the phrase "waiting by the phone"?

As I was praying, I saw a man sitting by the phone (I didn't see his face), but He was waiting there with a grieving heart. I soon understood it was a father (our Father) who was sitting by the phone waiting for His sons and daughters to call. He just wanted to hear their voice. He wanted to say hello and wanted them to know how much He missed talking to them. How much He missed listening to their struggles, their disappointments, their hurts and their pain. He wanted to let them know how much He loved them, and He was grieving because He wanted to comfort and counsel them. He wanted to help them with the problems they were facing. He wanted to give them answers that would not only change their circumstances, but change them. Hour after hour went by, yet there were very few phone calls. I could hear Him say, "If they would only call."

So many of us think about praying and sadly, the majority of the time we don't. Here is what is written in Jeremiah 29:12: "When you call me and come and pray to me, I will listen to you." (CEB) He said that He'll listen.

One of the frustrations we all experience is when we're pouring out our heart, and the person we're speaking to doesn't really listen. When God listens to us, at the voice of His little boy or girl, He's fully engaged. Not only does He listen, but He wants to help. In Psalm 86:7 it says, "Whenever I am in trouble, I cry out to you, because you will answer me." (CEB) I love that it says, "WHENEVER I AM IN TROUBLE." It doesn't limit the number of times I can call Him. He doesn't say, "Well, you called yesterday" or "You called an hour ago." He says, "Whenever."

Then comes the assurance and confidence we all need - "HE WILL ANSWER." Yet here is where we might get confused or discouraged. There is a way in which we want God to answer us, but often He doesn't answer us the way we want Him to.

We get frustrated and discouraged because He doesn't answer us right away. We want the answer now. I had to realize that He was God and not "Tinkerbell" with her little magic wand. I also had to realize that my solution is frequently the wrong one. This often leads us to think that God doesn't answer prayer, which is wrong because He does, but not in the way we always want.

It's like a child coming to one of their parents and asking to borrow the car to help their friend. The problem is that your child is 13, has never driven a car, and to do so would be illegal. To top it all off, it's two o'clock in the morning. The answer: no.

Then comes the next question: can you take me? At this point as a parent you must evaluate all the facts, even those which may be left out. Several answers could be "No," "Later," ("How much later? Tomorrow?" they'll surely ask.) "Let me think about it." "Is your homework done?" And often before we get the answer, other things have to happen first.

The following verse gives us the approach we need to embrace. Psalm 17:6: "I am crying aloud to You, O True God, for I long to know Your answer. Hear me, O God. Hear my plea. Hear my prayer for help." (Voice) The key is "I LONG TO KNOW YOUR ANSWER." To be honest, there are times I don't like His answers, but in reality, answers from heaven are simply amazing. He gives us answers we would've never thought of. Imagine - supernatural answers!

One of my faults and frustrations is that I really dislike delays, but how thankful I am that God has my very best in mind when he delays the answer. We call this a "divine delay." If God doesn't answer right away, I'll wait, or because of time constraints, I'll make my decision based on biblical truth, not on my feelings or what I want. Often, I know the answer, because I sense it inside of me.

The answer inside me is something God placed in me as His creation. Many people call it "our knower." The challenge is doing what we know we should do and not what we want to do. Why ask God for help if we're only going to do it, as Frank Sinatra sang, "my way?"

Often when we pray for help, we have a limited perspective of what's really going on or other possibilities that may exist to answer the predicament we're in. Thus our minds limit and restrict many incredible answers, even supernatural ones.

If you ask me if I wanted my own answer or a supernatural one, I would shout, "GIVE ME A SUPERNATURAL ANSWER!" That's exactly what's written in Jeremiah 33:3: "Call to me and I will answer you. I'll tell you marvelous and wondrous things that you could never figure out on your own." (Message Bible)

Sign me up for this! We're desperate for His answers.

Listen, Our Father is still waiting by the phone. He would love to hear your voice!

Day 280

THOUGHT OF THE DAY: Remorse verses repentance

Though the words remorse and repentance seem to mean the same thing, they actually don't. In the Greek, remorse is metameletheis, which means to feel or express sincere regret or remorse about one's wrongdoing or sin. It also means mental regret.

When someone feels badly about something, they may automatically say, "I'm sorry," but more often than not they may actually exhibit little or no change in their behavior, and may even repeat it.

Then there's the word repent, which in the Greek is metamelomai, which simply means to turn around. It was a military term that described a soldier marching in one direction and then doing an about-face. It means to change one's mind, i.e. to repent: to wholeheartedly amend with abhorrence one's past sin: to change the way one acts and with it to make a sincere effort to change both actions and attitudes.

A person who has remorse is one who feels badly about what they've done, while a person who repents is a person who not only feels badly, but actually tries to change their actions. How many sorries have we said to people? Though we may feel sorrowful, if we have no real desire to change, we're likely to repeat our actions. Frankly, neither "I'm sorry" nor five cents hold much worth.

On the other hand, when a person repents, they not only say, "I'm sorry" but will more often than not ask you to forgive them. There will be a deep and sincere effort to truly change. It doesn't mean that they won't stumble, but if they do, they'll continue to work at turning around.

In Matthew 27:3 we read the account of Judas who betrays Jesus. Some translations wrongly interpret the Greek to say that he repented, but he actually didn't. The NIV says, "When Judas, who had betrayed him, saw that Jesus was condemned, he was seized with remorse and returned the thirty pieces of silver to the chief priests and the elders." The idea that Judas was remorseful rather than repentant is made clear in Matthew 26:24: "The Son of Man will suffer what the Scriptures say will happen to him. But it will be very bad for the one who hands over the Son of Man to be killed. It would be better for him if he had never been born." (ERV)

I know that personally I'm tired of people saying, "I'm sorry" but not changing. Yet I must continue to love and encourage them as best I can. I also have to be aware that I myself must go beyond saying, "I'm sorry." I must repent. I must change. It is one thing to know what I should do and another thing to actually live it out. I know that trying to modify my behavior won't work. I need the Holy Spirit who lives in me to do the work I can't. The Holy Spirit is called the Helper, and I know that I'm in desperate need of his help.

What if all of us lived a life of repentance rather than of remorse?

Day 281

THOUGHT OF THE DAY: Walk with me

As soon as I awoke this morning I said, "Good morning, Father."

Immediately I thought of Enoch and what's written about him in Genesis 5:23-24. In verse 23 it tells us that Enoch lived to be 365 years old. Then verse 24 in the Amplified Bible Classic Edition says, "And Enoch walked [in habitual fellowship] with God." The Voice Bible says, "Enoch had such a close and intimate relationship with God" and the (TLV) says, "Enoch continually walked with God." Genesis 6:9 uses the same words regarding Noah: "Noah walked with God."

You're being invited to walk with God!

As I lay there something happened inside of me. I blurted out "WALK WITH ME." I then recalled Psalm 37:23: "The Lord guides us in the way we should go and protects those who please him." That is pretty powerful. God will guide us in the way we should go, not the way we want to go. Then He promises us that He'll protect us.

Sign me up!

In John 8:16 Jesus said, "If I did judge, I would judge fairly, because I would not be doing it alone. The Father who sent me is here is with me." (CEV)

Imagine for a moment that we all have the capacity to make the right decisions because WE ARE NOT ALONE. We have two minds: a carnal/natural mind and a spiritual mind. What could we accomplish if we'd walk in our spiritual mind, realizing that God (the Holy Spirit) is continually with us? Take a moment right now!

What if everyone walked with God? Perhaps more to the point, what if you and I walked with God?

There's a loud voice this morning, and it's saying, "I want to walk with you." From the very beginning we see that God's intention was to personally walk with man and to have a real relationship with him. In Genesis 2:19-20 we read how God created all the animals and brought them to Adam to give them names. Hey Adam, what do you want to name this animal - God and Adam just hanging out. God had to have laughed at some of the names Adam gave to the animals. Can't you see the Lord teasing him about some of them? Can't you hear the Lord say to Adam, "Are you sure you want that name?!"

You were created to walk with God! You were created not to be alone! Created to have a real relationship with him!

Can you hear Him ask, "Will you walk with me?"

Sign me up!

Day 282

THOUGHT OF THE DAY: He is near

My THOUGHT OF THE DAY comes from verses from Pastor Carlo Thomas, my friend and the man of God I've worked with for 21 years. He's an incredible person, a humble servant to all and one who's made more sacrifices to preach the heart of God than anyone I know. Currently he started 21 days of prayer with all the pastors who relate to him and/or consider him their pastor. They're praying twice a day: once at 5:30-6:00 a.m. and again from 9:30-10:00 p.m. Every day he sends verses to meditate on.

Our problem is not necessarily avoiding the Word, but spending too little time considering what the verses are saying. We read with our intellectual (natural) rather than spiritual mind. Paul writes about this concept in 1 Corinthians 2:14. Let's consider what he's saying, for it's so true. "But a natural person does not accept the things of the Spirit of God. For they are foolishness to him and he is not able to understand, because they are spiritually examined." (DLNT) Our natural mind can't perceive or receive what God is trying to say, because our intellectual mind gets in the way.

The following verses are so encouraging. God tells us He is near. Wow, how wonderful is that! Then comes the "but." The but is that we have to do something. We have to respond. It's great that God is near. My questions become, "Where is He?" and "What do I have to do?"

We can be told that someone is giving away hundred dollar bills a block from where we are, but if we don't make the effort to go there, then we won't receive the benefit of receiving what is freely available.

The first verse we need to "muse" over is Psalm 145:18-19: "The Lord is near to all who call upon Him, to all who call upon Him sincerely and in truth. He will fulfill the desires of those who reverently and worshipfully fear Him; He also will hear their cry and will save them." (AMPC)

Okay, God is near. Great. But I have to call upon Him with sincerity and tell Him the truth. The result will be that in His time He'll give me the desires of my heart if it's what's best for me. The psalmist also speaks to our honoring God and having a reverent attitude towards Him. The Lord is not like a slot machine where you put in a coin and pull the lever to get a result. He is a person, and like any person, needs to be approached in the right way.

The second verse is from Isaiah 55:6: "Turn to the Lord and pray to him, now that he is near." (GNT) Again, He is near. Do we really understand/perceive that? GOD IS NEAR! What do I have to do? I have to reach out to Him and then talk to Him. He's listening and will answer. It would be like hanging out with a number of friends in one room and hearing that God is in the other room. You can stay with your friends or go to the other room where God is - where He is, by the way, waiting for you!

Now the last verse is written by Jeremiah after the destruction of Jerusalem when the majority of people were taken 900 miles away to live in captivity for 70 years. Before they're taken to Babylon, hundreds, if not thousands of people starve to death, as the water supply was cut off from the city. Imagine watching this happen to your son or daughter. How would these desperate people have responded? How do WE respond in hopeless/desperate times? Jeremiah wants to remind them that, "The Lord is wonderfully good to those who wait for him, to those who seek for him. (Lamentations 3:25 TLB)

Did we hear that? Can we accept what is said? God is WONDERFULLY GOOD to those who wait and those who seek him. Two keys: continually waiting and seeking.

Please take some time with these verses and let the Holy Spirit speak to you about things in your life and what God is trying to say to you. What the Holy Spirit shows one person about their life may be different from what he'll show another person. Please go back and reread the verses.

Yes, he is near! But...?

Day 283

THOUGHT OF THE DAY: Your prison cell is open

I went to bed somewhere around 9:30 last night and slept until 3:30 this morning. As I awoke, my mind was filled with so many thoughts that I felt like I was in a library, and the librarian was handing me topics to look up and read.

One of my questions is why we're still in prison. When Jesus' ministry first started after John the Baptist was imprisoned, the very first thing Jesus said and read aloud in the temple was from Isaiah 61:1 and Luke 4:18: "The Spirit of the Lord is on me. He has chosen me to tell good news to the poor. He sent me to tell prisoners that they are free." (ERV) Read that again: "HE WAS SENT TO TELL PRISONERS THAT THEY ARE FREE."

We have to grasp the depth and significance of this. The very first thing he says is that his Father has sent him to tell prisoners they were free. All of us at one time or another have been in prison (and too many still are). Jesus says we're free to leave. Yet why are so many of us still being held captive?

In some cases, people don't know that Jesus came to pay the debt for their imprisonment. While some of us have been put in prison by others, many others of us have put ourselves in prison, and still others are there because they feel they deserve to be. They're held there by guilt and shame and an underlying belief that they deserve to be held captive.

Know that Jesus has paid the price for us to be released from our various prisons. There isn't a prison cell that he doesn't have a key to. Some don't know that the prison doors are open, while others have been in prison so long that's all they know.

My heart breaks as I see prison cells open and people still sitting in their cells. John 10:10 says that "Jesus said that he came to give us life." Living in a prison cell isn't living the life he intended. If you're still in prison, then take a look - I see Jesus coming your way.

There are two accounts in Acts where Peter is in prison. In the first it says that "at night Peter was sleeping, bound with two chains between two soldiers; and the guards before the door were keeping the prison. Now behold, an angel of the Lord stood by him, and a light shone in the prison; and he struck Peter on the side and raised him up, saying, 'Arise quickly!' And his chains fell off his hands." (Acts 12: 6-7)

I find it interesting that the angel had to give Peter a slap as if to say, "Hey Peter, get up and get out of here." Perhaps we too might need a "dope slap" as if to say, "Come on, the prison cell is open and the chains that held you prisoner no longer bind you."

In the second story, Peter's in prison again, but this time with Silas and many others. In Acts 16 and in verse 26 it says, "Suddenly there was a great earthquake, so that the foundations of the prison were shaken; and immediately all the doors were opened and everyone's chains were loosed." There was a supernatural earthquake that caused prison cells to open and chains on prisoners to fall off, yet the prisoners were fine! Crazy stuff.

I'm telling you that if you missed the last earthquake, get ready, because another one is coming. In fact, I can feel the ground beginning to shake. In John 8:36 John writes, "So if the Son sets you free, you will be absolutely free." (GW)

Listen, your prison cell is open or soon will be. Please don't stay in your cell!

Day 284

THOUGHT OF THE DAY: Your tomb is opened

The other day I wrote that our prison cells were open. At the same time, I also saw graves being opened and people coming back to life.

In all our lives we've experienced some sort of death. Pain, disappointment, betrayal, life circumstances, our own decisions and those of others, have deeply affected our lives. How many times have you felt that something in your life has died or been lost and in that area there's no longer any hope?

While in prison at least there's some hope of someday getting out, but when we experience death or loss, we tend to believe there's no way any life can come from the grave that we're in. It's a place of hopelessness, where we feel that something has died in us.

I want to tell you that I've seen numerous graves in my life open and God bring new life to that which was dead. In the book of John, Lazarus dies and has been in the tomb for four days. Lazarus' sisters Martha and Mary are deeply grieving along with a large contingency of other people. In John 11 Jesus is escorted to Lazarus' tomb where he's told that four days have passed since Lazarus has died. In verse 39 it says, "Lord, by this time there is a stench, for he has been dead four days." In other words, not only are we grieving, but the whole thing stinks – there's no way life can come from death.

Picture Jesus outside the tomb suddenly blowing everyone's mind. Standing there he calls Lazarus out. We read in John 11:43: "He cried with a loud voice, 'Lazarus, come forth!' " and the next verse says, "And he who had died came out bound hand and foot with grave clothes, and his face was wrapped with a cloth. Jesus said to them, 'Loose him, and let him go.' "

You see, as much as Jesus is calling us out of our graves and tombs, we're still in need of getting help.

I want you to picture your tomb and Jesus standing in front of it calling your name (YES, YOUR NAME). Okay, you're alive but still in need of having people carefully remove your burial bandages.

Yes, we can be alive and still be bound.

Before Jesus called Lazarus from the tomb, he had people roll away the large rock in front of it. You might be thinking that there's no one who can roll the stone away from your personal tomb, but consider the possibility that there are already people playing this role - people around you who even at this moment are rolling the stone away because they care, love you, and want to see you "live again."

If there's no one to roll your stone away, God will roll it away Himself. I just love the picture of the angel sitting on top of the stone that was rolled away. It's as if the angel was smiling and saying, "Well, that was no big deal."

Beyond this, here's the incredible truth - stones and tombs can't stop the Lord from restoring life to us. Referring to the death of Jesus, we read in Matthew 28:2, "And behold, there was a great earthquake; for an angel of the Lord descended from heaven, and came and rolled back the stone from the door, and sat on it."

I'm persuaded that God wants to do what you might think is impossible. He's standing in front of your tomb and saying, "I will breathe life in you again."

Your tomb is open.

Day 285

THOUGHT OF THE DAY: Walking in the Spirit

Not to oversimplify things, but there are two realms that exist at the same time.

One is the natural realm in which we live with our five senses: "sight (ophthalmoception), hearing (audioception), taste (gustaoception), smell (olfacoception or olfaception), and touch (tactioception).

The other is the spirit realm where we have the capacity to enter a place outside our senses which is just as real as the natural. Many believe that the five senses in the natural are also the same in the spirit. I can personally attest the truth of this, having experienced in the spirit sights, sounds, smells, and tastes.

Paul talks about the natural man and the spiritual man. In 1 Corinthians 2:4 we read, "But the natural, nonspiritual man does not accept or welcome or admit into his heart the gifts and teachings and revelations of the Spirit of God, for they are folly (meaningless nonsense) to him; and he is incapable of knowing them [of progressively recognizing, understanding, and becoming better acquainted with them] because they are spiritually discerned and estimated and appreciated." (AMPC)

Simply stated, when we think and live with our natural mind, we cannot receive or perceive spiritual things. In fact, Paul writes in Romans 8:7 that "the carnal mind is enmity against (at war with) God; for it is not subject to the law of God, nor indeed can be." (NKJV) Our natural/carnal mind literally fights with the concepts and precepts of God, because it CANNOT perceive or receive matters of a spiritual nature.

When we think and act with our natural senses we'll miss and not comprehend the spiritual realm. Most importantly, we won't be able to sense the presence of God nor will we perceive what's taking place in and around us.

One of the most challenging verses in the bible is found in Galatians 5:16: "But I say, walk habitually in the [Holy] Spirit [seek Him and be responsive to His guidance], and then you will certainly not carry out the desire of the sinful nature [which responds impulsively without regard for God and His precepts]." (AMP) This verse tells me that if I continually/habitually have my mind on the things of God, I won't make carnal decisions. Oh Lord, help us! We act as if we're light switches, shifting continually between carnal and spiritual. Perhaps we should just tape the switch in one position!

Imagine with me if we all walked in the Spirit on a continual basis, what we could we be hearing, seeing, and perceiving. Our problem is that we're inconsistent. We live the majority of our lives carnally, and then we're frustrated that we can't perceive what God is doing.

I'm convinced that there's an open door available to us. I believe God is waiting for us to respond. We read this in Revelations 4:1 "Then as I looked, I saw a door standing open in heaven, and the same voice I had heard before, which sounded like a mighty trumpet blast, spoke to me and said, 'Come up here and I will show you what must happen in the future!'"

Can't you sense that there's an open door? Aren't we sensing the call to spend time with the Lord? The result will be - HE WILL SHOW US! He will show us the past, present, and future. We'll have wisdom, insight, understanding, discernment, peace, joy, hope, and more.

What if we all spent our lives walking in the Spirit? The door is open! We need to respond! We can do this! Honestly, just think of the life we could live. Imagine how the Holy Spirit would use us! Imagine the lives we would touch!

We have to abandon carnal thinking and living!

Day 286

THOUGHT OF THE DAY: What's in your hand?

Moses has been instructed by God to deliver Israel from Egypt, yet his first mistake is the same one we often make - he starts looking at what he can do, not what God can do.

Why is it that when God speaks to us about doing something, we immediately begin looking at what's possible for us, not God? Over and over again we make this mistake. We're flawed in our ability to trust God, and sadly, it applies to the small as well as big things in our lives.

God sees (I like that) the mess that His people are in and makes it clear what He will do. Exodus 3:7-8: "And the Lord said: 'I have surely seen the oppression of My people who are in Egypt, and have heard their cry because of their taskmasters, for I know their sorrows. So I have come down to deliver them out of the hand of the Egyptians.' "

Here's Moses' response in verse 11. Are you ready for this? "Who am I that I should go to Pharaoh, and that I should bring the children of Israel out of Egypt?" Yup, it's all about us. Here is our Father's response to him in verse 12: "I will certainly be with you." Over and over again through the entire bible God says to us: "I WILL BE WITH YOU."

You might think that would be enough for Moses (and for us in our lives). But no, Moses begins the "what if" mental gymnastics. From chapter 4:1 Moses says, "But suppose they will not believe me or listen to my voice; suppose they say, 'The Lord has not appeared to you.' "

So how does God respond to Moses' "suppose/what if" question? Verse two says, "So the Lord said to him, 'What is that in your hand?' Moses replies, 'A rod.' " For Moses and for us, God simply instructs us to use what we have and stop looking at what we lack.

Moses viewed the rod as insignificant. He saw instead what he had in the natural. God can and does take the natural things we have and turn them into the supernatural. We just have to let Him.

It's really simple - WHAT'S IN YOUR HAND?

Day 287

THOUGHT OF THE DAY: Just take the next step

If I'm 15 feet from a door that I want to open and walk through, how do I get there? The answer is - one step at a time.

I'm a planner. I like everything figured out in advance. As much as this is a good trait to have, it also has its weaknesses. The first is that I may have everything so etched in stone that I can easily miss God's plan as I focus too much on my own. The second weakness is that when I don't have a plan, I don't take any steps, and if I don't take steps, I can stay stuck.

It's the times when I don't have all the answers that I need to consider simply taking the next step I see. This requires faith. Leaning too much on a plan diminishes our need to trust God moment by moment.

I love what it says in Hebrews 11:8: "By faith Abraham obeyed when he was called to go out to the place which he would receive as an inheritance. And he went out, not knowing where he was going." Notice here that God was faithful to show Abraham that it was time to move on and take the next step towards his future. The appropriate response is to obey what we believe He's showing us and not worry about all the details.

I feel that so many of us are stuck, and the Holy Spirit is shouting - TAKE THE NEXT STEP! Don't wait another minute. If you don't know where you're going, then you're at the perfect place. The promise that God gave to Moses applies to us. "I will certainly be with you." (Exodus 3:11)

TAKE THE NEXT STEP...

Day 288

THOUGHT OF THE DAY: Words

One of the more difficult issues we all face on a consistent basis is what we say, what comes out of our mouths. Every time we say or hear something, it has some sort of effect on our life.

In Proverbs 18:21 it says, "Words kill, words give life; they're either poison or fruit—you choose." (MSG) Most translations say" life and death are in the power of the tongue." Notice it says to choose.

I believe we don't realize what power each of us has in our words. It can be one or several, but each word spoken has the capacity of being a blessing or bringing devastation. James 3:5 says, "So also the tongue is a small thing, but what enormous damage it can do." (TLB) It goes on to say in verse 10: "And so blessing and cursing come pouring out of the same mouth. Dear brothers, surely this is not right!"

James says that every man is guilty of saying things he shouldn't. While this is true, it doesn't give us permission or an excuse.

I don't like being hurt by words, so why should I use words to hurt others? We have all heard sayings like, "If you can't say something good/nice then don't say anything at all," or "People who live in glass houses shouldn't throw stones."

Yet all of us are guilty. Why? Often we use words to defend ourselves. We've been hurt so much that our reaction to even the smallest perceived offence is to lash out, the pain in our heart and soul often revealing itself in our speech. And sadly, once we say something, we can't take it back.

So we're faced with a choice. Are we going to continue to say things that are hurtful and negative, or are we going to choose to speak life and blessing? A few final verses say, "Whatever a man sows he reaps" and then Proverbs 26:27: "If you dig a pit, you will fall in; if you start a stone rolling, it will roll back on you." (CEV)

If we're tired of falling into pits, tired of getting crushed, tired of hurting others and being hurt - then let's choose our WORDS!

Day 289

THOUGHT OF THE DAY: What's being stolen?

Over the last number of days, I've kept on hearing, "What has the enemy stolen? What have we allowed him to steal?"

Thieves are clever and often subtle. They can break into your home without your knowing, and until you realize something is missing, you won't even know they were there.

What are you missing, may I ask? Your peace? Your joy? What about some relationships? Hope, maybe? Are you despondent, depressed, disappointed, disheartened, discouraged? I would suggest that we haven't yet recognized that the enemy of our soul has found a way to steal what Jesus came to give us.

John 10:10 is likely familiar to you: "The thief's purpose is to steal, kill and destroy. My purpose is to give life in all its fullness." How did the enemy find a way in? Matthew 13:24-25 suggests one answer. The Parable of the Wheat and the Tares says, "Another parable He put forth to them, saying: 'The kingdom of heaven is like a man who sowed good seed in his field; but while men slept, his enemy came and sowed tares among the wheat and went his way.' " (NKJV)

The problem is that they were sleeping. Let's unpack that.

Matthew 25:5 speaks about the 10 virgins and the oil for their lamps. What is the crux of the problem? Delay. Verse five: "But while the bridegroom was delayed, they all slumbered and slept." Has delay been the issue?

Then we have Ephesians 4:27:

EXB: "Do not give the devil a ·way to defeat you [foothold; opportunity]"

GNV: "Neither give place to the devil"

GW: "Don't give the devil any opportunity to work"

GNT: "Don't give the devil a chance"

HCSB: "And don't give the devil an opportunity"

ICB: "Do not give the devil a way to defeat you"

Then there's the Amplified Bible:

"And do not give the devil an opportunity [to lead you into sin by holding a grudge, or nurturing anger, or harboring resentment, or cultivating bitterness]."

There are at least three ways the enemy steals from us - when we're sleeping in general, when there's delay and we "fall asleep," and third, when we open the door to him through holding a grudge, nurturing anger, harboring resentment, or cultivating bitterness.

Then, there's David's situation as he served in the kingdom, and Satan came with vengeance. Read first Samuel 30, and let's respond the way he did: by encouraging himself, seeking God for a plan, and following it by finding where the enemy was and then attacking. The result was that David recovered everything the enemy had stolen!

What's being stolen and why? Do something about it.

Day 290

THOUGHT OF THE DAY: There's another bus

As I'm getting ready to go to the overflow homeless shelter, this thought floods my mind: "There's another bus."

What in the world does that mean?

So many people feel like they've missed their opportunity. They made the wrong decision and in so doing missed what could have been. We've all heard the voice in our heads and even coming from others, "It's too late." According to whom, we might ask?

Well, it wasn't too late for Moses. It wasn't too late for Sarah and Abraham and for Zacharias and Elizabeth (parents of John the Baptist). All of us have a time table that we've constructed in our minds. Such and such, we think, has to happen by such and such a time. As we look back, haven't we all discovered that most of the time we really weren't ready when we thought we were? And yes, there have been times too when we just missed the opportunity.

All too often when we feel we've missed the opportunity or the open door, discouragement and depression grip us, which, in turn, lead to hopelessness.

For a moment I want you to picture yourself at a bus station. For whatever reason you missed the bus. You can either go home or stay at the station to catch the next one. When I was younger, I would take buses from New Hampshire to Massachusetts. I can remember more than once either missing the bus or having the bus routes cancelled due to bad weather. On more than one occasion I had to spend hours and even one time, the entire night, waiting for another bus to come and pick me up. Ever spend days in an airport waiting to catch the next plane?

Here's our choice: we can leave the bus station, train station, or the airport, or we can simply wait for the next opportunity. It's true that it's often lousy waiting and can even become an opportunity to gripe, complain, or get discouraged, disappointed, or depressed, but we need to ask ourselves how all of that can possibly help.

Here's what Paul says in Philippians 4:11: "I've learned to be content in whatever situation I'm in." (GW) Notice that he referred to the PROCESS. Yes, he had to LEARN...

While you're waiting for the next bus, you can complain and be depressed or feel sorry for yourself. You can leave the station and blame someone, or...you can choose to have confidence that another bus is on the way.

Hey, what's that I see? It's another bus coming to pick you up. The bus will stop, the door will open. There's only one thing left to do and that's to get on board.

Before you boarded you might have seen the destination sign on the front reading "XXXX Special." Where the Xs are, put your name. This bus has come just for you!

Day 291

THOUGHT OF THE DAY: Are you trapped?

How many times do we feel trapped and simply want a new beginning? All too often we're like coal miners stuck inside the mines we're excavating.

We've all read the real-life stories. I can't begin to imagine the thoughts, emotions, and fears running through the minds of those to whom this has happened. Perhaps the greatest cry is, "I just want to get out."

Ever feel this way?

Often the deep pit we're in is the "pit of our past." Though we can be rescued, we still continue to relive the memories, our past decisions and sins haunting us. We may be officially out of the pit, but we're still stuck in the deep, dark hole of our minds.

But wait, I have great news!

Our God doesn't remember our pasts. His word says that He can't. Not only does He declare us innocent, He DOES NOT REMEMBER!

When you read Isaiah 49:15, I ask you to not just read the words, but picture our Father/God sitting down, looking at you, and whispering these words. "I, even I, am the One Who takes away your sins because of Who I am. And I will not remember your sins." (New Living Translation) Not only will He take away our sins, but He says, "I WILL NOT REMEMBER!"

Who in your life needs this fresh start?

Listen to the words of Jeremiah as he pours out his heart in Lamentations 3:55: "I called out your name, O God, called from the bottom of the pit. You listened when I called out, 'Don't shut your ears! Get me out of here! Save me!' You came close when I called out. You said, 'It's going to be all right.' " (MSG)

Can we hear that? "It's going to be all right."

No matter where we are or what's going on in our lives, our Father will not forget us. Isaiah 49:15: "Is it possible for a mother, however disappointed, however hurt, to forget her nursing child? Can she feel nothing for the baby she carried and birthed? Even if she could, I, God, will never forget you." (Voice)

One of my favorite verses is when Noah is shut up in the ark. We can just imagine what's going on in his mind. God certainly knew. Genesis 8:1 says, "Then God remembered Noah."

God remembers you, and He forgets / blots out your past.

Are you trapped? Then know this, "It's going to be all right."

Day 292

THOUGHT OF THE DAY: Jesus loved him

Yesterday during service Pastor Steve mentioned the parable of the Good Samaritan, which on my own I had just begun to reflect on. I would encourage you to do the same. It's loaded with insights that are worthy of gleaning and embracing.

To recap the story, a rich young ruler comes to Jesus and asks the "million-dollar" question. "What must I do to inherit eternal life?"

Why is it our natural propensity to look at what we can do, even in the face of Jesus having done all of it for us?

It seems that receiving His free gift is harder than we might expect. Rather than doing things to effectively "earn" our salvation, it's completely about receiving what Jesus accomplished on the cross.

Getting back to the story, Jesus answers him and the young man responds by saying (my words) "Hey, I'm good. I've been doing that all my life." Even though Jesus knew the young man was sincere, He could also see that something was lacking.

Perhaps like the young man, we feel like we're doing okay yet are unaware of the areas we're lacking or falling short in our lives. There's something we have to know. It's found in Mark 10:21. Multiple translations say, "And Jesus, looking at him, loved him."

Can we grasp this? Jesus knows where we're falling short. He knows everything about us, and He looks at us with LOVE because His focus is His love for us, not our faults and where we're falling short.

Jesus wants us to know that HE LOVES US. Yes, we're falling short, but HE LOVES US.

Day 293

THOUGHT OF THE DAY: It's time to start again

It was during the life of Haggai the prophet that the time had come to once again rebuild the temple. The people had started working on the project some 16 years earlier, but all kinds of resistance surfaced. There was resistance that came from others, but most of the opposition came from inside the ranks. They were struggling with themselves.

The circumstances that Israel was facing mirror the resistance that all too often crops up in our own lives. Israel was trying to rebuild the temple that had been destroyed, just as we're sometimes trying to recover from our own devastation. We finally begin to put our lives together and are making headway when everything comes to a grinding halt. We meet resistance from other people, but if we're honest, the biggest hinderances to rebuilding our lives are our own issues. We start out well and then stop, having endless cycles, it seems, of starting and stopping.

How can we break the cycle? We need something to hold onto, and frankly, it can't be our own strength or will power. We need something, and that something is God's promise to us found in Haggai 1:13: "I am with you, says the Lord." Over and over God says this. We just have to begin really believing that He means it.

We're His children, and He doesn't abandon or give up on us. Even when we ourselves give up, He is still present saying, "I am with you." Just as Israel stopped working on the temple for 16 years, God spoke through Haggai and said, "It's time to rise up and build again."

God is speaking to us again today - Rise up, rebuild your life. I'm with you.

Israel would do well, then would be a mess. Over and over again Israel would repeat the cycle. Over and over again God reached out to His children. During the time of Zephaniah, Israel was a wreck, and God again spoke to them and said: "The Lord your God is with you. He is like a powerful soldier. He will save you. He will show how much he loves you and how happy he is with you. He will laugh and be happy about you." (Zephaniah 3: 17, ERV)

In the middle of their mess He said, "I am with you. I will fight for you and bring you through every battle. I will show you how much I love you."

And listen, God doesn't change! He is speaking once again - I'M WITH YOU! It doesn't matter how much time has passed.

ITS TIME TO START AGAIN!

Day 294

THOUGHT OF THE DAY: Where is our passion?

Have our hearts grown cold? Are we eager to meet with God? Are we jumping out of bed and running to our prayer closets? Are we enthusiastic on Sunday morning knowing that we'll encounter the presence of God? Do we delight in doing the will of God? Are we excited to hear the great and mighty things God is doing around the world? How about what God is doing in our local church?

Where is our fire?

Can you remember the days when you were compelled to find God? The days you were compelled by the Holy Spirit to do and say all kinds of things? Twice we find Paul using this term. Here is what's written about him.

Acts 18:5: "When Silas and Timothy had come from Macedonia, Paul was compelled by the Spirit, and testified to the Jews that Jesus is the Christ."

Acts 28:19: "But when the Jews spoke against it, I was compelled to appeal to Caesar, not that I had anything of which to accuse my nation." Paul was compelled to go to Rome, even knowing he would be killed there.

What compels us, I ask?

Has someone or something put out your fire or even stolen it? I remember the old Vineyard song "Light My Fire Again." With tears running down my cheeks I have my hands outstretched. Here is that song: https://youtu.be/dOrthdHtf64

Day 295

THOUGHT OF THE DAY: I think I just saw Easter hop past me

A survey about the real meaning of Easter was taken in April 2014, and most people reported it as "candy." No surprise then that according to the Pew Research Center, by 2050 the percentage of Christians in America will have dropped by 66 percent.

Americans are expected to shell out a combined $16.4 billion on multicolored plastic eggs, chocolate bunnies, marshmallow Peeps, and other holiday staples – a figure up from $15.9 billion the year before.

Peeps' manufacturers say it takes roughly six minutes to make one marshmallow Peep chick. Assuming this time frame is standard for all the Peeps consumed around Easter, it would take a combined 150 million hours, or more than 17,000 years, to make all of the Easter Peeps consumed.

If jelly beans are more up your alley, know that the National Confectioners Association says that 16 billion are made for the Easter season each year. Assuming you can comfortably grab 20 jelly beans in a single handful, it would take 800 million hands to hold those beans.

The White House on Monday will host the 137th annual White House Easter Egg Roll, a tradition that goes back to 1878 with President Rutherford B. Hayes. The number of people expected to attend this year will be 35,000.

During the Easter season online shoppers are expected to spend $221.00 per family versus $140.62 for those who shop retail.

Oh, I think I just saw Easter hop past me...

Day 296

THOUGHT OF THE DAY: What do you see?

In Mark eight we read the story of a blind man who was brought to Jesus in the town of Bethsaida. After Jesus "had spit on his eyes and put His hands on him, He asked him if he saw anything." He responded by saying, "I see men like trees, walking." Then Jesus prayed again, and his sight was fully restored.

So here's a question that I'm often asked by the Holy Spirit that I'll pass on to you: "What do you see?" When I'm asked this, it seems that the Holy Spirit is trying to tell me that I'm missing something. So I pray and ask, okay, what am I not seeing? All too often I begin to get a glimpse of something, but more often than not, I stop there and fail to see what the Holy Spirit wants me to, thus continuing to see things in a distorted way.

I'm writing this thought, because I'm hearing that all of us have areas in our lives where we're blind. Our vision, our perception, our perspectives, and our opinions are particularly vulnerable. Sadly, we're aware of some of those areas, but of others, we're clueless. Unfortunately, though, we're too often content in our blindness or our lack of truly seeing.

Jesus wants to spit in our eyes. Will we let him? Or will we continue to give ourselves the liberty to be stubborn, stuck, and yes, unwilling to change? In Luke 6:39 it says, "And He spoke a parable to them: 'Can the blind lead the blind? Will they not both fall into the ditch?' " In Matthew 15:14 it says, "If the blind leads the blind, both will fall into a ditch."

Because of our blindness we're hardly capable of fully leading others.

Is it time to see?

Day 297

THOUGHT OF THE DAY: His voice

This morning I awoke to a bellowing whisper that grew louder and louder. This voice is being heard in every valley, every mountain, every desert, city, town, and village. There's not a place on earth that His voice isn't being heard today. What is this voice saying?

Listen, you can hear it. Take a moment. What do you hear? His voice is thundering, yet full of love! His voice is pleading, yet inviting.

Can you hear it?

Over and over it's like a voice echoing in a canyon. The air is filled with mercy and compassion. I've never heard His voice like this before. Can you hear it? Oh, "The mercies of the Lord are from everlasting to everlasting." (Psalm 103:17) I'm filled with awe and wonder. Can you hear what He's saying?

These same words were spoken from a cross on a hill called Golgotha and are spoken every day to all humanity. What is this voice saying? You can hear, "IT IS FINISHED, it's completed. it's done, it's accomplished, it's consummated!" The Greek better renders it, "YOUR DEBT HAS BEEN PAID IN FULL."

Can you hear it?

Day 298

THOUGHT OF THE DAY: Relentless expectation

Over the past few weeks and especially today, I've had this nagging sense that I can't identify. All day I've been asking what it is. Finally, just a few minutes ago I heard one word. The word is expectation. That's it. I'm sensing God is about to do something. Are you sensing the same thing?

Also during the day I was hearing, "Don't let the devil steal from you." Steal what, I asked? There was no immediate answer, but I continue to pursue the Lord on the matter.

What IS clear to me is how often all of us have allowed the enemy to steal our sense of expectation, which is woven into our dreams and the things God has promised all of us. He steals these through discouragement.

We have to be sick and tired of letting the enemy steal our dreams, steal our promises, steal our expectations.

The difficulty is that our indwelling Holy Spirit measures time differently than our natural minds or flesh do. When we read the word "soon" in the Bible, we think in terms of a short period of time, which is funny because in reality, it often means years. Like in Philippians 4:5 it says, "The Lord is near (at hand) [He is coming soon]." (AMPC)

Then there is James 5:8: "You, too, must be patient. Don't give up hope. The Lord will soon be here." (GW) "The Book of James is probably the oldest book of the New Testament, written perhaps as early as A.D. 45, before the first council of Jerusalem in A.D. 50."

The point is, we have to cling to HOPE! We have to hold onto what we've been promised. Hold on to your expectations!

Perhaps all of this can be summarized by this one verse in John 11:40: "Didn't I tell you that if you keep trusting, you will see the glory of God?" (CJB)

There it is, we have to keep on trusting and WE WILL SEE THE GLORY OF GOD. WE WILL SEE OUR EXPECTATIONS FULFILLED!

Day 299

THOUGHT OF THE DAY: What will you hear today?

Perhaps one of the things we hear and say often is that we haven't heard from God. We are living in an age, no, I take that back; man has always lived in a time that he's needed to hear from God.

I believe many of us attribute not hearing from God to His not speaking. I can hear myself saying, "God's being quiet right now; He's not talking. This can sometimes be true; a verse in Amos spoke to me today about this very thing. Amos 8:11: " 'Behold, the days are coming," says the Lord God, 'That I will send a famine on the land, Not a famine of bread, Nor a thirst for water, But of hearing the words of the Lord.' " (NKJV)

Wow! It was like God standing on top of a mountain declaring these words to us. The problem is not that God isn't speaking, though; it's that we're not hearing.

Why? Here's a short list. We don't pray; we're too distracted, too busy, aren't still, are inpatient, unwilling to wait, already know what we want to do, and are overwhelmed with the circumstances we're in. You can add to the list. Yes, Amos said there would be a famine in hearing.

We all know the phone number 537 364 2433 (Jeremiah 33:3) which says, "Call to Me, and I will answer you, and show you great and mighty things, which you do not know." We all want this, but the key is calling and then believing He'll answer.

Here is a question – where was Jeremiah when God said this? Jeremiah 33:1: "Moreover the word of the Lord came to Jeremiah a second time, while he was still shut up in the court of the prison." Yes, many times when we're in a difficult place we're encouraged to call on God (make the phone call).

So the problem more often than not isn't that God isn't speaking. It's in our hearing. Our Father wouldn't speak if He didn't want us to hear. He says, "Call to Me, and I will answer you, and show you great and mighty things, which you do not know."

What will you hear today?

Day 300

THOUGHT OF THE DAY: Oh...

Now you'd imagine that after 44 years of preaching I would've learned this by now. As I write I can hear a faint chuckle and can see a big grin. The chuckle is getting louder. I can sense that Abba is pleased.

If we stop learning and growing that's when we're edging into dangerous waters. So you're probably wondering what I've learned. Well, since Sunday or perhaps beginning at the end of last week, I started musing about what I should speak about on Easter Sunday. I went back and reread the account of Jesus' resurrection in all four gospels, asking the Holy Spirit to show me something that I'd missed over the years. I heard nothing. In fact, yesterday I was becoming frustrated so stopped praying, confident that in His timing He'd show me something at some point before I opened my mouth on Easter morning.

So I continued to muse with the Lord, and then He said this to me: "You're praying for a message when instead you should ask for my heart!" OH... He was right. Lesson (hopefully) learned.

Are we asking for a word, or should we instead be asking for His heart?

By the way, it was 5:00 a.m. this morning, after one of those I-can't-fall asleep nights, that He gave me His heart for Easter. I can see Him smiling.

Perhaps you don't have to wait 44 years to learn that's it's not about the message. It's always about His heart.

Day 301

THOUGHT OF THE DAY: Breath of God

I pray that you would feel the breath of God (phuema) this morning and that you would receive this breath. For surely He has drawn near and wants to, this Easter, enable and empower you to fulfill His calling on your life. John 20:21 says, "As the Father has sent Me, I also send you." (NKJV)

We read in John 20 that it was evening when Jesus drew near to them and breathed on them (phuema). It is better translated he "blew" on them and said, "Receive the Holy Spirit." The Voice Bible says, verse 22: "Now He drew close enough to each of them that they could feel His breath." The verse continues and says, "Jesus (said): "Welcome the Holy Spirit of the living God.' " The Cambridge Bible says "(Receive ye) or, take ye, implying that the recipient may welcome or reject the gift: he is not a mere passive receptacle."

This is so funny. I can't remember how many times I've told people to "take it" while I was praying for them. I would say this because I could sense that they weren't receiving/taking in what the Holy Spirit was attempting to put in them.

The next time you're prayed for - TAKE IT! You may have a physical manifestation when you do - like falling to the ground - just like the many people I prayed for had when they decided to "take it."

May your Easter be filled with His presence. Holy Spirit, breathe on us!

Day 302

THOUGHT OF THE DAY: God shows up on Easter
Works of the Holy Spirit: Easter, March 27th
Yesterday was a supernatural day. The Holy Spirit walked into the sanctuary at two services. Yes, I said two services. At 10:30 we met at the

301

Porch, and at 12:30 I was in a Spanish Church on Pleasant Street. The guest speaker at both services was the Holy Spirit.

In John 20, Jesus walked through the locked door into the room the disciples were hiding in. Yesterday Jesus walked into two churches and changed all of our lives.

Many of us had areas that we've kept locked. But yesterday Jesus unlocked those doors. Just as the disciples were filled with fear, we too are often held captive by our fears, but yesterday Jesus walked into our lives and replaced fear with peace.

Where people were hopeless, he breathed hope.

Where there was despair and depression, he breathed on people, overwhelming them with his love and his affection.

As Jesus himself was in a tomb, yesterday Jesus set people free from their own tombs that they might enjoy life.

Jesus showed his disciples his hands and his side. Yesterday Jesus came and invited us all to have a greater revelation of him. There was a spirit of revelation that filled the room and our lives.

As Jesus said, "As the Father has sent me; I send you," yesterday he anointed people and sent them out to preach the Gospel of the Kingdom.

Yesterday the power of God swept through both church services. People wept, and some crumbled and fell under the power of God.

I was honored to be a part of this supernatural Easter, and while I don't want to seem ungrateful, I don't want to live in yesterday. The Lord spent yesterday setting us free, healing our wounds, imparting hope, giving us a deeper revelation of him. Why? That we may not only live lives filled with peace and joy, but that we could be His sons and daughters declaring His goodness to those to whom He sends us.

Easter March 27, 2016 - the Holy Spirit came and breathed on us, but there was only one condition. We had to receive it, or as the Cambridge Bible says, we had to "take it."

Day 303

THOUGHT OF THE DAY: More on Easter

Works of the Holy Spirit: More news from Easter

Yesterday in the afternoon I called the man who translated for me Easter Sunday at the Spanish Church. Whenever I minister in another church, I usually call the next day to see how they felt about the ministry and if they have any questions.

When the Spanish translator answered the phone, he was very exuberant, talking so fast that I had to "parrot" what he was saying so that I didn't misunderstand. The funny thing is that when he answered the phone, he called me "Bishop," which is how the pastor introduced me on Sunday. He gave me that title because of the churches I've planted and my itinerant traveling. It's so funny to hear it.

He told me that the pastor and the entire church were blessed with what the Holy Spirit did on Sunday. He said that when he was on the floor (he was there for a while), that the Holy Spirit showed him a number of painful episodes from his childhood and healed his heart. He wasn't aware of how profoundly these episodes had affected his life. In his broken English he spoke about his wife who's the worship leader. During the time I was praying with her, I could see the Holy Spirit touching her and knew that the Lord wanted to go even deeper. So he told me to take off my suit jacket and put it on her shoulders. As soon as I did, she collapsed. Her husband spoke of the things that the Holy Spirit did, her life transformed by the power of God.

In our own church (the Porch) both Pastor Tom and Pastor Steve told me how they could feel the power of God flow out of them. When I watched the video of the service, I could literally see the Holy Spirit on Pastor Tom. As we spoke about Easter, he told me how prophetic words he was speaking penetrated people's lives and how many broke down. Literally he was seeing lives supernaturally changed in the few moments people stood there in front of him.

When I spoke to Rece who was on the platform, she told me that no one remained in their seats, that everyone was in the aisle waiting for prayer. She reported that in all her years she'd never seen a response like that. Remember, this was Easter Sunday.

I can't begin to tell you the joy that floods my heart when I hear of all the things the Holy Spirit did on Easter. To be an eye witness of the transforming power of the Holy Spirit is overwhelming, so much so that I just have to raise my hands and worship him.

We want to declare what Paul writes in 1 Corinthians 2:4-5: "And my speech and my preaching were not with persuasive words of human wisdom, but in demonstration of the Spirit and of power, that your faith should not be in the wisdom of men but in the power of God." (NKJV)

Can I have an amen?

"Call to me and I will answer you. I'll tell you marvelous and wondrous things that you could never figure out on your own." (Jeremiah 33:3)

Take the time! Open the door! Today!!!

Day 304

THOUGHT OF THE DAY: I don't remember

Over the past few days I've been considering the things the Lord would have me share this weekend in New York. I've also been musing with him over the passing of a young woman of God.

There's a verse in James 2:13 which says: "Mercy triumphs over judgment." I can look back on my walk with the Lord and recognize that for a number of years I didn't understand that our God DELIGHTS IN MERCY (Micah 7:18). Take a moment. The God who knows everything about us DELIGHTS - HEAR THAT - DELIGHTS IN MERCY.

Micah 7:18 from the Amplified Bible says, "Who is a God like You, who forgives wickedness and passes over the rebellious acts of the remnant of His possession? He does not retain His anger forever, because He [constantly] delights in mercy and lovingkindness."

Close your eyes and say, "He constantly delights in mercy and lovingkindness." I just love the word "delights." If He delights in mercy, then I should delight in mercy, not only for myself but towards others. And if we don't receive His mercy, how can we give it? If our Father just loves showing mercy, then we should as well.

And then there's Isaiah 43:25: "I, I am he who blots out your transgressions for my own sake, and I will not remember your sins." (ESV)

The other day I was praying and was recounting and remembering my past. I began thinking about my sins from the distant past and yes, my recent past. I began thanking God for forgiving me, and then He said to me, "I don't remember." Even now my heart leaps knowing that His mercy triumphs over judgement. He not only truly delights in mercy, but if that isn't enough, God DOES NOT REMEMBER OUR SINS.

I had to take a moment to simply lift my hands. I didn't utter a word. Praise Him that He doesn't even remember!

Day 305

THOUGHT OF THE DAY: Tomorrow

I'm so tired of "tomorrows!" What do I mean?

I hear people share with sincere hearts what they want to do or what they believe God intends for them. You can hear the excitement in their voices. Yet...nothing really happens. Why is that?

There are actually too many reasons to list them all, but here are a few:

- The enemy comes and steals the seed through procrastination, discouragement, busyness, doubt, other people's opinions, fear, lack of finances, our past, etcetera.
- We fail to truly honor what we believe God has shown us.
- We don't take small steps or even one step to activate what we believe.
- The thought of what may be multiple steps overwhelms and discourages us.
- We think and think but take no action.
- We focus on circumstances and not on the Lord.
- We see obstacles and not Jesus.
- Like Peter, we take a step but lose our focus.

Everything in me screams - Take the next step! You can do it!

Too often we're like the cripple at the pool of Bethesda in John 5:7. When the water was stirred, he said, "I have no man to put me into the pool when the water is stirred up." Stop waiting for someone else, I want to cry! Sure, there are multiple steps - JUST TAKE THE NEXT ONE!

STOP TRYING TO FIGURE IT ALL OUT.

When Abraham was told to leave where he was, it says in Hebrews 11:8: "By faith Abraham obeyed when he was called to go out to the place which he would receive as an inheritance. And he went out, not knowing where he was going."

Tell Annie that I'm no longer going to wait until tomorrow to sing. I'm going to take a step TODAY! All of heaven is behind You!

Day 306

THOUGHT OF THE DAY: Survey says

Years ago I used to watch Family Feud. When one of the contestants would answer a question, the host of the show would respond "Survey says_____."

So let's follow suit by taking a survey. The question is... is today's church hot or cold? Question number two: Are you hot or cold?

I will refrain from sharing my perspective. But I will say that like Elijah, I have seen a "cloud the size of a man's hand." I know it's about to rain. In fact, there are a few sprinkles falling. Do you have eyes to see?

If you're looking with your natural eyes, you'll be blind to it! Luke 17:20 describes being asked about God's coming kingdom. "He answered them and said, 'The kingdom of God does not come with observation.'" I believe we haven't understood that while the kingdom is here, it isn't yet complete. We're trying to see something in the natural, when in reality it can only be seen with spiritual eyes. It's like going to a 3D movie and not wearing the special 3D glasses.

I believe we're about to see the fulfillment of Isaiah 44:3: "For I will pour water on him who is thirsty, and floods on the dry ground; I will pour My Spirit on your descendants, and My blessing on your offspring." Did you see the condition that is placed on receiving the rain?

Question three: Are you thirsty? Survey says _____.

Day 307

THOUGHT OF THE DAY: I tell you with tears in my eyes

As I wrote the "survey says" entry the other day, I had to fight back tears!

Observing the general condition of today's church leads me to conclude that it is neither hot nor cold. So if it's not hot or cold, what is it? Let's all say this together - Lukewarm! Oh, Father, once again! Would you please provoke, stir, fill us! Without your Spirit we'll continue to be complacent. I'm crying out that in your mercy you do again what you have done in the past!

I love the church! I love the people of God! In Isaiah 60:1-5 it says,

Arise, shine;
For your light has come!
And the glory of the Lord is risen upon you.
For behold, the darkness shall cover the earth,
And deep darkness the people;
But the Lord will arise over you,
And His glory will be seen upon you.
The Gentiles shall come to your light,
And kings to the brightness of your rising.

Please read this again. Understand that it means that people can see the glory of God on you and the unspeakable results!

Cry out and know Psalm 126:5 which says, "May those who sow in tears reap with shouts of joy!" (RSVCE)

The seeds for shouts of joy are tears!

Day 308

THOUGHT OF THE DAY: Time for honesty

This morning when I woke up the Holy Spirit spoke to me.

Immediately I took the thought and began to think about others in relationship to what He'd given me. In fact, as I write this, I'm deeply saddened that I first thought of others. I gave it brief and I mean brief consideration, but I didn't see how it really applied to me. At this point

I'm really not writing to anyone but myself. Perhaps you might gain some insight as well.

As I'm writing this, I'm deeply troubled by my thinking of others first. My spiritual viewing screen is getting bigger. It's like going from a 19 to a 60-inch television screen. I don't like what I'm seeing. Then Luke 6:41-42 comes crashing into my mind: "And why quibble about the speck in someone else's eye—his little fault—when a board is in your own? How can you think of saying to him, 'Brother, let me help you get rid of that speck in your eye,' when you can't see past the board in yours? Hypocrite! First get rid of the board, and then perhaps you can see well enough to deal with his speck!" (TLB)

Yup. Honesty time.

My first thought this morning was about how people profess their faith, are great at serving, giving, teaching, etcetera, but when it really comes down to loving others, they fail. I am more than included in this, particularly where honesty about certain relationships is concerned. How about you?

Honesty time.

If I wasn't convicted enough at this point, I was led to 1 Corinthians 13:1-7 in the Message Bible. It says:

If I speak with human eloquence and angelic ecstasy but don't love, I'm nothing but the creaking of a rusty gate. If I speak God's Word with power, revealing all his mysteries and making everything plain as day, and if I have faith that says to a mountain, "Jump," and it jumps, but I don't love, I'm nothing. If I give everything I own to the poor and even go to the stake to be burned as a martyr, but I don't love, I've gotten nowhere. So, no matter what I say, what I believe, and what I do, I'm bankrupt without love. Love never gives up. Love cares more for others than for self. Love doesn't want what it doesn't have. Love doesn't strut, Doesn't have a swelled head, Doesn't force itself on others, Isn't always 'me first,' Doesn't fly off the handle, Doesn't keep score of the sins of others, Doesn't revel when others grovel, Takes pleasure in the flowering of truth, Puts up with anything, Trusts God always, Always looks for the best, Never looks back, But keeps going to the end.

Honesty time...

Day 309

THOUGHT OF THE DAY: "I feel like I'm king of the mountain!"

It's been a long time since I read Habakkuk 3:17-18, but this morning it's caused me to shout and has lifted my spirit. Indeed joy has filled my soul, reminding me of the greatness of our God. Oh Father, write this on the tablet of our hearts! Cause us to remember and to declare these verses.

Habakkuk 3:17-19 (Message Bible)
Though the cherry trees don't blossom
and the strawberries don't ripen,
Though the apples are worm-eaten
and the wheat fields stunted,
Though the sheep pens are sheepless
and the cattle barns empty,
I'm singing joyful praise to God.
I'm turning cartwheels of joy to my Savior God.
Counting on God's Rule to prevail,
I take heart and gain strength.
I run like a deer.
I feel like I'm king of the mountain!
Oh ya, "I feel like I'm king of the mountain!"

Day 310

THOUGHT OF THE DAY: No new word

What is the Holy Spirit speaking today? The same thing He was saying yesterday.

One of the problems we face is always looking for a new word. The difficulty is that we don't fully glean, comprehend, understand, and grasp what the Lord is trying to show us. We say, "Oh that was a good word" and then immediately begin looking for another one. We therefore never fully receive all that could have been ours. It's a lot like an all-you-can eat buffet. We eat and not too soon after, we're hungry again.

Have you ever considered that while we want to go on to the next word, God purposely doesn't open a new door (give a new word) because He's encouraging us to see the value of what He's already shown us?

Most of our circumstances haven't changed from yesterday. The cherry trees still haven't blossomed, the strawberries still aren't ripe, the worms are still eating the apples, the wheat still isn't growing, no sheep have miraculously shown up, and there still aren't any cattle in the barn. No, life hasn't changed from yesterday.

But, have we gleaned the response God is looking for? Habakkuk said: I'm singing, doing cartwheels of joy, because I know God's purposes for my life will prevail! He's trying to teach us that when everything is upside down, we should be declaring that we're king of the mountain.

The problem is that it's hard to be king of the mountain when we've pitched our tents in the valley.

Day 311

THOUGHT OF THE DAY: Digging ditches

I just love the way the Holy Spirit brings clarity and understanding to the things we go through. As you might recall, over the past few days my emotions have been upside down. Like all of us, it causes me to pursue the Lord and ask what's going on and why.

During these times we can become vulnerable to Satan's lies. How can that happen? When we're seeking answers, Satan likes to interject his own theories, and it takes some time to sort out and discern between the Holy Spirit and Satan. That's why it's good not to draw conclusions too quickly and to continue to weigh what we're hearing. This is difficult in the midst of our emotions feeling out of control. All in all, I really dislike these times!

I do know this: God is faithful and always shows us what's going on. It may take time, but as it says in Psalm 139, "He knows our frame." Yes, He really knows us!

So I got up very early Sunday morning at about 3:15 a.m. I spent the time musing and pursuing without getting an answer. At 5:30 I went back to bed and slept until 7:30. A short time after I got up again and sat down to pray.

As I did, the Lord had me turn to Second Kings chapter three, which is the story of Jehoshaphat seeking an answer about going to war. When God answers him through Elisha, he's told to dig ditches. Verse 16: "Thus says the Lord 'Make this valley full of ditches.' " The context was that Jehoshaphat wasn't to pursue fighting the battle using normal methods of warfare, but to dig ditches, and God would fill them with water so when the enemy looked into the valley, the water would look like blood. This would cause the armies of Moab to think that Israel was at war with their allies, and to appear as if they'd killed one another off. Meanwhile Moab thought they would just march in and take all the "spoil," all this an ambush by which the armies of Moab were defeated.

So how does that relate to me? It says that when they'd dug the ditches, that God filled them with water. Verse 17: "For thus says the Lord: 'You shall not see wind, nor shall you see rain; yet that valley shall be filled with water.' " Often God uses subtle methods to accomplish His purposes.

In order for the Holy Spirit to answer me and fill me, I have to dig spiritual ditches. In digging them I'm not only filled with God's Spirit, I'm given insight as to what's happening and what to do. Simply put, when we pursue God, in His time He'll fill us and grant us the insight we need.

If we're troubled, oftentimes the key is to dig a ditch so God can fill us and give us His insight and strategy.

Perhaps you're in the process of digging a ditch or need to consider doing so...?

Day 312

THOUGHT OF THE DAY: Stay behind

Good morning. I pray that you can hear our Father's invitation to come and meet with Him and once there, to linger.

In Exodus 33 Moses and Joshua met with God in what was called the Tabernacle of Meeting. God would meet with Moses as a friend, which is a pretty amazing concept. When Moses finished, he left, but Joshua stayed behind.

Exodus 33:11: "The Lord spoke to Moses face to face like a man speaks with his friend. Then Moses would go back to the camp, but his helper, Joshua son of Nun, always stayed in the tent."

Perhaps it was Joshua's ALWAYS STAYING BEHIND that prepared him to lead Israel into the Promised Land.

May I encourage you to stay behind and linger?

Day 313

THOUGHT OF THE DAY: It's beginning to rain

We've felt a shift in the winds of the Spirit signifying that change is taking place, and I heard this morning, "It's beginning to rain." It's a warm spring-like day, and there's a light rain falling that's kissing the early spring flowers. The flowers are in need of the rain in order to grow and allow their colors to be bright and brilliant. It's as if the flowers have been waiting for the rain, because without it, they'd fail to meet their fullest potential.

I believe we too have been waiting for the rain. It's been a long winter, and we've anticipated spring. In the Song of Solomon 2:11 it says, "for winter has passed." In verse 12 it says, "The flowers appear on the earth; The time of singing has come, And the voice of the turtledove is heard in our land."

Haven't we been waiting for spring? Haven't we been waiting for rain? Well, light rain is falling.

I remember that when I was a child, I'd love to go out on warm spring days, especially when the light rain would fall. I can remember leaping and sticking out my tongue to catch a few of the droplets. I experienced such joy as I stretched out my arms and would twirl around, enjoying the moment with a full and satisfied heart.

So this morning this little boy is going to leap, putting my arms out wide. I'm going to twirl around and yes, stick my tongue out because I'm thirsty for the rain of God.

The great thing is that this is only the beginning of the rain He'll pour down.

Day 314

THOUGHT OF THE DAY: You're incredible

If only we could believe the voice that thunders from heaven. Can you hear it? It's the voice of our Father standing and declaring, "YOU'RE INCREDIBLE."

When are we going to start believing just how amazing each of us is? For too long we've allowed the voices that surround us to belittle us and tear us down.

I'm so in love with Ephesians 2:10: "For we are God's masterpiece, created in the Messiah Jesus to perform good actions that God prepared long ago to be our way of life."(ISV) Close your eyes and hear - you are God's masterpiece.

When God was creating the heavens and the earth, He stood back and looked at what He'd created and said, "That's good." I believe that when each of us were created, that Our Father stood back, and looking at each one of us, said, "Oh, what an incredible masterpiece! I will always love you."

Could it be that once we begin to grasp these realities, we'll recognize in others the Father's masterpiece?

Can you hear His voice today? He's saying,

"YOU'RE INCREDIBLE."

Day 315

THOUGHT OF THE DAY: Don't ask Him to come

For most of my walk with the Lord I often prayed, "Lord, come." While that might sound right, it's actually not. Why?

It's because God is omnipresent, which simply means He's everywhere all the time. Since this is true, why would I need to ask Him to come? I now pray, "Lord, help me/others to sense/discern your presence." Right now, He's not only all around you, He's in you. You and I are never alone; God is never absent from our lives.

I was reading the Psalms the other day and came across this beauty: "Just as Jerusalem is protected by mountains on every side, the Lord protects his people by holding them in his arms now and forever." (Psalm 125:2 - CEV) Oh, to think that He actually holds us in His arms!

Then there's Isaiah 43:2: "When you pass through the waters, I will be with you; And through the rivers, they shall not overflow you. When you walk through the fire, you shall not be burned, Nor shall the flame scorch you." (NKJV)

Oh Lord, you declare "I will always be with you." Can we pause for a moment and take that in?

There are so many other verses. Here is Hebrews 13:5: "For he himself has said, 'I will never desert you, nor will I ever forsake you.'" The word "never" in this passage is almost too much for us to grasp. But we should try...

Don't ask Him to come; He's already with you and in you!

Day 316

THOUGHT OF THE DAY: Open arms

I wasn't out of my bed but a few seconds this morning when I saw the Lord coming towards me with His arms outstretched as wide as they could be.

Picture for a moment Him coming to you with outstretched arms and a smile that says "I love you." Think of it: HE is coming to you. From an old Air Supply song I could hear the phrase, "So now I come to you with open arms."

Each day, whether you've stumbled or not, the Father is in pursuit of you. I can hear Him whisper, "I'll complete the work in you!" It reminds me of Philippians 1:6 from the Amplified Bible "I am convinced and confident of this very thing, that He who has begun a good work in you will [continue to] perfect and complete it until the day of Christ Jesus [the time of His return]."

Yes, HE WILL PERFECT AND COMPLETE EACH OF US.

I have to laugh as I write this because I well know that He has funny methods to get the "project" done. No, the things He allows are NOT the methods I would use, but that's why He's God, and I'm not!

As I sit here writing I can hear, "Only believe." Twice in the gospels Jesus said it, and listen to the phrasing, "Do not be afraid; only believe." (Mark 5:36 and Luke 8:50) No matter where you've been, where you are today, or where you'll be tomorrow, don't let fear stop you from listening to the word and REJOICING in the truth - His arms are open wide, and He'll perfect each of us.

Have a supernatural day!

Day 317

THOUGHT OF THE DAY: Just three simple questions

What if we lived out the answers to the three questions the Holy Spirit asked me and that I shared yesterday in church?

Hopefully you'll read each answer slowly and live your lives walking them out.

1. How will they know we are disciples of Jesus?

• John 13:35: "By this everyone will know that you are My disciples, if you have love and unselfish concern for one another." (AMP)

• "By this shall all [men] know that you are My disciples, if you love one another [if you keep on showing love among yourselves]." (AMPC)

2. What does love look like?

• 1 John 3:16: "This is how we know what real love is: Jesus gave his life for us. So we should give our lives for each other as brothers and sisters." (ERV)

• "We know what true love looks like because of Jesus. He gave His life for us, and He calls us to give our lives for our brothers and sisters." (VOICE)

3. Did Jesus give us a commandment?

• John 15:12: "This is my command: Love one another the way I loved you. This is the very best way to love. Put your life on the line for your friends." (MSG)

• "This is My commandment, that you love and unselfishly seek the best for one another, just as I have loved you." (AMP)

• "Everyone will know you as My followers if you demonstrate your love to others." (VOICE)

Just three simple questions!

Day 318

THOUGHT OF THE DAY: Hold on

It was impossible to put into words what I was feeling and sensing over the last two days. Feelings of hopelessness and disappointment overwhelmed me, and I felt weary in waiting. Yet something inside of me was saying, "Hold on." Indeed, while my emotions were saying one thing, God's faint voice was saying "Hang in there." It's the classic war between our mind and our spirit.

So I got up this morning and heard "I cannot lie," from Titus 1:2 where it says, "God, who cannot lie." (NKJV) Then I'm reminded of Hebrews 10:23: "So let us seize and hold fast and retain without wavering the hope we cherish and confess and our acknowledgement of it, for He Who promised is reliable (sure) and faithful to His word." (AMPC)

It says, "LET US SEIZE, HOLD FAST, NOT ALLOWING YOURSELF TO WAVER." Why? Because our "God is FAITHFUL TO HIS WORD."

As I'm musing over this, I begin to feel a shift inside of me. What's that going on? Hope is rising. Oh, He is faithful.

Then I hear part of a song from the 1960s: "dada dadan't dada." It's supposed to be the beat and the voices of Sam and Dave who wrote the song in 1966. The song is called "Hold On, I'm Coming." The chorus says simply, "Just hold on, I'm comin' Hold on, I'm comin." The song starts out "Don't you ever feel sad. Lean on me when the times are bad, when the day comes, and you're down, in a river of trouble and about to drown. Just hold on, I'm comin', Hold on, I'm comin'."

That's where we cling to what God has promised us. Abba is faithful! This is only a valley bringing us to the mountain!

Hold on; help is on the way!

Day 319

THOUGHT OF THE DAY: Where are you?

In Genesis 3:9 it says, "Then the Lord God called to Adam and said to him, "Where are you?" (NKJV)

For the past two days I've been hearing, "Where are you?" It's caused me to stop and ask myself - Where am I, and then allow the Holy Spirit permission to show me. Yes, even show me things I really don't want to see in each area of my life.

The psalmist wrote in Psalm 139:23: "Search me, O God, and know my heart; Try me, and know my anxieties." (NKJV) The Message Bible puts it this way: "Investigate my life, O God, find out everything about me; Cross-examine and test me, get a clear picture of what I'm about."

"Are you pursuing your dream" is the question which came to mind. I thought of Joseph, who in spite of horrific obstacles, held on to his dream. He was faithful to God and man wherever he was because he knew that "God was with him." Am I doing everything I can to pursue the dreams that God has put in my heart?

Quickly a multitude of names and faces passed before my eyes. I was overwhelmed and even as I write this, my heart is heavy, tears in my eyes. Oh Father, call out to them with a loud and clear voice! Tell some to come home and others to rekindle their dreams, putting an unquenchable fire and passion in their hearts that they can't extinguish. Remind them of who they are and be relentless in your pursuit of them. Show them how Satan has lied to them and taken them off course. Show them the way back. Shout to them from 1 John 2:27: "But the anointing which you have received from Him abides in you." (NKJV), "As for you, the anointing that you received from him remains on you" (CEB) and from the Amplified Bible, "As for you, the anointing [the special gift, the preparation] which you received from Him remains [permanently] in you."

Oh, please rekindle your dreams; wherever you are, step towards them. It's not too late. The gift(s) in you are still there. You were created to fulfill the dreams/callings He put into your hearts. OH PLEASE, can't you hear Him calling, "Where are you?" His hand is, as Isaiah 65:2 says, "outstretched all day long." Show us Father, that you're bigger than any obstacle, that NO MATTER WHERE WE ARE - WE CAN RETURN TO OUR FIRST LOVE. THE LORD HAS NEED OF YOU! MY HEART IS PLEADING... Where are you?

Day 320

THOUGHT OF THE DAY: You are so beautiful

I was riding in my car Tuesday when out of nowhere I started to sing the song, "You Are So Beautiful" by Joe Cocker. I've never been a Joe Cocker fan, so you can imagine how surprised I was when I continued to sing the chorus over and over again. The lyrics are very simple: "You are so beautiful to me, You are so beautiful to me, Can't you see?"

Then what hit me was the question the chorus ends with: "Can't you see?" It was at that moment that I realized that no, I don't see that I'm beautiful to our Father.

Growing up, one of our children had the wackiest hair. In many pictures their hair was just horrific. Yet despite their hair, I still recognized what a beautiful child the Lord had given us. Our child was beautiful!

Riding in my car the Holy Spirit was asking me - Brian (substitute your own name), can't you see how beautiful you are? Yes, our Father sees through different eyes. He sees beyond all of our sins, weaknesses, and personality flaws. He sees beyond what we are and what we're doing or not doing and sings, "You Are So Beautiful to Me!"

Until we can begin seeing how beautiful we are, we'll be unable to see how beautiful others are. It ties into the second part of Matthew 22:39, which reads, "You shall love your neighbor as yourself."

So if God loves us as we are and sees us as beautiful, what right do we have to hold a lesser perspective of ourselves? When we do that, we're in danger of putting our opinion and perspective above our Father's.

Today as I write this, I can hear singing! "YOU ARE - YOU ARE SO BEAUTIFUL TO ME!"

Day 321

THOUGHT OF THE DAY: He will do it

I awake on certain days, and all my shortcomings, weaknesses, and imperfections greet me like the morning sun. I'm tired and weary when such imperfections gaze back at me. It's like waking up and staring in a mirror. Sometimes the mirror is of the magnifying variety, when every blemish I have is exaggerated.

"Blemishes be removed!" I want to declare. When this doesn't happen, the temptation is to apply spiritual make-up, which only covers the blemishes; it doesn't make them disappear.

In reality, though, the cover stick needs to be thrown away altogether.

As for doing the real job of changing, the plain truth is that I am unable to change myself. I always think I can, however, which is when a voice comes, saying, "I will complete the work I started." Philippians 1:6 from the Amplified Bible, Classic Edition, says it this way, "And I am convinced and sure of this very thing, that He who began a good work in you will continue until the day of Jesus Christ [right up to the time of His return], developing [that good work] and perfecting and bringing it to full completion in you."

Silly me, thinking I can do what's only possible for God. Psalm 138:8 says it too:

• "The Eternal will finish what He started in me. Your faithful love, O Eternal One, lasts forever; do not give up on what Your hands have made." (VOICE)

• "The Lord will perfect that which concerns me; Your mercy, O Lord, endures forever; Do not forsake the works of Your hands." (NKJV)

• "Finish what you started in me, God. Your love is eternal—don't quit on me now." (MSG)

• "The Lord will complete what his purpose is for me. Lord, your gracious love is eternal; do not abandon your personal work in me." (ISV)

That settles it. He will complete us. He will continue to work in us right up until the day Jesus returns. So let's stop striving and rest in what He's promised.

Though I'm incomplete; I'm simultaneously complete. Rest, for He's at work in us!

Philippians 2:13: "[Not in your own strength] for it is God Who is all the while effectually at work in you [energizing and creating in you the power and desire], both to will and to work for His good pleasure and satisfaction and delight." (AMPC)

- "For it is God who is producing in you both the desire and the ability to do what pleases him." (ISV)

HE WILL DO IT...

Day 322

THOUGHT OF THE DAY: Put away your tin cup

When I awoke this morning, I grabbed a cup of coffee and went and sat before the Lord. Hmmm - I guess coffee is allowed in the sanctuary.

I wasn't there but a moment when I felt the Lord say, "I have been waiting for you." I couldn't help but feel that He's always waiting for us! I then saw thousands of faces all struggling to find a way into God's presence. Quickly my mind went to Acts 3:2 where we find the following, "And a certain man lame from his mother's womb was carried, whom they laid daily at the gate of the temple which is called Beautiful, to ask alms from those who entered the temple."

Did you see where the lame man went to beg? He went and sat outside the temple. Sadly, too many people only go to church to beg. I'm hearing, "Put away your tin cup." Can you hear the sound of a spoon hitting a tin cup? "Put the tin cup away; you're my sons and daughters."

It's time to put away our begging mentality, banish it completely from our thinking. Hebrews 4:16 (AMP) says, "Therefore let us [with privilege] approach the throne of grace [that is, the throne of God's gracious favor] with confidence and without fear, so that we may receive mercy [for our failures] and find [His amazing] grace to help in time of need [an appropriate blessing, coming just at the right moment]."

Did you see the world "privilege"? It's our privilege (our inheritance) that we can come "boldly" as many translations put it. Here in the Amplified it says (watch this) "with confidence." "Without fear or fearlessly." So do we need to beg? No! We can "OBTAIN," or this says, "receive." It doesn't say "hope to receive."

So put away your tin cup! Here in the presence of God (with a cup of coffee) we can find mercy and "His amazing grace" in our time of need. I love that it says that when we do this, the blessing will be manifested in our lives, "coming just at the right moment," it says. While we immediately receive, it often takes a "moment" to see and feel the manifestation of the help we need. There's no mention whatsoever of begging – in fact, it's quite the opposite!

So grab a cup of coffee, and PUT AWAY YOUR TIN CUP! Abba is waiting for YOU!

Day 323

THOUGHT OF THE DAY: Not my will

Imagine with me for a moment the effect of every son or daughter doing the Father's will and not their own.

Jesus was confronted with this choice in the Garden of Gethsemane, and every day we're continually confronted with the conflict between our will and the will and heart of our Father. Some choices and decisions are easier than others, times when it's not as hard to lay our will aside.

At others, however, it's really difficult. It's an extremely rare occasion when our struggles can remotely compare with Jesus'. Here is how the Amplified Bible puts it in Matthew 26:39, "And after going a little farther, He fell face down and prayed, saying, 'My Father, if it is possible [that is, consistent with Your will], let this cup pass from Me; yet not as I will, but as You will.'"

Again, imagine the impact it would have on our culture, in each of our relationships, not to mention the effect of the witness to outsiders. In fact, if we succeeded in successfully putting God's will above our own, the term "hypocrite" could be eliminated from people's opinions of us.

I'm reminded that in Acts 5:40-41 the apostles were beaten because they refused the request of the religious leaders to stop preaching Jesus. The New King James Version says, "When they had called for the apostles and beaten them, they commanded that they should not speak in the name of Jesus, and let them go. So they departed from the presence of the council, rejoicing that they were counted worthy to suffer shame for His name."

They rejoiced!

Father, replace our hesitation to do your will with rejoicing. Let us be the answer Jesus was praying for in Matthew 6:9-10, "Our Father in heaven, Hallowed be Your name. Your kingdom come. Your will be done on earth as it is in heaven."

Father, we pray "not our will."

Day 324

THOUGHT OF THE DAY: One of those days

Every once in a while, you have one of those days when you're overrun by a slew of negative feelings, all of them beginning with the letter D. You feel...

Discouraged, depressed, disheartened, disappointed, dismayed, demoralized, despondent, dejected, defeated, deflated, distressed, disparaged, desperate, disturbed, drained, disillusioned, dumbfounded, dispirited, dashed, defeated, disquieted, downhearted, dismal, defeated, dreary, dreadful, disenchanted, disgruntled, dissatisfied, deserted, disconnected, displeased, downcast, and down in the dumps.

Then in less than 24 hours God turns everything around, making a way where there seemed to be NO WAY! You sit and watch as His love for you turns the hearts and minds of men. He makes possible from impossible and exceeds your wildest imagination. You sit and watch His Spirit sweep favor through the whole room.

It's incredible that our Father can see us at the Red Sea or at the boundary of the Jordan River. Not only does He see us, but He has a plan to get us to the other side.

By the way, a good word of counsel is to allow yourself to wait because a lot can change within 24 hours.

Day 325

THOUGHT OF THE DAY: Friend

I don't know what's going on. I was asking the Lord about what He wanted to say and heard nothing! Then about an hour later I started singing, "You've Got a Friend" by James Taylor. Crazy. While I do like James Taylor, his songs are not typically on my radar screen.

Have you ever looked at the lyrics?

"You've Got A Friend"

"When you're down and troubled and you need a helping hand
and nothing, whoa, nothing is going right.
Close your eyes and think of me, and soon I will be there
to brighten up even your darkest nights."

Can we hear Jesus speaking this to us?

"You just call out my name, and you know wherever I am
I'll come running to see you again.

Winter, spring, summer, or fall, all you have to do is call and I'll be there, yeah, yeah, you've got a friend."

How about this coming from Jesus' mouth...?

"If the sky above you should turn dark and full of clouds
and that old north wind should begin to blow,
keep your head together and call my name out loud.
Soon I will be knocking upon your door.
You just call out my name, and you know where ever I am
I'll come running to see you again.

Winter, spring, summer, or fall, all you have to do is call and I'll be there."

How about this?

"Hey, ain't it good to know that you've got a friend? People can be so cold.

They'll hurt you and desert you. Well, they'll take your soul if you let them,

oh yeah, but don't you let them.

You just call out my name, and you know wherever I am

I'll come running to see you again."

Yup. Jesus once again.

"Winter, spring, summer, or fall, all you have to do is call, Lord, I'll be there, yeah, yeah, you've got a friend. You've got a friend.

Ain't it good to know you've got a friend. Ain't it good to know you've got a friend.

Oh, yeah, yeah, you've got a friend."

Honestly, I haven't spent a lot of time thinking about the fact that Jesus called us friends! In John 15:15 he said, "No longer do I call you servants, for a servant does not know what his master is doing; but I have called you friends, for all things that I heard from My Father I have made known to you."

There are definitely times when you just want to talk to your closest friend. You want to share your state of mind, your disappointment, and your struggles, knowing that no matter what you say, they'll continue to love you! You look in their eyes and their expression says, "I know, I'm here for you," or "Sure, you messed up, but it doesn't matter to me."

Today I started reflecting on Jesus as my friend! I'm just beginning to ponder all that this means. Would you join me?

Jesus, you are my friend!

Day 326

THOUGHT OF THE DAY: Seems to be a simple choice

This morning I was cleaning and considering a number of thoughts that popped into my mind. While scrubbing the stove I heard, "Can you smell the stink?" Right away my nostrils didn't smell anything, but I knew my spirit would discern it.

Immediately I knew what God was saying. He was referring to the not-so-subtle pride and self-righteousness I indulge in way too often.

It surfaces when I believe others should think the way I do, or even act or react the same way. I place a very high value on my way and my opinion, discounting other perspectives as incorrect or less than. Even though there's a very fine line between feeling comfortable with your own perspective and not placing value on someone else's, I have no right to insist that others see it "my way."

I was reminded of Proverbs 6:16-18. From the Amplified Bible it reads, "These six things the Lord hates; Indeed, seven are repulsive to Him. A proud look [the attitude that makes one overestimate oneself and discount others." I honestly didn't go on and look at the other six, because I needed the truth of this one to sink in. I wonder how deeply we let the Lord speak to us about our pride and self-righteousness?

The image of a proud look really spoke to me. We kid ourselves when we believe we can disguise this attitude so that others can't see our pride and self-righteousness. Who are we kidding, anyway?! Whether or not someone can see it isn't the issue, though. The issue is that it's in our hearts.

The word says that God dwells with those who are contrite and humble. Isaiah 57:15 from the ESV says, "For thus says the One who is high and lifted up, who inhabits eternity, whose name is Holy: 'I dwell in the high and holy place, and also with him who is of a contrite and lowly spirit, to revive the spirit of the lowly, and to revive the heart of the contrite.' "

So here is our choice. We can either be haughty and proud or humble and contrite. We can have God's dwelling place or can be in a place He hates.

Seems like a simple choice.

Day 327

THOUGHT OF THE DAY: Let us give thanks

I was outside this morning a little before 5:00 a.m. Three of our dogs needed to do their morning business.

I was surprised how light it was. The air was warm, and there was a gentle breeze blowing. It was quite spectacular. As I walked toward the mailbox to get our morning paper, I was filled with wonder as I became aware of all the noises that filled the air. Numerous birds were chirping; various insects were making noises, and ducks were on the pond.

As I found myself really enjoying this brief time outside so early in the morning, a question and answer came flying into my mind. The question was - what is all of creation doing right now? The answer came immediately - praising "ME," meaning God. They were giving thanks and declaring His goodness. It was as if the entire atmosphere was filled with one voice singing in harmony. It was much like listening to an orchestra with its brass and percussion sections, its violins, flutes, and harps all worshipping.

Scripture is filled with admonitions about giving thanks, and in that moment, I became aware of my own need to join with creation. All too often I see what God isn't doing and focus on that instead of stopping to celebrate what He is doing right in my midst. I'm shaking my head because you'd think by now I would be walking in greater gratitude.

Psalm 136:1: "Oh, give thanks to the Lord, for He is good! For His mercy endures forever." Verse 4: "To Him who alone does great wonders, for His mercy endures forever, verse 20: "Oh, give thanks to the God of heaven! For His mercy endures forever." (NKJV)

Where would we be without His mercy? His unconditional love? His goodness, His kindness, His forgiveness?

I think I will go now and join all of creation by spending some time in giving our Father thanks! Let us give thanks to the God of heaven and earth!

Perhaps you can join me?

Day 328

THOUGHT OF THE DAY: Complaining

Yesterday morning as I opened my front door and went down a few steps, I noticed that several of our rhododendrons had bloomed overnight. Gazing at them, I began to hear the Hallelujah Chorus. I looked at the rhododendrons on the right and then turned to the left. I could hear the perfect harmony of the chorus. I heard the bass section, the tenors, the altos, and the sopranos. I stood on the stairs and listened and began to smile.

As I drove to church, I sensed that something inside had shifted. As we began to worship, the Lord started to speak to me about complaining and worrying. Honestly, how much time do we spend complaining? How much of our day is consumed by worrying?

I remembered the complaining of the Israelites almost immediately after being delivered from slavery in Egypt. We too have been delivered from our bondages, and yet like Israel, begin focusing on our lack rather than on all that God has done and given us.

In Exodus 16 it says that the people started complaining just a few days after their release because there was no food to eat. The supplies they had taken from Egypt had been consumed. We read in verses 3-4: "For you have brought us out into this wilderness to kill this whole assembly with hunger. Then the Lord said to Moses, 'Behold, I will rain bread from heaven for you.' " (NKJV)

Think about this: God provided supernaturally. Yet like Israel, they got tired of eating manna day after day, three meals a day, and became unhappy with God's provision. It was good at first, but then the complaining started again. They took their eyes off the supernatural provision, and suddenly what God was providing wasn't "good enough." Would we have complained if we were in the same position? You bet.

In 1 Corinthians 10:5 it says, "With most of them God was not well pleased." (NKJV) Why? Because among other things, they complained. Can we say then that God is not pleased with our frequent complaining? (And what in the world does this have to do with my rhododendrons?!)

We need to stop complaining and start filling our mouths with thanksgiving. We need to rejoice in what God has and is providing. The reality is that complaining robs our joy and our peace and creates an atmosphere that shuts out the presence of God.

Paul writes in Philippians 4:11: "I've learned by now to be quite content whatever my circumstances. I'm just as happy with little as with much, with much as with little. I've found the recipe for being happy whether full or hungry, hands full or hands empty." (Message Bible) The Amplified Bible says, "For I have learned to be content [and self-sufficient through Christ, satisfied to the point where I am not disturbed or uneasy] regardless of my circumstances."

Holy Spirit, help us find contentment in our circumstances. Fill our mouths with gratitude that causes us to worship. When we begin to complain, speak to us. Forgive us.

Though it's raining out, and the windows are shut, I can hear the Hallelujah Chorus. It's God inviting us to join in.

Enjoy your supernatural day!

Day 329

THOUGHT OF THE DAY: Off to Romania: June 1, 2016

It's 5:45 p.m. and I'm sitting in Logan Airport. Al picked me up just before 3:00, but it took us over two hours to get here. Thankfully Al suggested that he pick me up early in case of traffic. Yes, Al heard the Lord - pick him up early.

The last few days have been a struggle to prepare to go. One word summarizes it - obstacles. Obstacles serve as distractions and thus frustrations. All during this time you can feel your flesh wanting to express itself.

In John 6:63 Jesus said, "The Spirit is the one who gives life; human nature is of no help!" (NET) I have to remind myself of this over and over again. Many translations say "the flesh profits nothing." Choosing to live in the Spirit requires work and determination. I can say that the more we choose in one direction or the other, it becomes easier.

Life is so much about making choices. Moses in speaking to Israel in the wilderness said in Deuteronomy 30:19: "Today I am giving you a choice of two ways. And I ask heaven and earth to be witnesses of your choice. You can choose life or death. The first choice will bring a blessing. The other choice will bring a curse. So choose life! Then you and your children will live." (ERV)

Yup. Our choices have far-reaching consequences.

Oh Lord, help us to choose life!

Day 330

THOUGHT OF THE DAY: I lift my hands

As I sat down on my office chair this morning, I was overwhelmed with a desire to raise my hands and begin declaring the goodness of our God.

God, there is no one like you! I will shout and declare at the top of my lungs Deuteronomy 33:26: "There is no one like the God of Jeshurun (Israel), Who rides the heavens to help you, And in His excellency on the clouds." (ESV)

I would climb the highest mountain this morning to say THANK YOU! Thank you for your grace and mercy. Thank you that you have said it is finished (our debt is paid in full). Thank you that it was because of the joy set before you that you endured the cross and that I've come to know that joy. Thank you for your mercy that's as high as the heavens are above the earth. Thank you that you cannot lie and that your word is true. Thank you that the grave couldn't hold you and that Satan couldn't defeat you. Thank you that you are the God of comfort. Thank you for your people who reach out and encourage and love us in the day of our grief and sorrow.

I will declare Jeremiah 31:12 that we "shall come and sing in the height of Zion, Streaming to the goodness of the Lord." Yes, we will come running to you. The Message Bible says,

The people will climb up Zion's slopes shouting with joy, their faces beaming because of God's bounty— Grain and wine and oil, flocks of sheep, herds of cattle. Their lives will be like a well-watered garden, never again left to dry up. Young women will dance and be happy, young men and old men will join in. I'll convert their weeping into laughter, lavishing comfort, invading their grief with joy.

Only you, oh Lord, can fill our mouths with laughter and turn our grief into joy. Yes, I lift my hands and say I LOVE YOU!

Day 331

THOUGHT OF THE DAY: Under authority

While in Romania I began weaving leadership concepts among the other things I was sharing. Over the next few months I'll be sharing some of those concepts and principles with you.

I'll start by saying that if you want to be a good leader, you first have to be a good follower. This means examining what the scriptures say about submission. In the New Testament the primary Greek word for submit is hypotássō (from hypó, "under" and tássō, "arrange") – properly, "under God's arrangement," taken from Bible Hub Commentary. From the Blue Letter Bible it says this: "This word was a Greek military term meaning 'to arrange [troop divisions] in a military fashion under the command of a leader.' " In non-military use, it was "a voluntary attitude of giving in, cooperating, assuming responsibility, and carrying a burden." My favorite definition for submit means "to be ordained under."

To truly understand and embrace submission, it's vital to view it as birthed from divine order. We read in John 6:38: "For I have come down from heaven, not to do My own will, but the will of Him who sent Me." Then John 4:34 says from the Amplified Bible, "Jesus said to them, 'My food is to do the will of Him who sent Me and to completely finish His work.' " Jesus submitted. How are we doing with it? It's possible to be submitting on the outside but not on the inside. So are we really submitting, I might ask?

Perhaps that's enough to consider for now. Holy Spirit, show us how this applies to our lives. Help us to see that submission is a major component of your kingdom. Reveal to us that we're all under divine authority. Tomorrow we'll touch on being submitted under those whom we're not exactly fond of...

Day 332

THOUGHT OF THE DAY: Good morning, Father

Oh Lord, thank you that you're always around us and in us. Help us to know you! Thank you that as with Daniel, you respond to our words. From Daniel 10:12: "Then he said to me, 'Fear not, Daniel, for from the first day that you set your mind and heart to understand and to humble yourself before your God, your words were heard, and I have come as a consequence of [and in response to] your words.' " (AMPC) Wow! If we could only believe this!

My heart is full as I declare Psalm 116:9: "I will walk before the Lord in the land of the living." (NKJV) Yes, "for in Him we live and move and have our being." (Acts 17:28 NKJV)

Oh, help us to know and believe 1 Kings 10:9: "Blessed be the Lord your God, who delighted in you. In the appointed time you will bring us into the promise land (the place where He will fulfill all that he has promised)." Numbers 14:8: "If the Lord delights in us, then He will bring us into this land and give it to us, 'a land which flows with milk and honey.' " Oh Lord, you will bring us into our tomorrow!

Thank you that you had Paul write in Romans 4:21 that he was "fully convinced that what He had promised He was also able to perform." (NKJV) Then again in 2 Timothy 1:12: "For I know whom I have believed and am persuaded that He is able to keep what I have committed to Him until that Day." (NKJV)

Oh Lord! My heart is full as I say, "Good Morning, Father!"

Day 333

THOUGHT OF THE DAY: Oh, I was glad

It's early Sunday morning, and I can't wait to go to the building we call church. I'm looking forward to seeing the people of the Porch and to worship. Psalm 122:1 captures my heart perfectly: "When they said, 'Let's go to the house of God,' my heart leaped for joy."

I sincerely hope that you have a place to worship that you can't wait to go to each week. It's the place where we're loved and where we love others. It's a place where we corporately find ourselves overwhelmed by the real and tangible presence of God. Oh, I so want this for each of you! It's not a place we only hope to meet with God, but rather a place where God's presence is manifest every time we gather.

Here's a thought from Haggai. He writes and tells the people of God that God was withholding the dew and rain and thus a draught occurred, because His people were not engaged in the establishing of the house of the Lord. Here it is in Haggai 1:7-10: "Thus says the Lord of hosts: 'Consider your ways! Go up to the mountains and bring wood and build the temple, that I may take pleasure in it and be glorified,' says the Lord. 'You looked for much, but indeed it came to little; and when you brought it home, I blew it away.' "Why?" says the Lord of hosts. 'Because of My house that is in ruins, while every one of you runs to his own house. Therefore the heavens above you withhold the dew, and the earth withholds its fruit.' "

Perhaps you want to give this some thought and pray for those to whom this might apply.

But as for me "When they said, 'Let's go to the house of God,' my heart leaped for joy."

Day 334

THOUGHT OF THE DAY: Don't give up

How many times have you wanted a breakthrough? How many times have you prayed, and sensing no movement, you got frustrated and stopped pounding on the door of heaven? How many times have we needed an answer? How many times have we so desperately needed the presence of God?

The answer for all of us is - too many. Why do we quit praying and pursuing when we need an answer from heaven? There are numerous answers. We get discouraged; we get frustrated; we get tired! But what if we persevered?

In Genesis 32:24 we read in the Amplified Bible: "So Jacob was left alone, and a Man [came and] wrestled with him until daybreak." Did you see that he was left alone?

Two things become clear: often our struggling with the Lord is best accomplished alone. Most of us don't like that, because no one is there to encourage us or give us answers. The second thing we're not fond of is answers that take a long time to come.

The key with Jacob is that he didn't stop struggling/wrestling until he got his breakthrough. He made his mind up. Genesis 32:26: "But he said, 'I will not let You go unless You bless me!' " (NKJV)

I'm not saying this is easy. I'm not saying it's not frustrating, discouraging, and tiring. Yet this I know: "He is a rewarder of those who diligently seek him." Yes, that's what Hebrews 11:6 says: "The one who draws near to God must believe that he exists and that he rewards people who try to find him." (CEB)

Haven't we all discovered that our wrestling with God is much easier when we can sense we're in His presence? Go ahead and create an atmosphere where God's presence is. Put on some worship music, pray in the Spirit, or go to a meeting where God's presence is manifest. (Solomon's Porch hosts such a meeting every two months called Peniel.)

Your breakthrough is near - DON'T GIVE UP!

Day 335

THOUGHT OF THE DAY: When things are a mess

Have you ever woken up with your emotions a mess?

When we do, we often go charging into the day with our thoughts and emotions twisted in a big bunch. As the day goes on, we react out of that negative place, and the result isn't good. When the evening comes, we're still a mess and then off to bed we go, only to wake up still feeling unsettled.

We need a selah moment.

The word selah appears about 74 times in scripture. Its primary meaning is to pause, to reflect, to meditate. In the Psalms you'll frequently find the word selah following a verse. The Holy Spirit wants us to pause there and stop and consider what we read and what it's saying to us. To immediately go on to the next verse means we'll likely miss the depth of the message.

When I'm studying or reading and come across a verse that resonates, I stop and glean what the Spirit of God is not only trying to show me, but wants to write on my heart.

An interesting fact is that there's an actual historical place that still exists today called Selah Petra. Massive stone walls encircle the city, making it nearly impossible to get to someone who may be hiding inside. There are those who say that during the Great Tribulation, people will go to Petra as a place of refuge.

Or could it be that our place of hiding is Jesus - our petra/rock?

We can't escape times of tribulation - when we're a mess. That's when we need to SELAH - pause, reflect, meditate, and find ourselves hidden in Him.

The final song of my sister's memorial service pierced my heart and caused me to say "All is Well." In the midst of the mess, "All is Well."

You might want to play this and declare "All is Well."

Day 336

THOUGHT OF THE DAY: What if we prayed Mark 16:20?

I've been sitting here this morning praying and pondering, telling the Lord that we need to see His power and glory.

I'm not sure, though, if we all want this power. It seems that so many are happy to attend church, sing a few songs, listen to another sermon, and return home only to repeat the pattern over and over again.

Many people who've seen the power of God in the past appear to have a "been there, done that" attitude. Others want a safe church where they can bring their friends and not have to worry that the power of God will show up. They don't want to hear people praying in tongues, have anyone shout, and oh, please don't have anyone fall down when they're prayed for. So essentially, they want to reach people through their intellect. Yes, they want the family church.

Now if Jesus came to your church, what would you like him to do? If people were demonized, would you have a problem if they fell down and started manifesting? How would you handle people falling backwards to the ground like what happened in the garden? Remember when Jesus saw the soldiers and asked them who they were looking for, and they said "Jesus"? When he responded that he was Jesus, just as He said it, they all fell backwards to the ground.

Last time I looked, the great commission was still in the Bible. It says in Mark 16:15-18:

And He said to them, "Go into all the world and preach the gospel to every creature. He who believes and is baptized will be saved; but he who does not believe will be condemned. And these signs will follow those who believe: In My name they will cast out demons; they will speak with new tongues; they will take up serpents; and if they drink anything deadly, it will by no means hurt them; they will lay hands on the sick, and they will recover." NKJV)

Lord, you said signs would follow. Therefore, I pray for this and hope you will as well. Mark 16:20: "And they went out and preached everywhere, while the Lord kept working with them and confirming the message by the attesting signs and miracles that closely accompanied [it]." (AMPC)

Amen. (So be it.) Lord, please work in our midst.

Will you join me in praying this?

Day 337

THOUGHT OF THE DAY: Would Jesus attend your church?

Much of the day yesterday I pondered this thought. I haven't done it yet, but in my head, I began writing a list of reasons why Jesus would attend the church over which I'm senior pastor.

So why don't we get a piece of paper and begin to write the various reasons why or why not Jesus would attend our church. Let's think together for a moment.

- Will the Holy Spirit be present?
- Will the Holy Spirit be allowed to lead the meeting?
- Will there be a real sense of love and affection for everyone who is there?
- In comes the stranger. He looks very peculiar. Does he get greeted?
- Will there be a spirit of judgement there? (Remembering with this one, the story of the woman they brought to Jesus who had been caught in adultery)
- Will there be worship or just contemporary music?

- Will we hear the voice of God or the voice of man, the latter which ends up being just another sermon? It may be full of ideas, but our hearts don't burn when we hear them, (like what happened to the two disciples on the road to Emmaus) (Luke 24:13)

Okay, so this list is just a beginning. I'm wondering what role I play in all of it.

Hmmm… Would Jesus attend our church?

Day 338

THOUGHT OF THE DAY: He came running

As I sat down to worship this morning, I clicked on YouTube and before even one note was played, I saw the Lord running towards me. I was standing in a field and could see the Father running towards me with a huge smile on His face and a look of affection.

So often we hear how we must run to the Lord. That we must pursue Him. While this is true, we haven't fully embraced Genesis 3:8: "And they heard the voice of the Lord God walking in the garden in the cool of the day." (BRG) Can you see him coming towards you? This is what we were created for - to walk with our Father. Adam and Eve knew it was the Father, and so it had to have been a common occurrence.

We need to recognize it as an ordinary day - the Father pursuing them just as He pursues us. It says Enoch walked with God. Moses is told by the Lord that His presence would go with him (Exodus 33). Can we comprehend that walking with God, hearing His voice, and being surrounded by His presence shouldn't be a once-in-awhile experience, but an everyday reality?

For many years we were looking forward to going to heaven so we could enjoy the Father's company. How sad that the revelation of being with Him each day was hidden from us. But now we understand! Right now, close your eyes - He's right there!

Yes, can you see Him running? He's running towards YOU…

Day 339

THOUGHT OF THE DAY: I heard a whisper

As I sat down to review my e-mails and consider what I was going to write for the THOUGHT OF THE DAY, I heard a whisper that sent chills through my body, and I can hear it even now!

It's a whisper that one would hear early in the morning in a beautiful valley surrounded by mountains. One where the entire valley can hear the echo.

The whisper has a warm and loving tone, yet is clear and full of strength. Can you hear it? There it is again. The whisper that's not only echoing through the valley, but echoing over all the nations of the earth. There it is again.

I asked the Lord why He's continuing to whisper the same thing over and over. He said "Because I want everyone to hear, I want everyone to embrace what I'm saying and to carry what I'm saying wherever they go. I want them to whisper - YOU ARE FORGIVEN... IT IS FINISHED... YOUR DEBT HAS BEEN PAID IN FULL!"

I heard a whisper. Did you?

Day 340

THOUGHT OF THE DAY: Wilderness training
Have you been to the wilderness lately?

We often view our time in the desert or wilderness as negative. We don't want to be there and spend much of our time trying to escape instead of allowing the Holy Spirit to mentor and train us there.

John the Baptist was the first prophet to speak since Malachi. A period of 400 years had passed. Where did John get trained? Where did he minister? The answer to both of these questions is in the wilderness.

• Mark 1:4: "John came baptizing in the wilderness and preaching a baptism of repentance for the remission of sins." (NKJV)

• Luke 3:2: "While Annas and Caiaphas were high priests, the word of God came to John the son of Zacharias in the wilderness." (NKJV)

I often say, "Good enough for Jesus, good enough for me." Well after Jesus was baptized in water and in the Spirit, where did God send Him.? The answer is – to the wilderness.

• Luke 4:1: "Then Jesus, being filled with the Holy Spirit, returned from the Jordan and was led by the Spirit into the wilderness." (NKJV)

My flesh would like to think that one trip to the wilderness should suffice. Yet the wilderness tends to be the place where the Holy Spirit does the best work in us. It's like a master potter continuing to mold and fashion the most beautiful vase that can be filled - over and over again.

It seems like we've all been been making more visits to the wilderness lately.

Oh Lord, help us to connect the wilderness with the place where the Holy Spirit wants to teach, train, and mentor us, the place where He'll both put things in and take things out.

Look at Luke 5:16: "So He (Jesus) Himself often withdrew into the wilderness and prayed." (NKJV) We see here that Jesus would purposely go to the wilderness to pray. What do you think He prayed for? I'll let you fill in the blanks.

Welcome to the wilderness!

Day 341

THOUGHT OF THE DAY: Where would we be?

It's Independence Day weekend, and my mind and heart are on overdrive. I've been sitting here musing with the Lord and the two of us have been on quite the emotional journey.

I've taken a stroll from 1970 to 2016 - some 46 years. There have been some amazing high points and some very painful low points. Yet through it all I can say that the Lord has been faithful, kind, forgiving. full of mercy, gracious, loving, encouraging, and empowering. He has never once abandoned or forsaken me!

When I felt He let me down I realized later that He knew better than me, and yes, that all things do work together for good. Yes, He is the God who redeems - everything. Whether I myself was in a good place, He has always been there. No matter life's circumstances, I knew He was near. I knew that He would hear my prayer and answer me in His time and in His way, which at times I didn't like, but it turned out that He was right. Where would we be without Him?

Wherever you are today, be encouraged that you are loved. No matter where you've been or where you are today, He's there with you. Just see yourself like Adam and Eve hanging out with the Lord. He knows what we're thinking. He knows our heart and emotions. Despite the times we've been angry, frustrated, disappointed or unhappy with Him, or even bewildered or confused, never once, not even for a moment, did He give up on us. He knows the secrets of our hearts, our flaws, like self-righteousness, pride, stubbornness, anger, and unforgiveness to name but a few, and how we continue to stumble in these and other areas. Yet He is with us! Where would we be without Him?

I just closed my eyes and heard Him whispering. Whatever He has promised He will bring to fulfillment. Yes, He'll even redeem our poor choices, our stubbornness, and our sin. I love the way the Message Bible interprets Psalm 139:7: "Is there any place I can go to avoid your Spirit? to be out of your sight? If I climb to the sky, you're there! If I go underground, you're there! If I flew on morning's wings to the far western horizon, You'd find me in a minute— you're already there waiting! Then I said to myself, 'Oh, he even sees me in the dark! At night I'm immersed in the light!' It's a fact: darkness isn't dark to you; night and day, darkness and light, they're all the same to you."

Where would we be without Him?

I just got a picture in my mind of walls that have been constructed around some hearts, and I see the Lord taking the walls down one brick at a time.

Oh, Father, your goodness is overwhelming! Where would we be without you!

Day 342

THOUGHT OF THE DAY: We don't have a political problem; we have a spiritual problem

It's Saturday morning, and very early I received a phone call about the demonstrations and shootings that took place last night. Yesterday I watched about three hours of news covering the Dallas shootings.

I heard commentator after commentator, special guests on Fox News, politicians, the attorney general, President Obama, and others talking about politics, gun control, and racial division.

I didn't hear one voice identify the real reason, however, the root cause of all of it. Sure, everything that was mentioned had merit, but it wasn't and isn't the true cause of America's condition.

I would venture to say that all of us have our own opinions and responses. Hopefully we've all quickly come to 2 Chronicles 7:14: "If My people who are called by My name will humble themselves, and pray and seek My face, and turn from their wicked ways, then I will hear from heaven, and will forgive their sin and heal their land."

We need prayer – at home and in our churches. Tomorrow at our church (Solomon's Porch), we are giving the entire service to prayer and worship. Hopefully churches across America and throughout the world are doing likewise. But why wait for tomorrow? You might want to pray after you read this.

A little-known fact is that during the American Revolution, prayer was heard in the hallowed halls of Congress.

The following is a lengthy article from Charisma News dated July 7, 2016.

"Washington continually sought to instill in his troops faith and reverence toward God." (Joye~/Flickr/Creative Commons)

JoomlaWorks "DISQUS Comments for Joomla!" (v3.4) starts here:

How could the ragtag American colonists face the mighty British war machine that was at its peak of power and dominance? They found the answer in prayer. As the Catholic scholar, William Novak, says, "In all moments of imminent danger, as in the first Act of the First Continental Congress, the founding generation turned to prayer."

The First Congress Opens with Prayer
The first meeting of the First Continental Congress took place on September 5, 1774. Delegates traveled from as far north as New England and from as far south as South Carolina to discuss how to deal with the growing British oppression. They were particularly concerned that British troops had occupied the city of Boston and closed its port.

Someone proposed that they begin their deliberations with prayer. Two delegates, however, opposed the motion on the grounds that they were such a diverse religious group, including Anglicans, Puritans, Presbyterians and Quakers, that it would be impossible for them to pray together.

Samuel Adams, a Puritan from Boston who had been impacted by the Great Awakening, arose and said that he was not a bigoted man and that he could join in prayer with any person of piety and virtue who loved his country. He went on to say that, although he was a stranger to Philadelphia, he had heard of an Anglican minister, a Rev. Jacob Dusche, who was such a man, and he proposed that they invite him to come and lead them in prayer. Adams' proposal was approved and Dusche was asked to preside over a time of Bible reading and prayer.

As the elderly, grey-haired Dusche stood before the Congress, he began by reading the entire 35th Psalm, which powerfully impacted everyone present. It is a prayer of David for deliverance and begins with the words, "Plead my cause, O Lord, with my adversaries; fight those who fight me." The Psalm ends with praise for God's deliverance.

As the Psalm was read, a unique sense of God's presence filled the room and tears flowed from many eyes. John Adams wrote to his wife, Abigail, of the impact of the Bible reading and prayer on the delegates. He wrote, "Who can realize the emotions with which they turned imploringly to heaven for divine interposition and aid. It was enough to melt a heart of stone. I never saw a greater effect upon an audience. It seems as if heaven had ordained that Psalm to be read that day. I saw tears gush into the eyes of the old, grave pacific Quakers of Philadelphia. I must beg you to read that Psalm."

After reading the Psalm, Dusche began praying for the delegates, for America, and especially for the city of Boston and its inhabitants who were under siege. As he began praying, the Anglicans, such as George Washington and Richard Henry Lee, knelt in prayer, according to their custom. The Puritans, according to their custom, sat with bowed heads and prayed. Others prayed according to their own, unique customs. But although their outward manners differed, there was a singleness of heart and purpose as they all united in prayer for God's assistance and intervention for America.

The Congress and the Nation Prays:

Prayer continued to be a daily and vital part of the proceedings of the

Continental Congresses. When years later Benjamin Franklin called the delegates of the Constitutional Convention to prayer, he reminded them, "In the beginning of the contest with Great Britain, when we were sensible to danger, we had daily prayers in this room for Divine protection." Indeed, the Catholic scholar, Michael Novak, is correct when he says, "In all moments of imminent danger, as in the first Act of the First Continental Congress, the founding generation turned to prayer."[ii]

During the Revolutionary War, the Continental Congresses issued no less than 15 separate calls for special days of prayer and fasting. For example, during the fall of 1776, when the morale of the army and populace had sunk to an all-time low because of a poor harvest and hardship on the battlefield, Congress proclaimed December 11, 1776, as a Day of Fasting and Repentance.

Jonathan Witherspoon, a Presbyterian Reformer and member of the Congress, was deputized to write the proclamation, which was then approved by the rest of the Congress. It reads, in part:

WHEREAS, the war in which the United States are engaged with Great Britain, has not only been prolonged, but is likely to be carried to the greatest extremity; and whence it becomes all public bodies, as well as private persons, to reverence the Providence of God, and look up to Him as the supreme disposer of all events, and the arbiter of the fate of nations; therefore; RESOLVED, That it be recommended to all the United States, as soon as possible, to appoint a day of solemn fasting and humiliation; to implore of Almighty God the forgiveness of the many sins prevailing among all ranks, and to beg the assistance of his Providence in the prosecution of the present just and necessary war. The Congress do also, in the most earnest manner, recommend to the members of the United States, and particularly the officers civil and military under them, the exercise of repentance and reformation, and the strict observance of the articles of war, particularly that part which forbids profane swearing and all immorality, of which all such officers are desired to take notice.[iii]

There was an amazing change of circumstances after this day of prayer, with successes on the battlefield and the reaping of abundant harvests. There was, in fact, such a turnaround after this that in 1779 Congress issued a proclamation setting aside a day of thanksgiving, because "it hath pleased Almighty God, the father of mercies, remarkably to assist and support the United States of America in their important struggle for liberty."

The Congress then listed seven different accomplishments of God on the behalf of the nation, including "many instances of prowess and success in our armies" and "so great abundance of the fruits of the earth of every kind, as not only to enable us to easily to supply the wants of the army, but gives comfort and happiness to the whole people."[iv]

Washington Makes Prayer a Vital Part of the Colonial Army

The Second Continental Congress, which convened on May 10, 1775, asked George Washington to become commander-in-chief of the ragtag Colonial militias and to transform them into an army that could face the mighty British war machine. Washington accepted the call and began immediately to instill in the Colonial troops a very real faith in God, for as Novak says, 'Washington knew his only hope lay in a profound conviction in the hearts and daily actions of all his men that what they did they did for God, and under God's protection."[v]

Washington, therefore, issued an order that each day was to begin with prayer led by the officers of each unit. He also ordered that, unless their duties required them to be elsewhere, every soldier was to observe, "a punctual attendance of Divine services, to implore the blessing of heaven upon the means used for our safety and public defense." He also forbade all profanity and promised swift punishment for any who uttered oaths that would offend God or man.

Washington continually sought to instill in his troops,

faith and reverence toward God. While quartering at Valley Forge, during a particularly difficult part of the war, Rev. Henry Muhlenberg was able to observe Washington's conduct from his nearby Lutheran Church. He wrote, "Washington rode around among his army yesterday and admonished each one to fear God."[vi]

That Washington himself was a devout person in his private life was confirmed by Isaac Potts, a Quaker who lived near Valley Forge, Pennsylvania, when the Continental Army, led by Washington, was wintering there under much duress in 1774-75. Potts was a pacifist who opposed the war until he had a life-changing experience while riding through the woods one day during, perhaps, the bleakest period of the war. He said,

"I heard a plaintive sound as of a man at prayer. I tied my horse to a sapling and went quietly into the woods and to my astonishment I saw the great George Washington on his knees alone, with his sword on one side and his cocked hat on the other. He was at Prayer to the God of the Armies, beseeching to interpose with his Divine aid, as it was ye Crisis, and the cause of the country, of humanity and of the world. Such a prayer I never heard from the lips of man. I left him alone praying. I went home and told my wife I saw a sight and heard today what I never saw or heard before, and just related to her what I had seen and heard and observed. We never thought a man could be a soldier and a Christian, but if there is one in the world, it is Washington."[vii]

Washington's Farewell Prayer

The many prayers were heard and the Revolutionary War came to an amazing end. It officially ended on October 19, 1781 when General Cornwallis surrendered his entire force to Washington. In customary fashion, Cornwallis turned his sword over to Washington, and the weaponry of his troops was stacked in neat piles. As this occurred the British band played, "The World Turned Upside Down." For freedom-loving people everywhere, however, the world had been turned right side up.

Showing the influence of Christianity on the American populace and their leaders, there was none of the revenge and butchery that are so common in Marxist and Islamic revolutions. There were no tribunals to exact revenge, no reign of terror, and no bloodthirsty proclamations by the Continental Congress. The war ended and the patriots picked up their lives and moved on.

Having completed his call, Washington issued a letter of resignation as Commander-In-Chief to the Continental Congress. Then, he wrote what could be described as a pastoral letter, dated June 14, 1783, to the governors of the various states. This letter included his "earnest prayer" that is here quoted in part. He wrote,

"I now make it my earnest prayer that God would have you, and the State over which you preside, in his holy protection; that he would incline the hearts of the citizens ... to entertain a brotherly affection and love for one another ... and to demean ourselves with that charity, humility, and pacific temper of mind, which were the characteristics of the Divine Author of our blessed religion, and without a humble imitation of His example in these things, we can never hope to be a happy nation."[viii]"

Oh Lord, hear the prayer of a nation that has ignored and rejected you.

Day 343

THOUGHT OF THE DAY: Excuses

I want you to jump into a time capsule and picture yourself as Moses tending Jethro's flock on Mt. Horeb. It's an ordinary day until you spot the burning bush that's on fire but not being consumed. As if this isn't dramatic enough to get your attention, the Angel of the Lord shows up and tells you that you'll be used to deliver Israel from Egypt. (from Exodus)

God tells Moses in verse 10 that it's time to go. Moses comes up with the first of what will be four excuses. Excuse #1 in verse 11: "But Moses said to God, 'Who am I that I should go to Pharaoh, and that I should bring the children of Israel out of Egypt?' " - the "who-am-I" excuse. God gives him a lengthy answer. Then in Exodus 4:1 Moses has excuse #2: "But suppose they will not believe me or listen to my voice; suppose they say, 'The Lord has not appeared to you.' " - the what-if excuse? Remember here that the bush is still burning, and a voice is talking to him in the midst of the fire.

God must have thought that Moses needed more convincing, so He says to him,

" 'Put your hand into your robe [where it covers your chest].' So he put his hand into his robe, and when he took it out, his hand was leprous, as white as snow. Then God said, 'Put your hand into your robe again.' So he put his hand back into his robe, and when he took it out, it was restored [and was] like the rest of his body." (Exodus 4:6-7, Amplified Bible)

Now you might think that all this is sufficient to convince Moses, right? Guess again. Here comes excuse #3 in verse 10: "Moses replied, 'I have never been a good speaker. I wasn't one before you spoke to me, and I'm not one now. I am slow at speaking, and I can never think of what to say.' " (CEV) Ouch - have we ever thought or said this? God's response from the Common English Bible, "Now go! I'll help you speak, and I'll teach you what you should say." So Moses says sure, I'll go, right? No! Here is excuse #4: "Moses begged, 'Lord, please send someone else to do it.' " The old use-somebody-else excuse. (verse four, Contemporary English Bible).

We all saw the excuses, but do you think they were the real reason for Moses' responses? No. The excuses were only a cover up for his fear.

So, what is the root of our excuses?

Day 344

THOUGHT OF THE DAY: I am deeply loved

Oh, that we would understand the incredible parable about the people invited to the wedding feast from Matthew 22:1-10. The Greek verb used for invite here is "kalein," which has the sense of inviting an honored guest to dinner (Ragamuffin Gospel p. 24) Jesus' approach causes people to feel special and is far different then telling them they're going to hell.

Here is Matthew's parable from the Easy to Read Version:

Jesus used some more stories to teach the people. He said, "God's kingdom is like a king who prepared a wedding feast for his son. He invited some people to the feast. When it was ready, the king sent his servants to tell the people to come. But they refused to come to the king's feast." Then the king sent some more servants. He said to them, "I have already invited the people. So tell them that my feast is ready. I have killed my best bulls and calves to be eaten. Everything is ready. Come to the wedding feast." But when the servants told the people to come, they refused to listen. They all went to do other things. One went to work in his field, and another went to his business. Some of the other people grabbed the servants, beat them, and killed them. The king was very angry. He sent his army to kill those who murdered his servants. And the army burned their city.

After that the king said to his servants, "The wedding feast is ready. I invited those people, but they were not good enough to come to my feast. So go to the street corners and invite everyone you see. Tell them to come to my feast." So the servants went into the streets. They gathered all the people they could find, good and bad alike, and brought them to where the wedding feast was ready. And the place was filled with guests.

Lord, help us see what Thomas Merton and St. Augustine saw and embraced. Merton said, "A saint is not someone who is good but who experiences the goodness of God." And from St. Augustine: "My deepest awareness of myself is that I am deeply loved by Jesus Christ and I have done nothing to earn it or deserve it."

Day 345

THOUGHT OF THE DAY: A quote from Augustine of Hippo

"You aspire to great things? Begin with little ones." (Saint Augustine quoting Ancient Roman Christian Theologian and Bishop of Hippo, one of the Latin Fathers of the Church)

Day 346

THOUGHT OF THE DAY: We can't forget

I don't know about you, but every once in a while, I find myself being quite judgmental. I look at the choices and decisions of both the saved and unsaved and have a host of negative thoughts and emotions, most of which Jesus himself never had.

Do you find yourself the same way at times? It's important to be honest about this and call it what it is: self-righteousness and pride, neither of which are pleasing to the Lord.

The question is how can we avoid this trap. Is there something we can do? The answer is found in Isaiah 51:1: "Listen to me, you who look for righteousness, you who seek the Lord: Look to the rock from which you were cut and to the quarry where you were dug." (CEB)

We just need to remember who we were before we met Jesus and to remember all the decisions and choices we made while walking with Him. Think for a moment about all the times the Lord has forgiven us. Think of all the times He demonstrated His love and mercy toward us. All the times there were no consequences for our sin. All the times He covered our sin and we weren't exposed. Psalm 103:10 summarizes this well. From the Amplified Bible: "He has not dealt with us according to our sins [as we deserve], Nor rewarded us [with punishment] according to our wickedness."

WE CAN'T FORGET THE PLACE WE'VE COME FROM. WE CAN'T FORGET HOW GOD HAS DEALT WITH US...

Day 347

THOUGHT OF THE DAY: The church has lost its voice

At one time, the voice of the church mattered. What happened?

According to recent polls, 45% of Americans identify themselves as "born-again." If this is so, how have such small minority groups shaped the landscape of America, instituting several radical changes to our laws and culture over the past 40 years? Many things that used to be wrong are now considered right. How did things change so quickly?

I would liken the church to a person with laryngitis. Usually laryngitis starts out with difficulty speaking, but can progress to the point where a person loses their voice altogether. I believe we've lost our voice.

How did this happen? I would like to share what I see.

1. We have spent more time fighting each other (Christian against Christian) instead of fighting together against the real enemy.

2. After the doctrine of the rapture was introduced to the church, instead of standing against evil, people adopted a "we're-leaving-here" attitude, so it's not our problem.

3. At some point in time the church lost its passion. We've become the church of Laodecia. We are neither hot nor cold.

4. The church for the most part embraced the doctrine of cessationism, the belief that the gifts of the Holy Spirit ended with the apostles. This allowed unbelief to enter the church and in so doing, the

church stopped anticipating and expecting the power of God. Academia and reason replaced the Holy Spirit.

Perhaps the church needs to revisit Mark 16:2: "And they went out and preached everywhere, the Lord working with them and confirming the word through the accompanying signs." And Hebrews 2:4: "God also bearing witness both with signs and wonders, with various miracles, and gifts of the Holy Spirit, according to His own will."

The church needs to go back and read what the Church Fathers wrote well into the fourth century, about how the gifts of the Spirit and the power of God were still evident among believers.

Lastly, we're all waiting for the fulfillment of Joel 2:28-29: "And it shall come to pass afterward that I will pour out My Spirit on all flesh; Your sons and your daughters shall prophesy, Your old men shall dream dreams, Your young men shall see visions. And also on My menservants and on My maidservants I will pour out My Spirit in those days." We somehow missed the word "afterward."

What does afterward refer to? The answer is found in Joel 2:12-13: "Now, therefore," says the Lord, 'Turn to Me with all your heart, With fasting, with weeping, and with mourning.' So rend your heart, and not your garments; Return to the Lord your God, For He is gracious and merciful, Slow to anger, and of great kindness; And He relents from doing harm."

The key is for the church to repent. We can shake our heads in dismay at all the changes around us, but we have to admit we've lost our voice and then ask of ourselves the hard question – why?

Day 348

THOUGHT OF THE DAY: We have lifted off

Last night there was a rumbling that could be felt in the city of Fall River and the surrounding communities. The epicenter of this disturbance was located near the old Fall River airport, to pinpoint it more accurately, Calvary Temple, 4321 North Main Street, Fall River, Massachusetts. This morning there's talk of additional rumblings that are likely to occur.

Even as I write this, I can feel a number of aftershocks. It's like being at the shore line of the ocean and watching the waves reach the beach. The waves are getting bigger, and people are flocking to enjoy the crashing. As far as I can see they're standing at the edge of the water waiting for the next wave to hit. As they do, people are getting soaked, smiling and laughing as they anticipate the next wave. I can hear a broadcast coming from a very high tower, and it's reaching each and every community near the city of Fall River. Can you hear it? The voice is asking, "Will you come? Will you?"

Yes, last night a handful of churches gathered together to pray. For almost two hours we prayed and worshipped, the worship especially awesome. We officially started at 7:15, and before I knew it, I looked at my cell phone to check the time, and it was 9:00. At this point we were still a ways from ending. Because of the time, we did a readers-digest version of the remaining topics we'd agreed we'd pray for.

If this was lift-off, I wonder what God has in store for our future?

Day 349

THOUGHT OF THE DAY: Sunday Christian

I haven't written in a few days because I've been sorting through various emotions and really didn't get a particular thought to write about. This morning, however, this question popped into my mind.

What is a Sunday Christian?

A Sunday Christian is a person who attends church on Sundays on a regular or semi-regular basis. They sing songs and listen to announcements and the message. They might tithe or give. When they miss a Sunday, they may or may not bring the previous Sunday's tithe. After hearing Sunday's message, they retreat to their home and resume their normal activities. In between they might attend a bible study or cell group. They may also attend a men's or woman's group or perhaps a seminar or conference only to return home and resume their normal life. Sunday Christians don't usually give to missions on a regular basis. They're neither a part of missions nor do they support those who are.

Sunday Christianity is like the Dead Sea. The Jordon flows into it, yet nothing flows out. I liken Sunday Christians to those with spiritual constipation. They eat and eat and eat, and nothing comes out. So what I mean here is that we can go to church week after week, month after month, and year after year and then not actually do anything with what we hear. James puts it this way - James 1:22: "But be doers of the word, and not hearers only, deceiving yourselves."

This morning when I prayed, I asked the Lord to do something. His reply was "Why don't you do something?" I shook my head believing that if the church rose up, we could change the world. One of the very last things Jesus said was "GO." Are we going? Is my church going?

The Sunday Christian is happy to attend church instead of BEING the church. The question is "Am I a Sunday Christian?" If so, why?

The darkening reality of our times is in large part because we've become Sunday Christians!

Day 350

THOUGHT OF THE DAY: Prepare for war

Yesterday I was talking with a pastor, and we were both feeling uneasy. You know, that sense that there's a stirring in the Spirit? I described it as "a disturbance in the force."

I hope the Star Wars reference doesn't set anyone off. The point is that something is transpiring in the Spirit. War hasn't begun, but there's a sense that we need to be alert. I would rather be prepared for battle than be caught unaware.

In 1 Chronicles 20:1 it says, "It happened in the spring of the year, at the time kings go out to battle." Again in 2 Samuel 11:1 it says, "In the spring of the year, the time when kings go out to battle." Why did kings go to war in the spring? It was primarily to capitalize on the good weather. It's not a very good strategy to go to war in the middle of winter.

My sense is that we need to prepare for war. I say again – it's better to be prepared than to be caught unaware.

Paul writes in 2 Corinthians 2:11: "For we are not ignorant of his devices; lest Satan should take advantage of us." I want to encourage everyone to take a piece of paper and write down the devices Satan uses. Matthew 13:24 -25: "The kingdom of heaven is like a man who sowed good seed in his field; but while men slept, his enemy came and sowed tares among the wheat and went his way." Isaiah warns us about watchmen who sleep.

Being prepared is better than being asleep.

Day 351

THOUGHT OF THE DAY: Is that a disguise you're wearing?

I was awoken at 3:00 a.m. with this thought in my mind: we all put on masks and disguises. We're hiding our wounds, our insecurities, flaws, faults, and fears, because we want to be accepted, loved, and respected.

There is healing in the wind:

- Ephesians 1:6: He made us accepted in the Beloved." (NKJV)
- 1 Corinthians 15:10: "By the grace of God I am what I am." (NKJV)
- Psalm 139:14: "I will praise You, for I AM FEARFULLY AND WONDERFULLY MADE." (NKJV)
- Isaiah 53:5: "He was wounded for our transgressions, He was bruised for our iniquities; The chastisement for OUR PEACE was upon Him, and by His stripes we ARE HEALED." (NKJV)

Is that a disguise you're wearing?

THERE'S HEALING IN THE WIND!

Day 352

THOUGHT OF THE DAY: Psalm 23:5

For years we haven't been able to rest because we were so distracted and yes, sometimes preoccupied by what the enemy was doing. As I wrote a while ago, while we need to be aware of what devices and schemes the enemy uses against us, we can't be so preoccupied with the enemy that we're robbed of peace, joy, and rest.

I pray that we can comprehend Psalm 23:5: "You prepare a table before me in the presence of my enemies." What a wonderful picture! To me it's a visual of sitting down at an amazing dinner table enjoying dinner with the Lord and with friends and family while the enemy is all around us watching. It's such a picture of rest. The enemy all around us while we're having dinner – WE ARE AT REST...

Today I was with a group of people, and we could sense the enemy trying to infiltrate our circle. We could've spent a fair amount of time praying against him, but we simply declared that he couldn't harass us. Then I quoted Psalm 23:5: "You prepare a table before me in the presence of my enemies." Immediately the room was filled with peace and joy.

Yes, the Lord is our shepherd.

Day 353

THOUGHT OF THE DAY: One of my regrets

As we reflect back on our lives, there are things we'd like to go back and do differently. Though it's impossible to go back, we can go forward and attempt to live out and implement the things about which we've gained insight and conviction.

What do I want to do differently? I want to say, "Thank you. I appreciate you. Thank you for all your labor. I appreciate who you are. I'm grateful for your friendship, for your love, caring, and support." I want to say, "Thank you for giving me grace when I was wrong and when I failed. Thank you for your forbearing with love, for overlooking my glaring weaknesses and for forgiving me. Thank you for following me when my leadership was inadequate at best, and poor at others."

Col. 4:6: "Let the words you speak always be full of grace." (NIRV)

Perhaps the greatest thing I'd do is say with greater frequency, "I LOVE YOU!"

Day 354

THOUGHT OF THE DAY: Our provision

When we awoke this morning there was "divine" provision for each of us.

Close your eyes for a moment. There in front of each of us is our Father, smiling because before us is our daily bread. Everything we need for today has already been provided. Our problem is sometimes with seeing it; His provision isn't always what we expected or wanted – in essence, our inability to believe Matthew 6:8: "For your Father knows the things you have need of before you ask Him." Listen to the Message Bible's version: "The world is full of so-called prayer warriors who are prayer-ignorant. They're full of formulas and programs and advice, peddling techniques for getting what you want from God. Don't fall for that nonsense. This is your Father you are dealing with, and he knows better than you do what you need."

If we could begin believing that before we even opened our eyes today, that everything we "NEED" for the day was already provided. The key word here, of course, is "need." What we may perceive our needs to be is often vastly different from what our true needs are.

In the Hebrew, El-Shaddai means "the all-sufficient God." In Genesis 17:1 we read, "Jehovah appeared to Abram and said to him, 'I am the All-sufficient God.' " In the Names of God Bible it says, "When Abram was 99 years old, Yahweh appeared to him. He said to Abram, 'I am El Shaddai. Live in my presence with integrity.' "

When we perceive that our need is not provided, we begin looking elsewhere. I pray we can hear and embrace the words Boaz spoke to Ruth: "Then Boaz spoke to Ruth: 'Listen, my daughter. From now on don't go to any other field to glean—stay right here in this one.' " (Ruth 2:8 NKJV)

Our true provision comes from only one source. Yes, "He knows our need before we ask."

Day 355

THOUGHT OF THE DAY: Welcome to court

In 1 John 2:21 it says that if we sin, we have an advocate with the Father. The CEV says, "My children, I am writing this so that you won't sin. But if you do sin, Jesus Christ always does the right thing, and he will speak to the Father for us." According to Barnes Commentary, the term advocate is used frequently by Greek writers to express one (who is legally for us), who stands in a court room in our defense.

Here's the good news: Jesus has never lost a case. Picture yourself in a court room. We're all guilty because of our sin, but our advocate stands up and speaks to the Father and says, "Father, my blood paid for that sin." As quickly as the words leave Jesus' lips there's the sound of a judge's gavel hitting the block. The noise is heard throughout the room. Everything becomes silent, not a sound is heard, and then in a clear and distinct voice we hear the judge say – "NOT GUILTY!"

If the blood of Abel cries out from the ground, how much more the blood of Jesus? "The voice of your brother's blood cries out to Me from the ground." (Genesis 4:10) "But one of the soldiers pierced His side with a spear, and immediately blood and water came out." (John 19:34)

It's because of the blood of Jesus that we've been legally declared not guilty!

Welcome to court!

Day 356

THOUGHT OF THE DAY: Beyond forgiveness
What do I mean by "beyond forgiveness" you might ask?
I remember that when I first gave my life to the Lord, deep inside I had an incredible sense that all my sins past, present, and future were forgiven. I knew in my mind that I was no longer guilty. I had read in Micah: "You will cast all our sins into the depths of the sea." (7:19, ESV)

While I was rejoicing in all that Jesus had done for me however, I still had a guilty conscience. I knew that all my sins were completely forgiven and forgotten by God, but I was unable to fully enjoy Jesus' sacrifice for me because my conscience (along with Satan's reminders) continually ran through my head.

Then one day I read Hebrews 9:14: "Christ offered himself through the eternal Spirit as a perfect sacrifice to God. His blood will make us completely clean from the evil we have done. It will give us clear consciences so that we can worship the living God." (ERV) From that moment on, my life changed. No matter what I've done in the past or will do in the future, the blood of Jesus will continually cleanse my conscience. Praise God that my conscience is clean.

A short time later I read 1 John 1:8-9: "If we say that we have no sin, we deceive ourselves, and the truth is not in us. If we confess our sins, He is faithful and just to forgive us our sins and to cleanse us from all unrighteousness." It's pretty clear: in order to have a clean conscience, we have to continually confess our sins.

Yes, forgiven, but beyond forgiveness, we can have our conscience cleansed. Hallelujah!

Day 357

THOUGHT OF THE DAY: Lessons from Moses

In 1 Corinthians 10:11 it says that things written in scripture are meant to serve as examples by which for us to learn. Here's the verse: "All these things happened to them as examples—as object lessons to us—to warn us against doing the same things; they were written down so that we could read about them and learn from them in these last days as the world nears its end."

So, the question today is, why couldn't Moses enter the Promised Land? What hinders us from entering into the promises God has for us?

Let's read Numbers 20:7-8: "Then the Lord spoke to Moses, saying, 'Take the rod; you and your brother Aaron gather the congregation together. Speak to the rock before their eyes, and it will yield its water; thus you shall bring water for them out of the rock, and give drink to the congregation and their animals.' " (NKJV)

The instruction is clear: take your rod and speak to the rock. In the past God used the rod to accomplish His purposes. This time Moses was to take the rod but not use it. All too often we're told to do things in a new way but instead use old methods that we're comfortable with and that have worked in the past.

What else can we learn? Read Numbers 20:10-11: "And Moses and Aaron gathered the assembly together before the rock; and he said to them, 'Hear now, you rebels! Must we bring water for you out of this rock?' Then Moses lifted his hand and struck the rock twice with his rod; and water came out abundantly, and the congregation and their animals drank." (NKJV)

What do we see? First, he has a low opinion of the people he's leading, seeing himself as better. Secondly, he tells them that he and Aaron will provide water. He has lost sight of the fact that it was God's sufficiency, not his own, that would bring provision. It wasn't Moses' power; it was God's.

Moses was relying on himself, what he could do. Haven't we learned yet that it's not about what we can do, but what He can and will do? Moses is told to speak to the rock but instead, in his anger and frustration, strikes the rock twice. When we get frustrated and angry, we're in our flesh. Our flesh and our character flaws will often keep us from receiving the promises God has for us.

In Moses' case, keep in mind that it was forty or so years after this that his anger caused him to kill the Egyptian. What character flaw or flaws do we persist in that prevent us from receiving God's promises to us? More than ever, the Holy Spirit is trying to show us that it's not about our own ability, power, or strength.

Aren't we tired yet of relying on ourselves? Aren't we tired of using old methods to accomplish what God wants to do today? Have we not yet understood 1 Corinthians 11:29 that says just because we don't discern or view as sacred the Lord's body, that people are sick and dying? Indeed, our failure to honor the body of Christ has greatly hindered God's power, and worse, can actually prevent healing.

Here's my prayer for all of us: Lord, help each of us to see the Moses in us. Show us the lessons we can learn from Moses so we can fully enter our Promised Land!

(Now that you've finished, what did you just read?)

Day 358

THOUGHT OF THE DAY: The seldom-used gift

Can you remember the day that you were baptized in the Spirit? Can't you remember how excited you were when you learned that Jesus wanted that for you? Remember how you wanted the gift of praying in tongues and in the Spirit.?

We had read in Romans 8:26: "And the Holy Spirit helps us in our weakness. For example, we don't know what God wants us to pray for. But the Holy Spirit prays for us with groanings that cannot be expressed in words." (NLT) Remember all the times we didn't have words in English (or whatever your language is) to express what was needed? We knew we had to pray; we just didn't have the words. The Holy Spirit, though, enabled us to pray in the Spirit – to pray in tongues. Praise God for this incredible gift.

That being said, how often do you pray in the Spirit?

When we pray in the Spirit, we put away our natural mind and put on a spiritual one. When we do that, it's amazing what ideas and concepts fill our minds. Jude 20 says, "But you, beloved, building yourselves up on your most holy faith, praying in the Holy Spirit."

There are so many days when our faith level is low. It's as if our spiritual batteries need charging. During these times we doubt more, are more easily confused and bewildered, and in general are in a place of struggling.

Jude provides us with a simple answer: "Build yourself up by praying in the Spirit." There have been countless times I've been weary, discouraged, and even despondent and depressed. I wish I could say that during these times I always remember to pray in the Spirit. I don't. Remember after all, that the topic today is about the seldom-used gift, whether its infrequency is due to not knowing what to pray or not knowing we need to use it as a means to build ourselves up.

Yet even so, there have been innumerable times when I've walked around my office, my house, in the streets, in the car, or even in someone else's home, and I've remembered. The effect has been to raise my faith level. Indeed, we've been given this supernatural gift; we need to use it!

Let's step out of the natural and into the Spirit. Let's use this gift we've received. If you haven't been baptized in the Spirit, ask someone about it. Ask the Lord. It's important that we understand this gift!

Day 359

THOUGHT OF THE DAY: My heart weeps – please come home

Through the many years, my life has intersected with thousands of amazing and precious sons and daughters of God. All the same I admit that frequently, it hasn't been easy. He never said it would be. All of us have stumbled at times. There have been times when many of us have lost our way, but He's always been there - always loving, always forgiving, always full of grace and mercy. How can this be? It's really very simple - He loves us as a Father.

Over the last few years I've had days where I've just wanted to sit down and cry. Today is one of one of those days. How many people do we know who've been devastated by relationships, by churches, or by their own painful choices? How many people have we known who've loved God but who don't love the church?

There are literally thousands of people who fit in this category and who've lost their way. So many want to come "home" but don't know how and are so afraid that nothing has changed.

There are so many with gifts and talents that haven't been used in years. Some have never even scratched the surface of their anointing. Oh Lord, let there be true healing in your house. May the spirit of judgment be eradicated. Oh, please, come home!

I know I've said this before, but in the early 2000s Pastor Glenn Feehan wrote a song called "Calling Them Home." It was based on a prophetic word God had given for that year. It comes from Zechariah 10:8: "I will whistle for them and gather them, for I will redeem them; And they shall increase as they once increased." Can't you see the Father standing on the porch whistling for his children to come home because it's dinner time, a time of banqueting when the fatted calf has been prepared? He's prepared a table for His "kids." I can see people literally running to the Father's house; they can't wait to get there.

As each one arrives with tears streaming down their faces, not a word is spoken, His embrace and the kiss placed on each cheek or forehead says it all. Oh, Lord, we still don't comprehend the depth of your love for us. Everything we've been through can be salve for those who are hurting. Who knows better how to love and care for people than us?

Each has been gifted and anointed, but most of us have been held back because of past hurts, past pain, and an inability to see or comprehend what God had placed inside of us before we were born.

Can you hear the Father whistling? Please, come home!

Jeremiah 31:10-14:

Hear the word of the Lord, O nations, And declare it in the isles afar off, and say, For the Lord has redeemed Jacob, And ransomed him from the hand of one stronger than he. Therefore they shall come and sing in the height of Zion, Streaming to the goodness of the Lord—For wheat and new wine and oil, For the young of the flock and the herd; Their souls shall be like a well-watered garden, And they shall sorrow no more at all. Then shall the virgin rejoice in the dance, And the young men and the old, together; For I will turn their mourning to joy, Will comfort them, and make them rejoice rather than sorrow. I will satiate the soul of the priests with abundance, And My people shall be satisfied with My goodness, says the Lord. (NKJV)

Please come home! Please use everything within you, for you were created to be who and what you are. The time is now; the Father is calling!

Day 360

THOUGHT OF THE DAY: Can you hear?

As I sat before the Lord this morning, I asked him what he wanted me to write. Immediately I heard and saw 1 Samuel 3:10: "The Lord then stood beside Samuel and called out as he had done before, (notice God had previously attempted to speak) 'Samuel! Samuel! (know that God is relentless) I'm listening,' Samuel answered. (Such a simple response.) 'What do you want me to do?' " (CEV)

I could see the Lord standing beside each of us and speaking, but we don't understand what He's saying. In fact, we aren't very confident that He's even speaking to us, never mind sure of the particulars of His message. Samuel too had to go through a process before he understood that it was God speaking to him. I heard the Lord say, "Follow the example of Samuel" who said, "I'm listening" – "What do you want me to do?"

This morning or whenever you have your communion time (the time where we "hang out" with the Lord), He wants us to say, "I'm listening."

As I did that myself, I could sense my natural mind immediately begin to interfere with my capacity to hear and believe it was God's voice. Again, I saw Him standing beside each of us and speaking. He said, "Tell them to get a piece of paper and to write down what they heard."

There are four things, no, actually five, that we should do. Write down everything you hear in that moment, not just what you can believe for. This distinction is important, because often we only write down what we have the capacity to see ourselves doing, and the effect is to limit what God is saying and thus limit what God can do through us.

1. We must take the time.
2. We must believe the Holy Spirit will speak.
3. We need to write it down – write it ALL down.
4. We need to meditate on and mull over what we've heard.
5. We must attempt to do what we've heard, to activate it.

I don't want to write what I heard, because I don't want to influence what you'll hear. I would love to see all of you write a comment. Remember that what He says to one person, He might not say to you. What you need to hear is different than what someone else needs to hear.

As a postscript I will say that God has been repeating with frequency the same thing to me for a while. Dare to venture why?

"I'm listening" – "What do you want me to do?"

Day 361

THOUGHT OF THE DAY: I don't have time – later

This morning when I sat before the Lord and began speaking to Him, I immediately sensed grieving. There are many times when I think it's me grieving, but it's not me at all; it's the Spirit within me. Yes, the Holy Spirit grieves - Ephesians 4:30: "And do not grieve the Holy Spirit of God."

When I asked why my Spirit was grieving, the Lord began to speak to me, but it was different. He asked me if I had come with my "to do list" - you know, that list of instructions we give to God when we pop into His presence?

He said that there are many times we don't even say "Good morning." He spoke of all the times He's heard, "I don't have time. I'll pray later." He's grieved when He hears this, because He looks forward to spending time with us. He's grieved because we don't understand that as with Moses, He'd speak to us like a friend. Exodus 33:11: "The Lord would speak to Moses face to face, as one speaks to a friend." (NIVUK)

I don't know, but this morning God became more personal than I'd ever experienced. There was a longing which I can still feel. Paul expresses this concept in 1 Thessalonians 2:8, "affectionately longing for you." Paul was expressing the heart of God.

The Lord spoke about all the days He waited for us to come, how He wanted us to know how much He loved us. He spoke of the days when He had wisdom and understanding for us, but we never came. He said that He wasn't telling us this to make us feel guilty for what's been missed. Instead it was as if He was asking, "Can we go on from here?"

Perhaps we could say less and listen more?

I was reminded of Proverbs 18:24: "But there is a friend who sticks closer than a brother." (NIV) Even as I'm writing this, I'm grieving. I want this feeling to go away, but it needs to linger for a while, so I'll have a better chance of remembering what He's said this morning. There are times when God moves in my life, but I soon forget what happened. It becomes another day that I've failed to value what He's said and done and thus miss the fullness of what God has intended.

Yet He reminds me of all the times He has and will show us again what we've failed to remember. He says it's because He really loves us.

I'm reminded of Matthew 6:32: "For your heavenly Father knows that you need all these things" and then Matthew 11:28-30: "Come to Me, all you who labor and are heavy laden, and I will give you rest. Take My yoke upon you and learn from Me, for I am gentle and lowly in heart, and you will find rest for your souls. For My yoke is easy and My burden is light."

Come, learn, rest...

The song "How He Loves Me" has now filled my mind. This is the best way I can think of to end this. (YouTube - How He Loves Us - Kim Walker (Jesus Culture). Click on http://youtu.be/JoC1ec-lYps)

Day 362

THOUGHT OF THE DAY: One of the keys to receiving the spirit of revelation and being a carrier of the presence of God

• John 14:21: "Every man who knows my commandments and obeys them is the man who really loves me, and every man who really loves me will himself be loved by my Father, and I too will love him and make myself known to him." (Phillips)

• John 14:23-24: "If anyone loves Me, he will keep My word; and My Father will love him, and We will come to him and make Our home with him. He who does not love Me does not keep My words." (NKJV)

Did we see that it's because of our love that we obey? Our obedience is also an indicator of our love for the Lord. It's our love that will not only bring a Spirit of Revelation into our lives, but will also bring the abiding presence of God Himself.

Day 363

THOUGHT OF THE DAY: Hold on to your dreams

Thank you for taking the time to read the THOUGHT OF THE DAY. It is meant to encourage us on our journey. As I thought about what to write today, I believe I can best say it through what God said and did yesterday. Click on the link below – I know it will profoundly touch your life.

The worship is incredible – the song is about 23 minutes long and worth every second. Please carve out some time and listen. The word starts at approximately 23 plus minutes. God speaks about holding on to your dreams and how He restores shattered ones.

Thank you for allowing me to share this thought with you.

http://youtu.be/ZROZkdaWyxE

Day 364

THOUGHT OF THE DAY: Who hindered you?

Last Saturday night at our prophetic meeting, this word was shared with everyone in the room. The full verse is from Galatians 5:7: "You ran well. Who hindered you from obeying the truth?"

Paul was writing to the Galatians, and the Lord had the same word for us. There was a holy hush in the room. It was like everything came to a complete stop and the Holy Spirit was asking each of us what or who was deterring us from living out our lives in obedience. It wasn't like we weren't obeying doctrine; it was more about living out the lives we knew God had shown He had for us.

The question was posed in such a way that we sensed the Holy Spirit wasn't asking about Satan hindering us. 1 Thessalonians 2:18: "Therefore we wanted to come to you—even I, Paul, time and again—but Satan hindered us." Satan wasn't the problem. (NKJV)

Yes, there are times Satan hinders us, but the question wasn't pointing to Satan. If Satan isn't hindering us, then what or who is? All day today the Holy Spirit kept this question in my mind. At one point as I was praying in the Spirit I began to cry. I saw a picture of a father speaking to one of his children and crying. Sitting on a couch and between the tears, he was talking to his child and was asking, "What's hindering you" from fulfilling your dreams? What's stopping you from reaching your destiny?"

Who or what is stopping us from becoming who we should be? Who or what is stopping us from living out dreams that we've had for such a long time? Are circumstances hindering us, is it fear in general, fear of man in particular, is it our church, is it disagreements about doctrine within the church? If any of these is true, why are we allowing them?

Later in the morning as I drove my car and was using the time to "hang out" with the Lord, I again began to cry. I saw the same picture of the father on a couch crying, and without any anger in His quivering voice, the father was sharing with his child how much he loved them. It was breaking his heart to see his child not living their life to the fullest. He had his arms outstretched and drew the child toward him. He at first said nothing; he just held his child and tears were running down his cheeks. Then with a broken voice he said, "It's not too late. You can do it, and I will be right beside you to help you."

Whatever is hindering us; it's time to break free. All the resources of heaven are at our disposal. Our Father is in the chain-breaking business.

Day 365

THOUGHT OF THE DAY: "You are God who sees me and cares for me."

Remember the story in Genesis 16 where Hagar thought she was better than Sarah because she could bear children and Sarah couldn't? Tensions mounted, and Sarah began mistreating Hagar verbally, some of the commentaries even believing that Sarah would physically hit Hagar.

Finally, Hagar couldn't take it anymore, so she ran off with her 13-year-old son Ishmael. The story continues in verses 7-8: "Now the Angel of the Lord found her by a spring of water in the wilderness, by the spring on the way to Shur. And He said, 'Hagar, Sarai's maid, where have you come from, and where are you going?' She said, 'I am fleeing from the presence of my mistress Sarai.' "

So what was God's solution to this situation? Verses 9–10: "The Angel of the Lord said to her, 'Return to your mistress, and submit yourself under her hand.' Then the Angel of the Lord said to her, 'I will multiply your descendants exceedingly, so that they shall not be counted for multitude.' "

God was not into condoning abuse. What He wanted was reconciliation. He wanted Hagar to return and admit where she was wrong and yield to the authority of Sarah.

Here are some hard lessons:

1. Running away from the problem is not an answer.

2. Each of us needs to admit where we're wrong. If Hagar didn't despise Sarah, would Sarah have mistreated her? We're accountable for our own actions, not anyone else's. There is no doubt that God knew that if Hagar did her part, that Sarah would change.

A Daily Devotional

Please do not take this example and stay in an abusive relationship. In this story God knew if Hagar admitted her wrong and yielded to Sarah's position over her, it would work out. The point is to admit where we're wrong, change our attitude, and yield to those in authority. Isn't that what we would want our children to do?

3. God's provision of increase is not always where we would like it to be.

Verses 13-14: "Then she called the name of the Lord who spoke to her, You-Are-the-God-Who-Sees; for she said, 'Have I also here seen Him who sees me?' Therefore, the well was called Beer Lahai Roi; which literally means, "The well of the One Who Lives and Sees Me." The ERV translation says, "The Lord talked to Hagar. She began to use a new name for God. She said to him, 'You are God Who Sees Me.' She said this because she thought, 'I see that even in this place God sees me and cares for me!' "

I must admit that there have been numerous times when I've had to change my attitude and conduct and submit to authority. Though I didn't like it, what I did know was the truth of Isaiah 55:8-9 which says, " 'For My thoughts are not your thoughts, Nor are your ways My ways,' says the Lord. 'For as the heavens are higher than the earth, So are My ways higher than your ways, And My thoughts than your thoughts.' "

We need to always remember that no matter what we're going through, no matter how difficult our situation, we have a "God who sees and cares for us."

355

About the Author

Pastor Brian R. Weeks began ministering in 1972 and has served as a pastor to both youth and young adults. He also served as an associate pastor for 11 years, and then for 25 years as a senior pastor, apostolic missionary, and church planter. In March of 2017, he released Solomon's Porch to other leader-ship, but in order to remain part of the local church, continues to serve among its several pastors.

In 2008, Pastor Brian formed Brian Weeks Ministries to facilitate his call to travel nationally and internationally. His journeys have taken him to Haiti, Ukraine, India, Romania, the Dominican Republic, Canada, and Moldova. He has ministered in Evangelical, Charismatic, Episcopal, Catholic, Pentecostal, Dutch Reform, Vineyard, Methodist, Baptist, Anglican, Faith Churches, and other churches.

His ministry includes teaching and training leaders and pastors through pas-tors' conferences, youth conferences, and Bible Schools, as well as doing prophetic ministry in these same settings.

Pastor Brian has co-planted two churches and has planted three others. His most recent church plant was birthed on Christmas Eve 2009. With his rich and diversified experience, he loves encouraging and mentoring other pastors in the Holy Spirit, as well as helping them grow and develop their churches in-to their respective futures.

Pastor Brian's passion is to see lives transformed by the power and love of God. His strong desire is that God's sons and daughters would not only discover their gifts and talents, but more importantly, comprehend how much God de-lights in them and how affectionately they are loved, knowing full well that they were created for a divine purpose. Pastor Brian's prophetic ministry helps people grasp these realities and empowers them to take steps towards their to-morrows. One of his greatest joys is to see people delight in God's presence and cherish their relationship with the Lord and with His people.

In recent years Brian has come to understand his role as much like that of a father or grandfather. Paul writes in 1 Corinthians 4:15: "For though you might have ten thousand instructors in Christ, yet you do not have many fathers." He has found profound joy in both understanding and walking in this role.

BIBLE TRANSLATIONS

Amplified Bible (AMP)
Amplified Bible, Classic Edition (AMPC)
BRG Bible (BRG)
Christian Standard Bible (CSB)
Common English Bible (CEB)
Complete Jewish Bible (CJB)
Contemporary English Version (CEV)
Darby Translation (DARBY)
Disciples' Literal New Testament (DLNT)
Douay-Rheims 1899 American Edition (DRA)
Easy-to-Read Version (ERV)
English Standard Version (ESV)
Expanded Bible (EXB)
1599 Geneva Bible (GNV)
GOD'S WORD Translation (GW)
Good News Translation (GNT)
Holman Christian Standard Bible (HCSB)
International Children's Bible (ICB)
International Standard Version (ISV)
J.B. Phillips New Testament (PHILLIPS)
Jubilee Bible 2000 (JUB)
Lexham English Bible (LEB)
Living Bible (TLB)
The Message (MSG)
Names of God Bible (NOG)
New Century Version (NCV)
New English Translation (NET)
New International Reader's Version (NIRV)
New International Version (NIV)
New International Version - UK (NIVUK)
New King James Version (NKJV)
New Life Version (NLV)
New Living Translation (NLT)
New Revised Standard Version, Anglicised (NRSVA)
New Testament for Everyone (NTE)
Orthodox Jewish Bible (OJB)
The Passion Translation (TPT)

Tree of Life Version (TLV)
The Voice (VOICE)
World English Bible (WEB)
Worldwide English (New Testament) (WE)
The New King James Version (NKJV) was used for all verses not otherwise noted.

Made in the USA
Middletown, DE
26 July 2024

57936111R00203